ADVANCES IN
LIBRARY ADMINISTRATION
AND ORGANIZATION

Volume 5 • 1986

ADVANCES IN LIBRARY ADMINISTRATION AND ORGANIZATION

A Research Annual

Editors: GERARD B. McCABE
Director of Libraries
Clarion University of Pennsylvania

BERNARD KREISSMAN
University Librarian Emeritus
University of California, Davis

VOLUME 5 • 1986

 JAI PRESS INC.

Greenwich, Connecticut   *London, England*

CONTENTS

INTRODUCTION

This fifth annual volume offers papers on a broad range of subjects. Some of these papers are the products of extensive research; a few reflect practical experience. As intended professional reading, all offer some stimulation to thinking and reflecting on the ideas or experience they contain. Ideas can be either immediately provocative or employable. The same can be said of practical experience. A research report conveying a new idea to a reader becomes effective if it causes response through stimulation of further thought or prompts some positive, beneficial action. A narration of operational experience becomes effective if it too prompts similar thought or action. Information gained through reading can be stored or used very soon after its reception, options that remain with the reader. Introspective judgment will make the decision on the usefulness of the information. The individual reader exercising discretionary power will use, store, or further develop the received information through thought, dismissing notions, and given an appropriate amount of time, will develop reasoned thought into concepts perhaps of greater magnitude than those originally received. If this effect occurs, the intent is achieved.

Gerard B. McCabe
Editor

A LONGITUDINAL STUDY OF THE OUTCOMES OF A MANAGEMENT DEVELOPMENT PROGRAM FOR WOMEN IN LIBRARIANSHIP

Ruth J. Person and Eleanore R. Ficke

INTRODUCTION

In the past several decades much concern has been expressed about the status of women in management. Reflecting this concern, increased attention has been devoted to the subject within librarianship—a field in which historically women have been numerically dominant and yet men have held (and continue to hold) the majority of the managerial positions.[1] A number of authors explored this topic, including Braunagle,[2] Buck,[3] Dale,[4] Dworak,[5] Fennell,[6] Goldstein,[7] Heim,[8] Martin,[9] Rensel,[10] and Sukiennik.[11] Library professional associations also

Advances in Library Administration and Organization
Volume 5, pages 1–13
Copyright © 1986 by JAI Press Inc.
All rights of reproduction in any form reserved.
ISBN: 0-89232-674-3

sponsored short informative programs which addressed women's concerns about management. As McDonough[12] has cautioned, however, "progress against discrimination in society as well as in the professions cannot rely on the tacit assumption that solutions will automatically follow from awareness of the problem."

Therefore, in order to seek more concrete solutions to the problem of imbalance between the number of women in library management and the number of women in the profession, several continuing education programs focusing on the role of women in library management were developed. Although some of these programs were brief, others were extensive in their coverage and received support from federal and other funding agencies.

In spite of these efforts, the progress of women in library management has remained "agonizingly slow,"[13] leading to a possible assumption that such educational efforts were futile. The literature reports few assessments of management development programs for women, and library science educators have reported few longitudinal investigations of continuing education activities. Thus, an in-depth, long-term analysis was necessary to clarify an assumption of possible futility and to explore alternative hypotheses that program effects may have been long- rather than short-term and more indirect than original expectations suggested.

EVALUATING THE LONG-TERM EFFECTS OF A CONTINUING EDUCATION PROGRAM

A continuing education activity specifically directed at training "librarians in methods for the development of management potential in women" was selected for long-term analysis. This program (hereinafter called the Institute) was conducted in 1977 by an accredited graduate school of library and information science. The Institute focused on a week of intensive, interactive sessions addressing the image of women in librarianship, assertiveness training, effecting change, and leadership and management skills. Participants were encouraged not only to develop their own managerial skills but to enhance their ability to serve as catalysts for other women to do the same.

Using the Institute as the focus of examination, a study was designed to (1) explore the career patterns of the original 30 participants, (2) identify participants' contributions to the development of "managerial potential of women" in librarianship, (3) identify and analyze the overall effects of the Institute as a continuing education activity over a five-year period, and (4) develop suggestions for the development of a model educational program for women in library management.

METHODOLOGY

The study was conducted as a longitudinal analysis using the original group of participants in the educational activity. Both the benefits and drawbacks of conducting a longitudinal evaluation were weighed in selecting an appropriate data-collection methodology. Allowing the euphoria or hostility generated by an intensive experience to disperse over time permits a certain amount of distancing from emotional involvement in the activity and encourages objectivity.[14] On the other hand, if too great a time elapses between the original program and an analysis, participants might not recall in any detail changes that could be attributed to any educational program. Other efforts at longitudinal analysis suggested that a combination of written and direct personal approaches was the best way to elicit information that individuals may have difficulty remembering.[15]

The sample for the study consisted of the 30 original Institute participants, who represented a good cross-section of librarians in the United States (with the exception that all participants but one were women). These original participants were selected for the Institute from a field of applicants on the basis of their stated commitment to Institute goals, overall credentials, and the special project required for admission. Other selection criteria included the attainment of a balanced representation of types of libraries, managerial and nonmanagerial personnel, and geographical distribution. In order to have a means of comparison between the sample and female members of the profession at large, data concerning the composition of the sample were matched to those in Heim and Estabrook's 1978 study, *Career Profiles and Sex Discrimination in the Library Profession.*[16]

Original Institute participants represented all types of library employment. In 1977, they had an average of 13 years' experience and 16 participants held managerial positions. All but one participant held the first professional degree in library science and two were doctoral recipients. Broadly speaking, this sample corresponded to Heim's, although Institute members were at the high end of the scale in terms of professional and educational achievement.

The 30 original participants were contacted by letter and asked to complete a written questionnaire consisting of both closed and open-ended questions concerning their own career progress and the contributions of the Institute to their efforts. Additional information was received through resumes, letters, personal and telephone contact, and through a five-year reunion meeting.

The data were analyzed into the following categories: sample characteristics and changes over the intervening five-year period, career developments in the area of management, contributions to the general development of women in library management, and evaluation of the Institute itself. The informal communication network that evolved as a direct result of the Institute was also outlined and analyzed.

THE RESULTS: FIVE YEARS OF PROGRESS

The response for the survey was 80 percent, with three nonrespondents and three returns from secondary sources indicating that individuals had left the field of librarianship. In order to make a direct comparison between individuals over time, only the data supplied by the 24 primary respondents to the survey were used for analysis.

As reflected in Table 1, the overall regional distribution of the sample altered only slightly in five years, as did library employment distribution. The most noticeable change came in library education, where the number of respondents who became faculty members or administrators in library schools increased substantially for the sample size.

Table 2 reflects educational changes over the five-year period. In addition to changes in formal degree status, respondents also reported from 1 to 50 continuing education activities, with an average of 11. As outlined in Table 3, 17 individuals made significant improvements in their position, as indicated by title. Thirteen of those 17 accomplished this by moving to another organization, and 8 of the 13 by also moving more than 200 miles from their 1977 location. Although some individuals made no job moves in five years, others held as many as four additional positions, yielding an average of 1.2 positions held since 1977.

When asked to rate their career advancement over five years (on a scale of 1, *not at all,* to 5, *significantly*), the mean score given was 3.2 As Table 4 reflects, advancement and improvement were made by a majority of respondents in areas of salary, status, challenge, and responsibility. The lower levels of improvement in "number of people managed" and "size of library" reflected primarily faculty and staff assignments where these criteria were not relevant.

Table 1. Distribution of Participants by Place of Employment
(Type of Library)

	Percent reporting			
Type of Library	1977 (N = 30)	1978 (Heim study)	1977 (N = 24)	1982 (N = 24)
Academic	27	29.6	25	17
Public	23	30.8	25	25
School	13	17.0	8	4
Special/Federal	13	6.5	17	21
Library education				
Faculty/Admin.	7	1.9	8	21
Student (Full-time)	10	0	13	0
Network	0	14.2	0	4
State library	7	(other)	4	4
Unemployed	0	0	0	4

Table 2. Highest Level of Educational Attainment

	Percent reporting		
Degree	1977 (N = 24)	1978 (Heim)	1982 (N = 24)
B.S./B.A.	4	—	4
M.L.S.	70	86.9	45
2nd master's	17	8	30
Doctorate	8	2.5	21 (+ 2 in progress)

Other individual responses to the question of career improvement suggested that areas such as "freedom of decision-making," "enhancement of future potential and opportunities for development," and "quality of working life" all improved and were important to the respondents. Two individuals even indicated that their jobs were "more fun" than those in the past. The wide variety of added comments suggested that, while salary and number of people supervised had increased, these areas were only partially responsible for perceptions of advancement. Like Herzberg's findings, [17] new challenges and opportunities for development and growth were found to be important contributors to job satisfaction and feelings of improvement for this sample as well.

Table 3. Career Paths of Institute Participants

Those who, in 1977, were		Became in 1982	
Library directors/heads	9	Directors of larger libraries	3
		Managers of larger units	3
		Same position	1
		Temp. unemployed	1
		Faculty	1
Assistant directors	2	Library director	1
		Same position	1
Library managers (heads of service units, dept. heads, staff managers)	5	Assistant director	1
		Same position	2
		Library director	1
		Same position	1
Library staff	4	Library assn. director	1
		Assistant director	1
		Library manager	1
		Same position	1
Faculty		Faculty	
Professor	1	Same position	1
Assoc. professor	1	Professor	1
Students	2	Network director	1
		Faculty	1

Table 4.   Career Improvement
Measures

Measure	Percent reporting (N = 24)
Salary	92
Status	75
Challenge	70
Responsibility	55
Number of people managed	46
Size of library	38
No improvement	8

IMPACT OF THE INSTITUTE ON CAREER GROWTH

Terms used repeatedly to describe the contributions of the Institute to career and personal growth, such as *validation, peer identification, role models, support, networks,* and *new ideas,* describe gains similar to those reported by Bowker[18] for a women's program in the academic environment. Although Bowker felt that responses were ''scattered, idiosyncratic, and not clearly articulated,'' reported gains for Institute participants were more clearly articulated as indicated in Figure 1. Eighty-six percent of the respondents indicated that the Institute was helpful in ''advancing careers in management.'' On a scale of 1 (*very little*) to 5 (*very much*), respondents had a median score of three.

In addition to the personal gains outlined in Figure 1, increases were noted by 71 percent of the respondents in professional association leadership roles, 60 percent in publication activity, and 48 percent in continuing education participation. At least one-fourth of the respondents reported publication activity that occurred as a direct result of contacts made through the Institute.

Figure 1.   Positive Outcomes of the Institute

Contacts: Allowed the development of a support network, professional contacts, and interaction with women in similar managerial settings

Self-Awareness: Enhanced participants' sense of self, provided positive reinforcement, allowed some women to see themselves as professional managers for the first time, and helped some acknowledge and deal with ambition

Career vs. Job: Encouraged some women to think in terms of long-term career patterns rather than simply about holding a job, clarified career goals, and allowed participants to think in terms of changes needed in their own careers or about new options available

Management Concepts: Introduced new concepts about management, or reinforced assumptions already held

Development of Others: Made some participants acknowledge and explore their status as role models, encouraged several participants to undertake research related to women in management, and influenced the teaching of others

INCREASING THE MANAGEMENT POTENTIAL OF OTHER WOMEN

The second objective of the Institute was to encourage the participants to provide developmental opportunities for *other* women in librarianship—in other words, to form a nucleus of individuals who could initiate change. Although 24 individuals cannot change the nature of a profession, they can serve as role models, provide educational programs, and identify problems and solutions through research, writing, speaking, and teaching.

The importance of role models for the development of women in management has been affirmed in the literature. Futas and Vaughn note that in librarianship, in particular, the "lack of feminist women on library school faculties has deprived women of role models."[19] As potential role models, Institute participants greatly enhanced their understanding of the obligations of such a role. Within five years, the visibility of these 24 role models also increased substantially: more than half of the group held major and highly visible management positions, five were faculty members or library school administrators, and at least half headed major association committees.

Other means of helping women to develop management skills and knowledge included writing and educational program development. More than a dozen management programs for women were arranged by Institute participants; nearly 500 women were reached by such efforts. Eight of the participants also published materials related to women and management, most of which resulted from relationships developed at the Institute.

INDIRECT INSTITUTE BENEFITS: THE IMPACT OF NETWORKING

Sometimes the most valuable outcomes of an activity are ones that are not predicted. In 1977, there was little discussion of "networking." Therefore, development of a recognizable "network" of individuals linked together initially by a shared experience and then by shared history was an unanticipated but major outcome of the Institute. Candy[20] has suggested that "women in all roles . . . . need supportive relations, especially those of other women." An evolving network of Institute participants developed over time.

In each of the five years of the study, more than half of the 24 respondents had at least three contacts with other Institute participants, and seven had monthly contacts or more. Of the members of the Institute maintaining such contacts, the median number of others contacted was two and the median number of contacts per year was two. Six persons maintained contact with at least three others from the original group. Initial contacts were largely a result of professional meetings, collaboration on publications of mutual interest, program development, or work-related situations. The strengthening of this network also paralleled the growth of a women administrators' discussion group within a professional association in which a number of Institute participants took leadership roles.

Four distinct groups emerged in an analysis of the contact patterns among participants. One group was linked by geographic location, one was initiated through the desire to develop a discussion group in a professional association setting, one was allied by type-of-employment interests, and one by pre-Institute contacts. In all but one case, at least one individual served as a "linking pin" between the group and others. As Figure 2 suggests, three individuals were the primary focus of this linking pin concept. Because of their close relationships with each other, these three provided and received information about almost all of the other participants represented in Figure 2.

Researchers have identified differences between men and women in terms of work-related friendship and interaction. In particular, Hennig and Jardim[21] note that "friendship for men is a valued outcome of interaction on the job, that relationships are not ends in themselves [and that] males use the informal network for job advancement." These authors further note that regard for friendship as a "prerequisite for interaction" hampers rather than helps professional women. Although initial post-Institute contacts were made primarily for professional purposes, a number of those contacts evolved into more personal and supportive relationships. In other words, friendships evolved that were a "tangential phenomenon that develops during the pursuit of job-related goals,"[22] repeating the male pattern identified by Hennig and Jardim.[23]

CONCLUSIONS

From an analysis of participant information, three important results of the continuing education program represented by the Institute emerged. These included perceived contributions to career advancement through experiences outlined in Figure 1, contributons to the development of other women, and the development of a network.

Perhaps the most direct result of the Institute—one that should have far-reaching consequences in the years to come—was the creation of an opportunity for professional networking and interaction. Because it is a well-known fact that networking can be important for career development, the fact that the participants were able to develop their contact-making skills along these lines and sustain relationships for a considerable period of time is noteworthy. It should be remembered that Institute attendees, in almost all cases, were unknown to one another and came together for individual improvement, to fulfill their own expectations of career development, and to work toward Institute goals. The unexpected outcome of a strong support network became a highly valued result of such interaction. Whether this interaction will relate directly to job advancement in the future remains to be seen.

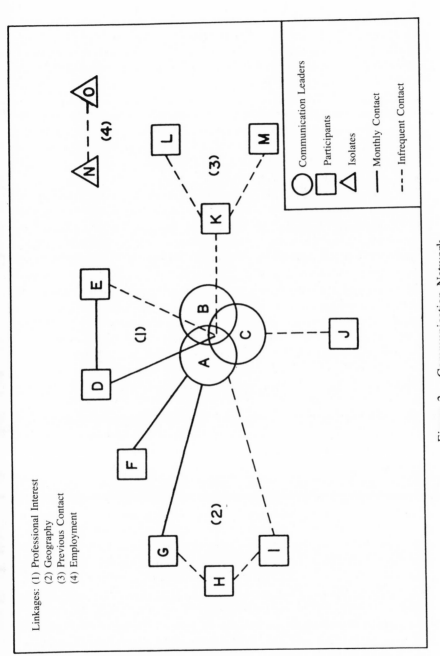

Linkages: (1) Professional Interest
(2) Geography
(3) Previous Contact
(4) Employment

Figure 2. Communication Network

9

Candy reports the "women in all roles . . . . need supportive relations, especially those of other women . . . Such groups can serve women in several ways. Behaviors needed for career success, and behaviors women were not socialized to perform, can be practiced. Problems can be solved. Experience and mistakes can be learned from."[24]

In his study of managers' working roles and the activities that describe those roles, Mintzberg highlights the role of "liaison" and defines the activities involved as "developing contacts with outside informers who can provide valuable information and favors when needed."[25] The network begun by the Institute participants is also one step in the individual development of liaison skills necessary to the successful practice of management in almost any organizational setting.

The Institute also fostered collaborativeness in terms of writing and programming efforts on the part of its attendees—an attitude needed by a profession with oft-divided interests. By attracting and fostering a diverse group of individuals who represented many types of employment backgrounds, the Institute offered testimony that there is indeed a common ground in library management. The fact that a cross-section of 30 individuals from many varied library settings could work together initially at an activity, form a network that still represents all types of libraries, and even suggest a second, higher-level follow-up activity, suggests that there must be a common level of sharing, at least among *women* in library management, that is enough to transcend type-of-library barriers.

Many results of a continuing education activity are highly individual and can be lost in group analysis. For example, the Institute experience helped one participant learn to regard her work life as a career rather than just a job. Another individual profited from learning to acknowledge and deal with ambition. The director of a large system discovered her need for a second activity, one that would place emphasis on more sophisticated techniques for handling difficult management problems, which she observed men deal with differently than do women.

At least one mark in educational programming is the support of participants for a replication of the activity for others. *All* of the participants in the study supported the idea of another Institute. Two-thirds also supported the idea of a second program for *themselves,* to build on what was learned at the original Institute and to further strengthen their contacts with one another. Reflecting the advancement of the original participants, suggestions for program activities were considerably more sophisticated than those covered by the initial Institute.

One of the most important outcomes of an analysis of an educational activity should be suggestions for the enhancement of future activities. One way to systematically make such suggestions is in the form of a model for future replication. Figure 3 suggests that there are two major elements in planning an educational activity designed to enhance the role of women in library management. The first element is the identificaton of appropriate content and the focus on skills and knowledge necessary for women to function effectively as library managers.

Figure 3.   Major Components to be Incorporated Into a Management Development Program for Women in Librarianship

Content: Skills and Knowledge	Educational Processes
(1) Management Skills and Knowledge —technical, human, and conceptual skills —nature of managerial work and role behavior —content areas: planning, organizing, human resource management, control, communication (2) Environmental Assessment Capabilities —understanding the service/NFP organization —analyzing the work place —understanding the overall organization of which an individual library is a part (3) Connector Efforts —identifying mechanisms for personal and professional support —developing strategies for the support of others —practicing coaching, mentoring, and communicating skills (4) Personal Assessment and Development —understanding the role of women in management —identifying career goals and choices —developing career decision-making skills —developing managerial socialization strategies	(1) Determining Learning Goals (2) Identifying appropriate learning techniques (i.e. lectures, case studies, studies, role play, games, discussion, audio-visual presentations, etc.) (3) Time, Place, and Format considerations (arranging human and material resources necessary to support learning techniques and content areas) (4) Developing Evaluation Mechanisms —short-term, immediate follow up —longitudinal study of participant career progress

The second element is that of educational process. Individual library educators and staff development specialists must determine the most appropriate techniques, times and places for enhancing content skills. Much of this decision will be based on the precise nature of the audience and the individual needs of participants, as well as on available resources and the objectives to be met.

If library educators wish to help future generations of women develop the skills and knowledge necessary to move into managerial roles and responsibilities, understanding the impact of specialized continuing education programs on their development will be critical. Given the years of experience and the age level of the respondents in this study, the next five-year period will be critical for their development in terms of management roles, contributions to the development of others, and general visibility. This study is thus envisioned as part of a continuous longitudinal examination of the impact of a continuing education program on its participants over time. It will be important to continue to track the progress of this group of women as they move through a period of continuous change in the profession and in society. This great knowledge "may help us to understand how some people survive and flourish under conditions of change while others falter or pay heavy personal costs. It may uncover new forms of adaptation that could be helpful to people if they were known."[26] It is critical that we have such information if we mean to help future generations of library managers to improve their own careers through management development programs.

NOTES

1.   Ella Gaines Yates, "Sexism in the Library Profession," *Library Journal* (December 15, 1979): 2615–2619.

2.   Judith Schick Braunagel, "Job Mobility of Men and Women Librarians and How it Affects Career Advancement." *American Libraries* 10 (December 1979): 643–647.

3.   Vernon E. Buck, "Toward Professionals Managing Professionals: A Case Study of Career Development for Women Librarians." In *The Evaluation of Continuing Education for Professionals: A Systems View*. (Seattle: Univ. of Washington, Division of Academic and Professional Programs, Continuing Education, 1979).

4.   Doris Cruger Dale, *Career Patterns of Women Librarians With Doctorates*. Occasional Paper #147 (Urbana, Ill.: University Of Illinois Graduate School of Library Science, 1980).

5.   Marcia Dworak, "Women in Public Library Management: How Do They Measure Up?" *Public Library Quarterly* 1 (Summer 1979): 147–160.

6.   Janice Clinedinst Fennell, "A Career Profile of Women Directors of the Largest Academic Libraries in the United States" (Ph. D. dissertation, Florida State University, 1978).

7.   Rachel K. Goldstein, "Women and Health Sciences Librarianship: An Overview." *MLA Bulletin* 65 (July 1977): 321–329; Goldstein, Rachel K. and Hill, Dorothy R. "The Status of Women in the Administration of Health Science Libraries," *MLA Bulletin* 64 (October 1975): 386–395; Rachel K. Goldstein and Dorothy R. Hill, "The Status of Women in the Administration of Health Science Libraries: A Five-Year Follow-up Study, 1972–1977;" *MLA Bulletin* 68 (January 1980): 6–15.

8.   Kathleen M. Heim and Leigh S. Estabrook, *Career Profiles and Sex Discrimination in the Library Profession* (Chicago: American Library Association, 1983).

9.   Jean Krieg Martin, "Factors Relating to the Representation of Women in Library Management" (Master's thesis, University of Georgia, 1978).

10.   Jeanne Rensel, "The Status of Women Librarians in Washington State, *PNLA Quarterly* 44 (Summer 1980): 18–25.

11.   Adelaide Reno Weir Sukiennik, "Training Women Library School Students for Greater Career Achievement" (Ph.D. dissertation, University of Pittsburgh, 1978).

12.   J.F. McDonough, "Discrimination in Social Work: Evidence, Myth and Ignorance," *Social Work* 24 (1979).

13.   Yates, "Sexism in the Library Profession," 2615–2619.

14.   Joan P. Bowker, "Attempt at Collectivity: Professional Confirmation and Support." In Barbara L. Forisha and Barbara H. Goldman (eds.), *Outsiders on the Inside: Women and Organizations* (Englewood Cliffs, N.J.: Prentice-Hall, 1981).

15.   See Bowker, "An Attempt at Collectivity" and Claire Selltiz et al., *Research Methods in Social Relations* (New York: Holt, Rinehart and Winston, 1959).

16.   Heim and Estabrook, *Career Profiles*.

17.   Frederick Herzberg, *Work and the Nature of Man* (New York: New American Library, 1966).

18.   Bowker, "An Attempt at Collectivity."

19.   Elizabeth Futas, and Susan Vaughn, "Workshop on Education." In *Women in a Woman's Profession: Strategies* (Chicago: American Library Association, 1974).

20.   Sandra E. Candy, "Women, Work and Friendship: Personal Confirmation and Support." In Barbara L. Forisha and Barbara H. Goldman (eds.), *Outsiders on the Inside; Women and Organizations* (Englewood Cliffs, N.J.: Prentice-Hall, 1981).

21.   Margaret Hennig, and Anne Jardim,. *The Managerial Woman* (Garden City, N.Y.: Doubleday, 1977).

22.   Candy, "Women, Work and Friendship."

23.   Hennig and Jardim, *The Managerial Woman.*

24.   Candy "Women, Work and Friendship."

25.   Henry Mintzberg, *The Nature of Managerial Work* (New York: Harper & Row, 1973).

26.   Elizabeth Douvan, "Changing Roles," *Michigan Alumnus* (October 1982): 4–7.

VOLUNTEERS IN LIBRARIES

Rashelle Schlessinger Karp

INTRODUCTION

The concept of volunteerism is not new; volunteers have been successfully supporting social institutions for years. Historically, volunteers have worked in the areas of prison care and reform,[1] child advocacy,[2] family services,[3] counseling,[4] job training,[5] suicide prevention,[6] rehabilitation and probation,[7] law enforcement,[8] teaching,[9] and many others.

But in spite of the overwhelming case presented in the literature of other fields *for* volunteerism, librarians have resisted the concept. This is amply demonstrated in the library literature, which is primarily devoted to debating the "should we's" of volunteerism as opposed to the "how's." Assuming that at the least, volunteerism is inevitable, and may in fact be desirable, it is helpful to first define the term, and then to examine some pros and cons, administrative concerns, and appropriate uses of volunteers.

Advances in Library Administration and Organization
Volume 5, pages 15–32
Copyright © 1986 by JAI Press Inc.
All rights of reproduction in any form reserved.
ISBN: 0-89232-674-3

DEFINITION OF VOLUNTEER

The old Department of Health, Education and Welfare defined a *volunteer* as a "person who contributes his personal service through an agency's human services program. He is not a replacement for paid staff, but adds new dimensions to the agency's services and symbolizes the community's concern for the agency's clientele."[10]

The *Florida State Statutes*[11] define four types of volunteers:

1. "Volunteer" means any person who, of his own free will, provides goods or services to any state department or agency, with no monetary or material compensation.
2. "Regular service volunteer" means any person engaged in specific voluntary service activities on an ongoing or continuous basis.
3. "Occasional service volunteer" means any person who offers to provide a one-time or occasional voluntary service.
4. "Material donor" means any person who provides funds, materials, employment, or opportunities for clients of state departments or agencies, without monetary or material compensation.

The Adult Education Association defines a volunteer as "the non-paid person who gives time to furthering the purposes of an organization . . . [he is] . . . either less centrally responsible or less adequately trained, but may also be more highly trained in the limited area in which he volunteers than a professional worker with whom he serves."[12]

Lindeman, writing for the Council of National Organizations for Adult Education, defines a volunteer in terms of what he or she does: volunteers "keep Democracy alive. They epitomize freedom and are to our society what the Bill of Rights is to the Constitution which governs us. The health of a democratic society may be measured in terms of the quality of services rendered by citizens who act 'in obedience to the unenforceable.' "[13]

Community service professionals have defined volunteer service as "a chance to realize one's potentialities, by giving of oneself as one human being to another."[14]

And the *Social Work Yearbook* defines volunteers rather emotionally as "the keepers of the public conscience, dedicated to the amelioration of human suffering and the righting of human wrong."[15]

By disregarding motivations as a crucial part of the definition of a volunteer, a simple definition, and the one this article assumes, is that volunteers are "individuals who freely contribute their services, without renumeration, to public or voluntary organizations."[16]

THE PROS AND CONS OF VOLUNTEERS IN LIBRARIES

The two accepted spellings of the word—*volunteerism* or *voluntarism*—could be analogous to the dichotomy in librarians' attitudes toward it.

Marshall of the Brooklyn College in New York records the objections to volunteerism in a speech delivered to librarians at a workshop on volunteers:

> Volunteerism undermines staff morale, denigrates the work of professional staff, exploits workers, volunteers, and the public alike, disrupts the organization, and threatens the future of the institution itself. [For] if volunteers did not leap into the breach created by failure to fund essential services . . . then funding for paid workers would be found.[17]

The library literature debates these issues, focusing on 10 major conflicts: (1) value of services, (2) public support, (3) obligations, (4) cost effectiveness, (5) staff morale, (6) exploitiveness, (7) obedience to the unenforceable, (8) job security, (9) professionalism, and (10) essential and nonessential tasks.

Conflict 1: Value of Services

One objection to volunteerism raised by librarians is that the use of volunteers lowers people's estimates of the value of a service. Corbett states that "so long as the layman sees so many libraries run by unqualified staff . . . he will have little esteem" for their value.[18] Farrington also writes about the value of service question when he states that since "library service has ceased to be offered as a philanthropic gesture" librarians should not be drawn from within the ranks of philanthropists.[19] Taber[20] and Schumacher[21] indicate that if the public only comes in contact with the "untrained custodian" (Taber's definition of volunteer), who has been initiated into the "mysteries of librarianship" (Schumacher's phraseology), then the image of the librarian as a valuable professional suffers. Levine states that people pay for what they value and conversely value what they pay for. She also insists that a librarian's use of volunteers reflects a lack of commitment to the service. This leads her to ask: If we, as librarians aren't convinced that a service is worth paying for, then how can we be convinced that it is worth providing at all? And, ultimately, if we are not convinced of the necessity to provide a service, then how can we convince the public to support it?[22]

It seems that the question here should not be one of money, but rather one of support, whatever its form. If a service is highly valued, support in the form of energies and time expended often indicates an even greater estimate of worth than a commitment of money. As for the fear that initiating a volunteer into the "MLS Mystique"[23] will somehow lower estimates of the librarian's worth—

experience has shown that in actuality, the opposite happens. As the volunteers do more work and learn more about the methods and needs of the profession, they also become increasingly aware of the necessity for more training and the value of the professional librarian.

Conflict 2: Public Support

Another objection to volunteerism is that it weakens public support because it causes the public to become apathetic about its responsibilities to the library. This, in turn may have disastrous effects at budget time, when instead of receiving monies to upgrade, create, or just maintain a vital service, a library director is told to solicit more volunteers.[24]

In response to this, librarians and other professionals call attention to the advocacy roles that volunteers assume. Deckoff indicates that volunteers are an institution's best advocates, because they live in the community and know how to best mobilize support from within it.[25] Gray calls volunteers a necessary "bridge" to the community because they create needed support for institutional programs.[26] Trainer echoes these sentiments when she states that a satisfied volunteer creates superb public relations.[27] And Tucker neatly characterizes this relationship when she says that volunteers provide "a lifeline between the expertness of the professional and the experience of the people."[28]

Conflict 3: Obligations

Some librarians correlate an administrator's decision to use volunteers with administrative laziness. These librarians claim that it is much easier to solicit volunteers than it is to mobilize public support during budget crunches[29] and that this is why so many administrators choose to enlarge their libraries' resources through the use of volunteers. It is felt that an organized effort to convince funding authorities of the need for services guarantees a better chance for the survival of the services than does the use of volunteers. Levine agrees with these thoughts, as she suggests that the only appropriate place to employ volunteers is lobbying for funds in the political arena, rather than in the library itself.[30]

Finally, Levine claims that the use of volunteers inevitably has adverse effects, because when the volunteers depart (as they always do), they leave a legacy of work behind them that paid staff will not be able to continue. It is therefore the librarian's obligation to build a broad base of support for services, not a legacy of selfless devotion.

Advocates of volunteerism refute the administrative laziness contention by stressing the time and energy required to select, train, and supervise volunteers.[31] Contrary to the contention that administrators should employ volunteers only as political allies, most supporters of volunteerism feel that the volunteer fills a dual role by performing internal services as a member of the library staff while at the same time filling an advocacy role as a fundraising member of the community.[32]

Conflict 4: Cost Effectiveness

Other criticisms of volunteerism center around claims that it is not cost effective. Many librarians feel that the investment required to train volunteers is far greater than the return.[33]

There is a paucity of actual research in the field of librarianship to support or reject this hypothesis, but most librarians who have successfully used volunteers intuitively feel that the return far surpasses the investment.[34] One study of a two-year program at Prince William Public Library in Virginia did conclude that in the first year of a program, volunteers were as costly (in management time) as paid staff, but that as the volunteer program progressed, management time decreased, thus making a volunteer work force increasingly cost efficient.[35]

Conflict 5: Staff Morale

Marshall voices the opinions of many when she says that using volunteers who have been trained at great expense means that the librarian is faced with yet another problem: "protecting his investment—giving volunteers choice assignments instead of dog work just to keep them from leaving."[36] In her opinion, this phenomenon causes a decline in staff morale.

The key here is good management. Deckoff points out that management often tends to be a little too "gentle" in handling volunteers. He claims that administrators must tell volunteers clearly what is to be done, how, and when. "It is better [for management] to err on the side of firmness [because] volunteers want authority figures, not servants."[37]

Conflict 6: Exploitiveness

Many groups are against volunteerism because they feel it is exploitive,[38] and in particular, exploitive of women.[39] For example, NOW (National Organization for Women) opposes volunteerism in libraries because such work by women is an "extension of household work. Change-directed activities" (like working for NOW) are valid volunteer activities for women, but "socially-oriented activities [like library work] merely reinforce the economic dependence of women by preventing them from earning money of their own."[40]

Not paying for service may constitute an exploitation of the service provider, but the benefits of volunteerism are not one-way.[41] Recent studies suggest that volunteerism fulfills many different needs for women, including (1) the need for primary work; (2) the need for something supplemental to primary work or to provide variety to a paying job that may be dull or routine; (3) the need for a vehicle to facilitate career entry or retraining; (4) the need to acquire status outside of the home; (5) the desire for social contact with adults; and (6) the need for a sense of personal power.[42] In fact, some state governments are beginning to recognize volunteer work as experience when applications are evaluated for employment.[43] It is therefore felt that the exploitation works both ways: the librarian may be exploiting the volunteer in order to accomplish institutional goals, but the volunteer also exploits the institution in order to satisfy special needs that motivated his or her offer to volunteer in the first place.[44]

Conflict 7: "Obedience to the Unenforceable"

Many librarians feel that the nature of the volunteer's status precludes any real control on the part of administration (there are no monetary rewards attached to the volunteer's performance). This causes volunteers to be unreliable, unmanageable,[45] and to be more likely to quit if they are not totally happy with the work environment.[46]

Once again, the answer is good management and careful, thorough preparation, in order to continue the trend of the 1980s toward less turnover of volunteer staff.[47]

Conflict 8: Job Security

Many professionals fear that volunteers will replace them[48] and some claim that no new positions will be funded where volunteers are successful.[49] Still others believe that volunteers are really job hunters in disguise, who will step into professional positions that they helped establish as volunteers.[50] It is, in part, this concern for job security that led the Library Association to adopt a very strict policy on volunteers. The *Library Association Record* states:

> Voluntary work should not be used as a substitute for the work of paid staff . . . There have been occasions in the past, where, without proper consultation, voluntary activity has been implemented which has threatened the jobs of paid staff and/or has had repercussions on earnings levels . . . Whilst the Association has no desire to disparage the motives of those who have traditionally provided supplementary services on a voluntary basis and who may wish to do so when library services are threatened by financial cuts, it is constrained, in present circumstances to resist the introduction of voluntary workers.
>
> The use of volunteers in periods of high unemployment is undesirable because of the risk to paid employment and the livelihood of individuals. The Association cannot condone the action of any of its members who engage themselves in voluntary work arising from the loss of paid jobs in any sector of the economy.[51]

Gale rebuts these claims by showing how patient libraries in hospitals were pioneered by farsighted volunteers who saw the need for them even before the library profession did. She goes on to say that these volunteers advanced the work themselves, recognized when they needed a professional, and then fought for the concepts until patients' libraries won departmental status in health care institutions and professional status in librarianship.[52] Stephan states that as volunteers work in a position and become convinced themselves of its importance, they also become very vocal in fighting for the establishment of paid positions where there had been none before.[53] Often cited as examples of this phenomenon are Friends of the Library groups and Boards of Trustees.[54] Detweiler and others add that paid positions are often established because volunteers expose the public to a service that then becomes valuable.[55] She points out that our unwillingness to employ volunteers "creates a vacuum into which others may step," with decisions and actions that adversely affect us as librarians.[56]

Finally, Warner argues that at least volunteers call attention to the value of new positions by filling them before they can be funded. She also asks a pertinent question: If a volunteer does fill an unfunded position one year and it isn't funded the next, can the librarian be sure that this happened *because* the position was filled by a volunteer? Warner claims that the funding might not have been provided anyway. But at least, with volunteers, the service was provided and the clients didn't suffer.[57]

Conflict 9: Professionalism

Librarianship's Status

One of the prevailing ideas about and perhaps the biggest objection to volunteerism is that use of volunteers detracts from librarianship's status as a "profession," and even gives the impression that no real qualifications are needed to perform the librarian's duties.[58] Objections to library volunteers centering around themes of professionalism are voiced over and over again in the literature. As early as 1942, Farrington wrote (about volunteers in hospital libraries) that administrators "look with suspicion upon any profession which purports to be professional but which allows amateurs to carry out the duties . . . [of] trained personnel."[59] And, in an editor's note written the same year (about a wartime economy), librarians were warned that "city officials who see librarians using . . . volunteers to fill vacancies will, after the war, think that any person will do, and . . . efforts to raise standards will be suddenly thwarted."[60] Thirty-four years later, Flanagan reiterates this fear by claiming that the use of volunteers in libraries damages the profession. These kinds of fears also led to the establishment in 1975 of an organization called CLOUT (Concerned Librarians Opposing Unprofessional Trends), which warns that volunteers devalue the role of professionals in the library.[61]

For the most part, supporters of volunteerism do not directly deal with this conflict. Instead, most proponents of library volunteerism first acknowledge the professional versus nonprofessional dilemma, and then point out the beneficial changes that volunteers can effect. The implication here seems to be that if the benefits derived from volunteers are great enough, this is justification for not worrying about their alleged threat to professionalism.

One librarian deals with the question by posing what she considers to be an even greater threat. She acknowledges the concern for professionalism, but then goes on to say that even more threatening is the thought of other specializations filling the vacuum left by the absence of librarians—volunteer or professional. As an example, she cites the hospital, where many "library-type" services are being managed by other specialties (nurses, activity directors, etc.), because there is no library or librarian. She claims that competent volunteers can pave the way for professional librarians.[62]

Professional and Nonprofessional Tasks

As noted previously, librarians have difficulty accepting volunteers because of threats they may represent to professionalism. However, even if the professional decides that these perceived threats can be minimized through good management, and that the benefits justify the risks, yet another problem must be resolved—defining specific tasks to be professional or nonprofessional.[63]

In an attempt to retain professionalism while maintaining a core of volunteers, much of the literature would limit volunteers to the performance of nonprofessional tasks.[64] Unfortunately, however, this same literature fails to properly define the term. For example, some hospital librarians believe that patient–librarian contact falls strictly under the definition of professional duties,[65] while other hospital librarians have cited cases where volunteers provided the patient contact as a nonprofessional, but beneficial extension of services.[66] This ambiguity confuses the debate even as librarians struggle to determine which tasks are nonprofessional (and thus appropriate for volunteers) and which tasks are professional (and thus not within the domain of volunteers).

Many examples of this confusing problem can be found by examining some of the jobs currently being performed by volunteers:

Development of graphic arts displays[67] and public relations campaigns[68]   Some practitioners feel that these tasks are not within the traditional domain of the professional librarian. However, library school curricula often emphasize the use of graphic arts and media as public relations techniques. Implicit in these courses is a belief that the cultivation of such skills is vital to the librarian's professional responsibility to actively promote the library.

Document preparation, including sorting, shelving, mending, and helping in the cataloging department   It is generally believed that the proper performance of these duties does not require a professional degree, and so they have traditionally been delegated to volunteers. However, in many libraries, the cataloging volunteer files into the card catalog and may even assign subject headings. Here again the lines between professional and nonprofessional labels become confused as librarians argue about the degrees of professionalism required for adequate performance.

Outreach services[69]   Many librarians consider outreach a delivery service that can adequately be performed by volunteers. However, what if the volunteer not only delivers materials, but also chooses them[70] and makes suggestions to the readers?[71] When the mechanical task of delivering materials develops into reader's advisor and reference services, many librarians would argue that the job should no longer be classified as nonprofessional.

Storytelling and general programming[72]   The same definitional problems exist here, as some feel that storytelling is an art that can be mastered without professional training, while others teach courses in it.

The same types of arguments can be offered concerning the use of volunteers to run genealogy programs,[73] to develop oral history programs,[74] to act as circulation assistants,[75] to provide library tours,[76] to produce materials in special formats,[77] to develop special collections and research projects,[78] to tutor,[79] to form talent pools,[80] to serve nursing homes and provide special equipment to the disabled,[81] to supervise other volunteers,[82] and even to run the whole library.[83] As Flanagan points out, the real question is this: Do volunteers know what they're doing and should they be doing it?[84]

Conflict 10: Essential and Nonessential Tasks

In an attempt to simplify the definitional tasks involved in determining appropriate tasks for volunteers, some librarians add yet another dimension to the criteria: essentialism. By claiming that volunteers should only perform nonessential services, librarians compound the definitional problems, because they must now apportion library jobs into professional and nonprofessional categories, and also into essential and nonessential categories.

This additional dimension brings up a basic philosophical issue. If a job is nonessential, then why do it at all? Librarians who advocate employing volunteers only for nonessential services condemn these services to defeat even before they are started. The key here is sound policy making that includes a well-defined philosophy of service. A library policy endorses a detailed mission statement that clearly identifies all service activities in which the library will engage. In this way, the librarian defines *all* of the library's services as essential and self-defeating definitions disappear.

USING VOLUNTEERS EFFECTIVELY

The "Guidelines for Using Volunteers in Libraries" adopted by the American Library Association (ALA) in 1971 begins by citing some benefits derived from the use of volunteers: (1) enhancement of community support, utilization and public relations, (2) potential recruitment into the profession, and (3) fresh approaches and added talents. Seventeen principles are listed as caveats for those librarians who recruit volunteers. In summarized form they include the following major caveats: the use of volunteers requires comprehensive prior planning, good administration, and contractual clarity; the use of volunteers should be considered a temporary measure pending employment of staff; volunteers should not displace or supplant established staff; volunteers must be recognized and awarded meaningful duties; and library services must be planned bearing in mind the possible termination of unavailability of volunteer help.[85]

The ALA Guidelines provide broad principles of management for a volunteer program. The literature provides some more specific guidelines, which are divided into six major areas:[86]

I. Plan and Prepare
   A. Determine the needs of the organization with the entire staff.
      This will include prioritizing needs and developing a time table for getting tasks done.
   B. Make sure that you and your staff feel that volunteers are the answer.
      After clearly determining what jobs need to be done, the librarian may find that volunteers will not be able to achieve the desired goals.
   C. Determine what kinds of volunteers are needed and how they will be motivated.
      This requires a knowledge of the kinds of people who frequently volunteer. A typology follows:
      1. Service-oriented volunteers: The volunteer is primarily devoted to others or doing things for others.
      2. Issue/cause oriented volunteers, or "loners": The volunteer is primarily concerned with a specific public issue, usually involving a change in society.
      3. Consummatory or self-expressive volunteers: The volunteer is primarily interested in enjoyment of activities for his or her own sake and for the sake of self-expression or realization, without any major focus on altruism.
      4. Occupational/economic self-interest volunteers, often called career volunteers: The volunteer is primarily interested in furthering his or her occupational and/or economic interests.
      5. Philanthropic/funding volunteers, or good-work volunteers: The volunteer is primarily concerned with raising funds for the benefit of the organization.[87]

Obviously, these categories overlap to some degree, but the fact remains that how well the volunteer performs in specific jobs will be affected by his or her motivations, and by how well the library administrator can meld the volunteer's and the institution's goals.

D. Determine costs and secure funds for the program. Although the volunteers are unpaid, they are not a free source of help; there are substantial indirect costs in terms of recruitment, training, and supervision, and substantial direct costs such as transportation and printing.

E. If the program is to be a sizeable one, a paid coordinator should be assigned.

F. Obtain approval and support statements from governing bodies and unions in writing.

Written statements will clarify the parameters of the program, and its funding sources. They will also provide a structured way to approach union officials, who may be very hostile to the concept of volunteerism.[88]

G. Be aware of legal responsibilities to your volunteers.[89] Some states have interpreted their Workers Compensation Acts so as to allow certain volunteers worker compensation benefits. The Pennsylvania Workers Compensation Act (PWCA), for example, defines "employee" as "All natural persons who perform services for another for a valuable consideration." Penn. Stat. Ann. Tit. 77, Sec. 22 (Purdon Supp. 1982). Section 1031 of the Act, as interpreted by the Pennsylvania courts, recognizes that "certain classes of volunteers who [perform] public services merit compensation under the PWCA for injuries received while carrying out their Good Samaritan activities." *Guffey v. Logan,* 563 F. Supp. 951, 957 (E.D. Penn. 1983). Librarians considering the employment of volunteers should check whether their volunteers should be covered by their workers compensation insurance.

H. Make sure that, in your estimate, the time and efforts devoted to the volunteer program will be balanced by substantial results.

II. Recruit

A. Prepare job descriptions for each position.

These should be prepared in consultation with the entire paid staff. This will not only clarify what the volunteer is to do, but should also help to diminish staff fears of being displaced and/or replaced.

B. Explore sources of volunteers.

Before advertising generally, explore the sources that already exist formally within the community. If there are no appropriate sources, than a carefully planned advertising campaign (which properly presents the library's image) should be developed and implemented.

C. Interview candidates.

It is critical here that the librarian possess a clear concept of job param-

eters and competencies, in order to make the interview a good
screening process. It should be remembered that the interviewer does
not have to accept everyone, and that each volunteer brings a special set
of skills to the job which qualify him or her for specific responsibilities.[90]

III. Orient

  A. The interview has already begun the process of orientation, because it
      included a thorough description of the job.
  B. Orient the recruit to the organization, its general purpose, goals, objec-
      tives, philosophies, rules and regulations. It should be emphasized that
      because this person will represent the organization, he or she should
      understand it properly.
  C. Introduce the volunteer to the staff, and give a thorough tour of the
      building.
      These introductions demonstrate the librarian's high estimate of the
      volunteer's potential to the library, and help establish esprit de corps.[91]

IV. Train and Supervise

  A. The volunteer must be told the identity of his or her supervisor.
  B. The supervisor must be accessible to the volunteer, especially in the
      early stages of the relationship.
  C. Duties should be clearly demonstrated, and with patience.[92]
  D. The volunteer should be updated on agency news and policy changes,
      and follow-up to ensure that confusions do not persist is imperative.[93]
  E. Volunteers should be encouraged to participate professionally and so-
      cially in the working group.
  F. Volunteers should be made aware of evaluation procedures that pertain
      to their performance.

V. Evaluate

    Volunteers should be evaluated at specified intervals using a rating scale
    approved by the library administration. These evaluations should be kept
    in a personnel folder that can later be used to provide job references,
    reminders to recognize special achievements, and (if necessary) docu-
    mentation for dismissal.

VI. Recognize

    The volunteer's "paycheck" is recognition, which may be accomplished in
    many ways, limited only by the creativity of the supervisor. However, it is
    equally important to "keep the contributions of both volunteers and paid
    staff in perspective. [Agencies] make great efforts to recognize and honor
    volunteers who are performing essentially the same service as paid employ-
    ees who receive little or no special recognition. Such contradictory reward
    systems can sabotage effective volunteer service if antagonism develops be-
    tween paid staff members and volunteers."[94]

Nichols[95] sums up the "dos and don'ts" of using volunteers very nicely:
Do plan carefully.
Do coordinate.
Do select carefully.
Do diversify, or match the volunteer to the task.
Do train.
Do integrate volunteers into the staff.
Do reward volunteers.
Do evaluate.
  [but]
Don't use volunteers to replace paid staff.
Don't underestimate volunteers.
Don't forget that how volunteers see us is important because they are our best public relations.

WHAT ABOUT THE FUTURE?

Develop Manuals For the Effective Use of Volunteers

Since the appearance of the 1971 ALA Guidelines, many guides on the "care and handling" of volunteers have been published. However, many librarians feel that there is still a great need for the profession to produce a definitive manual dealing with the problems involved and their solutions. Jenkins[96] points out the need for national and state level leaders to upgrade standards for providing library service to include a recognized role for the volunteer. He also feels that library schools should conduct workshops and include coursework in their curricula on the use of volunteers in libraries. (Warner polled library schools in 1972 and found that most do not recognize the subject as essential for study.) Jenkins further states that librarians should budget formally for volunteers and that library volunteers should be organized on state and national levels, as they are through the American Hospital Association.

Make a Real Commitment to Volunteers

The employment of library volunteers indicates a high level of commitment to service. Volunteers can and should provide the diversification needed to help librarians respond to the many needs of the community. The "right" volunteer (carefully supervised) can infuse a program with high levels of motivation, expertise, and stimulation—qualities that are always valuable. Paid staff will probably never be the complete answer, because there may never be a time when all the necessary services are adequately funded. However, if volunteers are to be service providers, then they should be so all the time, and not merely in reaction to circumstances that force their acceptance by the profession. Librarians should not, as the ALA says, consider volunteerism a temporary measure, pending the employment of staff. This kind of reasoning degrades the volunteers' status to mere "stopgap" until something or someone better comes along. Any volunteer program (and, in fact, any program) operating within a conceptual framework that only half endorses it is doomed to failure. Commitment to the service demands a commitment to the volunteers who perform it.

Take a Serious, Impartial Look at Volunteerism

We must stop being paranoid about the survival of our profession as a profession. Librarianship is highly diversified and includes many specializations. Therefore, there is always room for people with special subject expertise, or even special personality traits. The librarian cannot be everything. He or she must acknowledge this fact, excel in the areas of professional specialization for which he or she has prepared, and allow others to fill complementary roles, even if these people are not librarians.

Redefine Our Philosophies of Service

A successful volunteer program depends on a firm commitment to the philosophies that underlie it. In order for volunteers to be actuated and fulfilled by a volunteer program, the librarian must be fully committed to the services that the volunteers are providing. This means that benefits obtained from volunteers should not be defined in terms of extension of services, but should be defined in terms of basic services. A library policy must embrace a clear philosophy of service, which defines all programs under the jurisdiction of the library as basic and essential. Thus, when one of the basic services included in the library's mission statement is not funded, justification for using volunteers will come directly from the library's written philosophy. We must commit ourselves to an "ideal" and honor our commitments with actions that include volunteers.

CONCLUSION

The profession of librarianship debates the issues of volunteers in libraries, focusing on 10 major objections: volunteerism (1) lowers the value of service; (2) weakens public support; (3) indicates administrative laziness; (4) is not cost effective; (5) lowers staff morale; (6) exploits women; (7) is an unreliable source of labor; (8) threatens job security; (9) threatens librarianship's status as a profession; and (10) should be limited to nonessential status.

A strong commitment to service and the service providers, along with good management, can prevent many of these undesirable effects. But more important, we must have more confidence in ourselves and must be willing to accept help from the communities we serve. Then, and only then, can volunteerism rightfully become a more potent and positive force within our profession.

REFERENCES

1. H. Barr, *Volunteers in Prison After Care* (London: Allen and Unwin, 1967); R. J. Berger et al., *Experiment in a Juvenile Court: A Study of a Program of Volunteers Working With Juvenile Probationers* (Ann Arbor: Institute for Social Research, University of Michigan, 1975); J. J. Kiessling, *The Ottawa Juvenile Court Volunteer Program* (Ottawa: Information Canada, 1972); S. J. Ellis and K. H. Noyes, "Citizens Inside. Supporting Teamwork," *Corrections Today* 45 (June 1983): 48 + .

2. *Volunteers in Child Abuse and Neglect Programs, A Special Report From the National Center on Child Abuse and Neglect, 1978* (Washington, D.C.: ERIC Document Reproduction Service, ED 161 203, 1978).

3. J. Edwards, *The Vanishing Dichotomy: The Public vs. The Private Family Service Agency: Implications for Black Families* (Washington, D.C.: ERI Document Reproduction Service, ED 173 476, 1977); H. Ganong and M. Coleman, "Evaluation of the Use of Volunteers as Parent Educators," *Family Relations* 32 (January 1983): 117–122.

4. M. Kahn et al., *The Open Door: A Campus Peer Counselling Center* (Washington, D.C.: ERIC Document Reproduction Service, ED 146 502, 1977); G. O. Lenihan and L. Jackson, "Social Need, Public Response: The Volunteer Professional Model for Human Services Agencies and Counselors," *Personnel and Guidance Journal* 62 (January 1984): 285–289.

5. D. Gottlieb, "VISTA, Pepsi, and Poverty," *Society* 9 (February 1972): 6–7.

6. S. Helig et al., "Role of Nonprofessional Volunteers in a Suicide Prevention Center," *Community Mental Health Journal* 4 (August 1968): 287–295.

7. R. J. Lee, "Volunteer Case-Aid Program—A Community Responds," *Crime and Delinquency* 14 (October 1968): 331–335; L. K. Niedenthal and R. E. Sinnett, "Use of Indigenous Volunteers in Rehabilitation Living Unit for Disturbed College Students," *Community Mental Health Journal* 4 (April 1968): 232–249; P. M. Shields et al., "Using Volunteers in Adult Probation," *Federal Probation* 46 (June 1983): 57–64.

8. I. Scheier et al., *Using Volunteers in Court Settings: A Manual for Volunteer Probation Settings* (Washington, D.C.: Department of Health, Education and Welfare, 1968); "Volunteers in Policing (symposium)," *Police Chief* 49 (May 1982): 18–46.

9. M. Skjoiten and R. Bartlett, "Student Volunteers as Group Leaders in Elementary Schools," *Children* 15 (November/December 1968): 225–228; B. DaSilva, *Practical School Volunteer and Teacher Aid Programs* (New York: Parker, 1974); S. T. Gray, "How to Create a Successful School/Community Partnership," *Phi Delta Kappan* 65 (February 1984): 405–409.

10. Mrs. R. Starkey, "Library Pals Volunteering for PALS," *Texas Library Journal* 51 (Spring 1975), p. 26.

11. *Florida State Statutes* (1980 Supplementary Pamphlet), art. 110, sec. 501, p. 161.

12. "Workshop on . . . the Volunteer," *Adult Leadership* 3 (November 1954), p. 13.

13. E. Lindeman, *The Volunteer*, as cited by A. K. Stenzel in *Volunteer Training and Development: A Manual for Community Groups* (New York: Seabury Press, 1968), p. 5.

14. A. K. Stenzel, *Volunteer Training and Development: A Manual for Community Groups* (New York: Seabury Press, 1968), p. 5.

15. E. Schenefield, "Citizen and Volunteer Participation," in *Social Work Yearbook* (New York: National Association of Social Workers, 1960), p. 157.

16. National Association of Social Workers, "Volunteers," in *Encyclopedia of Social Work*, Vol. 2, 7th ed. (Washington, D.C., 1977), pp. 1582–1590.

17. L. Trainer, "METRO Workshop on Volunteers in Libraries Sparks Controversy, Offers Practical Advice," *American Libraries* 7 (December 1976): 666–667.

18. E. V. Corbett, "The Layman Looks at Librarianship," *Library World* 44 (October 1941): 43–45.

19. A. Farrington, "Hospital Library Volunteers, No," *ALA Bulletin* 37 (September 1943): 261–263.

20. F. T. Tabor, "What Price Volunteers?" *Wilson Library Bulletin* 15 (November 1940): 269.

21. M. Schumacher, "Hospital Library Volunteers, Yes," *ALA Bulletin* 37 (September 1943): 258–260.

22. E. Levine, "Volunteerism in Libraries," *Bay State Librarian* 69 (Summer 1980): 11–14.

23. A. J. Anderson et al., "Why Not Volunteers? (Solving the Problem of Staff Reduction," *Library Journal* 108 (May 1, 1983): 883–884.

24. A. Flanagan, "Some Thoughts on Survival in the Seventies: or Two Views of the Volunteer Dilemma." *Catholic Library World* 48 (October 1976): 112–115.

25. M. J. Deckoff, "The Volunteer: Key to Successful Fund Raising," *Independent School* 43 (October 1983): 34–38.

26. S. T. Gray, "Working with Volunteers," *VocEd* 57 (June 1982): 49–51.

27. L. Trainer, "METRO Workshop on Volunteers in Libraries Sparks Controversy, Offers Practical Advice," *American Libraries* 7 (December 1976): 66–667.

28. M. P. Tucker, "Volunteers for the Library," *California School Libraries* 44 (Winter 1973): 21–22.

29. A. Flanagan, "Some Thoughts on Survival in the Seventies: or Two Views of the Volunteer Dilemma." *Catholic Library World* 48 (October 1976: 112–115.

30. E. Levine, "Volunteerism in Libraries," *Bay State Librarian* 69 (Summer 1980): 11–14.

31. Sister M. M. Cribben, "Browsing: Library Volunteers Projects," *Catholic Library World* 46 (November 1974); 181.; C. Kies, "And What Have I Done What For?" *Catholic Library World* 48 (October 1976): 102–102; N. Savage, "Volunteers in Libraries." *Library Journal* 101 (December 1, 1976): 2431–2433; G. Cooper, "Plan for Reductions," *Library Journal* 108 (May 1, 1983): 884.

32. "Edmonton Lauds Its Volunteers at Tenth Year Birthday Party," *Library Journal* 108 (October 1, 1983): 1834.

33. "Volunteers in Libraries: Comments to Marjery Quigley," *Library Journal* 67 (May 1, 1942): 401. N. Savage, "Volunteers in Libraries," *Library Journal* 101 (December 1, 1976): 2431–2433.

34. E Greer, "Volunteers in the Chapel Hill Public Library," *North Carolina Libraries* 32 (Spring 1974): 25–27.

35. B. Longeway, "Examining Volunteer Expenses," *American Libraries* 10 (January 1979): 10.

36. L. Trainer, "METRO Workshop on volunteers in Libraries Sparks Controversy, Offers Practical Advice," *American Libraries* 7 (December 1976): 2432.

37. M. J. Deckoff, "The Volunteer: Key to Successful Fund Raising," *Independent School* 43 (October 1983): 37.

38. K. A. Henderson, "Women as Volunteers." *The Humanist* 44 (July/August 1984): 26–27 + .

39. K. Nyren, "News in Review, 1981." *Library Journal* 107 (January 15, 1982): 139–150.

40. E. Bolger, "Volunteerism, Take It Out of My Salary," *Ms.*, (February 1975): 71–74.

41. P. C. O'Neill, "New Volunteer Venture is a Two Sided Service." *Phi Delta Kappan* 65 (October 1983): 145–146.

42. E. Howarth, "Personality Characteristics of Volunteers," *Psychological Reports* 38 (1976): 855–858; J. R. Jenner, "Participation, Leadership, and the Role of Volunteerism Among Selected Women Volunteers," *Journal of Voluntary Action Research* 4 (October-December 1982): 27–38.

43. "Volunteers in Libraries: Reports from all Over," *Library Journal* 107 (January 1, 1982): 20.

44. L. Lucas, "Volunteers: Altruists or Prima Donnas?" *Public Libraries* 19 (Fall 1980): 87–89.

45. M. P. Tucker, "Volunteers for the Library," *California School Libraries* 44 (Winter 1973): 21–22.

46. J. L. Pearce, "Job Attitude and Motivation Differences," *Journal of Applied Psychology* 68 (November 1983): 646–652.

47. "Volunteer Use Up in Phoenix," *Library Journal* 107 (October 1, 1982): 1804.

48. S. R. Gale, "Volunteers and Patient's Libraries," *Catholic Library World* 48 (October 1976): 116–118.

49. S. Stephan, "Assignment: Administrative Volunteer," *Catholic Library World* 48 (October 1976): 104–107.

50. L. Trainer, "METRO Workshop on Volunteers in Libraries Sparks Controversy, Offers Practical Advice," *American Libraries* 7 (December 1976): 666–667.

51. Library Association, "Library Association Policy on Unpaid Volunteers," *Library Association Record* 84 (February 1982): 72.

52. S. R. Gale, "Volunteers and Patient's Libraries," *Catholic Library World* 48 (October 1976): 116–118.

53. S. Stephan, "Assignment: Administrative Volunteer," *Catholic Library World* 48 (October 1976): 104–107.

54. F. Warnscholz, *Making the Most of Volunteers and Friends in Libraries* (Nebraska: Nebraska Library Commission, 1978).

55. M. J. Detweiler, "Volunteers in Public Libraries: The Costs and Benefits" *Public Libraries* 21 (Fall 1982): 5.

56. M. J. Detweiler, "Volunteers are One Option," *Library Journal* 108 (May 1, 1983): 883–884.

57. A. S. Warner, *Volunteers in Libraries: LJ Special Report #2* (New York: Bowker, 1977).

58. A. J. Anderson and others. "Why Not Volunteers? [Solving the Problem of Staff Reduction]," *Library Journal* 108 (May 1, 1983): 883–884.

59. A. Farrington; "Hospital Library Volunteers, No," *ALA Bulletin* 37 (September 1943): 261–263.

60. "Volunteers in Libraries: Comments to Marjery Quigley," *Library Journal* 67 (May 1, 1942): 401.

61. J. Carvalho, "To Complement or Compete? The Role of Volunteers in Public Libraries," *Public Library Quarterly* 5 (Spring 1984): 35–39.

62. S. R. Gale, "Volunteers and Patient's Libraries," *Catholic Library World* 48 (October 1976): 116–118.

63. J. Carvalho, "To Complement or Compete? The Role of Volunteers in Public Libraries," *Public Library Quarterly* 5 (Spring 1984): 35–39.

64. V. C. Stanton, "Volunteers, Another View: How Do the Volunteers Feel About their Work?" *Wisconsin Library Bulletin* 74 (September 1978): 235–236.

65. A. Farrington, "Hospital Library Volunteers, No," *ALA Bulletin* 37 (September 1943): 261–263.

66. M. Schumacher, "Hospital Library Volunteers, Yes," *ALa Bulletin* 37 (September 1943): 258–260.

67. M. M. Seguin and J. Jarlsberg, "Vintage Volunteers in the Library," *Catholic Library World* 48 (October 1976): 109–111.

68. G. K. Logan, "Volunteers for Publicity," *Louisiana Library Association Bulletin* 10 (March 1947): 72–74; "Volunteers in Libraries: Guards, Public Relations, Outreach," *Library Journal* 102 (October 1, 1977): 1996; "Hayden, Colorado Survey Finds People Love their Library," *Library Journal* 107 (November 15, 1982): 430–431.

69. M. LeClair-Marzolf, "Fairly Boring Jobs for Young People [reprinted from Main Entry, February 1981]" *Unabashed Librarian* 38 (1981): 2–5.

70. "Many Outreach Services Depend on Volunteers," *Library Journal* 99 (November 1, 1974): 2795.

71. L. Moussa, "Volunteers Offer Library Service to Shut-ins," *Catholic Library World* 48 (October 1976): 119–121.

72. E. A. Petgen, "Inside to Outside and Back Again," *Southeastern Librarian* 16 (Summer 1966): 107–112; Inglewood California Public Library, *Volunteer Assistance in the Library* (California: Inglewood California Public Library, 1975); I. L. Blair, "Medford Storytelling Guild: or Volunteers, Unlimited," *Emergency Librarian* 10 (November–December 1982): 19–20.

73. "LSCA Funded Volunteer Program Catches on in Carroll County," *Library Journal* 107:

500+; C. McKinley, "Volunteer Efforts Recognized at Laramie County," *Wyoming Library Roundup* 37 (Summer 1982): 50–51.

74. B. Taylor, "Volunteers Aid Oral History Project." *Focus on Indiana Libraries* 29 (Spring 1975): 23.

75. "Proposition 13 Spurs Use of Volunteers in Ventura," *Library Journal* 104 (May 1, 1979): 996; "Libraries of All Types Depending on Volunteers," *Library Journal* 100 (February 1, 1975): 254.

76. "Docents at Los Angeles Public: an Elite Volunteer Corps," *Library Journal* 108 (October 15, 1983): 1917.

77. D. B. Pfeifer, "Meeting the Needs of the Physically Handicapped," *Library Occurrent* 22 (August 1968): 289–290.

78. M. P. Parsons, "One Library's Volunteers," *Wilson Library Bulletin* 18 (September 1943): 34–35+.

79. "METRO Studies Volunteer Use; Tucson Urges Program," *Library Journal* 101 (July 1976): 1480–1481.

80. M. M. Seguin and J. Jarlsberg, "Vintage Volunteers in the Library," *Catholic Library World* 48 (October 1976): 109–111.

81. "Need for Volunteers Cited: New Projects Reported," *Library Journal* 99 (September 1, 1974): 2026.

82. "One Volunteer Experiment," *American Libraries* 5 (May 1974): 231–232.

83. W. W. Sannwald and C. M. Hofmann, "Practicing Librarians: Volunteerism in Ventura County," *Library Journal* 107 (ie 105) (March 15, 1980): 681–682; M. J. Detweiler, "Volunteers in Public Libraries: The Costs and Benefits" *Public Libraries* 21 (Fall 1982): 5.

84. A. Flanagan, "Some Thoughts on Survival in the Seventies: or Two Views of the Volunteer Dilemma." *Catholic Library World* 48 (October 1976): 112–115.

85. American Library Association, Library Administration Division, "Guidelines for Using Volunteers in the Future of Libraries" *American Libraries* 2 (April 1971): 407–408.

86. K. Dodson, "Help! The Answer Can Be Volunteers," *Idaho Librarian* 32 (July 1980): 112–115.

87. E. Stanton, *Clients Come Last* (Beverly Hills, CA: Sage Publications, 1970).

88. "Volunteer Projects: Reports from the Field," *Library Journal* 104 (February 1, 1979): 341.

89. "Legal Status of Volunteers Clarified in Florida," *Library Journal* 104: (November 1, 1979): 2274.

90. M. Whipple, "Creative Use of Volunteers [at Acton Public Library]," *Connecticut Libraries* 24 (Spring 1982): 15–16.

91. "Volunteerism," in E. Silverman, *101 Media Center Ideas,* (Scarecrow, 1980) pp. 157–177.

92. M. A. Hoaglund, Sister "Library Skills—Caught or Taught! [Instruction to Volunteers]," *Catholic Library World* 53 (November 1981): 173–175.

93. A. Vafa, "Volunteer Literacy Tutors Must Have Training and Support," *Canadian Library Journal* 37 (August 1980): 267–269.

94. L. Lucas, "Volunteers: Altruists or Prima Donnas?" *Public Libraries* 19 (Fall 1980): 87–89.

95. B. M. Nichols, "Enrich Your Library with Volunteer Programs," *Show Me Libraries* 31 (August 1980): 24–26.

96. H. Jenkins, "Volunteers in the Future of Libraries," *Library Journal* 97 (April 15, 1972): 1399–1403.

THE HISTORY OF PUBLISHING AS A FIELD OF RESEARCH FOR LIBRARIANS AND OTHERS

Joe W. Kraus

INTRODUCTION

Most writers who have reviewed what has been written on the history of book publishing in this country have lamented that too little research is being done. My complaint is not about the lack of interest in the subject—in fact there has been a quickening of interest during the past 10 to 15 years—but that so few librarians are involved. This paper is a brief for the writing of American book publishing history by librarians. Some librarians have made contributions, to be sure, but they are not many and they generally come from the ranks of rare book librarians. Why librarians shy away from research on the history of the book, which is still their basic stock in trade, is a phenomenon which I shall not speculate on here. My purpose is rather to suggest that librarians are neglecting a sub-

Advances in Library Administration and Organization
Volume 5, pages 33–65
Copyright © 1986 by JAI Press Inc.
All rights of reproduction in any form reserved.
ISBN: 0-89232-674-3

ject in which they have both a proprietary interest and an opportunity to use the bibliographical knowledge that comes with their professional education.

In my attempt to persuade the unconvinced and to support those already committed to the study of publishing history, I will summarize some of the current activities pertaining to the history of the book and review the research of the past 15 years pertaining to the history of American book publishing. Fifteen years is neither an arbitrary period nor one of convenience; it is the time that has elapsed since the coverage of G. Thomas Tanselle's *Guide to the Study of United States Imprints,*[1] a work that will be alluded to repeatedly. My emphasis will be on American publishing history rather than on the larger subject, the history of the book, but because printing is closely linked with publishing—the functions were inseparable until well into the nineteenth century—a selection of books and articles published since 1970 on printing, binding, book illustration, and design and some titles on the business of publishing are included.

RENEWED INTEREST IN THE HISTORY OF THE BOOK

Whether or not librarians are interested in the history of the book, scholars from other fields are and they have taken the lead in a new wave of interest during the past decade. The impetus for much of this attention is Lucien Febvre and Henri-Jean Martin's *L'Apparition du Livre,* published in 1958 but not translated into English until 1976.[2] The book is not merely another summary of the history of printing from moveable type in Western Europe, although that subject is synthesized skillfully; it is also a study of the book as a force for cultural change. It is the latter emphasis of the book that has influenced a generation of historical scholars in France and has had a considerable impact on English and American scholarship. Collectively, the French influence bears the attractive, almost seductive, name *l'histoire du livre,*[3] a term that has come to signify something more than a smooth-flowing phrase in a different language.

Anglo-American scholarship on the history of the book derives from a literary rather than an historical tradition. W. W. Greg and R. B. McKerrow, pioneers in the development of analytical bibliography, became bibliographers in order to determine the correct or most nearly correct texts, from among a bewildering array of early printings of Elizabethan and other early English plays. A "correct text" in this instance means one printed precisely as the author intended. McKerrow's *Introduction to Bibliography for Literary Students,*[4] which influenced scholarship for 20 years after its publication in 1927, emphasized that textual study is dependent on the bibliographical study of books and that to be a bibliographer one must know as much as possible about the printing and publishing practices of a period. It is an oversimplification to say that the French approach to the history of the book is concerned with the book as a conveyer of ideas whereas the Anglo-American approach considers the book as an artifact, but this distinction seems to lie at the heart of the matter. An English scholar, John Feather, has stated it much better: "It is not merely that the one is textual and analytical while the other is historical and sociological; it is rather that the one took the book as its starting point while the other approached it tangentially."[5]

The difference, however it may be expressed, has led to a skirmish of words between advocates of the two points of view. Robert Darnton, in *The Business of Enlightenment; a Publishing History of the Encyclopédie, 1775–1800,* for example, speaks of "aficionados savoring bindings, epigones contemplating watermarks, *erudits* preparing editions of Jane Austen" in American rare book rooms "but no ordinary, meat-and-potatoes historian attempting to understand the book as a force in history."[6] In his 1981 Hanes Lecture, Tanselle sought to reconcile the differences between the French and Anglo-American models and to suggest a methodology that would combine analysis of the physical book with study of the book industry in the context of social, economic, cultural, and intellectual history.[7] Feather has also attempted to resolve the conflict by pointing out that the differing approaches can be explained at least in part by historical differences in the publishing practices and the records available in France and England.[8] What seems to be emerging from this discussion is a broader-based view of the study of the history of the book that will encourage research by scholars from a number of disciplines related to the book. Fortunately, one does not have to choose between the French and Anglo-American points of view, but this conflict is worth noting at this point because American researchers tend to be impatient with the bibliographical spade work that must be done before one can begin to make generalizations about the impact of books published in any given period.

Although the contribution of the Febvre–Martin book is acknowledged in Elizabeth L. Eisenstein's *The Printing Press as an Agent of Change* published in 1979,[9] the impetus for her book came from a broad sweep of authorities. Her analysis of these sources shows convincingly that printed books have not been given fair consideration by historians of science and religion as agents of change. Professor Eisenstein's book and her lectures and papers have sparked new interest in this country and have called the attention of historians to a field of research that they have tended to overlook.

In 1980, two conferences on the history of the book were held in this country. "Books and Society in History" sponsored by the ACRL Rare Books and Manuscripts Section met in Boston in June, and in October "Printing and Society in Early America" was sponsored by the American Antiquarian Society in Worcester, Massachusetts. The ACRL Conference had a decidedly international flavor with six participants from the United States, two from France, two from West Germany, and one from Great Britain. In general, the papers reflect the French emphasis of *l'histoire du livre,* particularly in the introductory session by Darnton, "What is the History of Books?" But in the introduction to the volume in which the papers were published, Tanselle stresses the importance of analyt-

ical bibliography in the study of the history of the book. The conference concluded by adopting a ringing "Statement of the History of the Book" which begins:

> The history of the book is fundamental to the historical study of society, but we are far from
> understanding the factors that have shaped the writing and dissemination of books. These
> factors have changed over time and have varied from one cultural area to another; hence the
> impact of the book has been ever-varied and changing. The attempt to understand the
> influences of changes in book production and dissemination is particularly demanding. In the
> first place, one needs to know the basic facts of what was printed, by whom and for whom.
> Detailed bibliographical studies, dictionaries of printers, and inventories of both public and
> private libraries are among the time-consuming, exacting and fundamental studies that are
> needed.[10]

The statement concludes with an appeal for cooperation among scholars of all
countries and for the support of libraries, governments, foundations, and other
institutions.

The American Antiquarian Society Conference was defined by the collecting
interests of the society, which emphasizes materials printed in the United States
prior to 1876.[11] Seventeen papers were presented by contributors from four countries, on the topics of the book trade, reading habits, music printing, subscription
book publishing, and the impact of print in early America. Research on the history of the book is nothing new to the American Antiquarian Society, of course.
Since its founding in 1812 by Isaiah Thomas, the author of the first history of
printing in America, the society has sponsored such works as the *Bibliography of
American Newspapers, 1769–1820* by Clarence S. Brigham, and dozens of other
bibliographical works have been published in the *Proceedings* of the society or
as separate publications. The significance of this conference was its
organizational focus and, in the words of David Kaser, "a body of like-minded
colleagues with whom to discuss . . . investigations," The latter point is particularly important, Kaser continues, because the Organization of American Historians tends to view the work on history of the book as precious, whereas the
American Library Association has been "tolerant but unhelpful," the Modern
Language Association has at times been "downright hostile," and the Bibliographical Society of America "has always favored the European book over the
American."[12]

In June 1983, the American Antiquarian Society announced a Program in the
History of the Book in American Culture.[13] The first annual James Russell
Wiggins Lecture, "On Native Ground: From the History of Printing to the His-
tory of the Book,"[14] by program chairman David D. Hall, inaugurated the activi-
ties on November 9. On October 31, 1984, James M. Wells of the Newberry
Library gave a second lecture, "American Printing; the Search for Self-
Sufficiency." A Conference on Needs and Opportunities for Research in the His-

tory of the Book in American Culture was held in November 1984. The Albert Boni Fellowship is available to support short-term research at the society and additional residential fellowships are available. The long-range goal of the program is the publication of a major, multivolume, collaborative history of the book in America sometime in the 1990s.

A related project is the Center for the Book, established at the Library of Congress in 1977. The ambitious goal of the center is to provide a "program for the investigation of the transmission of human knowledge and to heighten public interest in the role of books and printing in the diffusion of knowledge."[15] Although the center was authorized by Congress, the library was left to seek funding from individual and corporate gifts to carry on the program. One gift established the Englehard Lecture series, which has attracted some notable American and English scholars to speak at the library, among them Nicolas Barker, Philip Hofer, Elizabeth L. Eisenstein, Edwin Wolf 2nd, Ian Willison, Robert Darnton, Dan H. Lawrence, James D. Hart, William Barlow and Anthony Rota. In March 1985, John Feather lectured on "The Book in History and the History of the Book." Symposia, lectures, and other publications of the center include *Literacy in Historical Perspective* (1983) edited by David Cressey, *On the History of Libraries and Scholarship* (1980) by Ian Willison, and *A Nation of Readers* (1982) by Daniel Boorstin. A guide to the resources of the Library of Congress for the study of the history of books is being prepared by Alice D. Schreyer, and plans are under way to index the unpublished copyright records for 1790–1870 in the Library of Congress, as a joint project with the American Antiquarian Society and the Bibliographical Society of America.

Other indications of interest in the history of the book that can only be mentioned in passing include establishment of the American Printing History Association in 1974, the beginning of its journal, *Printing History,* in 1979, and the New York Public Library's popular lecture series on printing and the arts, started in 1983 and continued in 1984 with a grant from the Carl and Lily Pforzheimer Foundation. The Hanes Lecture Series, sponsored by the Hanes Foundation for the Study of the Origin of the Book at the University of North Carolina at Chapel Hill, has already been mentioned as the source of Tanselle's comments on the study of the history of the book. Five lectures have been given since the series was started in 1980.

WHAT IS THE HISTORY OF PUBLISHING?

The programs, lectures, and publications mentioned so far pertain to the history of the book rather than to the history of publishing but the difference is more a matter of emphasis than of content. Michael Sadleir's definition of publishing history, quoted by Sir Frank Francis in his Richard Shoemaker Lecture in 1971, is a good starting point for considering the scope of the subject.

> Publishing history . . . includes every incident, mishap or change of policy which may occur in the life of any book from the moment when a contract is made for its publication to the moment (maybe many years later) when it goes finally and irrevocably off the market, even the last copy of a remainder issue having been sold.[17]

He goes on to suggest that the bibliographer (and the researcher in publishing history, we may add) needs to understand the relationship between author and publisher, the type of contract in use at that time, the processes of book manufacture—paper, typography, illustration, binding, and endpapers—methods of selling, the sequence of later and cheaper editions and their physical qualities. This definition, coming from a noted English bibliographer and collector of nineteenth-century English novels, emphasizes the literary aspects of publishing. The cultural historian would add that the study of any period of publishing history must be related to the social, economic, and cultural stirrings of the time.

The wide-ranging scope of the history of publishing is at the same time a delight and a despair of researchers. Publishing a book today involves the work of a host of specialists—literary agent, publisher's reader, editor, compositor, designer, copywriter, illustrator, printer, binder, reviewer, salesman, bookseller—to name some of them. Each of the specialists exercises some influence on the appearance and life of a book. Some specialities have emerged fairly recently in our times and the history of their origin and development is a subject for study in itself.

BIBLIOGRAPHY OR HISTORY?

Darnton's mischievous comments on the tendency of American bibliographers to overemphasize detailed descriptions of the paper, binding, and typography of a book reflect an attitude shared by others. Is it necessary to be a bibliographer to write good publishing history? The question is moot, I believe. It is not necessary to compile full-dress bibliographies of every American publishing firm. The majority of the books that have been published are of no great literary merit or historical significance in themselves and scholars of a future generation are unlikely to be concerned over the precise words and punctuation of the text of every book. But they will want to know the circumstances that determined which books were published and which ones were not. Whether analytical bibliography is the goal or not, the writer of publishing history needs to have the same grasp of the details of printing and publishing history as the bibliographer. That is to say, he or she must know as much as possible about how a book was produced, how it was sold, and how it was received by the readers. What both the bibliographer and the writer of publishing history must know about the physical book is covered well by the two present-day manuals on bibliography; Bowers' *Principles of Bibliographical Description* and Gaskell's *New Introduction to Bibliography*.[18] Both books place considerable emphasis on printing on a hand press and need to be supplemented by more recent papers on such topics as the bibliographical description of paper, patterns of binding cloth, color identification, identification of type faces, and similar matters. These topics are covered in Tanselle's *Selected Studies in Bibliography*.[19]

BIBLIOGRAPHIES

The sources for studying the history of American book publishing are scattered but there are some guides. Tanselle's bibliographical essay "The Historiography of American Literary Publishing,"[20] published in 1965, superseded earlier reviews of the literature by Rollo G. Silver and David Kaser.[21] All are worth reading to gain the viewpoint of three productive scholars in the field. Tanselle's indispensable *Guide to the Study of United States Imprints,* a two-volume, classified bibliography of books, articles, theses, and other printed sources has already been mentioned. No bibliography is ever complete, but Tanselle's *Guide* omits little of importance. It will be the starting point for any study of publishing history in the United States. The references that follow in this essay do not include books and articles published before 1970, the cut-off date for Tanselle's *Guide*. Each section that follows should be preceded by the unwritten sentence: "In addition to the books and articles listed in Tanselle's *Guide,* the following are worth your attention."

For the years since 1970, this list is reasonably comprehensive on the history of publishing, less so on the history of printing, and it is highly selective on the remaining subjects. All relevant library science dissertations and those from other fields that could be identified by using the index to *Dissertation Abstracts International* are included. Master's theses, a rapidly disappearing product of American library schools, have not been included; citations are readily available in Shirley Magnotti's two compilations.[22] I have excluded references on the private press and on periodical publishing, not because of any antipathy to those subjects but because the former is well reported in the book collecting journals and the latter in the bibliographies of journalism. Finally, works on the history of publishing in Canada and in Central and South America are not included.

ANNUAL BIBLIOGRAPHIES

Several attempts have been made at an annual bibliography of books and articles on the history of the book in this country, but all have been discontinued for one reason or another. *Studies in Bibliography*[23] included an annual "Selective Checklist of Bibliographical Scholarship" for the years 1949 to 1971. The checklist was published two years after the date of coverage, i.e., the checklist for 1949 is found in *Studies in Bibliography, 1951. Proof,*[24] a yearbook published by the University of South Carolina Press, included a "Register of Current Publications" of which Section 7, "Printing, Binding, Publishing and Bookselling," is useful for the four years the yearbook was published, 1971–1974. *BiN; Bibliography Newsletter,*[25] published by Terry Belanger as a one-man enterprise since 1973, is useful and entertaining but it is not a comprehensive review. An ambitious *Annual Report of the American Rare, Antiquarian and Out-of-Print Book Trade*[26] included a bibliographical essay, "Trends in Bibliography," for 1978–1979—its first and only year of publication. *ABHP; Annual Bibliography of the History of the Printed Book and Libraries,*[27] published at The Hague under the auspices of the Committee on Rare and Precious Documents of International Federation of Library Associations, includes some books and articles on American printing and publishing. The first volume was issued in 1973 (covering publications of 1970). The *Bibliographie der Buch- und Bibliothekgeschichte* (BBB),[28] first published in 1982, includes some references pertaining to England and America although it is primarily concerned with the history of books and libraries in German-speaking countries.

The *Index to Reviews of Bibliographical Publications*[29] serves as a kind of annual review of separately published bibliographical works. In 1980, it indexed the reviews published in 369 periodicals, considerably more than any individual can keep up with easily. A new annual, *Rare Books 1983–84,*[30] includes bibliographical essays on descriptive and analytical bibliography, books about books, and periodicals for collectors, dealers, and libraries. With luck, we may have a continuing bibliography again.

PERIODICALS

To keep up to date on recently published articles, however, one needs to scan the current journals long before any annual bibliography includes them. Tanselle's 1973 summary article on periodicals pertaining to bibliography[31] is still a useful guide for earlier titles and for a table indicating the journals indexed by one of the common indexes to periodicals. A more recent summary written from a somewhat different point of view can be found in *Rare Books, 1983–84*, referred to previously.

A spate of new library journals has appeared since 1973 but most of them are concerned with library management and services. One of them, *Special Collections,*[32] may contain articles pertaining to printing or publishing history. Some changes in a few of the earlier journals and some new ones in other fields should be mentioned. The *Bulletin of Research in the Humanities*[33] is the new name of the *Bulletin of the New York Public Library;* the journal is now published quarterly by the library and the State University of New York at Stony Brook. The

American Book Collector[34] now appears in a new series with a new format and longer articles than appeared in the earlier series. An author index[35] to Cannon's *Bibliography of Library Economy, 1876–1920* increases the usefulness of a little-used source indexing some articles pertaining to the history of publishing. *AEB,* a new journal, carries the explanatory subtitle, *Analytical and Enumerative Bibliography*;[36] it is primarily concerned with analytical bibliography and textual studies but carries some articles and reviews about publishing history. Other new journals include *Fine Print,*[37] a handsome journal published in San Francisco, and *Printing History,*[38] the research journal mentioned earlier, and *APHA Letter,*[39] the news bulletin of the American Printing History Association. *ICARBS*[40]—the title is the location symbol for the library of the Southern Illinois University at Carbondale—is a fine example of the periodicals published by libraries and friends of libraries containing articles based on their special collections.

Journals published outside the United States having some material of interest include the *Papers*[41] of the Bibliographical Society of Canada and, from England, *Publishing History,*[42] the *British Library Journal,*[43] the Printing Historical Society *Journal*[44] and *Bulletin,*[45] and the *Antiquarian Book Monthly Review.*[46] *Quaerendo,*[47] a journal published in Amsterdam, in English, contains some articles of interest. A new indexing service, the *American Humanities Index,*[48] indexes a number of bibliographical periodicals not covered by the older *Humanities Index.*

COPYRIGHT

Copyright records are highly important in investigating the history of publishing because the date when a book was deposited for copyright provides a *terminus ad quem* for the date of publication. Unfortunately, publishers sometimes fail to send the required two copies to the Copyright Office and in such instances one must rely on the date the book is listed in the *Weekly Record*[49] or dates of advertisements and announcements in book trade and other periodicals. For books entered after 1901, the date can be determined easily by consulting the *Catalogue of Copyright Entries,*[50] but the records for books entered for copyright from 1891 to 1901 are less satisfactory, and for books entered for copyright before 1891 the records are unpublished and scattered. Tanselle's article, "Copyright Records and the Bibliographer,"[51] unravels this tangle of sources. William S. Kable has edited the South Carolina District copyright records before 1820[52] and an article by Roger E. Stoddard illustrates the use of early copyright records for American books of poetry and some of the problems that arise.[53] John Y. Cole's article[54] on the history of the Library of Congress Copyright Office will explain much about the practices of the early period and the resulting records. Barbara Ringer's

Bowker Memorial Lecture in 1974[55] gives the viewpoint of the current scene by the Register of Copyrights.

Most of the many books and articles of the past eight years are concerned with the copyright law revised in 1976 and the problems that arise from unauthorized reproduction of copyrighted materials on photocopying machines. The Commerce Clearing House compilation[56] includes the text of the law along with reports and commentaries. Earlier major revisions to the copyright law were made in 1891, when copyright was extended to foreign authors of books published and manufactured in the United States; in 1870, when the Copyright Office was established in the Library of Congress, and in 1831, when copyright protection was lengthened to 28 years. A list of the important dates and events in the development of American copyright, compiled by Benjamin W. Budd,[57] and a bibliography of articles on copyright compiled by Matt Roberts,[58] will help to fill in the details. The conflicts between opposing interests in copyright legislation were numerous and bitter during the nineteenth century. James J. Barnes has written about one of them, the unsuccessful attempt to gain passage of a copyright treaty between the United States and England in 1854.[59] A general historical article stressing the legal aspects of copyright legislation has been written by Magavero.[60]

REFERENCE BOOKS

For an understanding of the technical terms of the book trade and of book manufacturing, Roberts and Etherington's *Bookbinding and the Conservation of Books*,[61] Glaister's *Glossary of the Book*,[62] and David M. Brownstone and Irene M. Franck's *Dictionary of Publishing*[63] will be helpful. The *Bookman's Glossary*,[64] now in its sixth edition, is also a handy guide. Kurian's *Directory of American Book Publishing*[65] gives the ancestry of existing firms and brief, but sometimes inaccurate, histories of discontinued publishers. Hackett's *80 Years of Sellers*[66] gives annual summaries from the first use of the term in 1895. The *American Book Trade Directory*[67] gives some historical information about publishers; the *Publishers Directory*[68] has more comprehensive lists. Annual summary volumes are published by *AB; the Bookman's Weekly*,[69] the *Publishers' Weekly*,[70] and Knowledge Industry Publications.[71] The *Bowker Annual*[72] has been the most consistent in its reporting since 1956 and it includes occasional articles of particular interest, such as a summary of the number of book titles published from 1879 to 1979.[73]

SOURCES

Ideally, the history of a publishing firm should be written from a study of the business and editorial records of the firm; occasionally a writer has this opportunity. Ellen B. Ballou's history of Houghton Mifflin[74] and Jack Wayne O'Bar's dissertation on the Bobbs-Merrill Company,[75] for example, were written largely from company files. But far more often, the business records of a publisher are destroyed and only the letters of a few well-known authors find their way into the manuscript collection of a research library.

A few research libraries have acquired the papers of some publishers. The Columbia University Library has the papers of Harper & Brothers, Random House, and W. W. Norton; it also has smaller groups of papers from D. Appleton & Company, Roberts Brothers, and from individuals in the book trade: publishers Joseph Pulitzer, George Haven Putnam, M. Lincoln Schuster, and literary agents Paul Revere Reynolds, James Oliver Brown, Harold Ober, Annie Laurie Williams, and Curtis Brown.[76] The Harper papers have been microfilmed as have those of a number of British publishers.[77] The Henry Holt[78] papers in the Princeton University Library, those of the Open Court Publishing Company[79] are at Southern Illinois University, Carbondale, and the Knopf archives are at the Humanities Research Center, University of Texas, Austin. The Library of Congress has the papers of many individuals—authors, publishers, editors, artists, and designers[80]—whose letters will throw some light on publishing practices of recent times. The *National Union Catalogue of Manuscripts*[81] will reveal the location of those in the Library of Congress and in any of the cooperating libraries along with a brief description of the scope of the collection. *American Literary Manuscripts; a Checklist of Holdings*[82] will provide the location of collections of authors' correspondence but little description beyond a count of the number of items and the dates covered by a collection. Lee Ash's *Subject Collections*[83] provides an abbreviated listing of individual and company papers, whereas R. B. Downs' *Library Resources of the United States*[84] lists published bibliographies that locate copies of books on many subjects, including publishing history. The book collection gathered by Douglas C. McMurtrie,[85] now largely at Michigan State University, and the Typographic Library and Museum of the American Type Founders Company, now at the Columbia University Libraries,[86] have been described.

The Columbia University Oral History Program has interviewed a number of individuals in the book trade—Bennett Cerf, B. W. Huebsch, Oscar Ogg, and Cass Canfield, for example—and the Microfilm Corporation of America's microfilm edition of these transcripts is available in many libraries.[87] Other oral history programs, particularly those on the West Coast, have interviewed printers, designers, and publishers.[88]

GENERAL HISTORIES OF PUBLISHING

John Tebbel's encyclopedic four-volume *History of Book Publishing in the United States*[89] provides a summary of what is known about a publisher or a period in publishing. There are errors of detail in Tebbel's work, which is based largely on book trade periodicals, but the historical sweep is convincing and the footnotes lead you to his sources. The footnotes are sometimes the most interesting section of the book for they are plentiful and they often suggest other topics that need to be studied. Joseph Blumenthal's *The Printed Book in America*[90] surveys the history of American book publishing by examining 70 outstanding examples with notes by a master printer. Madeleine B. Stern's *Books and Book People in the Nineteenth Century* and her *Publishers for Mass Entertainment in Nineteenth Century America* continue her studies of lesser-known publishers, printers, booksellers, and authors started in her earlier book, *Imprints on History.*[91] An article by Harlan and Johnson gives a good summary of recent trends in American book publishing.[92]

The colonial book trade has been surveyed in recent writing, somewhat superficially in Boston[93] and New Orleans,[94] more thoroughly in New York City,[95] South Carolina,[96] and Virginia,[97] and the role of women printers and publishers in the American colonies is the subject of three books.[98] Tanselle has made a careful estimate of the probable number of books published by American colonial printers.[99] Donald Farren's dissertation[100] on subscription book publishing in the eighteenth century explores a previously neglected aspect of publishing in the United States.

Dissertations by Bennett[101] and Detlefsen[102] deal with printing and publishing during the Civil War, one by Sereiko[103] examines the Chicago booktrade after the 1871 fire, and another by Russell Duino[104] traces the history of publishing and bookselling in Cleveland. Susan Otis Thompson's *William Morris and American Book Design* provides an expert survey of book typography at the turn of the century and a rationale for considering the impact of the Kelmscott Press. An earlier, briefer version in *The Arts and Crafts Movement in America: 1876–1916*[105] is interesting because it places books alongside examples of Arts and Crafts furniture, pottery, glassware, and other objects of the movement. In Philadelphia, a series of articles on publishing from 1876 was published by the Drexel University Library School.[106] A series of lectures given at Gallery 303 in New York City gives reminiscences of some printers and designers of this century,[107] among them Will Bradley, Bruce Rogers, Will Ransom, T. M. Cleland, Victor Hammer, Fred Anthoensen, and Edwin and Robert Grabhorn.

HISTORIES OF PUBLISHING FIRMS

Not all books and articles on individual publishers that have appeared since 1970 can be classed as scholarly, but the ones listed here will at least add some information not previously known. There are a half dozen first-person narratives. Hiram Haydn[108] (who worked for Crown, Bobbs-Merrill, Random House, Athenaeum, and Harcourt Brace), Cass Canfield[109] (Harper & Row), Henry Regnery[110] (Henry Regnery Company, William Targ[111] (World Publishing Company and G. P. Putnam's Sons) and Bennett Cerf[112] (Random House) have published their recollections. All are witty, urbane and calculated to set the record straight. Alfred

A. Knopf did not write a book but some autobiographical pieces[113] and at least one book by a long-time staff member have appeared. A well-illustrated 175th anniversary history was published by John Wiley & Son[114] and the 200th anniversary of Lea and Febiger and its antecedent firms was celebrated by the publication of a history.[115]

The colonial period of American printing and publishing has been studied more carefully than any other period, but there are still subjects to be explored. Benjamin Franklin,[116] David Hall,[117] Matthew Carey,[118] Hugh Gaine,[119] James Parker,[120] Robert Wells,[121] and the Babcocks[122] are the subjects of recent books or dissertations. The availability of the microform edition of *Early American Imprints* and *American Bibliography; a Preliminary Checklist*[123] in many libraries makes it possible to study the imprints of a printer–publisher or of a locality without endless travel to other libraries. Use of the Eighteenth Century Short Title Catalogue will aid research in this period greatly as this project becomes more widely known.

It is perhaps inevitable that such personalities as E. Haldeman-Julius,[124] publisher of the little blue books, and the flamboyant Elbert Hubbard[125] will always attract the attention of both popular and scholarly writers, but the old-line publishing firms, Harper,[126] Appleton-Century,[127] and Henry Holt,[128] have not been neglected and a number of books about Max Perkins,[129] the noted editor at Scribners, have appeared recently. Hubert Howe Bancroft's publishing activities have been carefully studied[130] as have a number of lesser-known publishers of the nineteenth century: Henry Altemus,[131] Abraham Hart,[132] Judge Publishing Company,[133] Walter Neale,[134] and the Charles L. Webster Company.[135] Susan Geary's study of popular novels in the nineteenth century[136] is an interesting approach to publishing history in a period before the best-seller concept had become important. The revival of interest in fine printing in the 1890s and the attempts to establish the same high standards in commercial publishing have received considerable attention. In addition to Susan O. Thompson's book, mentioned previously, articles on the Arena Publishing Company,[137] the Master printer Theodore L. DeVinne,[138] reminiscences of Stone and Kimball and their times,[139] and a series of articles on the printing revival in Boston[140] have appeared in the last 15 years. Books on Copeland and Day[141] and on Way and Williams[142] were published. Twentieth-century publishers studied recently include B. W. Huebsch,[143] Horace Liveright,[144] Coward McCann,[145] and Modern Library.[146] A biography of Mitchell Kennerley[147] is under way.

MUSIC PUBLISHING

Although some general publishers issue books of music, most music is published by a fairly small group of companies. The *American Music Handbook*[148] lists 135 publishers, including general publishers in existence 10 years ago, most of whom are still active, sometimes under different names today. How music is published is explained in two short books: Leonard Feist's *Popular Music Publishing*[149] and one describing general music publishing and the work of one publisher, C. F. Peters.[150] A short history of Boosey and Hawkes appeared in a recent number of *Opera News*.[151]

The sources of information about music publishing are not well known among nonmusicians. D. W. Krummel offers a number of additions to Tanselle's *Guide* and has estimated the number of items that have been published in the United States.[152] A special issue of *American Music*[153] on music publishing in America, edited by Krummel, should be suggestive to researchers. Richard J. Wolfe's standard work on the history of early music publishing in America[154] has been supplemented by a paper given by Crawford and Krummel for the American Antiquarian Society 1980 Conference.[155] Papers on Isaiah Thomas as a music publisher[156] and on Andrew Wright[157] have also been published. The technical problems of determining dates of early published music have been summarized by Krummel for the Committee for Bibliographical Research of the International Association of Music Libraries.[158] Research on later music publishing has touched on topics such as early activity in the Middle West[159] and the history of ASCAP.[160]

CHILDREN'S BOOK PUBLISHING

Children's book publishing as a separate speciality dates from as recently as 1919, when Louise Seamen Bechtel was appointed head of the Children's Department of the Macmillan Company. For the more recent history of the speciality, Robin Gottlieb's bibliography[161] lists the books and articles covering the period 1919–1976. *Phaedrus; an International Journal of Children's Literature*,[162] published since 1973, provides a fine medium for historical and comparative studies of children's literature but nothing on the publishing history of books for children has appeared in it.

REGIONAL PUBLISHING

Most books are published in New York, but an increasing number of small publishers can be found in unexpected corners of the United States. Information about them is not likely to be found in the usual sources, although a search through the conventional indexes has turned up a number of articles, perhaps a representative sample. More information could be found in regional and local newspaper articles. The sample includes two articles on textbook publishing in the Ohio River Valley[163] and one article apiece on the Rio Grande Press of Glorieta, New Mexico,[164] Alan Swallow of Denver,[165] the Northland Press of Flagstaff, Arizona,[166] Arkham House of Sauk City, Wisconsin,[167] and the Superior Publishing Company of Seattle, Washington.[168] Dissertations have been written on Ralph Fletcher Seymour[169] of Chicago and two West Coast printer–publishers, Paul Elder and Taylor & Taylor.[170]

ALTERNATIVE PUBLISHING

The most recent phenomenon in book publishing, although no means a new idea, is publishing by the author. More than 50 books on how to publish your own book are listed in *Books in Print*. There are many reasons for the current revival: increased costs of printing and distribution, the emphasis by many publishers on best-selling works, availability of inexpensive offset presses, and a desire to publish books that will appeal to a limited audience and are difficult to place with conventional publishing firms. For these and other reasons, the movement has boomed and, although this rebirth has not been going long enough to have much of a history, the movement cannot be ignored. One of the most interesting of the current books on self-publishing is entitled *The Passionate Perils of Publishing;*[171] the twofold appeal of the book is its ardent espousal of both self-publishing and feminist books. The *Publish-It-Yourself-Handbook*[172] includes articles by Anais Nin, Leonard Woolf, Alan Swallow, and other well-known people on their printing and publishing experiences. The *Tri Quarterly* featured articles on two small publishers in a special issue on current writing.[173] The movement has its own journal, *The Small Press Review,*[174] a current bibliography, *The Small Press Record of Books in Print,*[175] now in its sixth edition, and its own apologist, Richard Kostelanetz, (see *The End of Intelligent Writing).*[176]

OTHER SPECIAL PUBLISHERS

Paperback publishing, no longer a phenomenon, has inspired three general histories,[177] books on two publishers—Dell[178] and Bantam,[179] a dissertation,[180] an anthology of articles about paperback publishing,[181] and a quarterly magazine for collectors of paperbacks.[182] Publishing by and for ethnic groups in the United States may be one of the least known aspects of publishing history. German publishing in the United States,[183] Jewish publishing,[184] and black publishing[185] have been studied but many other groups have publishing histories that have not been recorded. The publishing activities of emigrant groups is sometimes studied by writers in the mother country before the activity is noticed by writers in the host country. An article on Finnish-American publishing by a professor at the University of Turku[186] is one example. Publishing for religious groups is closely related to ethnic publishing and in many instances the functions overlap. Publishing for the America Lutheran Church[187] and the Lutheran Church, Missouri Synod,[188] for example, include materials in foreign languages for members who had not yet mastered English. In the American Baptist denomination[189] and in the Adventists,[190] the publication body was an essential part of the educational ministry. For these reasons and others, publication has been a important feature of most religious groups, but the history of religious publishing is still largely unwritten.

The number and variety of publishing enterprises in this country is remarkable. Some are very well organized. University presses have their own organization, handbook,[191] and journal.[192] Although there is no recent attempt to write a historical study of the influence of the American University Press on American scholarship, Carroll G. Bowen has written a suggestive introductory article.[193] Accounts of the early history of Columbia University Press[194] and of the University of California Press[195] have been written by directors of those presses and a dissertation on the latter press[196] has been completed. Libraries are sometimes publishers,[197] as are book collectors' clubs[198] and, in a earlier time, railroads.[199] Micropublishing has become an established trade, considerably older than the word that now describes it, with competing companies and a history.[200] The scholarly reprint business, which flourished after World War II, is the subject of a recent book that includes a chapter on the history of the genre.[201] Not much research has been done on publishers who specialize in books on a particular subject. A study of law book publishers[202] and Roger E. Stoddard's series of articles on play publishers[203] are exceptions. Finally, useful studies have been made on the publishing history of a single book[204] or a single author.[205]

THE BUSINESS OF PUBLISHING

Librarians view books as purveyors of ideas, but publishers must see books as items to be sold for profit. Even the most idealistic publisher or bookseller is subject to the practices of the marketplace, and anyone who presumes to write the history of the book must be acquainted with the peculiar marketplace of books. Two symposia, Publishers and Librarians; a Foundation for Dialogue (1983)[206] and Perspectives on Publishers (1975)[207] provide glimpses of the field of publishing as seen by groups of academic observers in two decades. A study of the industry was made by a team of sociologists headed by Lewis A. Coser,[208] and two publishers, Curtis Benjamin[209] and Herbert S. Bailey, Jr.,[210] have written thoughtfully about their craft. Books by Harald Bohne,[211] John P. Dessauer,[212] and Howard Greenfeld[213] explain how the publishing business works. An older but better book in many ways, *What Happens in Book Publishing*, edited by Chandler B. Grannis,[214] is still useful. And two reformers, Leonard Shatzkin[215] and Thomas Whiteside,[216] have given their views on some of the current problems of book publishing.

PRINTING, BINDING, AND ILLUSTRATION

The best book on the making of a book today is Marshall Lee's *Bookmaking*,[217] which has good illustrations of all steps in the process. Unfortunately, no similar books exist on earlier periods of printing. Colonial printing has been studied with great care, but the nineteenth century, when many mechanical innovations were introduced, is not as well understood. A great deal of help will be provided by a series of reprints of volumes on paper, binding, printing, and typesetting in the

Nineteenth Century Book Arts and Printing History Series.[218] Bibliographies by Winckler[219] and Brenni[220] will be helpful in selecting other books and articles for study.

Concerning individual printers and how they worked, the correspondence between D. B. Updike and Stanley Morison[221] will provide information on two leading printers of our time. Biographical accounts of lesser-known printers appear frequently in *Printing History*.[222] Reilly's *Dictionary of Colonial American Printers' Ornaments*,[223] John Bidwell's survey of Caslon ornaments in American books,[224] *The Common Press* by Harris and Sisson,[225] and Philip Gaskell's census of extant wooden presses are examples of the detailed studies available on the colonial period of printing.[226] The Englehard Lecture given by Edwin Wolf 2nd at the Library of Congress is an interesting survey of early printing offices.[227]

Rollo G. Silver[228] and Stephen Botein[229] have written on the economic problems of the colonial printer. Silver's research on the work of the nineteenth-century printer[230] continues to shed light on this subject. John Bidwell[231] has studied the paper sizes produced for printers. Michael Winship has reviewed what is known about the use of stereotyping;[232] Silver has traced the introduction of the process into this country.[233] The presses used are described in Moran's comprehensive book.[234] Two histories of R. Hoe and Company[235] and accounts of the web press[236] and the Columbian,[237] Pearl,[238] and Napier presses[239] have been published. Directories of type foundries in the United States[240] and in New York City[241] are available. Madeleine B. Stern has traced an early machine designed to produce wood type to Isaac Singer of sewing machine fame.[242] Ray Nash's chapter on ornamental type in America appears in the new edition of Gray's *Nineteenth Century Ornamented Type Faces*.[243] The important step of introducing typesetting machines has been studied by Huss[244] and Mary Biggs traced the part played by women in typesetting.[245]

A bibliography on bookbinding by Brenni[246] will serve as a guide to some of the books and articles on this subject. The history of machine book binding has been written by Frank Camparato[247] and Sue Allen has studied patterns of machine-stamped bindings and decorated endpapers in the nineteenth century.[248] Verner W. Clapp's summary of research on the causes of deterioration in book paper and remedies available to paper manufacturers is important.[249]

Brenni's bibliography on book illustration[250] will locate some information on specific illustrators. There are surveys of illustrators by Hornung,[251] Pitz,[252] and Meyer.[253] A new edition of Mantle Fielding's classic, *American Engravers on Copper and Steel*, is being issued by the American Antiquarian Society.[254] An important change in the techniques of illustration is traced in David Woodward's account of the decline of wood engraving in the nineteenth century.[255] Jefferson Dykes has identified the work of 50 Western illustrators in books and periodicals.[256] Museums are giving increased attention to American illustrators—for example, the 1970 Winterthur Conference Report, *Prints in and of America to 1850*,[257] and catalogs of exhibits of the work of illustrators published by the Boston Museum of Fine Arts,[258] the Delaware Art Museum,[259] the Brooklyn Institute of Arts and Sciences Museum,[260] and the Grunwald Center of the University of California at Los Angeles.[261] Detailed unpublished studies of the work of Bruce Rogers[262] and Will Bradley,[263] and of Walter Crane's[264] influence on American books have been completed.

IS THERE ANYTHING LEFT TO BE DONE?

Although the number and variety of recent publications relating to the history of book publishing in the United States is remarkable, many aspects of the subject are still untapped. Indeed, a list of topics that remain to be studied would rival this paper in length. Some have already been mentioned: publishing by religious groups and ethnic bodies, children's book publishing, publishers that specialize in a specific subject, regional publishers, and the emergence of such specialities as literary agent, designer, editor, and book reviewer in the publishing trade. A few hours browsing through Tebbel's *History* and Tanselle's *Guide* will reveal that no satisfactory histories exist for most of the major publishing houses in this country, among them Scribners, Little Brown, E. P. Dutton, McGraw-Hill, and Macmillan, for example.

The publication of art nouveau books at the turn of the century has received a fair amount of attention recently, but what of the publishers of Socialist-Labor-Marxist books at that time? An account of Chicago publisher Charles H. Kerr was published in a Italian journal,[265] not an American one. American writing of the 1920s has been the subject of many critical and analytical works but little has been written on the venturesome young publishers who encouraged the authors of that period. Someone with a knowledge of business history might apply that knowledge toward an understanding of the financial organization of publishing firms and their traditional high rate of failure. One librarian, Estelle Jussim, combined her knowledge of photography and books to write two books relating to the history of publishing.[266] Librarians with similar competence in art, in music, and in educational media could make useful studies of the history of publishing enterprises that specialize in these subjects. And, of course, basic bibliographies of the books produced by a particular publisher, of those printed in a locality, or of any period in the mid–nineteenth century that is inadequately covered by our book trade bibliography would be welcome. The choice of topics is limited only by one's imagination and industry; what research will be done by librarians, and what by others, remains to be seen.

NOTES AND REFERENCES

Abbreviations

AASP	Proceedings of the American Antiquarian Society
AB	AB; Bookman's Weekly
ABC	American Book Collector
BSAP	Papers of the Bibliographical Society of America
JHL	Journal of Library History
JPHS	Journal of the Printing Historical Society
LQ	Library Quarterly
PH	Printing History
Pub H	Publishing History
PULC	Princeton University Library Chronicle
PW	Publishers' Weekly
QJLC	Quarterly Journal of the Library of Congress
SB	Studies in Bibliography
SP	Scholarly Publishing

1. G. Thomas Tanselle, *Guide to the Study of United States Imprints* (Cambridge; Belknap Press, 1971).

2. Lucien Febvre and Henri-Jean Martin, *L'Apparition du Livre* (Paris: Albin Michel, 1958). Translated as *The Coming of the Book; the Impact of Printing, 1450–1800* (London: NLB; Atlantic Highlands, N.J.: Humanities Press, 1976). A fine review is that by James M. Wells in *Review* 1 (1979): 309–319. He also reviewed the original work in the *Library Quarterly* 29 (July 1959): 201–204.

3. For a summary of this scholarship see Wallace Kirsop, "Literary History and Book Trade History: The Lessons of *L'Apparition du livre*," *Australian Journal of French Studies* 16 (1979): 488–535, and Raymond Birn, "Livre et Société After Ten Years: Formation of a Discipline," *Studies on Voltaire and the Eighteenth Century* 15 (1976): 287–312.

4. Ronald B. McKerrow, *An Introduction to Bibliography for Literary Students* (Oxford: Clarendon Press, 1927). An earlier version of this book was entitled "Notes on Bibliographical Evidence for Literary Students and Editors of English Works in the Sixteenth and Seventeenth Centuries," *Transactions of the Bibliographical Society* 12 (1913): 213–318. W. W. Greg's writings on bibliography appear in his *Collected Papers*, J. C. Maxwell, ed. (Oxford: Clarendon Press, 1966).

5. "Cross-Channel Currents; Historical Bibliography and *l'histoire du livre*," *Library* 6th Ser., 2 (March 1980): 4.

6. Quoted by G. Thomas Tanselle, *The History of Books as a Field of Study* (Chapel Hill: Rare Books Collection/Academic Affairs Library, University of North Carolina at Chapel Hill, 1981), p. 3.

7. Tanselle, *History*, pp. 13–14.

8. Feather, "Cross-Channel Currents," pp. 4–5.

9. Elizabeth L. Eisenstein, *The Printing Press as an Agent of Change* (Cambridge: Cambridge University Press, 1979). A one-volume paperback reprint was published in 1980 and a revised edition, *The Printing Revolution in Early Modern Europe* (Cambridge: Cambridge University Press, 1983). The revised edition omits many of the interesting bibliographical footnotes in the earlier work.

10. *Books and Society in History; Papers of the Association of College and Research Libraries Rare Books and Manuscripts Preconference, 24–28 June 1980, Boston, Massachusetts*, Kenneth E. Carpenter, ed. (New York: Bowker, 1983), pp. xi–xii.

11. Ten essays from the Conference papers were published in *Printing and Society in Early America*, William L. Joyce, David D. Hall, Richard D. Brown, and John B. Hench, eds. (Worcester: American Antiquarian Society, 1983).

12. Review of *Printing and Society in Early America*, *LQ* 54 (April 1984): 199–200.

13. *The Book; Newsletter of the Program in the History of the Book in American Culture*, No. 1–, November 1983– (Worcester: American Antiquarian Society) is the current source for information on the program.

14. David D. Hall, "On Native Ground; From the History of Printing to the History of the Book," *AASP* 93, Pt. 2 (1983): 313–336.

15. The quotation is from the enabling legislation, Public Law 95-129, 95th Congress, approved by the President October 12, 1977. See also John Y. Cole, "Books, Libraries and Scholarly Traditions," *SP* 13 (October 1981): 31–43, and "The Center for the Book in the Library of Congress," in *Rare Books, 1983–84*, edited by Alice D. Schreyer (New York: Bowker, 1984), pp. 149–151.

16. Five lectures were published in *QJLC* before this fine journal was discontinued. No. 1, Nicolas Barker, "The Invention of Printing; Revolution Within Revolution," *QJLC* 35 (April 1978): 64–76; No. 2, Philip Hofer, "The Early Illustrated Book," ibid., pp. 79–81; No. 3, Elizabeth L. Eisenstein, "In the Wake of the Printing Press," *QJLC* 35 (July 1978): 183–197; No. 4, Edwin Wolf 2nd., "Origins of Early American Printing Shops," ibid., pp. 198–109; No. 5, Robert Darnton, "Work and Culture in an Eighteenth-Century Printing Shop," *QJLC* (Winter 1982): 34–47.

17. Michael Sadleir, "The Development During the Last Fifty Years of Bibliographical Study of Books of the Nineteenth Century," in *The Bibliographical Society, 1892–1942; Studies in Retrospect* (London: The Bibliographical Society, 1949), p. 154. Quoted in Sir Frank Francis, *Bibliographical Information in Manuscript Collections* (New Brunswick, N.J.: Rutgers University Graduate School of Library Science, 1972), p. 154. For another view of the scope of the subject, see Morris Eaves, "What is the 'History of Publishing'?" *Pub H* 2 (1977): 57–77.

18. Fredson Bowers, *Principles of Bibliographical Description* (Princeton: Princeton University Press, 1949); Philip Gaskell, *A New Introduction to Bibliography* (Oxford: Oxford University Press, 1972). For Bowers's criticism of Gaskell's book see "McKerrow Revisited," *BSAP* 67 (1973): 109–124.

19. G. Thomas Tanselle, *Selected Studies in Bibliography* (Charlottesville: Published for the Bibliographical Society of the University of Virginia by the University Press of Virginia, 1979). See also his "Book-Jackets, Blurbs, and Bibliographies," *Library*, 5th Ser., 26 (June 1971): 91–134.

BIBLIOGRAPHIES

For additional references see Tanselle, *Guide*, vol 2, pp. 888–894.

20. G. Thomas Tanselle, "The Historiography of American Literary Publishing," *SB* 18 (1965): 3–39.

21. Rollo G. Silver, "Problems in Nineteenth-Century American Bibliography," *BSAP* 35 (1941): 35–47; David Kaser, "The Booktrade and Publishing History," in *Research Opportunities in American Cultural History*, John Francis McDermott, ed. (Lexington: University of Kentucky Press, 1961), pp. 140–154.

22. Shirley Magnotti, *Master's Theses in Library Science, 1960–1969* (Troy, N.Y.: Whitston Publishing Company, 1975) and *Master's Theses in Library Science, 1970–1974* (Troy, N.Y.: Whitston Publishing Company, 1976).

23. *Studies in Bibliography*, vols. 3–26; 1950/51–1973. (Charlottesville: Bibliographical Society of the University of Virginia). The checklists for 1949–1954 were reprinted with a cumulated

index in *SB* 10 (1957) and those for 1956–1962 were reprinted with a cumulated index in an unnumbered volume in 1966.

24. *Proof; the Yearbook of American Bibliographical and Textual Studies,* vols. 1–3, 1971–1974 (Columbia: University of South Carolina Press); vol. 4, 1975 (Columbia, S.C.: J. Faust & Co.).

25. *BiN: Bibliography Newsletter,* vol. 1–, 1973– (New York: Terry Belanger, 21 Claremont Ave.). It became a two-man enterprise with the January/February 1983 number but publication dates are still uncertain.

26. *Annual Report of the American Rare, Antiquarian and Out-of-Print Book Trade, 1978–79* (New York: B.C.A.R. Publications, 1979).

27. *ABHP; Annual Bibliography of the History of the Printed Book and Libraries,* vol. 1–, 1970– (The Hague: Nijhoff).

28. *Bibliographie der Buch– und Bibliotheksgeschichte,* vol. 1–, 1982– (Bad Iburg, W. Germany: Horst Meyer).

29. *Index to Reviews of Bibliographical Publications,* vol. 1–3, 1976–1979 (Boston: G. K. Hall); vol. 4–, 1980– (Troy, N.Y.: Whitston Publishing Company).

30. *Rare Books, 1983–84,* Alice D. Schreyer, ed. (New York: Bowker, 1984).

31. G. Thomas Tanselle, "The Periodical Literature of English and American Bibliography," *SB* 26 (1973): 167–191.

32. *Special Collections,* vol. 1–, 1981– (New York: Haworth Press). Quarterly.

33. *Bulletin of Research in the Humanities,* vol. 81–, 1978– (New York: New York Public Library and State University of New York at Stony Brook). Quarterly.

34. *American Book Collector,* new series, vol. 1–, 1980– (New York: Moretus Press). Bi-monthly.

35. Anne Harwell Jordan and Melbourne Jordan, eds., *Cannon's Bibliography of Library Economy, 1876–1920; an Author Index with Citations.* (Metuchen, N.J.: Scarecrow Press, 1976).

36. *AEB; Analytical & Enumerative Bibliography,* vol. 1–, 1977–. (DeKalb, Ill.: Bibliographical Society of Northern Illinois). Quarterly.

37. *Fine Print; a Review for the Arts of the Book,* vol. 1–, 1975–. (San Francisco: Sandra D. Kirshenbaum). Quarterly.

38. *Printing History; the Journal of the American Printing History Association,* vol. 1–, 1979–. (New York: APHA). Semi-annual.

39. *APHA LETTER,* no. 1–, 1974– (New York: APHA). Bi-monthly.

40. ICARBS, vol. 1–, 1973– (Carbondale, Ill.: Friends of the Morris Library, Southern Illinois University Library) Semi-annual.

41. *Papers of the Bibliographical Society of Canada.* vol. 1–, 1973–. (London, Ont.: BSC). Annual.

42. *Publishing History,* no. 1–, 1977–. (Cambridge: Chadwyck-Healey, Ltd.). Semi-annual.

43. *British Library Journal,* vol. 1–, 1975–. (Oxford: Oxford University Press). Semi-annual.

44. *Journal of the Printing Historical Society,* vol. 1–, 1980– (London; PHS). Annual.

45. *Bulletin of the Printing Historical Society,* no. 1–, 1980– (London: PHS). Three times a year.

46. *Antiquarian Book Monthly Review,* vol. 1–, 1974– (Oxford: ABMR Publications). Monthly.

47. *Quaerendo; a Quarterly Journal from the Low Countries Devoted to Manuscripts and Printed Books,* vol. 1–, 1971– (Amsterdam: Nico Israel). Quarterly.

48. *The American Humanities Index,* vol. 1–, 1975– (Troy, N.Y.: Whitston Publishing Company). For additional titles and descriptions see *Library and Library-related Publications,* Peter H. Hernon, Maureen Pastine, and Sara Lou Williams, eds. (Littleton, Col.: Libraries Unlimited, 1973).

COPYRIGHT

For titles published before 1970 see Tanselle, *Guide,* pp. 303–306.

49.   *Weekly Record,* vol. 1–, 1974– (New York: Bowker). Part of *Publishers Weekly* before 1974.

50.   *Catalogue of Copyright Entries,* July 1, 1891– (Washington: U.S. Government Printing Office).

51.   G. Thomas Tanselle, "Copyright Records and the Bibliographer," *SB* 22 (1969): 72–124. Also in Tanselle, *Selected Studies in Bibliography,* pp. 93–174.

52.   William S. Kable, "South Carolina District Copyrights, 1794–1820," *Proof* 1 (1971): 180–198.

53.   Roger E. Stoddard, "A Provisional List of U.S. Poetry Copyrights, 1786–1820 and a Plea for the Recovery of Unlocated Copyright Registers," *PBSA* 75 (1981): 450–483.

54.   John Y. Cole, "Of Copyright, Men and A National Library," *QJLC* 28 (April 1971): 114–136.

55.   Barbara Ringer, "The Demonology of Copyright," *PW* 206 (November 18, 1974): 26–30.

56.   Commerce Clearing House, *The Copyright Revision Act of 1976; PL 94-553* (Chicago: CCH, 1976).

57.   Benjamin W. Budd, "Notable Dates in American Copyright, 1783–1969," *QJLC* 28 (April 1971): 137–143.

58.   Matt Roberts, *Copyright; a Selected Bibliography of Periodical Literature* (Metuchen, N.J.: Scarecrow Press, 1971).

59.   James J. Barnes, *Authors, Publishers and Politicians* (Columbus: Ohio State University Press, 1974).

60.   Gerard Magavero, "The History and Background of American Copyright Law; an Overview," *International Journal of Law Libraries* 6 (1978): 151–158.

REFERENCE BOOKS

61.   Matt T. Roberts and Don Etherington, *Bookbinding and the Conservation of Books; A Dictionary of Descriptive Terminology* (Washington: Library of Congress, 1982).

62.   Geoffrey Ashall Glaister, *Glaister's Glossary of the Book: Terms Used in Papermaking, Printing, Bookbinding and Publishing,* 2d ed. (Berkeley: University of California Press, 1979).

63.   David M. Brownstone and Irene M. Franck, *The Dictionary of Publishing* (New York: Van Nostrand Reinhold, 1982).

64.   *The Bookman's Glossary,* 6th ed., Jean Peters, ed. (New York: Bowker, 1983).

65.   George Thomas Kurian, *Directory of American Book Publishing from Founding Fathers to Today's Conglomerates* (New York: Simon & Schuster, 1975).

66.   Alice Payne Hackett and James Henry Burke, *80 Years of Best Sellers, 1895–1975* (New York: Bowker, 1977).

67.   *American Book Trade Directory,* 1915– (New York: Bowker, 1915–).

68.   *Publishers Directory,* 1979– (Detroit: Gale Research Company, 1979–).

69.   *The AB Bookman's Yearbook,* 1954– (Clifton, N.J.: Bookman's Weekly, 1954–).

70.   *Publishers Weekly Yearbook; News, Analysis and Trends in the Book Industry,* 1983– (New York: Bowker, 1983–). The name was changed to *The Book Publishing Annual* with the 1984 edition.

71.   *U.S. Book Publishing Yearbook and Directory,* 1979/80– (White Plains, N.Y.: Knowledge Industry Publications, 1980–).

72.   *The Bowker Annual of Library and Book Trade Information*, 1955/56– (New York: Bowker, 1956–).
73.   Dorothy B. Hokkanen, "U.S. Book Title Output—A One Hundred-Year Overview," *Bowker Annual* (New York: Bowker, 1971), pp. 65–69.

SOURCES

For titles published before 1970 see Tanselle, *Guide,* p. xliii.

74.   Ellen B. Ballou, *The Building of the House; Houghton Mifflin's Formative Years* (Boston: Houghton Mifflin, 1970).
75.   Jack Wayne O'Bar, "A History of the Bobbs-Merrill Company 1850–1940, with a Postlude through the Early 1960s" (Ph. D. diss., Indiana University, 1970).
76.   Kenneth A. Lohf, "Treasures for Alma Mater: How Columbia University Acquired the Papers of Major New York Publishers and Literary Agents," *Manuscripts* 29 (1977): 102–109 and "The Brothers Harper and their Authors: Pictures from an Exhibition," *Columbia Library Columns* 24 (February 1975): 18–32.
77.   *The Archives of British and American Publishers*, series 1–3 (London: Chadwyck-Healy, Ltd./Somerset House, 1974–). This microform set includes George Allen & Co., 1893–1915; Swann, Sonnenschein & Co., 1878–1911; Kegan Paul, Trench, Trübner & Henry S. King, 1858–1912; Cambridge University Press, 1696–1902; Richard Bentley & Co., 1829–1898; House of Longman, 1794–1914; Elkin Mathews, 1811–1938, Grant Richards, 1897–1948 and George Routledge & Co, 1853–1902.
78.   Charles A. Madison, "Gleanings from the Henry Holt Files," *PULC* 25 (1966): 86–106.
79.   Claudia McKenzie Foster, "The Open Court Papers," *ICARBS* 2 (Fall 1975): 146–151.
80.   For example, see Herbert J. Sanborn, "The Cleland Papers," *QJLC* 20 (1963): 163–173.
81.   *The National Catalog of Manuscript Collections,* vol. 1– (Hamden, Conn.: Shoe String Press, 1959–1961; Ann Arbor: J. W. Edwards, 1962–). A volume has been published each year with cumulated indexes for 1959–1962, 1963–1966, 1967–1969, 1970–1974, 1975–1979, and 1980–1982.
82.   *American Literary Manuscripts; A Checklist of Holdings in Academic, Historical and Public Libraries, Museums and Authors' Homes in the United States,* 2d ed. (Athens: University of Georgia Press, 1977). For a review giving some shortcomings of this checklist see *Review* 1 (1979): 295–300.
83.   Lee Ash, ed., *Subject Collections: A Guide to Special Book Collections and Subject Emphases as Reported by Universities, Colleges, Public and Special Libraries and Museums in the United States and Canada,* 5th ed. (New York: Bowker, 1978).
84.   Robert B. Downs, *American Library Resources; a Bibliographical Guide* (Chicago: American Library Association, 1951). There are supplements for 1950–1961, 1960–1971, and 1970–1981 and a *Cumulative Index, 1870–1970.*
85.   Scott Bruntjen and Melissa L. Young, comp. *Douglas C. McMurtrie; Bibliographer and Historian of Printing* (Metuchen, N.J.: Scarecrow Press, 1979).
86.   David Walker Mallison, "Henry Louis Bullen and the Typographic Library and Museum of the American Type Founders Company: (D.L.S. diss., Columbia University, 1976) and *The History of Printing from its Beginnings to 1930; the Subject Catalog of the American Type Founders Company Library in the Columbia University Library,* 4 vols. (Millwood, N.Y.: Kraus International Publications, 1980).
87.   *Columbia University Oral History Collection; An Index to the Memoirs in Part 1 of the Microfilm Edition* (Sanford, N.C.: Microfilm Corporation of America, 1979) and *Oral History Guide*

No. 2; a Bibliographical Listing of the Memoirs in the Micropublished Collections (Sanford, N.C.: Microfilm Corporation of America, 1979).

88.   Patsy A. Cook, ed. *Directory of Oral History Programs in the United States* (Sanford, N.C.; Microfilming Corporation of America, 1982).

GENERAL HISTORIES OF PUBLISHING

For titles published before 1970 see Tansell, *Guide,* pp. 763–794.

89.   John Tebbel, *A History of Book Publishing in the United States* (New York: Bowker, 1972–1981).

90.   Joseph Blumenthal, *The Printed Book in America* (Boston: David R. Godine, 1977).

91.   Madeleine B. Stern, *Books and Book People in 19th-Century America* (New York: Bowker, 1978); *Publishers for Mass Entertainment in Nineteenth Century America* (Boston: G. K. Hall, 1980); *Imprints on History; Book Publishers and American Frontiers* (Bloomington: Indiana University Press, 1956) and "The Role of the Publisher in Mid-Nineteenth-Century American Literature," *Pub H* 10 (1981): 5–26.

92.   Robert D. Harlan and Bruce L. Johnson, "Trends in Modern American Book Publishing," *Library Trends* 27 (Winter 1979): 380–407.

93.   Benjamin Franklin V., ed., *Boston Printers, Publishers and Booksellers, 1640–1800* (Boston: G. K. Hall, 1980).

94.   John M. Goudeau, "Booksellers and Printers in New Orleans, 1764–1885," *JLH* 5 (January 1970): 5–19.

95.   Linda Markson Kruger, "The New York City Book Trade, 1725–1750" (Ph.D. diss., Columbia University, 1980).

96.   Calhoun Winton, "The Colonial South Carolina Book Trade," *Proof* 2 (1972): 71–87.

97.   John Edgar Molnar, "Publication and Retail Book Advertisements in the *Virginia Gazette,* 1736–1789" (Ph.D. diss., University of Michigan, 1978).

98.   Leona M. Hudak, *Early American Women Printers and Publishers, 1639–1820* (Metuchen, N.J.: Scarecrow Press, 1978); Richard L. Demeter, *Primer, Presses and Composing Sticks; Women Printers of the Colonial Period* (Hicksville, N.Y.: Exposition Press, 1979); Marjorie Dana Barlow, comp., *Notes on Women Printers in Colonial America and the United States* (Charlottesville: Hroswitha Club, distributed by the University Press of Virginia, 1976).

99.   G. Thomas Tanselle, "Some Statistics on American Printing, 1764–1976." In *The Press and the American Revolution,* Bernard Bailyn and John B. Hench, eds. (Worcester: American Antiquarian Society, 1980), pp. 315–363.

100.   Donald Farren, "Subscription: A Study of the Eighteenth Century American Book Trade" (D.L.S. diss., Columbia University, 1982).

101.   Stephanie Lee Mitchell Bennett, "The Impact of the Civil War on the Volume and Character of Publishing in the North, 1860–1869" (Ph.D. diss., University of Iowa, 1973).

102.   Ellen Gay Detlefsen, "Printing in the Confederacy, 1861–1865, A Southern Industry in Wartime" (D.L.S. diss., Columbia University, 1975).

103.   George Eugene Sereiko, "Chicago and Its Book Trade, 1871–1892" (Ph. D. diss., Case Western Reserve University, 1973).

104.   Russel Alfred Duino, "The Cleveland Book Trade, 1819–1912; Leading Firms and Outstanding Men" (Ph.D. diss., University of Pittsburgh, 1981).

105.   Susan Otis Thompson, *William Morris and American Book Design* (New York: Bowker, 1977); "The Arts and Crafts Book," in *The Arts and Crafts Movement in America, 1876–1916,* Robert Johnson Clark, ed. (Princeton: Princeton University Press, 1972), pp. 94–116.

106.   Thomas M. Whitehead, ed., "Aspects of Publishing in Philadelphia, 1876–1976," *Drexel Library Quarterly* 12 (July 1976); 1–98.

107.   Chandler B. Grannis, comp., *Heritage of the Graphic Arts; a Series of Lectures Delivered at Gallery 303, New York City under the Direction of Dr. Robert L. Leslie* (New York: Bowker, 1972).

HISTORIES OF PUBLISHING FIRMS

For titles published before 1970 see Tanselle, *Guide* pp. 405–762.

108.   Hiram Haydn, *Words and Faces* (New York: Harcourt, Brace, Jovanovich, 1974).

109.   Cass Canfield, *Up and Down and Around; A Publisher Recollects the Time of His Life* (New York: Harper's Magazine Press, 1971).

110.   Henry Regnery, *Memoirs of a Dissident Publisher* (New York: Harcourt, Brace, Jovanovich, 1979).

111.   William Targ, *Indecent Pleasures* (New York: Macmillan 1975).

112.   Bennett Cerf, *At Random; the Reminiscences of Bennett Cerf* (New York: Random House, 1977). Edited from the Columbia University Oral History Program's transcripts of interviews. See also John F. Baker, "Fifty Years of Publishing at Random," *PW* 208 (August 4, 1975): 25–31.

113.   Alfred A. Knopf, "Historian and Publisher," *American Heritage* 28 (April 1977): 100–106; "Publishing Clarence Day," *Yale University Library Gazette* 55 (January 1981): 101–115. See also Harding Lemay, *Inside, Looking Out; A Personal Memoir* (New York: Harper's Magazine Press, 1971).

114.   John Hammond Moore, *Wiley; One Hundred and Seventy-five Years of Publishing* (New York: Wiley, 1982).

115.   R. Kenneth Bussy, *200 Years of Publishing; a History of the Oldest Publishing Company in the United States, 1785–1985* (Philadelphia: Lea & Febiger, 1984).

116.   C. William Miller, *Benjamin Franklin's Philadelphia Printing, 1728–1766; a Descriptive Bibliography* (Philadelphia: American Philosophical Society, 1974).

117.   Robert D. Harlan, "David Hall and the Townshend Acts," *BSAP* 68 (1974): 19–38 and "A Colonial Printer as Bookseller in Eighteenth Century Philadelphia; the Case of David Hall," *Studies in Eighteenth Century Culture* 5 (1976): 355–369. Both supplement his earlier article "David Hall and the Stamp Act," *BSAP* 61 (1967): 13–37.

118.   James Gilreath, "Mason Weems, Mathew Carey and the Southern Booktrade, 1794–1840," *Pub H* 10 (1981): 17–49.

119.   Alfred Lawrence Lorenz, *Hugh Gaine; a Colonial Printer-Editor's Odyssey to Loyalism* (Carbondale: Southern Illinois University Press, 1972).

120.   Alan Dyer, *A Biography of James Parker, Colonial Printer* (Troy, N.Y.: Whitston Publishing Company, 1982).

121.   Christopher John Gould, "The Printing Firm of Robert Wells, with a Descriptive Bibliography of its Imprints" (Ph.D. diss., University of South Carolina, 1977).

122.   Jane Ellen Carstens, "The Babcocks: Printers, Publishers, Booksellers" (D.L.S. diss., Columbia University, 1975).

123.   *Early American Imprints (Evans) 1969–1800* (New York: Readex Microprint, 1955–1969). Another series based on Ralph R. Shaw and Richard H. Shoemaker, *American Bibliography; a Preliminary Checklist for 1801–1819* (Metuchen, N.J.: Scarecrow Press, 1958–1966) and Richard H. Shoemaker, *A Checklist of Imprints for 1820–* (Metuchen, N.J.: Scarecrow Press, 1964–) is being microfilmed.

124.   Richard Colles Johnson and G. Thomas Tanselle, "The Haldeman-Julius 'Little Books' as

a Bibliographical Problem,'' *BSAP* 64 (1970): 29–78 and ''BAL Addenda: Haldeman-Julius' Little
Blue Books,'' *BSAP* 66 (1972): 69–71; Mark Scott, ''The Little Blue Books in the War on Bigotry
and Bunk,'' *Kansas History* 3 (1978): 155–176; Abraham Blinderman, ''Haldeman-Julius and the
'Little Blue Books,' '' *AB* 62 (October 16, 1978): 2243–2250, reprinted in *AB Bookman's Yearbook,*
1978, Pt. 1, pp. 77–80; Dale Marvin Herder, ''Education for the Masses; the Haldeman-Julius Little
Blue Books as Popular Culture during the Nineteen Twenties'' (Ph.D. diss., University of Michigan,
1975).

125.   Robert L. Beisner, ''Commune in East Aurora,'' *American Heritage* 22 (February 1971):
71–77; Charles F. Hamilton, *As Bees in Honey Drown; Elbert Hubbard and the Roycrofters* (South
Brunswick, N.J.: A. S. Barnes Company, 1973); Bonnie Ruth Baker Thorne, ''Elbert Hubbard and
the Publications of the Roycroft Shop, 1893–1915'' (Ph.D. diss., Texas Woman's University, 1975).

126.   Peter S. Bracher, ''The Early American Editions of *American Notes;* their Priority and
Circulation,'' *BSAP* 69 (1975): 365–376; ''Harper & Brothers; Publishers of Dickens,'' *Bulletin of
the New York Public Library* 70 (Spring 1976): 315–335; Sidney P. Moss, ''Charles Dickens and
Frederick Chapman's Agreement with Ticknor & Fields,'' *BSAP* 75 (1981): 33–38; Rosalie Hewitt,
''Henry James, The Harpers, and The American Scene,'' *American Literature* 55 (March 1983):
41–47.

127.   Gerard R. Wolfe, *The House of Appleton; the History of a Publishing House and its Relationship to the Cultural, Social and Political Events that Helped Shape the Destiny of New York City*
(Metuchen, N.J.: Scarecrow Press, 1981).

128.   Seth Weiner, ''Thomas Hardy and His First American Publisher; Chapter from the Henry
Holt Archives,'' *PULC* 39 (Spring 1978): 134–157.

129.   John Kuehl and Jackson R. Bryer, eds., *Dear Scott/Dear Max; the Fitzgerald-Perkins Correspondence* (New York: Scribner, 1971); Clifford M. Caruthers, ed., *Ring Around Max; the Correspondence of Ring Lardner and Max Perkins* (DeKalb: Northern Illinois University Press, 1973);
Andrew Scott Berg, *Max Perkins; Editor of Genius* (New York: E. P. Dutton, 1978).

130.   Benjamin Draper, ''Hubert Howe Bancroft in Colorado,'' *Colorado Magazine* 48 (Spring
1971): 91–107; Harry Clark, *A Venture in History; the Production, Publication and Sale of the Works
of Hubert Howe Bancroft* (Berkeley: University of California Press, 1973).

131.   Hilda Bohem, ''Alice's Adventures with Altemus (and Vice Versa),'' *BSAP* 73 (1979):
423–442 and ''Erratum,'' *BSAP* 75 (1981): 103.

132.   Louis Ginsburg, *A. Hart; Philadelphia Publisher, 1829–1854* (Petersburg, Va.: Glade
Press, 1972).

133.   Jeffrey Wollock, ''Books of the Judge Publishing Company,'' *ABC* 20 (May 1970):
13–18.

134.   Robert K. Krick, *Neale Books; an Annotated Bibliography* (Dayton, Ohio: Press of
Morningside Bookshop, 1977).

135.   Frederick Anderson and Hamlin Hill, ''How Samuel Clemens Became Mark Twain's Publisher,'' *Proof* 2 (1972): 117–143.

136.   Susan Geary, ''The Domestic Novel as a Commercial Commodity; Making a Best Seller in
the 1850s,'' *BSAP* 70 (1976): 365–393.

137.   Roger E. Stoddard, ''Variety and Reform; B. O. Flower's Arena Publishing Company,
Boston, 1890–1896, with a Bibliographical List of Arena Imprints,'' *BSAP* 76 (1982): 273–337.

138.   Michael Koenig, ''DeVinne and the DeVinne Press,'' *LQ* 41 (January 1970): 1–24.

139.   Henry Regnery, ''Stone, Kimball and the *Chap-Book,*'' *Chicago History* 4 (Summer
1975): 87–95; Herbert Stuart Stone, Jr., ''Stone & Kimball; Some Personal Observations,''
Newberry Library Bulletin 6 (August 1978): 306–313; Gaylord Donnelley, ''The Influence of Stone
& Kimball on Chicago Printing,'' ibid: 314–321.

140.   Paul Shaw, ''Boston; Hub of Fine Printing Revival,'' *AB Bookmans Yearbook,* 1980, Pt.
2, pp. 11–24; ''William Morris' Vision Interpreted,'' and ''Morris, Updike and 3 American
Presses,'' ibid., 1982, Pt. 1, pp. 47–56 and 57–66.

141.   Joe W. Kraus, *Messrs. Copeland & Day, Boston, 1893–1899* (Philadelphia: George S.

MacManus, 1979): Estelle Jussim, *Slave to Beauty; the Eccentric Life and Controversial Career of F. Holland Day, Photographer, Publisher, Aesthete* (Boston: David R. Godine, 1981).

142.   Peter E. Hanff, "Way & Williams, Chicago, 1895–1898," *Quarterly News Letter of the Book Club of California* 42 (Summer 1977): 73–77; Joe W. Kraus, *History of Way and Williams, 1895–1898* (Philadelphia: George S. MacManus, 1984).

143.   James Gilreath, "The Benjamin Huebsch Imprint," *BSAP* 73 (1979): 225–243; Ann Catherine McCullough, "A History of B. W. Huebsch, Publisher" (Ph.D. diss., University of Wisconsin at Madison, 1979).

144.   Dorothy Commins, *What is an Editor ? Saxe Commins at Work* (Chicago: University of Chicago Press, 1978).

145.   Thomas Weyr, "Coward-McCann & Geoghegan," *PW* 213 April 3, 1978): 33–36.

146.   Gordon B. Neavill, "The Modern Library Series; Format and Design, 1917–1977," *PH* 1 (1979): 26–37; "The Modern Library and American Cultural Life," *JLH* 16 (Spring 1981): 241–252.

147.   Matthew J. Bruccoli, "Mitchell Kennerley; Entrepreneur of Books," *AB* 73 (March 19, 1984): 1079–1088.

MUSIC PUBLISHING

For titles published before 1970 see Tanselle, *Guide,* pp. 120–122 and index entry *Music*

148.   Christopher Pavlakis, ed., *The American Music Handbook* (New York: Free Press, 1974), pp. 625–648.

149.   Leonard Feist, *An Introduction to Popular Music Publishing in America* (New York: National Music Publisher's Association, Inc., 1980).

150.   Carolyn Sachs, ed., *An Introduction to Music Publishing* (New York: C. F. Peters Corporation, 1981).

151.   Hans Heinsheimer, "Great Publishing Houses, IV Boosey & Hawkes," *Opera News* 48 (March 17, 1984): 14–18. Earlier articles in the series dealt with European publishers: Schott, Breitkopf & Hartel, Ricordi, and Universal-Edition.

152.   D. W. Krummel, "American Music Bibliography; Four Titles in Three Acts," *Yearbook for Inter-American Musical Research,* 8 (1972): 137–193, and "Counting Every Star; or, Historical Statistics on Music Publishing in the United States," ibid. 10 (1974): 175–193.

153.   *American Music* I (December 1983): 1–110.

154.   Richard J. Wolfe, *Early American Music Engraving and Printing; a History of Music Publishing in America from 1787 to 1825 with Commentary on Earlier and Later Practice.* (Urbana, University of Illinois Press in Cooperation with the Bibliographical Society of America, 1980).

155.   Richard Crawford and D. W. Krummel, "Early American Music Printing and Publishing," in *Printing and Society in Early America* (Worcester, Mass.: American Antiquarian Society, 1980), pp. 185–227.

156.   Karl Kroeger, "Isaiah Thomas as a Music Publisher," *AASP* 86, Pt. 2 (1976): 321–341.

157.   Paul R. Osterhout, "Andrew Wright; Northampton Music Printer," *American Music* I (December 1983): 5–26.

158.   D. W. Krummel, comp., *Guide for Dating Early Published Music; a Manual of Bibliographical Practice* (Hackensack, N.J.: J. Boonin, 1974).

159.   Dena J. Epstein, *Music Publishing in Chicago before 1871; the Firm of Root and Cady, 1858–1871* (Detroit: Information Coordinators, Inc., 1969); Theodore Winton Thorson, "A History of Music Publishing in Chicago, 1850–1960" (Ph.D. diss., Northwestern University, 1961). Ernst C. Krohn, *Music Publishing in the Middle Western States before the Civil War* (Detroit: Information Coordinators, Inc., 1972).

160.   Bonnie Lee DeWhitt, "The American Society of Composers, Authors and Publishers, 1914–1933" (Ph.D. diss., Emory University, 1977).

CHILDREN'S BOOK PUBLISHING

For titles published before 1970 see Tanselle, *Guide,* pp. 78–79 and index entry *Children's Books*

161. Robin Gottlieb, *Publishing Children's Books in America, 1919–1976; an Annotated Bibliography* (New York: Children's Book Council, 1978).

162. *Phaedrus; an International Journal of Children's Literature Research,* vol 1– (Boston: Phaedrus, Inc., 1973–).

REGIONAL PUBLISHING

For titles published before 1970 see Tanselle, *Guide,* pp. 1–67.

163. Mauck Brammer, "Winthrop B. Smith; Creator of the Eclectic Educational Series," *Ohio History* 80 (1971): 45–59; David P. Anderson, "Cincinnati Publishers and the McGuffey Readers," Society for the Study of Mid-Western Literature, *Newsletter* 4 (1974): 12–13.

164. Richard N. Ellis, "The Rio Grande Press—Contributor to Southwestern History," *New Mexico Historical Review* 53 (July 1978): 271–174.

165. William F. Claire, ed., *Publishing in the West; Alan Swallow, Some Letters and Commentaries* (Santa Fe, N.M.: The Lightning Tree, 1974).

166. Paul E. Weaver, " 'Northland Press' and the Fine Art of Bookmaking," *Arizona Highways* 47 (October 1971): 33–46.

167. Sheldon Jaffery, *Horrors and Unpleasantries: A Bibliographical History and Collector's Price Guide to Arkham House* (Bowling Green, Ohio: Bowling Green State University Popular Press, 1982).

168. Ralph W. Andrews, "Pioneering Pictorial Histories; First Twenty-five Years of the Superior Publishing Company," *Journal of the West* 11 (April 1972): 367–378.

169. Kathryn M. Camp, "Ralph Fletcher Seymour and His Alderbrink Press (Chicago 1898–1965); a History and Checklist of his Publications" (Ph.D. diss., University of Chicago, 1979).

170. Ruth I. Gordon, "Paul Elder; Bookseller—Publisher (1897–1917); a Bay Area Reflection" (Ph.D. diss., University of California, Berkeley, 1977) and Anne Elizabeth Englund, "Taylor & Taylor, San Francisco Printers; the Early Period, 1896–1911" (Ph.D. diss., University of California, Berkeley, 1978).

ALTERNATIVE PUBLISHING

171. Celeste West and Valerie Wheat, *Passionate Perils of Publishing* (San Francisco: Bookleggers Press, 1978).

172. Bill Henderson, ed., *The Publish-it-Yourself Handbook* (Yonkers, N.Y.: The Pushcart Press, 1973).

173. *Tri Quarterly* 43 (Fall 1978). See especially Ted Wilentz and Bill Zavatsky, "Behind the Writer, Ahead of the Reader; A Short History of Corinth Books," pp. 595–613, Bill Henderson, "On Pushcart Press," pp. 614–623.

174. *Small Press Review,* vol. 1–, 1967– (Paradise, Calif.: Dustbooks).

175. *Small Press Record of Books in Print,* 1968– (Paradise, Calif.: Dustbooks). Annual.

176. Richard Kostelanetz, *The End of Intelligent Writing* (New York: Sheed and Ward, 1974).

OTHER SPECIAL PUBLISHERS

For titles published before 1970 see Tanselle, *Guide,* index entries *Paperback Books, Religious Books, Publishing by.*

177. Piet Schreuders, *Paperbacks U.S.A.; a Graphic History, 1939–1959,* translated from the Dutch by Josh Pachter (San Diego: Blue Dolphin Enterprises, 1981); Thomas L. Bonn, *Under Cover; an Illustrated History of American Mass-Market Paperbacks* (New York: Penguin, 1982) and Piet Schreuders, "The First Pocket Book," *PH* 5 (1983): 3–14; Kenneth C. Davis, *The Paperbacking of America; Two-Bit Culture* (Boston: Houghton Mifflin Company, 1984).

178. William H. Lyles, *Putting Dell on the Map; a History of the Dell Paperbacks* (Westport, Conn.: Greenwood Press, 1983).

179. Clarence Peterson, *The Bantam Story; Twenty-five Years of Paperback Publishing,* 2d ed. (New York: Bantam, 1975).

180. Michael Scott Barson, "The Paperback Explosion; an American Publishing Phenomenon, 1939–1980: (Ph.D. diss., Bowling Green State University, 1981).

181. Allen Billy Crider, ed., *Mass Market Publishing in America* (Boston: G. K. Hall, 1982).

182. *Paperback Quarterly; Journal of Mass Market Paperback History* vol. 1–, 1978– (Brownwood, Tex.: Paperback Publications).

183. Robert E. Cazden, *German Exile Literature in America, 1933–1950; a History of the Free German Press and Book Trade* (Chicago: American Library Association, 1970); "The German Book Trade in Ohio before 1848" *Ohio History* 84 (1975): 57–77, and "Johann Georg Wesselhoft and the German Book Trade in America," in *The German Contribution to the Building of the Americas; Studies in Honor of Karl J. R. Arndt,* G. K. Friesen and Walter Schatzburg, eds. (Worcester, Mass.: Clark University Press, 1977), pp. 217–234; Don Heinrich Tolzmann, "Minnesota's German-American Book Trade, 1850–1935," *ABC* (July/August 1974): 20–22.

184. Charles A. Madison, *Jewish Publishing In America; the Impact of Jewish Writing on American Culture* (New York: Sanhedrin Press, 1976).

185. Donald Franklin Joyce, *Gatekeepers of Black Culture; Black-Owned Book Publishing in the United States, 1817–1981* (Westport, Conn.: Greenwood Press, 1983) and James Frazier, "Black Publishing for Black Children; the Experience of the Sixties and Seventies," *Library Journal* 98 (November 15, 1973): 3412–3426.

186. Auvo Kostiainen, "Features of Finnish-American Publishing," University of Turku, Institute of General History, *Publications* 9 (1977): 54–70.

187. Karlin Lotars Ozolins, "Book Publication Trends in the American Lutheran Church and its Antecedent Bodies, 1967–1971" (Ph.D. diss., University of Michigan, 1972).

188. Albert W. Galen, "Concordia Publishing House's One Hundred Years," *Concordia Historical Institute Quarterly* 42 (1969): 157–170.

189. Lawrence T. Slaght, *Multiplying the Witness; 150 Years of American Baptist Educational Ministries* (Valley Forge, Pa.: Judson Press, 1974).

190. Donald R. McAdams, "Publisher of the Gospel; C. H. Jones and the Pacific Press," *Adventist Heritage* 3 (1976): 23–32.

191. Gene R. Hawes, *To Advance Knowledge; a Handbook on American University Press Publishing* (New York: Association of American University Presses, 1967), especially Chapter 2, "How University Presses Have Evolved," pp. 26–62.

192. *Scholarly Publishing,* vol 1–, 1969– (Toronto: University of Toronto Press).

193. Carroll G. Bowen, "The Historical Context of the University Press in America," *SP* 2 (July 1971): 329–349.

194. Henry H. Wiggins, "Early and Middle Years at Columbia," *SP* 14 (July 1983): 327–336.

195. August Frugé, "The Metamorphoses of the University of the California Press," *SP* 15 (January 1984): 161–176.

196.   Albert Henry Muto, "The University of California Press, 1893–1933," (Ph.D. diss., University of California, Berkeley, 1976).

197.   Jay K. Lucker, "Princeton University Library as a Publisher, 1953 to 1974," *PULC* 36 (Spring 1975): 201–216; Dana J. Pratt, "Publishing at the Library of Congress," *SP* 12 (July 1981): 329–337.

198.   Murray Blander, "The Bibliophile Society, Boston, Massachusetts," *Bulletin of Bibliography* 30 (July/September 1973): 136–140.

199.   Tom D. Kilton, "The American Railroad as Publisher, Bookseller and Librarian," *JLH* 17 (Winter 1982): 39–64.

200.   Alan Marshall Meckler, *Micropublishing; a History of Scholarly Micropublishing in America, 1838–1980* (Westport, Conn.: Greenwood Press, 1982); Allen B. Veaner, ed., *Studies in Micropublishing, 1853–1976; Documentary Sources* (Westport, Conn.: Microform Review, 1976).

201.   Carol A. Nemeyer, *Scholarly Reprint Publishing in the United States* (New York: Bowker, 1972): Earl M. Coleman, "Formation of a Reprint House," *AB Bookmans Yearbook* (1970): Pt. 1, pp. 5–6.

202.   Jenni Parrish, "Law Books and Legal Publishing in America 1760–1840," *Law Library Journal* 72 (Summer 1979): 355–452.

203.   Roger E. Stoddard, "A Guide to 'Spencer's Boston Theatre,' 1855–1862," *AASP* 79 (1969): Pt. 1, pp. 45–98; "Notes on American Play Publishing, 1765–1865," *AASP* 81 (1971): Pt. 1, pp. 161–190; "A Catalogue of the Dramatic Imprints of David and Thomas Longworth, 1802–1821," *AASP 84* (1974): Pt. 2, pp. 317–398 and "A Note on the Eldridge Publishing Co.," *Serif* 11 (Summer 1974): 44–45.

204.   James J. Barnes and Patience P. Barnes, *Hitler's Mein Kampf in Britain and America; A Publishing History, 1930–39* (Cambridge: Cambridge University Press, 1980); Waldemar H. Fries, *The Double Elephant Folio; the Story of Audubon's Birds of America* (Chicago: American Library Association, 1973).

205.   B. J. Sokol, "The Publication of Robert Frost's First Books: Triumph and Fiasco," *Book Collector* 26 (Summer 1977): 228–239; Anna Lou Samuelson Ashby, "A Publishing History of Christopher Morley" (Ph.D. diss., University of Texas at Austin, 1974).

THE BUSINESS OF PUBLISHING

For titles published before 1970 see Tanselle, *Guide,* pp. 763–794.

206.   "Publishers and Librarians; a Foundation for Dialogue," Mary Biggs, ed., *LQ* 54 (January 1984): 1–106.

207.   "Perspectives on Publishing," Philip G. Altach and Sheila McVey, eds., *Annals* 421 (September 1975): 1–215. Also published by Lexington Books (Lexington, Mass., 1976).

208.   Lewis A. Coser, Charles Kahushin, and Walter W. Powell *Books, the Culture and Commerce of Publishing* (New York: Basic Books, 1982).

209.   Curtis G. Benjamin, *A Candid Critique of Book Publishing* (New York: Bowker, 1977).

210.   Herbert S. Bailey, Jr., *The Art and Science of Book Publishing* (New York: Harper & Row, 1970).

211.   Harald Bohne and Harry van Ierssel, *Publishing; the Creative Business* (Toronto: University of Toronto Press, 1973).

212.   John P. Dessauer, *Book Publishing: What It Is and What It Does.* (New York: Bowker, 1974).

213.   Howard Greenfeld, *Books from Reader to Writer* (New York: Crown, 1976).

214.   Chandler B. Grannis, ed., *What Happens in Book Publishing* (New York: Columbia University Press, 1971).

215. Leonard Shatzkin, *In Cold Type; Overcoming the Book Crisis* (Boston: Houghton Mifflin, 1982).

216. Thomas Whiteside, *The Blockbuster Complex; Conglomerates, Show Business and Book Publishing* (Middletown, Conn.: Wesleyan University Press, 1981).

PRINTING—BINDING—ILLUSTRATION

For titles published before 1970 see Tanselle, *Guide,* index entries *Bookbinding, Illustrated books, Printing, Typography.*

217. Marshall Lee, *Bookmaking; the Illustrated Guide to Design/Production/Editing,* 2d ed. (New York: Bowker Company, 1979).

218. The Nineteenth Century Book Arts and Printing History Series includes the following volumes on American printing subjects:

Dard Hunter, *Papermaking in Pioneer America* (New York: Garland Publishing, 1980). Reprint of 1952 edition published by the University of Pennsylvania Press, Philadelphia.

Joel Munsell, *Chronology of the Origin and Progress of Paper and Paper-Making* (New York: Garland Publishing, 1980). Reprint of 1876 edition published by Joel Munsell, Albany, N. Y.

John Andrews Arnett, *Bibliopegia; or, The Art of Bookbinding in all its Branches* (New York: Garland Publishing, 1980). Reprint of the 1835 edition published by R. Groombridge, London.

James B. Nicholson, *A Manual of the Art of Bookbinding* (New York: Garland Publishing, 1980). Reprint of the 1856 edition published by H. C. Baird, Philadelphia.

R. M. Burch, *Colour Printing and Colour Printers* (New York: Garland Publishing, 1981). Reprint of the 1910 edition published by Baker & Taylor, New York.

Theodore L. DeVinne, *The Printer's Price List; a Manual for the Use of Clerks and Book-keepers in Job Printing Offices* (New York: Garland Publishing, 1980). Reprint of the 1871 edition published by F. Hart, New York.

R. Hoe & Company, *Catalogue of Printing Presses and Printing Materials* (New York: Garland Publishing, 1980). Reprint of the 1881 edition published by R. Hoe & Company, New York.

American Type Founders Company, *Specimens of Type, Brass Rules and Dashes, Ornaments and Borders, Society Emblems, Check Lines, Cuts, Initials and Other Productions of the American Type Founders Co.* (New York: Garland Publishing, 1981). Reprint of the 1896 edition published by the American Type Founders Company, Philadelphia.

Caleb Stower, *The Printer's Manual* and Edward Grattan, *The Printer's Companion* (New York: Garland Publishing, 1981). Reprint of the 1817 edition published by R. & C. Crocker, Boston, and the 1864 edition published by Edward Grattan, Philadelphia.

Cornelius S. Van Winkle, *The Printers' Guide; or, An Introduction to the Art of Printing* (New York: Garland Publishing, 1981). Reprint of the 1818 edition published by Cornelius Van Winkle, New York.

Thomas F. Adams, *Typographica; or, The Printer's Instructor* (New York: Garland Publishing, 1981). Reprint of the 1844 edition published by Thomas F. Adams, Philadelphia.

Thomas Lynch, *The Printer's Manual, a Practical Guide for Compositors and Pressmen* (New York: Garland Publishing, 1981). Reprint of the 1859 edition published by the Cincinnati Type Foundry.

J. Luther Ringwalt, ed., *American Encyclopaedia of Printing* (New York: Garland Publishing, 1981). Reprint of the 1871 edition published by Menamin & Ringwalt, Philadelphia.

John S. Thompson, *The Mechanism of the Linotype* and John S. Thompson, *History of Composing Machines* (New York: Garland Publishing, 1980). Reprint of the 1902 edition published by the Inland Printer Company, Chicago, and the 1904 edition published by the Inland Printer Company, Chicago.

219.   Paul A. Winckler, comp., *History of Books and Printing; a Guide to Information Services* (Detroit: Gale Research Company, 1979).

220.   Vito J. Brenni, *Book Printing in Britain and America* (Westport, Conn: Greenwood Press, 1983) and Vito J. Brenni, *Art and History of Book Printing* (Westport, Conn.: Greenwood Press, 1984).

221.   David McKittrick, ed., *Stanley Morison & D. B. Updike; Selected Correspondence* (New York: The Moretus Press, 1979).

222.   James J. Barnes, "Jonas Winchester; Printer, Speculator, Medicine Man," *PH* 5 (1983): 17–28; William M. Cubery, "The Memoirs of William M. Cubery," Robert D. Harlan ed., *PH* 4 (1982): 55–56; Madeleine B. Stern, "Every Man His Own Printer; the Typographic Experiments of Josiah Warren," *PH* 2 (1980): 11–20; Alexander Nesbitt, "A Life with Type and Letters," *PH* 2 (1980): 4–10; E. Richard McKinstry, "A Sketch of the Brief Printing Career of David Cree, 1784–1786," *PH* 1 (1979): 19–22; Stephen P. Ruggles, "The Autobiography of Stephen P. Ruggles," Rollo G. Silver, ed., *PH* 1 (1979): 7–17.

223.   Elizabeth Carroll Reilly, *A Dictionary of Colonial American Printers' Ornaments and Illustrations* (Worcester, Mass.: American Antiquarian Society, 1975).

224.   John Bidwell, "Some Caslon Ornaments in Some American Books," *PH* (1980): 21–25.

225.   Elizabeth M. Harris and Clifton Sisson, *The Common Press; Being a Record, Description & Delineation of the Early Eighteenth-Century Handpress in the Smithsonian Institution* (Boston: David R. Godine, 1978). See also Elizabeth M. Harris, "The American Common Press; the Restoration of a Wooden Press in the Smithsonian Institution," *JPHS* 8 (1972): 42–52 and "A Close Look at the 'Common Press' " *AB Bookmans Yearbook* (1978), Pt. 1, pp. 81–83.

226.   Philip Gaskell, "A Census of Wooden Presses," *JPHS* 6 (1970): 1–32.

227.   Wolf, "Origins of Early American Printing Offices." See Note 16.

228.   Rollo G. Silver, "Aprons Instead of Uniforms; the Practice of Printing, 1776–1787," *AASP* 87 (1977): Pt. 1, pp. 111–194.

229.   Stephen Botein, " 'Meer Mechanics' and an Open Press; the Business and Political Strategies of Colonial American Printers," *Perspectives in American History* 9 (1975): 127–225.

230.   Rollo G. Silver, "The Power of the Press: Hand, Horse, Water and Steam," *PH* 5 (1983): 5–16; "Violent Assaults on American Printing Shops, 1788–1860," *PH* 1 (1978): 10–18, and "The Convivial Printer: Dining, Wining and Marching, 1825–1860," *PH* 4 (1982): 16–25.

231.   John Bidwell, "The Size of the Sheet in America; Paper Moulds Manufactured by N. & D. Sellers of Philadelphia," *AASP 87* (1977): Pt. 2, pp. 299–342.

232.   Michael Winship, "Printing with Plates in the Nineteenth Century United States," *PH* 5 (1983): 15–26.

233.   Rollo G. Silver, "Trans-Atlantic Crossing; the Beginning of Electrotyping in America, *JPHS* 9 (1974/75): 84–103.

234.   James Moran, *Printing Presses; History and Development from the Fifteenth Century to Modern Times* (Berkeley: University of California Press, 1973).

235.   Frank E. Comparato, *Chronicles of Genius and Folly; R. Hoe & Co. and the Printing Press as a Service to Democracy* (Culver City, Calif.: Labyrinthos, 1979): Stephen D. Tucker, "History of R. Hoe & Company, 1834–1885," Rollo G. Silver, ed., *AASP* 82 (1972): Pt. 2, pp. 351–453.

236.   Rollo G. Silver, "Efficiency Improved; the Genesis of the Web Press in America," *AASP* 80 (1971): Pt. 2, pp. 325–350.

237.   James Moran, "How Many Columbian Presses did George Clymer and his Successors Make?" *JPHS* 13 (1978/79): 78–80.

238.   Stephen O. Saxe, "A Brief History of Golding & Co.," *PH* 3 (1981): 13–19.

239.   Rollo G. Silver, "Early Time-Sharing Project; the Introduction of the Napier Press in America," *JPHS* 7 (1971): 29–36.

240.   Maurice Annenberg, *Type Foundries of America and their Catalogs* (Baltimore: Maran Printing Services, 1975).

241.   Stephen O. Saxe, "The Type Founders of New York City, 1840–1900," *PH* 2 (1980): 4–19.

242. Madeleine B. Stern, "Isaac M. Singer's Type Machine," *PH* 1 (1979): 4–9.

243. Nicolete Gray, *Nineteenth Century Ornamented Type Faces, with a Chapter on Ornamented Types in America, by Ray Nash* (London: Faber & Faber, 1976).

244. Richard E. Huss, *The Development of Printer's Mechanical Typesetting Methods, 1822–1925* (Charlottesville: University Press of Virginia, 1973).

245. Mary Biggs, "Neither Printer's Wife Nor Widow; American Women in Typesetting, 1830–1950," *LQ* 50 (October 1980): 431–452.

246. Vito J. Brenni, *Bookbinding; a Guide to the Literature* (Westport, Conn.: Greenwood Press, 1983).

247. Frank E. Comparato, *Books for the Millions; a History of the Men Whose Methods and Machines Packaged the Printed Word* (Harrisburg, Pa.: Stackpole Company, 1971).

248. Sue Allen, "Machine-Stamped Bookbindings, 1834–1860," *Antiques* 115 (March 1979): 564–572 and "Floral-Patterned Endpapers in Nineteenth-Century American Books," *Winterthur Portfolio* 12 (1977): 183–224.

249. Verner W. Clapp, "The Story of Permanent/Durable Book Paper, 1115–1970," *SP* 2 (January, April, July 1971): 107–124, 229–245, 353–367. Also published as a supplement to *Restaurator* (Copenhagen: Restaurator Press, 1972), Supplement No. 3.

250. Vito J. Brenni, *Book Illustration and Decoration; a Guide to Research* (Westport, Conn.: Greenwood Press, 1980).

251. Clarence P. Hornung and Fridolf Johnson, *2000 Years of American Graphic Art; a Retrospective Survey of the Printing Arts and Advertising since the Colonial Period* (New York: George Braziller, 1976).

252. Henry Pitz, *200 Years of American Illustration* (New York: Harry N. Abrams, 1983).

253. Susan E. Meyer, *America's Great Illustrators* (New York: Harry N. Abrams, 1978) and *A Treasury of the Great Children's Book Illustrators* (New York: Harry N. Abrams, 1983).

254. Judy L. Larson, "Separately Published Engravings in the Early Republic," *PH* 6 (1984): 3–24. The *Catalogue of American Engravings* is the announced title of the new work.

255. David Woodward, "The Decline of Commercial Wood-Engravers in Nineteenth Century America," *JPHS* 10 (1974/75): 57–83.

256. Jefferson C. Dykes, *Fifty Great Western Illustrators; a Bibliographic Checklist* (Flagstaff, Ariz.: Northland Press, 1975).

257. *Prints in and of America to 1850*, John D. Morse, ed. (Charlottesville: University Press of Virginia, 1970).

258. *The Artist and the Book, 1860–1960, in Western Europe and the United States*, 2d ed. (Boston: Museum of Fine Arts, 1972).

259. *The Golden Age of American Illustration, 1880–1914* (Wilmington: Delaware Art Museum, 1972).

260. *A Century of American Illustration* (Brooklyn: Institute of Arts and Sciences Museum, 1972).

261. *The American Personality; the Artist-Illustrator of Life in the United States, 1860–1930* (Los Angeles: Grunwald Center for the Graphic Arts, UCLA, 1976).

262. Robert A. Tibbitts, "Bruce Rogers, American Book Designer" (Ph.D. diss., University of Chicago, 1969).

263. Roberta Waddell Wong, "Will Bradley: Exponent of American Decorative Illustration at the End of the Nineteenth Century" (Ph.D. diss., The Johns Hopkins University, 1970).

264. Frederick Daniel Weinstein, "Walter Crane and the American Book Arts" (Ph.D. diss., Columbia University, 1970).

265. Franco Andreucci, "Socialismo e Marxismo per Pochi Cents: Charles H. Kerr, Editore," *Movimento Operaio e Socialista* 3 (1980): 269–286.

266. Estelle Jussim, *Visual Communication and the Graphic Arts; Photographic Technologies in the Nineteenth Century* (New York: Bowker, 1974) and Estelle Jussim, *Slave to Beauty* (see Note 136).

THE RESPONSE OF THE CATALOGER AND THE CATALOG TO AUTOMATION IN THE ACADEMIC LIBRARY SETTING

Joan M. Repp

INTRODUCTION

It appears that profound changes are occurring in the creation and function of the catalog, as well as in the role and function of the cataloger. Although the catalog is changing markedly in form and scope, the purpose of the catalog—to provide access—remains constant. The tasks of the cataloger are also changing, incorporating many elements of management and supervision. The cataloger's basic responsibility, however, remains the same—to create the structure and content of the catalog. It is essential to explore the catalog and the cataloger's role from both historical and contemporary points of view in order to compre-

Advances in Library Administration and Organization
Volume 5, pages 67–89
Copyright © 1986 by JAI Press Inc.
All rights of reproduction in any form reserved.
ISBN: 0-89232-674-3

hend the magnitude of the changes and to gain some sense of what future roles and functions may be. The cataloger and catalog, creator and creation, are so closely allied that both must be examined simultaneously.

The impact of automation on the practice of cataloging is an invasive, unrelenting, and welcome one. Cataloging will never be the same. Although the sharing of expertise through the union catalogs was useful, the advent of shared cataloging in an on-line mode was truly the catalyst. The phenomenal growth and the acceptance of automation as applied in cooperative cataloging were due to the real need addressed, the foresight of the early planners such as Kilgour, and a number of other factors that enabled and accelerated the move. Major factors include explosion of computer technology itself with a dramatic rise in power and flexibility; the precipitous drop in attendant equipment costs; ease of installation; increasing relative ease of use. Supporting this effort from the cataloging perspective was the development of the MARC formats by the Library of Congress, the backbone of machine-readable cataloging, and the development of ISBD and ISSD formats to facilitate the international exchange of bibliographic data. These structures, coupled with the information explosion, which itself is at least partially a child of new methods of handling and disseminating information, necessitated a new set of internationally accepted cataloging protocols.

AACR2 has been hailed as the last preautomation cataloging code, and it carries within it a basic structure easily adaptable to the machine environment. The code has two major sections. Part one deals solely with the rules for creating the physical description of the piece in hand; part two deals solely with access points. The parallel is a clear one: database record and search terms. Whether or not AACR3 will dispense with the main entry, deemed by some as an "idea which has been overtaken by technology"[1] or whether main entry needs to be retained is still a matter of some debate in the literature.[2] Current professional literature has also provided a variety of viewpoints and scenarios on what the immediate future holds for the cataloging process, catalogers, and the traditional technical services department.[3] The development and application of totally machine-based cataloging appear theoretically possible given the development of artificial intelligence, natural language query, and the rule base that characterizes cataloging. This is suggested not only for descriptive cataloging but also for the selection and construction of access points and the construction of a classification number. Taking one more step, it may be possible to have "an expert system with full cataloging capability linked into an electronic publishing system, so that as a text is generated on-line, it can be passed through an expert-system cataloging process without any intellectual input from an intermediary."[4]

IMPACT ON CATALOGING DEPARTMENTS

The impact of automation on the cataloging process has been characterized by changes in organization, work flow, staffing patterns, and job responsibilities. One common organizational change was the merger of the cataloging and bibliographic searching units.[5] Another common response was the development of two tracks for the processing of new library acquisitions. Materials for which there was acceptable copy in the database were handled by one unit, identified variously as the editing, copy, or automated cataloging unit. Many libraries created copy cataloging units within their cataloging departments while others created separate departments for this activity.[6] Materials for which no copy could be found, or for which no acceptable copy was in the database, were routed to the original cataloging unit. "Acceptable" copy was locally defined and varied widely from library to library. The most restrictive accepted only MARC records that were an exact match.[7] Many libraries developed "white lists," mounted on the terminal, specifying cooperating institutions, in addition to Library of Congress, who input acceptable cataloging records. Records of those institutions not on the "white list" were rejected out of hand. Another variation on the change in work flow was observed, based on the amount of discretion the paraprofessional/ clerical at the terminal was permitted in editing selected fields. This practice appeared to be based on earlier staffing patterns established by working with proof slips or *National Union Catalog* copy.[8] As recently as 1983, one large research library using OCLC was still routing about 33 percent of its titles to the original cataloging unit. Routing of less than 10 percent, as reported by other research libraries in the same study, is the more likely pattern.[9] Another common response to the impact of on-line cataloging was the development of holding profiles by libraries. These resulted from patterns of database searching based on the nature of the material in hand, local demand, and the observed length of time it took for comparable records to show in the database. Some libraries reported holding material for up to one year before sending it forward for review and creation of the record by the professional cataloger, during which time acceptable copy for 85–95 percent of the material to be cataloged had been found.[10]

On Staffing

Because of the increased efficiency in the cataloging process and creation of the supporting files and records, many cataloging departments not only staffed differentially utilizing the paraprofessional more fully, but actually reduced staff.[11] One creative response was to transfer positions to an in-house retrospective conversion unit, responsible for creating a machine-readable file from the paper files, such as the shelflists, for later use in machine applications. These units were often staffed by paraprofessionals under the supervision of a professional cataloger, and were not intended to become a permanent part of library processing, but only to exist for the duration of the project.

On Work Patterns

Common sense dictates that workers have the files they frequently use located near or at their work stations. Because the traditional shelflist, given its bulk and complexity, is not duplicated throughout a library system (although parts of it may be, there is usually one and only one legal shelflist), the staff relying on this monumental file must be physically located where it is. Once a library's records are in machine-readable form, however, a variety of options are available for reproducing, fractionating, and manipulating the records by any number of preplanned or serendipitous factors. These may include format, subject, call number, or author, arranged alphabetically, numerically, or chronologically. The end product may be distributed in static form, such as COM or paper. These are relatively inexpensive to produce, readily reproducible, and can be updated with ease. The on-line presentation of this file, or a portion of this file is more current and may, in certain circumstances, be interactive as well. On-line interactive files are accessible from any location having a telecommunications link, even one as pedestrian as a home telephone. The machine environment then, has provided a degree of freedom not practical prior to its advent, in that library files, whether paper, film, or on line, can be made accessible in many locations. In addition to more flexibility in physical location, many library cataloging departments have changed from the traditional 8–5, Monday through Friday, work schedule in order to maximize utilization of costly terminals. Expanding the traditional work schedule also takes advantage of accessing databases when charges are lower based on peak and off-peak loads. System response times are also faster during off-peak hours.[12] This change in work schedules need not result in problems in staffing and supervision but may be viewed as an opportunity to use changing worker patterns, flextime scheduling, and part-time staffing to meet institutional needs.

On Machine Dependency

It is patently obvious that embracing automation wholeheartedly does result in machine dependency. When the system is down for a period of time, it can become very difficult to keep cataloging staff constructively occupied. Bibliographic searchers accustomed to the ease, speed, and convenience of major databases are not eager to use the NUCs, but prefer to wait until the database is again available. Major changes have also occurred in the way the individual worker structures work time and interacts with other employees with the integration of a terminal into the workflow. In a manual system, the worker controls the speed of the interaction; in a machine system the machine controls the speed of the interaction. The response time of a data-base terminal may be much slower than the worker wishes to work, and this leads to frustration and an attendant loss of attention, which can lead to an increase in errors. The opportunity for casual interaction with fellow employees is minimized. This, coupled with the machine setting the pace, can result in a feeling of the machine being in control, rather than the worker.

From an institutional point of view, once having committed itself, a library becomes dependent because there is no easy "way of reestablishing autonomy except at prohibitive cost, both direct, say in terms of recreating vacated positions, and indirect, in terms of seceding from an increasingly cooperative bibliographic world."[13] On the other hand, the same dependence on and rigidity (i.e., standardization) of the machine environment have resulted in freeing staff from extremely tedious, repetitious, and labor-intensive work that had to be done manually in the past, such as the recreation of cataloging records, and finishing and filing the cards.

IMPACT WITHIN THE INSTITUTION

An interesting development in library organization due to automation is the administrative realignment of the cataloging department (traditionally a technical-service area) with the circulation department (traditionally a public-service area) and the creation of "access services" to encompass both departments. A machine-readable record created by the cataloging department, either as a by-product of card production or as a separate process such as a retrospective conversion project, becomes the basis for an automated circulation system. An interdependency only casually recognized in a manual circulation system becomes critical in an automated circulation system. Questions such as who has responsibility for editing, maintaining, and linking records must be resolved.

On Service

A real possibility exists to materially improve patron access with a different form of catalog. Criticisms leveled at card catalogs include size, complexity, expense, limited information, lack of security, deterioration, and physical format limitations. All of these influence the effectiveness of the catalog as a public-access tool either directly (complexity) or indirectly (security). The prospect of an on-line public-access catalog as a replacement for the traditional card catalog is an intriguing one. Not only can patrons access information in different ways, but management reports unavailable before can aid in evaluating service, maintaining records, and assisting in collection analysis and development.

On the Professional Cataloger

Catalogers have been the butt of a number of jokes, some good humored, some barbed, many deserved, for their apparent propensity to make the cataloging record in general, and subject access in particular, as obscure as possible for the layperson.[14] The continuing debate regarding the value of faculty status for catalogers as a subset of academic librarians further clouds this intramural issue. Due to higher visibility, collection development responsibilities, and the growing role of bibliographic instruction, other academic librarians perform more in the model of a teaching faculty member than does the cataloger. The cataloger whose work results in a measurable number of units per month is in danger of being classed as a technician. The position has even been taken that the faculty status has caused difficulty for catalogers.[15] The role of the traditional cataloger, even within the traditional technical services structure, is becoming more and more that of manager and planner, with the paraprofessional assuming many of the functions formerly assigned to the cataloger. Comparison has been made between the function and role of professional cataloger and professional work in engineering and architecture.[16] The parallel is an excellent one when examining the growing importance of the paraprofessional in libraries and the industrial technologist in industry. In both cases, over the last 10 years the professional has moved into planning, administrative, and supervisory functions and a new class of highly skilled paraprofessionals has developed, assuming many if not most of the tasks formerly done by professionals. The use of support staff in the professions is not a new phenomenon, but the movement accelerated during the 1960s and 1970s due to a number of social, economic, and political factors.[17] From 1960 to 1975, the number of librarians in academic libraries increased from 9,000 to 20,100, or 123 percent; support staff in the same libraries during the same period increased from 9,000 to 35,600, or 295 percent.[18] The assumption of standardized cataloging by the paraprofessional has, then, freed the cataloger for the more difficult and esoteric cataloging, participation in library instruction programs, and interpreting the catalog to the end user. However, catalogers must remain librarians who are responsible for creating the bibliographic form and content of the catalog.[19]

It is unfortunate that the public-service professional working directly with the patron often does not appreciate the fact that the cataloger catalogs for a dual client base. One base is the patron who wishes to retrieve information rather than a specific work. In public libraries, this represents virtually the sole client base for nonfiction queries. In academic libraries, it is the undergraduate who most often seeks information rather than a specific work. These patrons are the subject seekers. They approach the collection with a subject question. Where they get the information, whether a book, journal, other serial, videotape, data file, or film is of less importance than the information itself. These are the clients most likely to seek the assistance of the public-service professional. The cataloger who applies the subject headings does not see, in most libraries, the end use of the product. The reference librarian who does see the end-user behavior often does not appreciate the complexities of applying the subject heading. This results in a real communication gap and mutual lack of appreciation on the part of each for the role of the other. Restructuring of traditional cataloging departments into Atkinson's tribal families, or the continued blurring of lines between technical services and public services, may serve to ameliorate this to some extent by making each group aware of the constraints within which the other must operate.

The second group, or client base, is the scholar, researcher, graduate student, or bibliographer who seeks a specific work. The search may center on a particular writer, researcher, or scholar whose work is under scrutiny, or may serve the internal needs of a particular library. Two questions must be answered: Does the collection contain this specific work? If not, what library does? It is most unfortunate that the professional cataloger has failed to make plain to his or her public service counterpart that the needs of scholars, researchers, and bibliographers are best met by accurate consistent physical description and access points excluding subject analysis, and that the penchant for detail and apparent obsession for accuracy are not self-serving or attempts at job security, but a legitimate, essential response to a real need for accuracy. The researcher, well acquainted with the ways of libraries, is more likely to pursue his or her search independently, and not seek the assistance of the public-service professional unless needed as an intermediary for an on-line data-base search. Even here, recent research suggests the sophisticated patron, for example, the researcher, feels quite capable of searching databases without an intermediary. Researchers perceive themselves to be more knowledgeable than any professional librarian about their area of expertise, and indeed well may be, although they may be less knowledgeable about how the discipline is structured and may not be familiar with the most useful techniques for accessing data in their field. One can conclude that the high number and high visibility of unsophisticated users as compared to the fewer numbers of researchers and their lower visibility, particularly in an academic setting, has contributed to the lack of appreciation for the cataloger's attention to detail.

ACCESS

The purpose of the cataloging function in a library setting is twofold: access and control. Access encompasses several areas including subject analysis, authorship, title, series, or any other term under which the material can be identified. Subject access in particular has received a great deal of attention recently by the library profession as a whole, and a considerable amount of library literature and research has been and is being devoted to the topic. This flow of literature has increased with the crisis—and that term is used advisedly—in subject analysis and access promulgated by the imminence of on-line public catalogs. Subject analysis/subject heading has never stabilized in the library world to the same extent that the physical description of the text has, as witnessed by the number and variety of subject lists, hierarchies, structures, and systems that have come and gone over the last 100 years. Currently the two most widely used and referenced lists, the Library of Congress Subject Headings and the Sears List of Subject

Headings, do not begin to meet the needs of highly specialized collections which, because of their narrow scope but considerable depth, require more detailed analyses. Indeed, the databases that hold data and information not under library control, such as ERIC and MEDLARS, have developed their own unique terms and structure, requiring search strategies very different from the traditional library protocols. These databases have of necessity generated specialized thesauri to provide the user with access to the data. There is debate as to whether the Library of Congress, and by extrapolation Sears subject headings, will be of any value in a machine environment, and subject access by some other method, such as the classification number, may be a more prudent and practical path to follow.[20] The prospect of applying different or additional subject terms that are both more readily manipulated in a machine environment to the 11 million records in OCLC, the bibliographic utility with the largest database at present, is staggering in terms of allocation of resources. That assumes, of course, that a thesaurus and search structure acceptable to all constituencies is possible. Subjects keep changing, like the ubiquitous influenza virus, mutating into a plethora of new topics, such as space medicine, or recombination of other topics, such as biochemistry. Although some of these are evolutionary changes and are social in nature, many of them are a true restructuring of knowledge due to our growing knowledge base. It seems fair to assume that as the information explosion continues and accelerates, this addition of subjects and restructuring of relationships between areas of knowledge and disciplines will also continue and accelerate. From a cataloging/control point of view, it becomes imperative that some sort of sensible, practical structure be imposed as soon as possible, to minimize cataloging agencies of all sorts and descriptions, not limited to the institutions we now call libraries, from riding off in all directions. Once the investment of time and personnel resources exceeds a certain point, it is very difficult to change direction.

Subject analysis, as uncomplicated as it appears today relative to what tomorrow holds, generates a great deal of interest because basically it is one of the three major points of interaction between the client and the system, whether the system is card, machine, or staff at the reference desk. Casual observation leads one to believe that at least as many, if not more, reference librarians lead the questioning patron to the shelf in response to query about a subject, as lead the patron to the card catalog. In this event, the reference professional is using his or her knowledge of the classification scheme as the subject access, not an assigned subject heading.

The subject term or terms applied to a work are important for the patron, but this is the least reliable and least useful retrieval point from a bibliographic-control point of view. An experienced bibliographer, attempting to verify the existence or ownership of a particular work, would use subject access as a last desperate resort, if at all. This lack of usefulness is not limited to technical services professionals. Reference librarians, unable to find material requested by a patron on a specific subject, occasionally invent book titles using the subject and look under title in the catalog. More often than not, the librarian finds a work with the subject term as the entry word or words, and then uses the tracings to discover the subject heading applied by the cataloger to that class of subject. At various times in the past, it has been seriously suggested that subject bibliographies, supplementing the catalog, may be a more efficient method of subject access than subject headings. In a manual environment, the labor intensity of creating and maintaining a subject bibliography precludes widespread use in this sense. An on-line environment, and good word processor, make the task much less formidable.

Other access points cause considerably less consternation, partly because they are more easily determined and are controlled by codes that have been relatively consistent throughout the history of modern librarianship, and in some cases, ancient librarianship as well. With the exception of corporate authorship, which has endured some changes, and the ambivalence catalogers seem to feel toward series as an access point, professionals, practitioners, and patrons all seem comfortable with the concept that the author's name is a useful and proper access point for his or her work, as is the title of the work. Here, too, one can argue pseudonym versus legal name versus best-known form of name in one's native country, but the basic premise still stands. The same is true of corporate authorship. There have been changes with AACR2 as to the scope of what merits corporate authorship, but the basic premise still stands that a corporate body is capable of "authoring" certain types of work, and that the corporate body can serve as a useful and deserved point of access. The form of these access points—direct entry, inverted, how to construct qualifiers and where to place them—varies with time and place but is still stringently controlled by the cataloging codes that have emerged over the years and are widely accepted.

The title is another access point that seems secure and inviolable. Although again one can debate how much of what on the title page is title proper and how much is subtitle, alternate title, or other title variations, most of these exceptions and aberrations have been examined and codified so that the decisions made at the point of cataloging are surprisingly consistent. One does not have the option of using or not using a title even if none exists.

Series as access point has fared less well mainly because of inconsistencies of application, the option of applying a series access point being left to a great extent to the judgement of the cataloger. As a result, the value of series as a point of control and retrieval is questionable at best. Many statements in current monographs and nonbook materials include the term *series* but the statement is of no bibliographic significance and deserves to be ignored. Card-catalog use studies indicate series as an entry point rarely is used by patrons.[21]

These then are the major access points a cataloger creates for patron use in constructing a cataloging record. Author and title are among the most secure access points, most highly controlled by current code, practice, and tradition, and they function as useful points of access for users in either machine or card environment. In a machine environment, the system-assigned control number, L.C.

card number, and ISBN or ISSN, are more highly controlled and specific but are of little or no value to most users other than technical services staff. Uniform title and alternate title are of some value, and in the case of music and the Bible, of inestimable value, but are generally less useful for other works. Even though other access points are consistent in their selection, construction, and application, they are applied less frequently and, in the case of series, virtually at the discretion of the cataloger. The subject as access point is the most troublesome and shows every sign that it will continue to be so in the machine environment.

CONTROL

From a library point of view, the cataloging record has an additional function. It is a method of inventory control; a precise, accurate, up-to-date record of what the library holds and where the work can be found. Accuracy and consistency in description of the work in hand have become more critical with the growth of union listings and projects, local, regional, national, and international. Unless the individual in charge of editing and compiling the union listing has complete and correct data on each entry, the listing will, of course, be inaccurate and misleading. The national chairman of RISM for Australia stated it succinctly at one point by saying she needed descriptive cataloging records done with sufficient accuracy so that she could know whether or not the cataloging record in front of her represents the same physical piece as the one held in a library half a world away. Fortunately, the physical description of the item in hand is the least controversial and most consistently reliable aspect of the cataloging record. Kilgour has been quoted as saying that descriptive cataloging today does not differ much from the cataloging practiced during the Middle Ages.[22] But even within the fraternity of catalogers, local practice sometimes prevails. Markuson has used the phrase "local petit point" to describe the fillips and fancies that grow up in any given library. Some are valid local practices, such as adding an X as the last element in a locally constructed call number developed from the Library of Congress schedules. This is done so that the local call number will never conflict with a call number assigned by Library of Congress. Or conversely, assigning an X as the last element in a call number assigned by Library of Congress, so the number will never conflict with a locally assigned call number constructed from the Library of Congress schedules. Both of these can be viewed as legitimate responses to a real problem. On the other hand, the assigning of X if the call number is created by a cataloger with an ALA degree and a Y if it is not appears to be fatuous.

CREATING THE RECORD

The cataloging record is in actuality quite elegant. Callemachus, according to library history the first cataloger, was also a poet. The parallels between the two products—the poem, particularly highly structured poetry such as haiku or the sonnet, and the cataloging record—are striking. Each seeks to identify an essence and to so describe it in words as to convey this essence to another. In poetry, the essence is a feeling; in cataloging, it is the description of a creative work. Both seek to use the perfect word in the perfect pattern to accomplish the task, with no wasted time or extraneous detail. The focus is clear and sharp. Protocols are defined and patterns are highly structured. The end product is, or should be, a concise accurate representation with every essential included in sufficient detail and all extraneous data excluded. The end users of this product, whether reading poetry or a cataloging record, need a degree of experience or sophistication to fully appreciate and benefit from what they see. Indeed, in the case of either a poem or a cataloging record, the end users may need training or assistance to comprehend and interpret the end product at all.

The cataloging record contains three major elements: description, access term, and call number. The first is a bibliographic description of the piece in hand, including format. The proliferation of formats are virtually unlimited because the creative human keeps finding new techniques and devices and reasons to capture, preserve, manipulate, and transmit information. Once the cataloger made the transition from printed matter to some other form, the burgeoning variety of formats and whether the record created was handled as a card, microform, or machine-readable data file, was of no real consequence. The second element, access, refers to the term or terms under which the bibliographic record may be located. They include the familiar author, title, and subject headings, and their variations. The third element, the call number, is probably the most critical element from a pragmatic point of view, because it is essential to retrieving the material. Call number is also the element where local manipulation is the most readily accepted because it is wholly site specific.

The creation of the record in the premachine environment, before shared cataloging through the bibliographic utilities, was highly labor intensive and therefore expensive. This was ameliorated to some degree by the cataloging available in hard copy through the *National Union Catalogs* and the various Library of Congress products, including cards. The maintenance of the records in card form, however, could not be shared, and each library had to alphabetize, file, revise, and perhaps ultimately withdraw each card placed in the catalog manually.

THE "NEW" CATALOG

Early microform catalogs merely reproduced the catalog card on microfilm. They had the advantage of being easily duplicated at a reasonable price, could be divided into subsets, and were easily transportable, providing a potential for wider distribution of the file. The major disadvantages were that they provided no more than the card catalog from which they were made, and provided less in that they could not be readily updated. In order to update, an entire new file had to be created, or separate supplements had to be provided. Later COM catalogs provided more flexibility, low cost, and ease of duplication, but still had the real disadvantage of being static, out of date as soon as they were produced. Despite this disadvantage, the COM market continues to grow at a constant 15 to 20 percent per year.[23] Having lived so long in the static environment of card or COM, it is difficult to imagine the changes possible with an on-line catalog. Certainly one has a right to assume it will minimally provide the same degree of access to material as the traditional catalogs do.

One of the major advantages for records maintenance in an on-line environment as opposed to a card environment is the capability to make global changes. As an example, in December 1980, a major bibliographic utility made plans to examine and modify headings in their database, which held 6,790,000 records in machine-readable form. This project was undertaken in order to bring the database into conformity with the new rules for headings as specified in AACR2. The conversion was expected to take 124 hours of continuous processing time based on an anticipated change in 8 to 20 percent of the records.[24] The actual change took twice as long because the earlier estimate proved to be low, and 39 percent of the records required at least one heading change. In all, the utility "made 3,716,740 modifications to about 2.7 million records."[25] It is patently obvious that this project could not have been accomplished in any other than an on-line environment.

Contents

As stated earlier, the purpose of the cataloging function from the library point of view is twofold, access and control. Library users, however, approach the collection from a very different point of view, namely, can I get what I need? The traditional card catalog does tell a patron what is owned, although not many libraries note detailed holdings such as missing volumes of a multivolume set on the public catalog records; however, it does not indicate whether or not the material is, in fact, available for the patron to use (it may be in the reference collection) or to check out (it may be at the binder). The on-line public-access catalog, on the other hand, can supply the patron with several kinds of information about the material at several levels from in-house terminals or terminals in remote locations, whether owned by the local institution or not, with a speed, accuracy, and convenience no other form of catalog possesses.

In addition to including a wider representation of the library's resources, more inclusive by type, location, or ownership, the on-line catalog can present data about the collection to the patron in various levels of detail or complexity. Availability of the material might also be included in this initial display. In a very real sense, selected elements of three fields—the public catalog card, the shelflist, and the circulation records—only one of which was readily available to the patron in the past, are being recombined. This can provide the patron with a different combination of data than the traditional card catalog can provide, one that has the potential to be much more useful to most patrons.

One of the most obvious tie-ins is the inclusion of the acquisition on-order record. The elegance here, from the processing point of view, is the creation of a single record, at point of order, that tracks the acquisition through the purchase and cataloging process. When processing is complete, the original record in the system can be edited at the time of cataloging or replaced with the finished cataloging record. Several systems presently on the market permit the downloading of the record from a major bibliographic utility, reformatting it into an order record. Not only is a single record created, but by piggybacking on a utility, keystroking is minimized.

The on-line catalog may also supply information such as detailed holdings, circulation status of each volume or copy, serials check-in records, and "declared missing but not withdrawn" statements. Additionally, it can readily reflect short-term relocation of cataloged material from its accustomed place due to transfer to reserve, removal for repair or binding, or longer-term relocation such as storage, long-term loan, or housing of the most recent edition in the reference collection. The record can also reflect location of uncataloged material in the backlog and, most commonly, circulation status of the material.

The on-line catalog also has the potential to contain all of a library's holdings, including serials, nonbook, and archival materials. Although it was always theoretically possible to do this, in a practical sense it did not occur due to a number of factors, including the difficulty of updating serials records and holdings manually and the nonstandard treatment accorded nonbook materials by many libraries. With the advent of AACR2, nonbook items have attained a degree of legitimacy they lacked in the past. Using standard cataloging and a bibliographic utility, machine-readable records in MARC format for nonbook materials are produced and can be readily accepted by an automated system. None of these developments in cataloging practice are unique to on-line catalogs, they just were less practical in a card environment. Other intriguing possibilities emerge such as loading files of neighboring libraries, regional collections, or union lists into a local catalog. A system dependent on hand filing, revising, editing, and correcting cards rather preemptorily precludes this possibility. An intriguing possibility has been suggested to acquire Magazine Index tapes, strip off the titles owned by a particular library, and load these tailored tapes into a local on-line catalog. They could be updated monthly, when the new Magazine Index tapes arrive, in a very practical way adding a subject index of current locally owned periodical articles to the catalog.[26]

Levels of Access

The initial abbreviated display—in all likelihood author, title, call number, publisher, and date—would not provide the scholar with sufficient bibliographic data to adequately identify the specific edition, issue, or impression he or she may seek, requiring a second level, available on demand, displaying more complete bibliographic data. A third level of display might be contents and/or history notes, or an abstract of the material. Theoretically, a fourth level could be the full text of the material itself. While possible, this is not practical at present because of limitations of both time and space; time to enter full text and space to store it, although this level of information access may well find its place in small highly specialized collections.

Differing levels of user sophistication can be accommodated on line. The use of menus and ample, simple-to-follow help screens are most useful for the occasional or novice user. These helps quickly become an annoyance to the sophisticated patron who is willing and able to use a command-driven system. Good system design can permit access to the data by patrons with either level of sophistication. The on-line environment can be much more accommodating than the card catalog in that it has the potential to accept and search key word, Boolean, or phrase in addition to any field previously indexed for searching.

Authority Control

The incorporation of authority control in the on-line system has received much attention, and represents one of the major differences between OCLC and other major bibliographic utilities. Maintaining authority control in a card environment required a substantial outlay of cataloging resources, and access to tools not available in all libraries. If the professional holds to the premise that "there can be no retreat from the demand that a catalog present to the user the complete works of an author, all of the various editions and representations of a work, and all of the library's holdings on a given subject or topic,"[27] authority control is essential. Interestingly enough, the card catalog attempted to but never totally succeeded in accomplishing this objective, because it would require a degree of inclusiveness (periodicals), and analysis (chapters and articles), no library can afford.

Authority control can be interpreted as having a dual function. Minimally, authority control will validate as legitimate a heading, term, or name. That is of some use in identifying a problem, but it does not tell the patron what to do next. This basic form of authority control is of more use to a cataloger or other staff member, who then can use other resources to assign the correct term. The second function of authority control is to provide an additional step, cross-referencing. This can be totally transparent, bringing up entries under the correct form with an explanatory note on the screen. Optionally the system can inform the patron that the term used is incorrect, that he or she must research under the correct term, and spell out the correct term for the patron. The system may also suggest additional related terms under which to search. Quite simply, these can be the *see* and *see also* records in the Library of Congress authority files, now available in machine-readable form.

Filing

In libraries, filing cards in the catalogs is a labor-intensive and therefore expensive process, occasionally characterized as subhuman. Libraries often require initial card filing, followed by revision by high-level paraprofessional or professional staff. In any collection, a misfiled card equals a missing book, particularly in a mark-it-and-park-it library. As catalogs become larger and entries more complex, the task of filing into the catalog takes longer and is more prone to error. The corollary to that is, of course, if it takes a professional to file it, where does that leave the patron? Finding the card is as complex as filing it. The ALA catalog-use study published in 1958 reported, "of the 203 sample searches conducted by staff members of participating libraries, 16 percent produced failures to locate entries for items that were actually in the catalog. Thus, on the average, the librarian user fared little better than the nonlibrarian user."[28]

The oft-repeated requirement that an on-line catalog be "user friendly" implies that the card catalog is "user friendly." Nothing could be further from the truth. Current card catalogs require minimally a knowledge of the hierarchy of the alphabet, building from there into a highly structured and controlled arrangement totally incomprehensible to the layman. A number of conventions have developed over the years in manual filing to make the patron's task simpler, such as interfiling *Mc* and *Mac* or spelling out *U.S., Dr., Mrs.*, etc. This process requires human interpretation at the point of filing and finding and generally works well enough. It does, however, assume the patron will know that the cards are filed as spelled out, not as written. Cards on which the entry line is a date present a variation on that same theme, but only the very sophisticated patron will anticipate these cards will not file in chronological sequence, which is logical, but will instead file *1800, 1500, 1700, 1600* because that is how they are spelled out. A high degree of ambiguity can arise with specialized terms, such as *.300 Vickers Machine Gun Mechanism*, which could file under *three, three hundred,* or *three-tenths*. Actually it files under *thirty calibre*.

The 1980 *ALA Filing Rules* are an excellent example of filing rules developed for a machine environment. They represent a radical change from any set of widely accepted filing rules used for the card catalog including the earlier ALA filing rules, the Library of Congress filing rules, and the many locally developed rules. Basically, entries will file "as is" rather than "as if." Because the machine is extremely literal, small errors that would be of virtually no account in a manual filing system, such as omitting the period after *Mr.*, will result in placing this entry out of order, preceding all other *Mr.* entries in the file. On a grander scale, a library accustomed to filing cards by heading, then heading followed by standard subdivisions, then standard subdivision followed by geographical term or parenthetical qualifier, will find these are interfiled as they read, regardless of type of subdivision or qualifier. Additionally the distinction of persons filing before places, filing before things, filing before titles, will also be lost and all these headings will interfile. Major similarities will remain, however. The arrangement will be basically alphabetical, nothing will continue to precede something, and subjects entries will file following the identical term that is not a subject entry. Although machines can be programmed to accommodate all the variations necessary to duplicate local practice, the decision to do so can only be characterized as reactionary and a waste of machine time and memory, because keyword searching, available on many on-line systems, provides a powerful complementary approach to material in addition to the alphabetic filing arrangement. The new rules are simple, logical, and consistent and should serve the patron well.

Maintenance

In an on-line catalog environment, card production will for all practical purposes cease to exist, although some limited card production may continue.[29] The halt in card production results in an immediate drop in card maintenance costs such as prefiling, filing in the catalogs, and revision. Labor costs for card filing and maintenance can vary widely depending on local procedures and levels of staff used, from $.33 to $2.73 per monograph cataloged. The $.33 figure was reported by a library utilizing only support staff.[30] Using the lowest figure, a library using a bibliography utility, adding 25,000 monographs annually, spends $8,250 in card filing and maintenance costs for personnel. To this must be added the cost of cards, approximately $.05 each at an average of 8.8 cards per title, or $11,000 per year.[31] This is a total card production of 220,000 cards per year. The standard 60-drawer card catalog case costs $2,000 and can accommodate 1,000 cards per drawer maximum. The total cost, then, of filing labor, OCLC card costs, and card catalog cases amounts to more than $26,000 per year. This figure can be considerably higher if procedures are more involved, different levels of staff are utilized, or more cards are produced per title. Some libraries have moved from detailed to cursory proofreading of cards and to correcting only those errors that will affect filing. Although the prospect of filing an incorrect card into the public catalog is distasteful, it is accepted as a trade-off to keep processing costs down and/or to increase the speed of processing.

Conversion and Linking

Any functioning on-line system assumes that at least a substantial portion of the library's records are in machine-readable form and loaded in the system. Obtaining machine-readable records in MARC format is possible as a by-product of cataloging through a bibliographic utility. Creating machine-readable records for previously cataloged materials, retrospective conversion (retrocon), and subsequent manipulation and loading of these records is not critical for an automated circulation system, but becomes critical for an on-line catalog for a number of reasons. Libraries that have frozen or closed their card catalogs in response to the adoption of AACR2, to get better control of filing backlogs, or for some other reason, find that patrons rarely use the card catalog. As a result, patron access suffers. Bibliographers and acquisitions staff cannot rely on the database as accurately reflecting the library's holdings, requiring a second look-up in the card catalog or the checking of various files to verify ownership of the materials. Retrospective conversion can be accomplished in a variety of ways, and the most effective method varies with the size of library, type of collection, condition of the shelflist, speed with which the project is to be completed and, of course, funding. There are now several responsible jobbers who will accept Library of Congress card numbers, author/title codes, or abbreviated bibliographic data on a floppy disk, match the records against their on-line files, and produce a full machine-readable record for a nominal fee. It is also possible to job the entire task, shipping the shelflist or a copy of the shelflist to the vendor providing the service. The vendor then matches or inputs the records as needed to produce the machine-readable file. Depending on when, by whom, and which database was used to produce the machine-readable file, further manipulation may be necessary. This may include checking for duplicates, correcting earlier headings to AACR2 forms and format, subject heading verification, and updating to achieve currency, as well as the creation of cross-referencing structures. The rapid and cost-effective creation of analytics, a real problem in the past, may soon be reaching a practical solution.[32]

Once retrospective conversion is substantially complete, and this has been identified by users as significant,[33] it is not essential to link the physical item to the bibliographic record with a bar or OCR coded label if one thinks of the on-line catalog in the same frame of reference as the card catalog. However, to effectively utilize the circulation function or use the system for internal inventory control, linking is essential.

TRANSITION

Patron acceptance of terminals as a means of accessing library collections has been surprisingly rapid. Resistance demonstrated by staff is due to a number of factors, including the personal threat always implicit in change, that of loss of job, status, or self-respect. In addition, technical services staff, catalogers in particular, worry about deterioration in the quality of records, and loss of control of the inventory and bibliographic control functions. This concern is legitimate and particularly worrisome to catalogers because they will have to clean up any disasters that occur. Some of these concerns can be at least partially defused during the needs-assessment phase of planning. A sensible, firm but flexible, tactful stance by administration is essential in the transition. Involving staff in the implementation and asking them to plan how to accomplish the necessary tasks can do much to minimize tension and concern. There are many other costs, both material and human, to developing and implementing an on-line catalog, in addition to the obvious ones of initial hardware and software acquisition costs. Site preparation, furniture, and safety systems such as fire, smoke, and water alarms are basically one-time costs. Maintenance contracts on hardware and maintenance agreements on software are continuing costs that tend to rise. Documentation and training must be provided and updated as changes occur. Supply budgets must be increased to cover paper, ribbon, tapes, or disks for duplication, backup, and storage. The acquisition of terminals is a sizable expense and, as the system proves its value, demand for services will increase, requiring more terminals. One rule of thumb for purchasing terminals is to purchase as many as you can afford. Another estimate is one terminal per 100 daily users.[34] Quantity requirements for public-access terminals can be determined with greater precision by applying formulae recently developed at Ohio State University in cooperation with OCLC.[35] Any studies based on current observed card catalog use must anticipate increase in patron demand in determining the number of terminals best suited to the library system.

The physical transition from the card catalog to an on-line catalog is a major one that a given library may not wish to accomplish in one fell swoop. The possibility of bringing up a partial on-line catalog—partial in terms of number of records, fullness of records, or currency of records (e.g., AACR2 headings and current subject headings)—is a real one that can be suitable in some situations. The problem of adequate access to all titles must then be addressed. Providing linkages between the on-line and closed or frozen card catalog is essential if the patron is to be well served, but this is difficult to achieve and justify. Confusion can be minimized by accepting a clear and logical break point between the old and the new and advertising this information. The break could be based on cataloging date or, alternatively, by publication date, a convenience for catalogers adopted in some libraries in response to the potential headings conflicts created by AACR2. The break could be based on format (e.g., monographs vs. serials vs. machine-readable data files). This again is easier for the professional than for the patron and assumes that information is suitably categorized by format. Another division could be by type of entry: name/title on line, subject on cards. This would continue the practice of divided card catalogs common in many libraries. All of these are temporary solutions at best, which may become permanent in large libraries unable to complete retrospective conversion projects.

CATALOG USE

The public catalog, whether card, film, on-line, or book, is a public-service tool designed and built for patron use, ideally without an intermediary. At the same time it should be recognized that ''to use a library requires more assistance than a catalog, even an interactive catalog, can provide.''[36] Two questions immediately arise regarding patron–catalog interaction. First, how many patrons use the catalog? Second, how successful are their searches? Results of several card-catalog studies conducted between 1938 and 1963 found "the number of patrons who consult the catalog at some time may vary from 50 to 97 percent of a library's general patronage, but that at any one particular time the range drops to 25 to 45 percent."[37] A more recent study, done in a small public library, indicated the removal of cards from the card catalog had no statistically significant influence on circulation.[38] Why this tool, viewed by librarians as essential, is used by such a relatively small percentage of patrons is a matter of some conjecture and concern. Additionally, much of the information on the catalog card is minimally used by the patron.[39]

In order to use a card catalog effectively, the patron must have certain skills and information. These may be taught formally, informally through handouts or assistance, or picked up through experience. Some of the skills are specific to card catalogs, such as the location of the call number on the card and the meaning and function of such obscure elements as the prefixes q and f. Others are applied from more broadly based learnings such as the hierarchy imposed on the arrangement of the cards by the alphabet. Studies of how patrons actually use card catalogs have been conducted in a variety of settings and over a relatively long period of time. All may be faulted to some degree in that the samples used were incomplete or biased, and in almost every case the conclusions must be qualified as being, to some extent, site specific. Several excellent summaries and reviews exist in the literature of studies done in this area from 1931 to 1979.[40] The preponderance of these studies, in excess of 100, were conducted in college and university settings, a high percentage of the populations studied were students, and in all but two cases the catalogs were card catalogs (as opposed to book, microformat, or on-line).

More recent studies, notably the OCLC *Research Reports* comprising the final report to the Council on Library Resources, have focused on the user in a machine environment.[41] Despite this significant change in format for the catalog, the information sought in the surveys is basically the same: who are the users, what information do they seek, how do they approach the catalog, and how well does the catalog meet their needs? In the past, catalog-use studies relied on a variety of techniques to gather data including questionnaires, observation, interviews, and circulation statistics. Direct observation and on-site interviews, the most reliable and useful methods for gathering data, are also very expensive and even then not totally reliable. It is now possible to monitor patron searches on line, to determine how a patron searches, strategies he or she uses, and errors he or she makes, timing the process with both date and time stamps entered automatically. Although this new method of monitoring patron searches needs to be refined, it does represent a significant advance in gathering data that can in turn be used to design catalogs that will be of greater value to the patron. This applies not only to the patron–machine interface with the on-line catalog, such as menu or command driven, but also to display options, search protocols, and so forth. It also provides the cataloger the opportunity to reevaluate how many and what kinds of access points are of value to the patron. Tradition can be very comforting and the "we've always done it that way" attitude is conservative and safe, in that it protects not only the integrity (that is, consistency) of the records, but also protects the cataloger from having to make a decision that may have long-range and unexpected ramifications. Catalogers quickly learn that to do one thing is impossible; the cataloging process and its attendant products are so interwoven in the fabric of information access, control, and dissemination that what appears to be a minor change can grow into a major project.

However, because of this reluctance to change, catalogers may be expending considerable time and effort ineffectively by continuing practices the patron no longer finds useful, and by not addressing changing needs. It is easy to continue to provide information the patron does not need, in a form that is not useful, because of communication breakdowns between cataloger and end user. As an example, the cross-referencing aspect of authority control, as opposed to validation, is of considerable interest at present. Some librarians feel it is essential to have the cross-referencing structure in a place to have a useful catalog. Others feel that key-word access and Boolian search capability will obviate the need for authority control. In other words, the argument is whether precoordination or postcoordination is more useful. A recent study of user behavior found, however, that authority records could not have helped 46 percent of the failed searches. Of this 46 percent, a simple program transposing first and second words as put in by the patron and searching again after the failure would have helped 21 percent.[42] The cataloger continues to create and apply subject headings rather than moving toward search terms. Although change needs to be approached slowly and with due concern for its outcome, a failure to change can have other serious consequences. The precoordinated subject-heading structure libraries have been using may not fit the efficiency of postcoordinated structure possible with boolean searching.

SUMMARY

Automation has presented libraries with the opportunity to radically alter the way materials and information are processed and made available to the user. Although the two basic purposes of cataloging—access and control—have not changed, how these purposes are accomplished has undergone radical change. As a result, restructuring has occurred within cataloging departments in the areas of organization, staffing, and workflow. The catalog is evolving into an instrument able to provide more flexible access to a broader spectrum of materials accessible from local and more remote locations.

The premise that the cataloging function in a given library can be successfully carried out by well-trained paraprofessionals using records created with the aid of artificial intelligence and brokered by a bibliographic utility is a fallacious one. The advent of automation has made the task of the professional cataloger more complex, no less so. In addition to creating a new bibliographic record, the cataloger must then overlay the coding system peculiar to the bibliographic utility serving the institution before the record can be entered in the database.

As information becomes available in format other than book, new procedures and codes must be developed and monitored to control these alternative formats and to provide appropriate access to their contents. Thus, the cataloger must remain the creator of the form and contents of the catalog.

Catalogers need to be careful, as they move into the future, to be at least as aware of and concerned with the patron's approach to library collections as they are with maintaining file integrity and control. Libraries appear to be moving, with the aid of automation, to forms of collection access that are far more flexible and have the potential to be more highly patron oriented than in the past. As a profession we need to move with deliberate speed toward maximizing the opportunity to create more efficient, effective, and therefore more useful access for patrons as a result of the conjunction of cataloging and automation.

NOTES AND REFERENCES

1. Michael Gorman, "AACR 2: Main Themes," in Doris H. Clack, ed., *The Making of a Code: The Issues Underlying AACR 2* (Chicago: American Library Association, 1980), p. 46.

2. Betty Baughman and Elaine Svenonius, "AACR 2: Main Entry Free?" *Cataloging and Classification Quarterly* 5 (Fall 1984): 1–10.

3. Michael Gorman, "On Doing Away with Technical Service Departments," *American Libraries* 10 (July/August 1979): 435–437; Robert P. Holley, "The Future of Catalogers and Cataloging," *Journal of Academic Librarianship* 7 (May 1981): 90–93; "The 'Catalogerless' Society," *American Libraries* 14 (December 1983):730; Martha Lawry, "A 'Word' for the Cataloger: Special Pleading or Definition of Function," *Journal of Academic Librarianship* 10 (July 1984): 137–140, among others.

4. Ann Clarke and Blaise Cronin, "Expert Systems and Library/Information Work," *Journal of Librarianship* 15 (October 1983): 289.

5. Peter Spyers-Duran, "The Effects of Automation on Organizational Change, Staffing, and Human Relations in Catalog Departments," in Daniel Gore, Joseph Kimbrough and Peter Spyers-Duran, eds., *Requiem For the Card Catalog* (Westport, Conn.: Greenwood, 1979), p. 31.

6. Joe A. Hewitt, *OCLC: Impact and Use.* (Columbus, Ohio: Ohio State University Libraries, 1977), p. 123.

7. Ibid., p. 73.

8. Ibid., p. 75.

9. Malcolm Getz and Doug Phelps, "Labor Costs in the Technical Operation of Three Research Libraries," *Journal of Academic Librarianship* 10 (September 1984): 215, 216.

10. Hewitt, *OCLC*, p. 69.

11. Spyers-Duran, *Effects of Automation*, p. 36.

12. Ibid., p. 31.

13. Murray S. Martin, "The Organizational and Budgetary Effects of Automation on Libraries," in Gerard B. McCabe and Bernard Kreissman, eds., *Advances in Library Organization and Administration* 2 (Greenwich, Conn.: JAI, 1983), p. 77.

14.   Sanford Berman, "The Automated Catalog and the Demise of the Cataloging Mystique Or, Here Comes the Catalog the People Always Wanted . . . Maybe," in Daniel Gore, Joseph Kimbrough and Peter Spyers-Duran, eds., *Requiem for the Card Catalog* (Westport, Conn.: Greenwood, 1979), pp. 65–70.

15.   Robert P. Holley, "The Future of Catalogers and Cataloging,' *Journal of Academic Librarianship* 7 (May 1981): 92.

16.   Ibid.

17.   Two excellent expositions of the evolution of library support staff are Charles W. Evans, "The Evolution of Paraprofessional Library Employees," in Michael H. Harris, ed., *Advances in Librarianship,* vol. 9 (New York: Academic Press, 1979), and Charlotte Mugnier, *The Paraprofessional and the Professional Job Structure.* (Chicago: ALA, 1980).

18.   Spyers-Duran, *Effects of Automation,* p. 38.

19.   Martha Lawry, "A 'Word' for the Cataloger: Special Pleading or Definition of Function?" *Journal of Academic Librarianship* 10 (July 1984): 138.

20.   See Michael Gorman, "The longer the number, the smaller the spine or, up and down with Melvil and Elsie," *American Libraries* 12 (September 1981): 498—499.

21.   Ben-Ami Lipitz, "Catalog Use in a Large Research Library," *Library Quarterly* 42 (January 1972): 136.

22.   Joseph A. Nitecki, *OCLC in Retrospect: A Review of the Impact of the OCLC System on the Administration of a Large University Technical Services Operations,* University of Illinois Graduate School of Library Science Occasional Papers, No. 123 (Champaign: University of Illinois, 1976), p. 25.

23.   Joseph R. Matthews, "Competition and Change: The 1983 Automated Library Systems Marketplace," *Library Journal* 109 (May 1, 1984): 857.

24.   "OCLC System to be down December 12–16 . . . AACR 2," *OCLC Newsletter* No. 132 (October 31, 1980): 7.

25.   "OCLC Converts Data Base to AACR 2 Form," *OCLC Newsletter* No. 134 (January 16, 1981): 4.

26.   This possibility was discussed by Joseph R. Matthews at the LAMA Institute, "Management of the Online catalog," Milwaukee, May 3—4, 1984.

27.   Maurice J. Freedman, "Must We Limit the Catalog?" *Library Journal* 109 (February 15, 1984): 324.

28.   F. W. Lancaster, *The Measurement and Evaluation of Library Services* (Washington: Information Resources Press: 1977), p. 24.

29.   As an example, Ohio State University Libraries continues to get a shelflist card because the LCS system does not permit ready access to all the shelflist information.

30.   Getz and Phelps, *Labor Costs,* pp. 211–212.

31.   OCLC charges $.0495 per card as of September 1, 1984, and estimated 5 cards per title in 1983. Local experience over a 3-year period averages 8.8 cards per title.

32.   Carrollton Press currently has an analytic retrospective conversion project under development.

33.   Carole Weiss Moore, "User Reactions to Online Catalogs: An Exploratory Study," *College and Research Libraries* 81 (July 1981): 300.

34.   Karen L. Horny, "Online Catalogs: Coping with the Choices," *Journal of Academic Librarianship* 8 (March 1982): 18.

35.   John E. Tolle, *Public Access Terminals: Determining Quantity Requirements* (Dublin, Ohio: OCLC, 1983).

36.   S. Michael Malinconico, "Catalogs & Cataloging: Innocent Pleasures and Enduring Controversies," *Library Journal* 109 (June 15, 1984): 1213.

37.   James Krikelas, "Catalog Use Studies and Their Implications," in Melvin J. Voigt, ed., *Advances in Librarianship,* vol. 3 (New York: Seminar Press, 1972), p. 199.

38.   William Aguilar, "Influence of the Card Catalog on Circulation in a Small Public Library," *Library Resources and Technical Services* 28 (April/June 1984): 183.

39.   Krikelas, *Catalog Use Studies,* p. 204.

40.   See: Karen Markey, *Research Report: An Analytical Review of Catalog Use Studies* (Columbus, Ohio: OCLC, Research Dept., Office of Planning and Research, 1980), ERIC Doc. ED 186-041; James Krikelas, "Catalog Use Studies," pp. 195–220.

41.   John E. Tolle, Karen Markey, and Neal K. Kaske, *Final Report to the Council on Library Resources,* (Columbus, Ohio: OCLC, 1983).

42.   Arlene G. Taylor, "Authority Files in Online Catalogs: An Investigation of Their Value," *Cataloging and Classification Quarterly* 4 (Spring 1984): 14.

ACCREDITED MASTER'S DEGREE PROGRAMS IN LIBRARIANSHIP IN THE 1980s

John A. McCrossan

INTRODUCTION

At the present time, successful completion of a master's program in librarianship that is accredited by the American Library Association is generally required for employment as a beginning professional librarian in public, academic, and special libraries. Moreover, a large proportion of school librarians (school library media specialists) and information specialists in other agencies also pursue the ALA-accredited master's program even though it is not always required for such positions.

An important exception to requiring the master's degree may be found in small libraries. Many small libraries, especially small public libraries and some types of small special libraries, will hire librarians who do not have the ALA-

Advances in Library Administration and Organization
Volume 5, pages 91–107
Copyright © 1986 by JAI Press Inc.
All rights of reproduction in any form reserved.
ISBN: 0-89232-674-3

accredited master's degree, often because they cannot afford professional salaries. However, once these libraries grow and secure additional funding they usually will employ at least one professional who has the master's degree.

It also needs to be pointed out that some serious legal challenges to the master's degree requirement have been raised in recent years, some based on affirmative action, as discussed below. Nonetheless, by and large most libraries of any size require the ALA-accredited master's for beginning professional positions. Sections of periodicals containing notices of open librarian positions offer considerable evidence of this fact. In a large majority of cases, such notices and advertisements indicate that the accredited degree is required. Barring further litigation and court decisions in favor of those without the degree, it appears that it will continue to be mandatory for most professional positions.

DEVELOPMENT OF PROFESSIONAL EDUCATION FOR LIBRARIANS

Historically, librarians learned about library work in a variety of ways, including (1) working in a library under experienced librarians; (2) reading library literature; and (3) participating in library association meetings. Education for librarianship is similar to education for some other professions in that it evolved from on-the-job training for high school graduates to the requirement that beginning professional librarians have a graduate degree in librarianship from a library science program located in an institution of higher learning.

From the mid-1920s to 1950, a bachelor's degree in library science represented the first professional degree for librarians. This was generally a second bachelor's degree. Some library schools also offered master's programs for those who wished to obtain leadership positions in the profession.

Beginning in 1949, a number of leading library schools dropped the bachelor's degree and adopted the master's as the first professional degree. In a few years, the one-year master's program became the standard and has remained so to the present time.

This development was the culmination of considerable soul-searching by the profession and of studies carried out in the early decades of this century. The most influential study, funded by the Carnegie Corporation and published in 1923, was prepared by C. C. Williamson. The report was very critical of the emphasis library education placed on routine technical matters, and Williamson argued that "no amount of training in library technique can make a successful librarian of a person who lacks a good general education."[1] He indicated that those being prepared for professional library work need a broad general education obtained in four years of college, followed by graduate study in a library school organized as a unit of a university rather than in a library.

Williamson also recommended the establishment of a system of accreditation to determine which library schools were equipped to provide quality library education. Following this recommendation, the American Library Association established the Board of Education for Librarianship in 1924. The board formulated standards for library education at various levels—graduate, undergraduate, summer schools, and library apprenticeship and training classes. Since that time, ALA has taken responsibility for accreditation of library education and has issued four sets of accreditation standards through the years. The most recent set, issued in 1972, is currently used to assist in evaluation of master's programs in librarianship; currently, the master's program is the only program which ALA accredits.[2] It was not until the 1950s that ALA accredited only fifth-year graduate programs. In 1970, ALA adopted "Library Education and Personnel Utilization"—a policy stating that first professional positions should require the master's degree.[3]

For a considerable time, the number of ALA-accredited library schools changed very slowly. In 1939, 30 accredited programs were in existence; in 1950, there were 36; and in 1960, 32.[4] A sizeable increase took place during the following years; by 1973, there were 58 accredited programs;[5] and as of 1984, 67 programs were accredited by ALA; 60 in the United States and 7 in Canada.[6]

Another event of great importance in the history of professional library education was the establishment of the Graduate Library School at the University of Chicago in 1926. The new school, begun with financial assistance from the Carnegie Corporation, offered programs leading to the master's degree and the doctoral degree and was intended to be, for librarianship, "analogous to the Harvard Law School and the Johns Hopkins Medical School."[7]

Not all library leaders enthusiastically endorsed the Chicago plan, however. In fact, many considered it unique in its emphasis on scholarly research and did not feel it was the best type of program for training the ordinary working librarian. Many of the schools continued to offer programs that were largely technical training, and it was not until the 1950s that these were abandoned in favor of graduate professional programs.

NUMBER AND SIZE OF MASTER'S PROGRAMS

During the past five years, the number of ALA-accredited master's programs in the United States and Canada has been approximately 65 or somewhat larger at any given time. In addition to ALA-accredited programs, many institutions, probably several hundred, offer one or more undergraduate or graduate courses in librarianship or educational media, many of which concentrate on preparation of school library media specialists.

Generally within recent years, approximately 30 such graduate programs have been associate institutional members of the Association of Library and Information Science Education (ALISE), known as the Association of American Library

Schools (AALS) until the name was changed in 1982. In 1985, the *Journal of Education for Library and Information Services* listed 17 associate institutional members.[8] (Only ALA-accredited programs may be full members of the association.)

Most master's degree programs in librarianship are quite modest in size when judged by number of students and faculty, and the number of degrees awarded has declined significantly in recent years. According to a 10-year summary report by Bidlack, a total of 6,752 master's degrees were awarded to graduates of ALA-accredited programs in 1971–1972. By 1981–1982, only 4,028 degrees were awarded to graduates of the accredited programs.[9] The unaccredited programs offered by associate institutional members of ALISE reported only 118 master's degrees being awarded.[10]

The decline in number of degrees granted is expected to end, and a small increase should be seen in the future. A major national survey, *Library Human Resources: A Study of Supply and Demand*, projects that some growth will occur in demand for beginning librarians to replace those leaving the profession to retire or for other reasons and to fill growing needs for professionals in special types of librarianship and information management.[11]

With approximately 65 to 70 programs accredited at any one time, this means that an average of about 60 master's degrees are awarded by each accredited institution each year. A few schools are very small and a small number are quite large, but the majority fall in the middle range. According to the most recent library education statistical report, 17 schools had 39 or fewer master's graduates and only 6 had 100 or more; the remaining 41 schools responding had between 40 and 99 graduates.[12] The same report indicates that programs not accredited by ALA are very small, with an average of 24 graduates during the year, the range being from 6 graduates in the smallest program to 65 in the largest. The latter figure is unusually high for an unaccredited program, but the program involved very recently lost accreditation.[13]

Size of the faculty is another of the greatest differences between the ALA-accredited programs and the unaccredited programs. The average accredited library school has 10 full-time faculty members. The 1984 library education statistical document indicated the number of full-time faculty ranged from a low of 3 in one school to a high of 28, the average being 9.97. The average for unaccredited programs was 4.5.[14]

Women constitute the majority of library school master's students—85 percent according to the *Library Human Resources* survey.[15] This is, of course, similar to the situation in librarianship itself, in which women make up a large majority. For a number of years there has been great demand for minority librarians, and library schools have made considerable efforts to attract minority students into their programs. These efforts have had mixed success, and blacks and other minorities make up probably no more than 10 percent of the total enrollment in the master's programs. The exact proportions, however, are difficult to determine, because the Canadian schools and some in the United States do not report the number of students by ethnic origin.

As noted previously, the number of master's degrees granted in library/ information science has declined significantly in recent years. Moreover, a number of library schools recently have closed or announced plans for possible closing, and a few others are being studied for possible closing or restructuring.[16] When universities experience continuing severe financial problems, as they have during recent years, university administrators look for ways to improve their financial situation, and one way is to close down programs that have low productivity, that is, relatively few students and research grants. Because library schools are low in productivity compared with some other educational offerings, they are subject to investigation for possible closure. It seems unlikely that many more library schools will be discontinued, because at present there are only one or two in each state. Moreover, the expected growing national emphasis on improvement in education at all levels will require greatly improved libraries and probably an increase in the number of librarians and information specialists.

LENGTH OF PROGRAMS

Most master's programs in librarianship take a full-time student one calendar year to complete; that is, two regular semesters or equivalent plus a summer session. Two years or more may be required for a part-time student in most library schools.

At one time, two years was standard for ALA-accredited master's programs; however, the one-year program became standard during the 1950s and has remained so in the United States until the present time. In recent years much discussion has taken place about the value of two-year as opposed to one-year programs. A conference attended by many of the deans and directors of accredited library schools was devoted to this topic, and the pros and cons of extended programs were discussed at some length.[17] Although almost all library schools in the United States have one-year master's programs, almost all Canadian schools have had extended programs for a number of years. The first Canadian school to inaugurate a two-year master's was McGill University, which in 1964 announced its intention to expand its program in order "to educate students to a more advanced level than in the past to meet the demand for graduates with specialized library training."[18] Most other Canadian schools had established extended programs by the mid-1970s.

The term "extended program" is probably a better one to use than "two-year program," as the latter is confusing. Some librarians, familiar with programs that take full-time students one calendar year or about 36 semester hours to complete, might assume that the longer programs under discussion would require two full calendar years or 24 months and about twice as many semester hours. Actually, such a program might require about 48—50 semester hours and take a full-time student two academic years—four semesters or a total of about 18 months of study.

Rationale for extending master's programs includes the argument that the one-year program is not sufficiently long to cover adequately traditional library science topics plus such growing areas of interest as information science, automation, services to specialized groups of users, and audiovisual materials and technology. Those favoring extension also indicate that a longer program would enable students to do a significant internship in a library and to take additional advanced and specialized courses, thus better preparing themselves for professional positions. Some who are skeptical about extended programs indicate that one year is a sufficiently long preparation for beginning librarians, that specialized training can be secured on the job or through occasional continuing education workshops or courses, and that an additional year of education would be better after the master's degree and some professional experience have been obtained. Thus the sixth-year post-master's program, rather than the two-year master's, might become standard. Experience has shown, however, that few librarians return to library school to pursue the sixth-year program, but that situation could change if employers provide motivation for them to do so, including financial incentives.

A major disadvantage of extended master's programs cited by some is that it might be prohibitively expensive for students, especially minorities. Would students be willing or able to pay the cost of two years of graduate study in order to obtain a position in a relatively low-paying profession such as librarianship? There are many good arguments on both sides, and general consensus has not been reached except in Canada, where the extended program is accepted.

ADMISSION REQUIREMENTS

Applicants for admission to the master's program must meet general university admission requirements and any additional requirements of the library school. Admission to graduate study frequently is dependent on the student's having received an undergraduate degree from an institution of higher education accredited by a regional accrediting agency and having maintained a 3.0 (B) average on all undergraduate work in the last two years of the undergraduate program. Completion of the Graduate Record Examination with an acceptable score is also often required for admission.

A small number of library schools indicate that students must meet a foreign language requirement, usually either by taking courses in a language or passing a language proficiency test. Some schools recommend that prospective students secure a broad undergraduate education in the arts and sciences, but they do not specify that students must pursue any particular undergraduate major. Other schools require students to solicit letters of recommendation from people who are knowledgeable about their potential, such as employers or professors, and some require a personal interview. It is generally recommended that students not take more than a minimum of library science courses at the undergraduate level. Library educators usually feel that students should receive a good general education as undergraduates before taking professional coursework.

PROGRAMS OF STUDY

The typical master's program includes one or more core courses—required basic courses all students must take—plus a variety of courses students choose as electives depending on their interests and career goals. Core courses are sometimes prerequisite to advanced courses; that is, a student must complete a particular core course before taking a particular advanced course.

Although in most schools the core consists of several separate courses, a few schools have adopted an "integrated core." The latter generally consists of one course covering different areas of study and carries credit equivalent to two, three, or more separate courses. Such a course is usually "team taught" by several faculty members with expertise in the different topics included.

Regardless of how the core is organized, areas covered generally include most of these topics: reference work and bibliography, information science, selection of library materials, cataloging and classification, foundations of librarianship, research methods, and library management. The goal is to introduce students to those topics with which all professional librarians should have some familiarity.

In the earliest library schools, all the coursework was required. As specialities grew, the core diminished and students were allowed to take electives covering various kinds of specializations. At the present time, the core constitutes approximately one-fourth to one-third of the content of most master's programs in librarianship. Elective courses frequently include advanced or specialized study of topics covered in an elementary way in core courses. For example, most library schools require a beginning course in reference and information sources and services, which introduces students to a variety of reference materials. Advanced elective courses may be offered giving in-depth coverage of particular subjects, such as a separate course devoted entirely to the study of reference/information sources in science and technology. There may also be one or more elective courses devoted mainly or entirely to information in a particular format, for example, computerized information services.

FIELD EXPERIENCE

Practicums or fieldwork experiences are available in a number of library schools as an integral part of the master's program, and "the 1980s are seeing an upsurge of attention to this topic."[19] Although not generally required of all students, those who elect such programs may receive the equivalent of two, three, or more

semester hours credit. Internships, which are generally longer and more intensive, are much less common except for students who need an internship for
school library media certification; the latter are frequently available through
colleges of education. Because of library funding problems, paid internships in
other types of libraries are quite rare.

The practicum or fieldwork experience generally is relatively short, usually
not more than several weeks of full-time work or a semester or two of perhaps
10–15 hours a week. An internship is frequently full-time and is often done after
other degree requirements have been completed. It may last from several months
to a year or more. Library trainee and work-study programs often are not
coordinated by a library school nor do students receive academic credit for
pursuing them; nonetheless, they can provide valuable experience for students,
as can regular part-time jobs in libraries.

In the early years of library education, practical work experience constituted a
sizeable and very important part of students' programs. Melvil Dewey, among
other leaders, was a strong proponent of such experience. In an 1879 article, he
indicated that the new librarian should be educated mainly by working as an ap-
prentice in a major library.[20]

In the ensuing decades, however, schools of librarianship became firmly established and the emphasis on practical experience declined substantially due to
various factors, including time limitations as the amount of coursework increased. C. C. Williamson's 1923 report also undoubtedly had great influence in
this regard. He argued that the program was too short to include experience in
addition to instruction and that the validity of the experience received by students
was questionable because practical work was often very poorly supervised.[21]

Since the late 1960s and early 1970s, however, a revival of interest in field
experience has occurred in library schools, perhaps related to the demands of
students and the subsequent attempts of universities to make education more relevant to the real world. In a 1973 survey, 60 percent of the schools responding
indicated that they had some sort of field experience available to their students.[22]
Another series of surveys, done at 3-year intervals from 1971–1972 to
1980–1981, showed a steady increase in schools offering field experience opportunities for their students. By the time of the 1980–1981 survey, only one school
reported that field experience was not available at all. The writer notes, however,
that fieldwork was not really an integral part of library school curricula because
only four schools reported that it was required of all students.[23]

JOINT MASTER'S DEGREE PROGRAMS

A number of library schools offer at least one joint degree program. Typically,
the student receives two degrees and must complete the equivalent of approximately one year of full-time study in librarianship and another year or more in

the other area, for example, music or public administration. At one or more institutions, other areas of study available in cooperation with library schools include chemistry, English, law, education, pharmacy, management, history/archives, instructional technology, art, and theology.

A major purpose of such programs is to better prepare librarians who are interested in certain specialities, such as law librarianship or music librarianship. Although students can and do prepare for these specialized types of librarianship without entering joint degree programs, the latter undoubtedly have some advantages, including a well-organized cooperative arrangement between a library school and the faculty of the other area concerned.

RESEARCH COMPONENT

Research is an important part of the master's curriculum. Students are exposed to research in separate courses devoted to research methods and in other courses in which they study published research or work on research projects in particular areas, for example, in a course on public librarianship in which students read and evaluate research and/or carry out research on some aspect of public library management or services.

One major goal is to prepare students to understand and evaluate published research reports about libraries and librarianship. It is also important that beginning librarians have some understanding of the research process and research literature so they can help library users who want to locate and use research materials. Master's students can also be prepared to do research themselves, but they would usually need considerably more training, such as that received in a doctoral program, to become really proficient researchers.

At one time a thesis was a common requirement for library science master's programs. Over the years, however, most library schools that had required a thesis dropped the requirement, although students may select it as an option. An informal survey done by Tryon suggests the reasons for abandoning the thesis requirement were (1) the one-year curriculum was too crowded and left little time for a thesis and (2) the number of students had grown so much that faculty could not supervise theses properly.[24]

Relatively few library school students write a thesis, but most of them write a number of research papers during their master's programs. Such papers may be done as class projects or as separate research studies unconnected with a particular class. Some of the reports may be somewhat similar to a thesis except that they do not have such rigorous requirements. Such reports can be excellent learning experiences for students because they can provide an opportunity to study specialized topics of interest in much more depth than they would generally be covered in a class.

COMPREHENSIVE EXAMINATIONS

Relatively few library schools require a comprehensive examination at the end of the master's program. If required, it may be written or oral or both, and it may cover a student's total program or a part of the program, (i.e., the core courses).

Faculty and student reaction to such an examination is generally mixed. One advantage frequently cited is that the examination provides strong motivation for students to review their master's program, and of course, a great deal of learning takes place during such an intensive review. A major disadvantage is the time required for such an examination, which is usually extensive, probably more or less comparable to the time devoted to one average course. It is sometimes argued that a student will benefit more from an additional course than from such an examination.

SALARIES AND JOB OPPORTUNITIES FOR GRADUATES

Traditionally, salaries of professional librarians have been quite modest. One major reason frequently cited is that librarianship has been largely a women's profession, and such professions have had considerably low pay scales compared with professions dominated by men.

The average salary for beginning professional librarians in 1982 was $16,583.[25] This is a substantial increase over the 1967 average of $7,505. When cost-of-living increases are taken into account, however, it can be determined that salary growth has not kept pace with the cost of living.[26] The average beginning salary in 1983 was $17,705. The increase from 1982 was significant, because "for the first time in many years, the increase in the average beginning salary was higher than the increase in the cost of living."[27]

What will happen in the future? Will librarians' salaries continue to improve slowly, significantly, or simply level off? There will probably be slow, modest improvement in the years ahead as society gives greater recognition to the value of library and information services and as more librarians become members of collective bargaining groups. Also, as women receive greater recognition and salary improvement in a variety of fields, the salary situation should also be improved in librarianship—a profession in which women constitute a large majority.

In recent years, placement has been good but not excellent. Most library school graduates have secured professional employment without great difficulty, but a minority have had some problems. The latter, in many cases, are placebound or have had unrealistic expectations as to type of library position they will accept. Thus a graduate who is unable to move to another area or unwilling to accept any but a very specialized type of position may have to wait some time before being professionally employed.

In the 1983 survey of placements and salaries, library school placement officers were generally quite positive about job opportunities for library school graduates. The report reads as follows:

There is a definite note of optimism about job vacancy listings for next year. For the first time in many years, a large number (29) of placement officers predict an increase in the number of listings. Estimates range as high as 67 percent.[28]

The writers of the survey, *Library Human Resources,* conclude that the market for beginning librarians and information specialists will improve somewhat in the future, one reason being the need to replace librarians who will retire or leave the profession for other reasons.[29]

In summary, it seems reasonable to assume that most library school graduates will be successful in obtaining a professional library/information position, but that a relatively small minority may experience some difficulty. It is probable that salaries will continue to improve somewhat, but not dramatically. It is also likely that a shortage of librarians will occur, particularly in some areas, because the number of library school graduates has declined so dramatically since the mid-1970s. Also, as previously noted, a significant proportion of librarians are of retirement age and will need to be replaced.

CHALLENGES TO THE PROFESSIONAL DEGREE REQUIREMENT

As mentioned earlier, in recent years some serious challenges have been raised to the requirement that professional librarians have a graduate degree from an ALA-accredited library science program. Through the years, some individuals have argued that other types of education and/or experience can prepare a person to function successfully as a professional librarian, for example, a master's or bachelor's degree in librarianship from a program not accredited by ALA; library experience; education other than library science; or a combination of the above.

Recently, the situation has become more critical, however, as (1) some government agencies have proposed dropping the master's requirement and (2) some individuals without the degree have challenged the requirement in the courts or before civil service commissions, sometimes on the basis of affirmative action.

Undoubtedly, the most significant challenge has come from the United States Office of Personnel Management (OPM). That office has been reviewing a number of federal government positions with the purpose of downgrading the educational requirements for some of them.

One major recommendation of OPM is that a person holding a master's degree in library science that requires less than two years of graduate study would be employed at a lower rank (GS7) rather than at the higher rank currently used (GS9). The entry-level salary for GS7, is, of course, much lower than that for

GS9. Because the vast majority of library science master's programs are only about one calendar year in length, the net result of implementing this recommendation would be that the majority of librarians hired by federal agencies would be employed at the lower rank and salary level.

Other OPM proposals call for transferring many professional duties to library technicians, allowing "entry into professional positions . . . with only a bachelor's degree and one year of experience."[30] In other words, the master's degree in librarianship would not be necessary for such professional employment.

Adoption of these recommendations could have a great effect on all types of libraries—public and private—throughout the United States. In discussing this matter, Robinson states the following:

> The OPM action would cheapen the M.L.S.—both its earning power and status for librarians both inside and outside the federal government. Any changes in standards for federal librarians will "trickle down" as accepted norms for state and local government, a process which will lead to the downgrading of professional librarians at state and local as well as the federal level. Professional library staff in public, school, and publicly funded academic libraries would feel the effect first, but it would not be long before staff in nonprofit and for-profit special libraries, and in private academic institutions, would begin to feel the effect.[31]

In a detailed analysis of the problem, Berger states the following about the Federal Office of Personnel Management's proposal:

1. OPM does not consider the master of library science degree to be the basic educational requirement for professional work in a library. A chief hallmark of all other professional series in federal service is recognition of a formal, basic educational requirement that must be met by all members of the profession. The proposed new standards would require only a baccalaureate that includes six undergraduate courses in "library-information service" in order to qualify for an entry-level professional job in a federal library. The library community has furnished OPM data showing that accredited baccalaureate programs for librarians (other than school librarians) do not exist today (and have not existed for 30 years).

2. Certain categories of nonprofessional on-the-job library experience are considered adequate to qualify for professional library work and are, therefore, substitutable for the formal education described earlier. However, OPM will not provide a test or some similar instrument by which the merits of paraprofessional experience in lieu of education could be measured.

3. OPM asserts that because the semester-hour requirements leading to the master's degree in library science have been reduced since the library standards were last revised (1966), today's MLS is less valuable to the federal government than are the master's degrees of other professions. Therefore, OPM would bring librarians holding the master's degree into federal service at a level of pay lower than the comparable level accorded similarly educated professionals in other fields. The library community has provided OPM data to prove that semester-hour requirements for the MLS have not changed in 30 years, nor were they or are they markedly different from those of other professions. Meanwhile, the standards for another professional series published during 1982 did not reduce the level of pay for beginning professionals holding master's degrees based on 30 to 36 semester hours of work.

4. Calibrations of the duties, responsibilities, and assignments for federal librarians are designated at lower levels of compensation than are comparable calibrations in either OPM's Primary Standard (used to measure the accuracy and adequacy of all OPM occupational standards) or OPM's standards for other professions. Although executive agencies of the federal government, the American Library Association, and Local 2910 of the American Federation of State, County, and Municipal Employees have called these discrepancies to OPM's attention, the same or similar ones reappear in subsequent revisions of the drafts.
5. Certain classification criteria have been omitted, specifically those that lead to assignments at the top step of the middle level of federal service. As a result, the promotional ladder provided by the standards will end at a point so low as to diminish seriously the chances for federal librarians to be considered for top positions in federal service. In contrast, classification standards published by OPM in 1982 for two other professions did include criteria at the top step of the middle level.

In effect, OPM's proposed new standards for the federal library-information service work force described librarianship as a profession in name only. The differences that divide OPM and the library community remain unresolved, despite repeated attempts by the library community to rationalize them.[32]

One of the best known cases of an individual who challenged the accredited master's degree requirement is that of Glenda Merwine. Merwine, who did not possess such a degree, applied for the professional position of librarian in Mississippi State University's College of Veterinary Medicine. She had previously worked in the university library as a paraprofessional, had a master's degree in secondary education, and had taken some school-library-oriented courses.

The library director informed her that she could not be considered for the position because she lacked the accredited degree, a requirement in the advertisement for the position. Of six applications before the search committee at the time the decision to employ was made, three applicants had completed ALA-accredited master's programs—one male and two female. Only those three were interviewed, and subsequently one of the three—the male—was hired. Merwine filed suit, charging discrimination, and the case came to trial in May 1983.

In a report on the case, Holley states that a number of extraneous issues were involved, but "the essential issue was whether or not Mississippi State University had a right to require the ALA-accredited master's degree as a condition of employment."[33] After much testimony at the trial, the jury decided in favor of Merwine and awarded her $10,000 in actual and punitive damages. In its decision, the jury indicated its opinion that Merwine was qualified to do the professional job.

Some months later, in December 1983, a judge overturned the jury's verdict, giving the opinion that there had not been intentional discrimination. He cited the fact that the employer had informed Merwine that only those with the accredited master's degree would be considered for the position. The judge's decision is being appealed and the final outcome is uncertain as of this writing.

Despite such attacks on the master's degree requirement, most libraries of any size currently specify that the degree is necessary for professional positions. Perusal of advertisements for professional librarians quickly reveals that the vast majority of libraries indicate that applicants must hold a master's degree from an ALA-accredited program.

This situation could change radically, however, if federal agencies downgrade the educational requirement for professional librarians or if courts find in favor of those contesting the degree requirement in significant cases. Holley discusses this danger as follows:

> I am concerned about legal attacks on appropriate educational standards. If we are concerned about excellence, we shall scarcely achieve it by dismissing sound professional education. I hardly see how we can talk about sophisticated library services unless we also talk about well educated librarians prepared to offer those services.
>
> What bothers me is that the OPM attack . . . and court cases denigrating professional library degrees may well be followed by attacks on degrees in other professions: journalism, social work, and nursing. The aim will be to downgrade the professions, especially those paying low salaries, to save money at all levels of government.
>
> In this country we have invested heavily in the sophisticated education of personnel. As a result we have competent and skilled workers [and can] provide services which are the envy of the world.[34]

TOWARD THE FUTURE

Librarianship has come a long way from the days when prospective librarians were educated mainly through practical experience. Graduate library schools are widely accepted, and most professional library positions require that applicants have a master's degree from an ALA-accredited library school. It is possible that in the future, the extended or two-year master's program may become a condition for professional library employment, especially for those in supervisory or specialized positions. This may not happen, however, unless librarianship becomes a better-paid profession, which will give students incentive to spend up to two years in graduate study.

Library school curricula have changed considerably through the years and will continue to change in the years ahead. One trend that comes to mind is increasing course offerings in information science/automation. As technology improves and users demand greater access to information, librarians will need more extensive training to respond to such demands. Moreover, increasing numbers of library school students want to prepare for information positions in government and industry, outside of traditional library settings, and they will need additional education in information services for such work.

Ironically, at a time when the library/information management profession is becoming more and more important to society, professional education is being threatened. The most serious problem, as noted earlier, is the attempt by some agencies, especially the federal Office of Personnel Management, to do away with the master's degree in librarianship as the basic educational requirement for professional library work. If this attempt is successful, the "trickle down" effect would be enormous, and many libraries throughout the United States—public and private—would follow OPM's example. Fortunately, there is still hope that OPM will not be able to implement its proposal, especially if public reaction and Congressional reaction is quite negative.

Recent years have seen an expansion of course offerings covering services to minorities, the handicapped, and the aging. This trend will surely continue as such groups increase their demands for adequate library service and as society attempts to improve programs for them. Reading and library-use patterns of such groups are in most ways similar to those of the population at large; however, librarians need to be aware of the ways in which they significantly differ.

Some areas that have been deemphasized in recent years in some library schools will need to receive a new emphasis. One such area is children's librarianship. At the present time, a critical shortage of children's librarians exists in some parts of the country, particularly for librarians having a good background in children's literature and programming. Because children constitute a very large proportion of library users (at least 50 percent in most public libraries, for example), more library school students will need to be well prepared to meet their needs.

Although many changes are desirable and necessary, one aspect of library and information services and of professional education for those services that should remain the same is the emphasis on librarianship as a helping profession dedicated to working with people—individuals and groups. In our time, institutions are becoming more and more impersonal and many people feel alienated from them. The library is one of the few institutions that takes great care in providing personalized services to women, men, and children from all walks of life. As long as this emphasis on helping people and providing desired services continues, the public will continue to use and support libraries and library education programs.

NOTES AND REFERENCES

1. Charles C. Williamson, *Training for Library Service: A Report Prepared for the Carnegie Corporation of New York* (Boston: Merrymount Press, 1923), 6.

2. American Library Association Committee on Accreditation, *Standards for Accreditation* (Chicago: The American Library Association, 1972), 2.

3. American Library Association, *Library Education and Personnel Utilization* (Chicago: The American Library Association, 1970) 2.

4. C. Edward Carroll, *The Professionalization of Librarianship with Special Reference to the Years 1940–1960* (Metuchen, NJ: Scarecrow Press, 1970), 62.

5. "Accredited Library Schools," Madeline Miele (ed.) in *The Bowker Annual of Library and Book Trade Information* 19th ed. (New York: Bowker, 1974), 323–325.

6. American Library Association Committee on Accreditation, *Graduate Library Education*

Programs Accredited by the American Library Association under Standards for Accreditation, 1972 (Chicago: American Library Association, 1984).

7. Frederick Keppel, "The Carnegie Corporation and the Graduate Library School: A Historical Outline," *Library Quarterly* 1 (January 1931); 25.

8. *Journal of Education for Librarian and Information Science* 26 (Summer, 1985) 63.

9. Russell E. Bidlack, "Summary and Comparative Analysis," in Timothy W. Sineath (ed.) *Library and Information Science Education Statistical Report 1983* (State College, PA: Association of Library and Information Science Education, 1983), SCA-3.

10. Agnes L. Reagan, "Students," in Timothy W. Sineath (ed.) *Library and Information Science Education Statistical Report, 1983* (State College, PA: Association of Library and Information Science Education, 1983), S-21.

11. Nancy A. Van House, Nancy K. Roderer, and Michael D. Cooper, "Librarians: Study of Supply and Demand," *American Libraries* 14 (June 1983): 370.

12. Agnes L. Reagan, "Students," in Timothy W. Sineath (ed.) *Library and Information Science Education Statistical Report, 1984* (State College, PA: Association of Library and Information Science Education, 1984), S-22-26.

13. Ibid., S-28.

14. Gary R. Purcell, "Faculty," in Timothy W. Sineath (ed.) *Library and Information Science Education Statistical Report, 1984* (State College, PA: Association of Library and Information Science Education, 1984), F-2.

15. Van House, Roderer, and Cooper, "Librarians," 362.

16. Esther Dyer and Daniel O'Connor, "Inside Our Schools: Crisis in Library Education," *Wilson Library Bulletin* 57 (June 1983): 860-863.

17. See Richard L. Darling and Terry Belanger (eds.), *Extended Library Education Programs* (New York: Columbia University School of Library Science, 1980).

18. Katherine H. Packer, "Educational Implications of the Two-Year Program in Library Science," in Darling and Belanger, *Extended Library Education Programs, 27.*

19. Margaret E. Monroe, "Issues in Field Experience as an Element in the Library School Curriculum," *Journal of Education for Librarianship* 22 (Summer/Fall 1981): 57.

20. Melvil Dewey, "Apprenticeship for Librarians,' *Library Journal* 4 (May 1879): 148.

21. Williamson, *Training for Library Service,* 64.

22. Roger C. Palmer, "Internship and Practicums," in Mary B. Cassata and Herman L. Totten (eds.), *Administrative Aspects of Education for Librarianship* (Metuchen, NJ. Scarecrow Press, 1975), 251.

23. Virginia Witucke, "The Place of Library Experience in Library Education: Trends and Current Status," *Journal of Education for Librarianship* 22 (Summer/Fall 1981): 75–76.

24. Jonathan S. Tryon, "Theses and Dissertations Accepted by Graduate Library Schools: September 1978 through August 1981," *Library Quarterly* 52 (October 1982): 360–361.

25. Carol L. Learmont and Stephen Van Houten, "Placements and Salaries, 1982: Slowing Down," *Library Journal* 108 (September 15, 1983): 1760.

26. Carol L. Learmont and Stephen Van Houten, "Placements and Salaries, 1981: Still Holding," in Joanne O'Hare and F. L. Schick (eds.) *Bowker Annual of Library and Book Trade Information,* 28th ed., (New York: Bowker, 1983), 288–289.

27. Carol L. Learmont and Stephen Van Houten, "Placements and Salaries, 1983: Catching Up," *Library Journal* 109 (October 1, 1984): 1805.

28. Ibid., 1810.

29. Van House, Roderer, and Cooper, "Librarians," 370.

30. Barbara M. Robinson, "Librarianship Under Attack," *Library Journal* 108 (February 15, 1983): 347.

31. Ibid., 347.

32. Patricia W. Berger, "The New Federalism: How It Is Changing the Library Profession in the United States," in Joanne O'Hare and F. L. Schick (eds.) *Bowker Annual of Library and Book Trade Information,* 28th ed., 1983 (New York: Bowker, 1983), 37–38.

33. Edward G. Holley, "The Merwine Case and the MLS: Where Was ALA?' *American Libraries* 15 (May 1984): 328.

34. Ibid., 330.

COLLECTION EVALUATION:
PRACTICES AND METHODS IN LIBRARIES OF ALA ACCREDITED GRADUATE LIBRARY EDUCATION PROGRAMS

Renee Tjoumas and Esther E. Horne

INTRODUCTION

While participating as members of the Learning Resources and Library Committee, the authors decided to examine the collection evaluation practices of library and information science (LIS) libraries.* The researchers believed that LIS libraries should serve as laboratories to assist students in bridging the gap between classroom theory and actual practice. (After all, if one were a builder of

*The Learning Resources and Library Committee is an advisory group comprised of faculty members, library staff, and student representatives organized for the purpose of assisting in the development of the library and information science collection.

Advances in Library Administration and Organization
Volume 5, pages 109–138
Copyright © 1986 by JAI Press Inc.
All rights of reproduction in any form reserved.
ISBN: 0-89232-674-3

bridges or tall edifices, one's own bridge ought to be as sound or one's own sky-scraper as sturdy.) Consequently, it was assumed that collection evaluation was a formalized procedure within LIS libraries.

A retrospective search of the literature, however, denied these assumptions. It did produce substantial evidence of the profession's concern about every one else's library (similar to the shoemaker's children going barefoot), but very little about collection evaluation practices of LIS libraries. Therefore, it seemed not only appropriate but necessary to ascertain if LIS library collections were being evaluated and, if so, to what extent and by what means. As a corollary, it was also of interest to know the circumstances in those cases where collections were not being evaluated.

BACKGROUND FOR THE RESEARCH PROBLEM

Concerning library school libraries, Kaser noted in 1964 that the literature revealed meager information about their collections. He also found no "consensus among library educators as to what they feel a library school collection must do for their students."[1] Furthermore, the ALA standards of 1951 and 1972 contained only brief evaluative guidelines. Library collections in 1951 were to be judged on "adequacy" of support given to the curriculum. In 1972, a collection was judged "adequate" if it supported the goals and objectives of the school.[2]

In 1972, Penner conducted one of the few collection evaluation studies related to LIS holdings in the literature. He studied two Canadian libraries using Orr's Document Delivery Test. Unfortunately, adequate records had not been kept, thereby limiting the usefulness of the study.[3] As late as 1978, Kiewitt reported that "little information has been gathered on the role and size of LIS libraries."[4] She reviewed several studies by various authors published between 1964 and 1978. These researchers were not truly evaluating collections per se but were interested in reference collections and in identifying reference sources in LIS collections.[5]

PRINCIPLES, CONCEPTS, AND RATIONALE

Collection evaluation, according to Mosher, "is a term applied to a number of techniques . . quantitative, simple or complex, costly or inexpensive, time-intensive or time-economic, one-time or ongoing, and can be applied to the study of the collections or collection efforts of any type of library."[6] In most cases, a combination of approaches or methods is the most useful in an evaluative or analytical situation.[7]

There are many reasons for carrying out evaluations of library collections, all of which have been summarized in the American Library Association's Resources and Technical Services Division guidelines: "Evaluations should be made to determine whether the collection is meeting its objectives, how well it is serving its users, in which ways or areas it is deficient and what remains to be done to develop the collection."[8]

As a basic principle, Lyle stated that "the purposes of evaluation are to provide a critical analysis of the program and operation of the library and to make such specific recommendations as seem appropriate."[9] Additionally, "each library must be judged by how well it performs the services required to meet the needs of its particular college (or school)."[10]

By the 1970s, most of the newer methods of evaluation used statistical procedures. Standards and other guidelines also utilized statistical approaches and formulas that yielded quantitative indications of adequacy.[11] However, Lyle cautioned in 1974 that evaluators should not rely on statistics, in and of themselves, because they do not truly reflect use in open-stack libraries. This consideration is especially important when conducting in-house use studies.[12]

Four general types of evaluation were used in the decade of the 1970s: impressionistic, checklist, statistical, and usage methods. Choice of method rested on the purpose and comprehensiveness of the evaluation process and on the effectiveness of the technique.[13] On the other hand, Rose notes that the most frequent methods of research were case studies, comparative statistics, and surveys.[14] In the area of book collections, the adequacy of monograph holdings was usually measured in quantitative terms, but this approach was misleading because most of these measures failed to account for the relative differences in book needs among the different subject areas in the curriculum.

Yancheff, writing in 1978, was concerned that nowhere in the professional literature did she find extensive use of computers to conduct analyses of collections numbering in the millions of volumes. For her, there was no excuse for not knowing what was in the library collection or how well it supported its goals and objectives.[15]

Broadus, while generally optimistic about collection evaluation, realized the shortcomings of each method. For instance, checklists tend to minimize needs and demands. Furthermore, all libraries are not exactly the same in their responsibilities and, therefore, they can not be compared. A high score of user satisfaction is also unreliable because it may say little about the quality of the collection.[16] Furthermore, Broadus states "To measure the ultimate value of the collection to the university and to society is simply beyond us and may always be so."[17]

What then is the good or utility of collection evaluation? Mosher states that "collection evaluation is an essential function of collection management."[18] It is an important part of collection development, that is, the acquisition and maintenance of materials with the library users in mind. An important side benefit of evaluation is that collection growth can be intelligently controlled.[19] In addition, evaluation can be accurate only if the library has clear mission and goal statements consistent with its parent organization and its users. In 1979, Holt also stressed the need for identifying university goals and philosophies.[20]

SURVEY OF THE LITERATURE ON EVALUATION METHODS

In collection evaluation, the professional literature cites numerous methods. Each approach can reveal important information about the condition of a library's holdings; however, each technique has its strength and weakness. The methods reviewed here are those that are most prominent in the field.

Impressionistic Method

The impressionistic method is entirely subjective and is not usually used alone. Customarily, evaluation is based on data gathered from personal examination of the shelves, the collection of a few quantitative measures, and the impressions of others. The method makes effective use of subject specialists, usually bibliographers and librarians, to gain impressions about the collection.[21] Unfortunately, there may not be such a person for every subject represented, and individuals, if found, may not agree. It is possible that some portions of the collection may interest no one, or that the expert in a particular area may not be aware of the holdings deficiencies or may be indifferent to them.[22]

Direct observation is practical but not very scientific. However, to the evaluator, an examination of the shelves will indicate size, scope, the depth of the collection, the duplication of materials, and incomplete journal runs.[23] Shelf-scanning, although simple, is a rewarding approach when combined with collection-development policy statements, faculty and student subject interest profiles, or subject-classification schedules. This method results in outlining the scope, currency, and physical condition of the collection.[24] The real disadvantage of this technique is that the materials may not be on the shelf. Therefore, the shelflist should always be consulted when checking the shelves.[25]

In-house Use

In-house use or in-library use deals with the utilization of library materials not recorded by circulation, which assumes that anything checked out is used outside the library. Lancaster, reporting on the findings of others studying in-house use, states that the ratio of in-library use to at-home use tends to remain relatively constant in a particular library, assuming no change has occurred in either the library or its users.

There are two ways of determining in-house use. One is to rely on the cooperation of all users in the library during a specified period of time. It is important for the reliability of this method, to determine through observation, what proportion of users actually cooperate by not shelving the materials they have used. A correction factor, therefore, can be calculated to understand the true level of in-house use. The alternative approach is to utilize a random sampling of users, locations, and perhaps time intervals. This procedure is seen by some to be more reliable than the previous method.[26]

By comparing circulation and in-library use data, Harris sought to evaluate the accuracy of recording in-house use. He found that the total amount of in-library use was underestimated and, furthermore, that this figure varied by subject areas in the collection. The number of books actually used was approximately 20 times higher than the official records indicated.[27]

McGrath conducted two correlation studies to test circulation data against in-house data. One correlation factor of .86 and one of .84 resulted and he therefore concluded that out-of-library use can be a reliable indicator of in-library use. Based on these results, he claimed that for predicting in-house use, a simple ratio of books taken out to those used in the library can be employed. However, because usage within narrow classifications had more variation, the out-to-in ratio was less reliable. Therefore, a regression line using the linear equation was perceived to be more reliable overall.[28]

Christiansen presents the advantages and disadvantages of in-house studies.[29] She cautions that "the extent to which patterns of in-library use parallel patterns of at-home use remains controversial."[30]

Compiling Statistics (Size, Costs, Editions, Etc.)

Statistics tell us nothing about quality. Goals do not translate into numbers and so it is not possible mathematically to measure the goals of the library or its community.[31] Nevertheless, statistics can tell us about the current size of a collection, its growth, and the monies expended for materials.[32] There is a positive correlation between collection size and the academic excellence of the institution. However, professionally competent librarians, good collection maintenance (vigorous weeding and good subject coverage), and prompt document retrieval are variables that are more important than size.[33] Based on collection size, one presumes that the larger the collection, the more likely it is to satisfy the needs of its users. If the library does not stay current it will decline in value, so it would seem that absolute size is not as good an indicator as rate of growth. However, growth rate may also be misleading, if obsolete items are not weeded. Percentage rate of growth penalizes the library pursuing an active policy of weeding.[34] Therefore, a better indicator of size is the number of unique titles.

In her method for quantitatively evaluating a current book collection, Golden stipulated that the subject coverage for each course had to be assigned an LC number. Then the books in the shelflist matching the LC number were counted and course enrollment figures consulted for demand. If only 10 books were found to be available for any one student, this ratio was considered to indicate a weak collection.[35]

What is the best indicator of size—total expenditures or volumes held? Research has shown that if all the volumes on the shelves and in circulation were counted, the actual number would as much as 20 percent less than the reported figures. However, when total expenditure is correlated with each of the other statistics (volumes added, material and binding expenditures, total salaries, staff size, volumes held, and total enrollment), an accurate picture of the collection size is obtained. When the total number of volumes is correlated with each of the other statistics, it too supplies an accurate picture of size.[36]

Interlibrary Loan and Unfilled Requests

Interlibrary loans are seen by Bonn to be similar to unfilled requests. If a library supplies 95 percent of client requests, its resources are perceived to be adequate, but if it borrows at a rate of 15 per cent or more, then the acquisition policy needs to be revised. When examining records in order to gain an insight into performance, it is much easier to review the unfilled requests than to count the filled requests. Also, it is assumed that unfilled requests represent those resources not available in the library.[37]

The interlibrary loans at California State University–Fullerton (CSUF) were investigated in order to determine their usefulness in evaluating the collection. The data analysis revealed that certain departments were not well served. Although it is possible to pinpoint collection weakness in departments and/or LC classifications, it was impossible to anticipate the need for a specific title. An equally difficult situation to predict was the changing subject demands stimulated by the hiring of a specialist by an academic department.[38]

Circulation Records

An excellent way to evaluate is to determine the "use factor." This figure can be calculated by developing a ratio of use to holdings in a specific subject class. This number is then expressed as a percentage demonstrating the relationship of the total number of volumes borrowed to the number of volumes held in a specific subject class. This "use factor" alerts one to overdeveloped as well as underused areas. Underuse can coincide with overborrowing from other libraries because of the age of that portion of the collection. Weaknesses, on the other hand, can occur because a category/categories of users has/have been ignored.[39]

Either Jain's "relative use" method or McGrath's "classified course technique" can also be employed to predict which parts of the collection are most and least used. The relative use method utilizes both collection and circulation samples in order to compare the expected use of a subset of the collection with its actual recorded use. The classified course technique attempts to demonstrate that books with classification numbers that match an overall institutional profile are more likely to be used than those that do not.[40]

Further uses derived from the analysis of circulation records are (1) retiring little-used portions of the collection; (2) identifying a "core" collection with which to satisfy a certain percentage of demands in the near future; and (3) locating underused and overused subject areas for collection development and heavily used titles for the purposes of duplication. Problems arise when many missing data are encountered due to replacement or loss of book cards and data labels.[41]

According to Trueswell, the last recorded circulation date of each volume appears to be the ideal statistic. From this statistic, he feels it is possible to identify the core collection. However, this method does not consider in-stack or browsing use.[42] One disadvantage of this method for analyzing circulation data is that it excludes in-house consultation and therefore does not represent actual use. It also does not take into account user failures or inaccessibility of heavily used materials, nor does it identify low use resulting from obsolescence or poor quality of the collection.[43]

Checklists

The oldest form of collection evaluation is to compare holdings against lists and bibliographies. There are four basic techniques: (1) checking with a sample of carefully selected bibliographies; (2) checking with journal-article bibliographies; (3) checking with basic lists of most-used, most-cited titles; and (4) rechecking the areas of revealed weakness.[44] Comer advises that one must be aware of two basic assumptions when choosing a list in order to fully understand the results. The first is that a list of certain core titles belongs in any existing collection. The second is that such a list represents the composite judgment of many specialists. Therefore, the evaluator must be sure that the list chosen is adequate to the purpose and appropriate to the type of library. There are no guidelines specifying particular lists that are adequate or appropriate.

Lists are relatively effective for a rough evaluation of adequacy and completeness of the collection. However, few subject bibliographies have been compiled for evaluating scholarly collections. Standard lists do not include esoteric materials and do not adequately evaluate a collection that must meet the needs of the university's curriculum. Unfortunately, some good works are not included on the list of recommended titles. For a complete evaluation, the list-checking method should be used in conjunction with other evaluation methods. A list is only valuable for estimating how well the collection matches the list. If large gaps are identified, then the evaluation may lead to an examination of selection policies.[45]

One can also take the complete list of a library's holdings in a specified area and compare those titles against book reviews and selection tools. If a title does not appear on any of the lists, then it is considered undesirable. If it appears on only one list, then it is of dubious quality. For public libraries, this method is useful for identifying titles that should be reviewed very carefully because they do not appear on any list.[46]

List checking is no more effective for evaluating the quality of a collection than the utilization of statistics. No credit is given for books not on the list but do fulfill local needs. The best measure of adequacy is the specialized, up-to-date, subject bibliography. Better still are the lists compiled with a particular library in mind and a well-defined purpose.[47]

To avoid the problem of dated and irrelevant lists, the holdings of peer institutions can be compared to provide a microlevel analysis based on the LC classification scheme. Sharp differences between peer situations may be found; nevertheless, by using LC classes to define holdings the problem of dated and irrelevant lists is avoided.[48]

The shortcomings of the checklist method include: (1) interlibrary loan is not taken into account; (2) possession of poor titles is not penalized and (3) special materials that are very important to a particular library may not appear on any list. These criticisms should come as a warning, suggesting caution in application.[49] ALA guidelines advise that "the list must match the objectives and type of collection a library has."[50]

Comparisons with Other Libraries

Evans is quite strong in his remarks on the use of this method of evaluation, which, in his opinion, accomplishes no more than the comparing of apples with oranges, because no objective criterion for evaluation is used. Institutions differ in their objectives, programs, and curricula. Furthermore, comparison is made almost impossible by the various ways in which libraries generate statistics about their collections.[51]

There are fundamental problems inherent in this method. For instance, is the catalog to be used for comparison comprehensive?[52] How is one to know, without evaluating the specific catalog selected as the evaluation tool? On the other hand, Knightly feels there is some value to this approach because attention can be drawn to areas badly needing correction.[53]

Standards

The ALA *Guidelines for Collection Development* detail the many advantages of applying standards. The biggest disadvantage of course, is that the minimum is regarded as the maximum.[54] Nevertheless, overall standards do have the effect of upgrading libraries. They provide a measure of the deficiencies, although they focus primarily on inputs rather than effectiveness.[55]

Since the 1940s, the standards have stressed quality, which is not easily defined. These standards have also emphasized institutional goals and objectives as the frame of reference within which the standards are to be applied. One area of dispute concerns the deliberate lack of specificity in most standards in both numbers and titles. For instance, what exactly is meant by "adequate support?"[56]

In order to reduce the conflict between regulation and freedom, which is basically irreconcilable, standards are worded in terms that are often vague. Interpreters are then needed to serve as judges who have sufficient background and knowledge but who are also biased and prejudiced. Despite this hazard, more institutions are meeting standards.[57]

Library standards exist for such professional training programs as law, medicine, and education. Brown notes that standards of regional accrediting agencies and state departments of education reinforced ALA standards for college libraries. Also, she found that the minimal meeting of ALA standards was the basis for awarding grants under the Higher Education Act, Title II (A).[58]

Formulas

The Clapp-Jordan formula is succinctly stated in the ALA *Guidelines for Collection Development*. In the case of academic research libraries, the Clapp-Jordan formula measures core collection as volumes per student, per faculty, per graduate field, per undergraduate honors program.[59] It identifies factors to which suitable weights can be assigned. These factors are student body (size and composition); faculty (size and involvement in research); curriculum (number of departments, courses, degrees granted, etc.); methods of instruction; study locations; geography of the campus; and the intellectual climate of the institution.[60]

Because the formula yields a minimum measure of the number of books considered adequate, this minimum is often interpreted by those controlling the funds of libraries as an optimum, thereby affecting acquisitions. It has been proposed that an annual growth rate be accorded of no less than 5 per cent.[61] McInnis demonstrates the Clapp-Jordan formula as a weighted sum of variables. The number of faculty members was adopted as the primary indicator of the collection size, because the influence on size is due more to research and graduate training than to the varying student enrollments. McInnis then conducted a regression analysis on the weighted formula with which he hoped to measure average relationships instead of a minimum standard. The regression analysis produced higher figures for the expected number of volumes. He therefore concluded his work by recommending the Clapp-Jordan formula as a suitable and reasonable conservative guide.[62]

Other researchers indicate that the Clapp-Jordan formula should take into account (1) the level of service desired in terms of immediate satisfaction; (2) the rate of obsolescence of volumes; (3) publication dates; and (4) the need for multiple copies.[63] Nevertheless, the Clapp-Jordan formula is definitely useful for planning, budgeting, and appropriating.[64]

The Washington State formula is based on the Clapp-Jordan formula. Both enrollment and curriculum factors are taken into account. Two elements of the Clapp-Jordan formula not included are an allowance of volumes per undergraduate major and volumes per honor student. These elements were considered too variable.[65]

The California State formula takes into account resource sharing by libraries and is based on the United States Office of Education Standards. Given a basic collection of 75,000 volumes for the first 600 Full Time Equivalent (FTE) students, 10,000 volumes are added for each additional 2,000 FTE students. Then 3,000 volumes are added for each subject field of graduate study and an additional 5,000 volumes for doctoral programs. From the total is subtracted 5 percent when the college is closer than 25 miles from a public institution of higher learning.[66]

Formula A of the Association of College and Research Libraries (ACRL) is also based on the Clapp-Jordan approach and is similar to the Washington State formula. The Clapp-Jordan allowance of volumes per honor student is omitted, and volumes are added per sixth-year-specialist degree field.[67]

Formula A of the ACRL recommends 85,000 volumes as being a basic core collection. One hundred volumes are added for each FTE faculty, volumes 15 volumes for FTE students, 350 volumes for undergraduates (major or minor), and 6,000 volumes for a master's program. Having determined the required number of volumes, Formula A assigns a grade: A for libraries having the required number; B for 80–99 percent; C for 65–79 percent; D for 50–64 percent.[68] Formula A, as presented in *College and Research Library News,* allows 3,000 volumes for a masters field with a doctorate, 6,000 volumes for a sixth-year specialist field, and 25,000 volumes for a doctoral field.[69]

The Beasley formula for potential public library service measures resources, population, circulation and research capability.[70] This formula is expressed as B = all resource material (may be weighted); P = population served; C = circulation; and S = study or research. Quality is not measured.[71]

The Voigt formula provides a method for determining an adequate acquisition rate for current materials on an annual basis. It also determines the acquisition rate for graduate fields, for undergraduate students, and for research programs with access to resource sharing with other libraries.[72] This model, unlike the Clapp-Jordan method, accounts for (1) differing material needs, (2) the impact of sponsored research, and (3) the impact of other research libraries in the area.[73]

Citation Analysis

This method of evaluation compares the holdings of the library to items cited in footnotes, bibliographies, or references recorded in papers, especially books and articles written by faculty or research staff. However, one cannot know whether or not the author limited him- or herself to the library being evaluated. The citations, furthermore, may relate to one area of the collection or to peripheral areas.[74]

Most recently, the focus of this approach has been used to determine core lists of primary journals and thus to identify serial titles for cancellation. Empirical data has shown that a relatively small number of core primary journals contain a large amount of literature on a subject.[75] According to Fitzgibbons, "citation researchers have tended to draw too many generalizations about their findings which may have caused much of the current skepticism concerning the application of this research area."[76]

Document Delivery Tests

The document delivery test (DDT) "assesses the capability of a library to provide users with the items they need at the time they need them."[77] It can be looked upon as a simulation of users in the library looking for a particular item.

The most difficult task in performing the DDT is the compilation of a set of citations that presume to reflect the document needs of the users. To test document delivery capability in one subject area is difficult, but when a wide spectrum of fields are to be evaluated, it is considerably more complex. The best way is to select a random sample from the sources cited by current authors in a field. Three hundred citations are pulled for a day, representing 300 users looking for specific items. The following questions are answered: (1) Is it in the collection? (2) If so, where is it physically located at the time of the test? Items not in the collection are obtained through interlibrary loan, to check the median time needed to obtain these materials.[78] Not only should the library of the user be tested, but also the lending library's capability of delivering documents to other libraries. A word of caution: To obtain meaningful results, DDT results *should be compared* with DDT results in other libraries or other units in the same library.[79]

LIS library personnel can find DDT useful in such areas as planning, management, and preparation for accreditation. First, a representative sample of document citations in library and information science is obtained; a randomly selected set of references then becomes a test sample with which to administer the DDT. The sources for the pool of citations include but are not restricted to dissertations and papers listed in *Library Literature, Documentation Abstracts, Computer Reviews,* and bibliographies in the *Annual Review of Information Science and Technology.* Other sources for these citations are the core journals in the field of librarianship and information science. The top 20 titles are considered to be sufficiently representative.[80]

"Searcher error," another consideration in DDT, gives inconsistent test results from one searcher to another. Furthermore, "sampling error" may occur when drawing samples from the same citation pool. Measuring capability by means of this test is not the same as evaluating the retrieval service. For all its weaknesses, the DDT is basically sound and applicable to many types of libraries.[81]

Use Studies

Libraries that have records of use available for 20 years or so can utilize these records to predict future use. Past use is a powerful variable.[82] Usually, use studies are more effective if more than one technique is used; for example, combining such approaches as circulation frequency, in-house use, and questioning of users. These findings will also indicate collection areas of little or no use, the need for duplicate titles, and changes in collection development policy or acquisition plans.[83]

The controversy over external utilization as an adequate measure of total use is well-documented in an article titled ''The University of Pittsburgh Studies Collection Usage: A Symposium.'' Schad does not agree with the study's assumption that external use is an adequate measure of total use.[84] Kent rebuts this contention about the relationship of in-house use to circulation by stating ''that external circulation data can be utilized with a high level of confidence to measure total book use in terms of books used at least once.''[85]

In the same article, Massman points out the pitfalls in relying only on circulation studies:

> The best such studies 20 years ago would not have predicted the present interest in ethnic studies, women's studies, and death, to mention a few areas which are currently of major concern. On the basis of circulation much could be discarded or never purchased which may be of great value next year or in 10 years. If the faculty, students, educational institutions, and society did not change, it would be much easier. Furthermore, older materials are looked at in a new light by each generation. One must also keep in mind, of course, that there are vast differences in the educational missions of various colleges and universities, and, therefore, there must be vast differences in the libraries which serve those educational missions.[86]

User Studies

According to the ALA *Guidelines,* the procedure for obtaining user opinions requires a survey of patrons or user groups. This method is subjective and often inconsistent. Also, user interest may be quite narrow.[87]

Finding out what users think is one way of evaluating the library's objectives or mission. User opinion, as feedback, affects the library's selection process; identifies strengths and weaknesses of the collection; reveals the types of users needs; trends in research; and changes in interest; and identifies contemporary demand.

Faculty evaluations of university collections can affect budgeting and the ability to draw new faculty and research members into the institution. Although public librarians have always been alert to user requests and to trends in circulation, not many seek their users' opinion on collection adequacy. By far the best evaluations are conducted by reference librarians. They are in touch with the library's users and know their library well.[88]

User opinion would seem to be a type of feedback routinely desired by managers but it is not often sought.[89] In part, this may be so because users are known to pay little attention to the collection and only become vocal about the absence of desired titles.[90]

Bonn developed a checklist utilizing background data about potential users and registered borrowers. His checklist contains a number of items concerning potential patrons' information needs, expectations, and capabilities for utilizing the collection or collections available to them. In the case of registered borrowers, the categories of actual use that were developed include subject class, language, types of materials, and services.[91]

Although opinion polls can give valuable information, their chief drawback is sample size. These samples must be large in order to derive reliable comparisons among libraries. Occasionally opinion polls do elicit the feelings of the population about libraries.[92]

Personal contact with users is better than mailed questionnaires, which have low return rates. A standard form for recording responses to standardized questions helps to create a lasting record. This approach is similar to the Bonn's checklist and can also serve as the beginning point for other types of evaluation.[93]

Surveys of user opinions can be as simple or complex as is needed to fit one's needs. Sometimes it is difficult to analyze and interpret the data and, furthermore, some users have difficulty in judging what is reasonable to expect from their library. However, "use and user studies can help determine objectively and systematically specific aspects of how the collection is being used and by whom."[94]

Shelf Availability Test

Generally speaking, a shelf availability test means just that: an item owned will be on the shelf when sought by the user. This test can attempt to include all users during a specified time period or it can focus on a random sample of users. Patrons are asked to identify the titles that they could not locate. These failures can be analyzed and the kind of failure identified. The findings yielded by such a test can reveal user search behavior and user attitudes.[95]

The function of availability analysis is to reveal library procedures requiring further study. It is important to understand the difference between unnecessary and justifiable delays,[96] because only about two-thirds of the items sought will be promptly found.[97] The use of failure slips provides a method for determining why a reader is experiencing failure, what book is being sought, and even the pattern of failure for certain volumes.[98] There are some disadvantages to this otherwise highly successful test. Its success depends on the cooperation of users. It can also be time consuming and difficult to carry out.[99]

Analysis of the Shelflist

A popular, simple, and useful measure, such as counting volumes by subject classification made from a shelflist card count, has significant drawbacks, especially if used alone. Shelflist measurement data is meaningful when compared with like data from similar libraries. Uses for the data, if accurately interpreted, are many. It can ascertain collection areas needing adjustment or more collection effort, it can justify book-budget requests, and provide a general view of the total collection. This approach also aids in planning cooperative collection development ventures. However, the technique is not particularly useful if more than one classification scheme has been used and if the classifications do not reflect curriculum programs.[100]

Another approach is for professors to describe their courses by using the LC classification scheme. It can readily be seen that this technique is reasonable for evaluating materials for the support of the curriculum. A bonus feature is that faculty learn about the importance of subject headings, classification, and the shelflist, which in turn assists them when doing research. Another benefit of this method is that the repetition of certain call numbers establishes a basis for weeding.[101]

If one records and tabulates the information provided by the shelflist, it is possible to describe the collection along these lines: publication date, country of origin, language of publication, publisher, edition, and format. This information, when analyzed, yields meaningful and evaluative results about the scope and usefulness of the collection.[102]

Analysis by Automated Methods

At Bucknell, circulation data by LC classification and academic department were analyzed through the use of computer-produced statistics.

> Circulation was compared to the number of volumes, which were then related to each department in order to determine how much the department was using the subject-related book collection. Circulation was also compared with the number of students in that particular department. Consequently, these two comparisons identified areas of the collection that were under- or heavily utilized.[103]

Several libraries now use computer-generated circulation data to weed collections, to determine supply and demand, and to order duplicate copies. At Arizona State University, the library circulation system provided data with which to devise "a formula to assess current utilization as well as the average number of volumes required per category of user to maintain the present level of user satisfaction."[104]

Computer-assisted analysis of circulation records can enable staff to reach conclusions about book use, the number of different borrowers for one book, the availability of a book, and the absence of the title from one or more reading lists. Computer analysis illustrates circulation histories of individual volumes and facilitates the replacement of damaged and worn-out copies. "Patterns of use in a large collection can be far more effectively and reliably monitored by computer-assisted analysis of circulation records."[105]

According to Lancaster, there are two major trends in the library field: the application of automation and the concern about evaluation. Automated systems can be designed with components to collect evaluative data on a continuous basis. This management-information module makes possible the collection of data that previously could be obtained only through one-time studies. This module can be added on to almost any system, even ones that have been operational for some time. One of the major benefits of the automated system is its ability to generate management information that has never before been available on a regular basis.[106]

METHODOLOGY AND INSTRUMENT DESIGN

After an extensive review of the professional literature, a two-part test instrument was prepared by the authors of this paper. The first part, to be completed by the chief administrative officer of each institution or by his or her delegate, consists of nine essential questions designed to elicit background data of each respective organization. The second part, to be answered by the librarian or an individual in charge of the LIS collection,** is composed of 15 items concerning the procedures applied to these specialized holdings. The primary objective of this last section was to collect information on how many LIS collections were being evaluated and to identify the methods utilized. The researchers were also interested in determining the number of collections receiving no analysis and in ascertaining the reasons for the lack of evaluation.

Of the 24 items in the questionnaire, only a few were open questions. The closed items were structured to generate four types of response categories: (1) statistical data; (2) "Yes" or "No" replies; (3) options where only one response was feasible from a choice of three answers; and (4) a menu of responses where one or more replies were possible.

To increase the validity and the reliability of the test implement, the questionnaire was reviewed by Dr. Elizabeth Stone, Dean Emeritus, and Dr. Raymond Vondran, Dean, both of the School of Library and Information Science at The Catholic University of America. In addition, the schedule of questions was also examined by Dr. Donald Shirey of the University of Pittsburgh. A number of revisions of the instrument were made in an attempt to improve the clarity of language and the appropriateness of each response category.

The population for this study consisted of all the accredited programs listed in the pamphlet entitled "Graduate Library Education Programs," published in March 1984 by the American Library Association. On May 5, 1984, questionnaires were mailed; however, The Catholic University of America was excluded for two reasons. First, this institution was the pilot test site, and second, to avoid entering a bias into the interpretation of the data, given that the researchers were a part of the teaching faculty. With this initial posting of the instrument, an introductory letter was addressed to the highest ranking officer for each school or department, explaining the researchers' objectives and their commitment that the

**In the questionnaire, LIS collection was identified as either a separate library or a collection where materials were held together on the topic of library and information science.*

data collected would remain confidential because the institutions' identities would remain anonymous.

Thirty-seven replies to the initial mailing were received. A second mailing was sent on June 21, 1984, to those who had not answered the first posting. Fifteen aditional responses were received as a result.

A total of 52 instruments (79 percent) were received; fourteen (21 percent) were never returned. Of those that were returned, four questionnaires (6 percent) were incomplete. In two cases (3 percent), administrators sent letters explaining why they elected not to participate in the study. In summary, 46 questionnaires (70 percent of the total population) provided the source of the data for this research project.

Because a questionnaire was used, the data were representative of the type collected using the survey research method. The answers recorded on the test instrument were extracted and initially placed on a spread sheet, to enable the researchers to view the spectrum of responses at one time. The matrix also provided a format by which the data could be organized. Each item was then analyzed by applying descriptive statistical methods. Certain responses for related items were also compared and contrasted to develop a profile of the most commonly occurring characteristics and to determine which cases were not part of the normal paradigm.

DATA ANALYSIS

"When was the department/school *first* accredited?," The responses to the first question tend to cluster in three distinct periods as displayed in Table 1. The data seem to demonstrate that the decades of the 1930s, 1960s and 1970s were the most active periods. In response to the question about the year in which these institutions were *last* accredited, 33 respondents (73.3 percent) indicated the span of time to be from 1980–1984, and 12 administrators (26.7 percent) indicated the five-year period between 1975–1979.

An investigation was conducted of the statistics regarding the 46 respondents (available in the *Library and Information Science Educational Statistical Report*

Table 1.   Years When Schools/
Departments Were First Accredited

Years of Accreditation	#	%
1920–1929	6	13.0
1930–1939	9	19.6
1940–1949	1	2.2
1950–1959	4	8.7
1960–1969	12	26.0
1970–1979	11	23.9
1980–present	1	2.2
Missing cases = 2 (4.3%)		

published by the Association for Library and Information Science Education in 1984). For Fall 1982, the number of full-time faculty members ranged as low as 5 and as high as 23; the median for all reporting institutions was 9.

The same analysis was applied to the figures representing part-time faculty for Fall 1982. The data revealed that a number of organizations had no participating part-time teachers, and in other cases, part-time members numbered as high as 27; the median number of part-time faculty was 4.

Utilizing the ALISE *Statistical Report,* a similar examination was conducted for Fall 1983 enrollment figures. For the 46 institutions included in this study, the total number of master's students ranged from 46 to 352, with the median calculated at 132. The number of doctoral students ranged from 7 to 52, with 15 identified as the median.

Concerning the LIS budget, 10 administrators (21.7 percent) indicated that financial control belonged to the school or department; whereas, 33 officials (71.7 percent) replied that it was managed by the campus library. In three cases (6.5 percent), the financial structure was different. Two respondents designated the materials budget to be the joint responsibility of both the department/school and the library. A third administrative officer noted that the LIS budget was coordinated by a management center working in close cooperation with the president's office.

In an open item, respondents were then asked to indicate to whom the library and information science librarian reported. From the answers provided, categories of university officials were identified. The rank order of the response frequencies for these categories is reported in Table 2.

The most frequently mentioned university officials to whom LIS librarians reported were library directors (34.8 percent) and school deans (17.4 percent).

Table 2. Rank Order of Responses: To Whom Does the LIS Librarian Report?

Official	#	%
Director/University Librarian/College Librarian	16	34.8
Dean/Director of School	8	17.4
No person designated/No separate collection	5	10.9
Assistant Director/Associate Director of University Libraries	2	4.3
Assistant Director of Public Services	2	4.3
Director of Humanities and/or Social Sciences Department	2	4.3
Assistant Director of Special Collections	1	2.2
Director of Division	1	2.2
Head of Reference	1	2.2
Provost	1	2.2
University Collection Development Officer	1	2.2
Head of Graduate Library	1	2.2
Head of Branch Library	1	2.2
Missing cases = 2 (4.3%)		

These replies parallel those of an earlier question, which found that LIS budgets were controlled primarily by university libraries and secondarily by schools and departments. In the third response category (10.5 percent), respondents indicated that no person was identified because there was no separate LIS collection. The remaining classes indicated by the respondents were particularly interesting because the data collected depicted the wide range and variety of administrators responsible for LIS librarians.

From the data assembled, it was determined that LIS collections were located within the same buildings as the classrooms (67.4 percent) or within walking distance (30.4 percent). Only in one case (2.2 percent) did an administrator indicate that the LIS collection was in a location that necessitated transportation.

These percentages correspond to the replies to another question: "How close is the physical location of the library in relation to the faculty offices?" Thirty-one officials (67.4 percent) reported that the collection was "in the same building" and 14 (32.6 percent) responded "within walking distance." The data seem to demonstrate that these collections are easily accessed by both faculty and students.

At this point in the analysis, the background information supplied by the administrators was completed. The second phase centered on the segment of the questionnaire answered by librarians or staff members responsible for LIS collections. In five cases however, this portion was completed by deans or department chairpersons because no separate collections existed. After these questionnaires were examined by the researchers, they decided to include these five test instruments in the analysis because of the completeness of the information contained.

Forty-two institutions reported the number of volumes contained in their collections. The smallest collection, containing 600 volumes, was identified as a reference library organized for the faculty. The researchers, therefore, excluded this collection from their analysis.

On the other end of the scale, six organizations supplied high figures ranging from 3,800,000 volumes to 280,000 volumes. After examining a variety of resources such as the *World of Learning* and *ALA Directory,* it was determined that these figures pertained to the overall campus holdings and not specifically to LIS collections. These figures were also excluded from the analysis because they were not appropriate.

Of the 35 remaining respondents, the number of volumes for their institutions ranged from 3,500 to 120,000, with a median of 29,000 volumes. In an additional step, 17 institutions were identified as having doctoral programs. The number of LIS volumes for these organizations ranged from 18,000 to 120,000, with a median of 49,000 volumes.

In analyzing the recorded serial holdings, the same responses as previously noted were excluded to insure consistent treatment of the data. Another case was also withdrawn because an incorrect reply, combining the number of journal titles with newsletter subscriptions, was supplied. In the remaining 34 institutions, the number of LIS journal titles ranged from 100 to 2,500 with a calculated median of 345. For the 16 organizations with doctoral programs, the median was 367 journal titles with a spread ranging from a low of 120 to as high as 1,600 titles.

To the query, "Has an evaluation of the collection been conducted?," 13 respondents (28.3 percent) answered "Yes" and thirty-three (71.7 percent) replied "No." Of the 13 positive responses, 2 were from institutions whose LIS collections were incorporated in larger campus holdings. Those who replied negatively were then asked to indicate why the evaluation did not occur and, in some instances, more than one reason was supplied. Twenty-six (78.9 percent) cited insufficient staff; 25 (75.8 percent) indicated lack of time; and 14 (42.2 percent) reported inadequate funds. Seven (21.2 percent) mentioned other reasons, including turnover in staff, a higher work priority, or the moving of the library to another location.

The remaining 13 respondents were then referred to the item asking, "For what reasons was the collection analysis conducted?" With some respondents supplying more than one reply, accreditation (53.9 percent) and weeding (53.9 percent) were the most frequently stated reasons, with 7 individuals selecting each of these categories respectively. The next most chosen category was "other" (46.2 percent), given by 6 respondents and included a variety of answers such as the following: to implement a doctoral program; to support a proposal for a federal grant; to sustain a changing curriculum emphasis. In another case, the evaluation was conducted in preparation for a merger of the LIS collection with an education library.

Five respondents (38.5 percent) indicated that the analysis was implemented to determine the adequacy of the collection, and three (23.1 percent) reported the evaluation was linked to storage activities. The remaining reasons chosen were to ascertain collection growth (15.4 percent) and to support the budget (15.4 percent).

The data seem to indicate that the predominance of collection evaluation activity occurred in the 1980s; this time period was recorded in all 13 cases. These replies parallel those in earlier items, because most institutions were reaccredited in the 1980s. Furthermore, of those who had conducted an analysis, 7 (53.9 percent) linked this activity to the accreditation process. In three instances however, individuals reported that activities also occurred in the 1970s, and one individual indicated that collection analysis had been conducted as early as 1969. In terms of the time period associated with these evaluation practices, 10 respondents (76.9 percent) indicated the span of 1 to 6 months and 3 (23.1 percent) replied it lasted from 7 to 12 months.

Four individuals (30.7 percent) responded that the examination of the LIS collections was implemented in conjunction with an analysis of other resources on campus. Nine people (69.2 percent) indicated that the evaluation was centered exclusively on the LIS holdings. In both of these situations, the 13 respondents also maintained that there were no extra budget allotments provided to support the analysis programs.

To the question, "Who conducted the evaluation?" all 13 individuals supplied answers. Seven (53.9 percent) indicated that the library staff members were responsible and 4 (30.7 percent) mentioned the joint involvement of the library staff acting in close cooperation with a faculty committee. Professors working alone were mentioned in one case (7.7 percent) and in another instance (7.7 percent), the librarian consulted the faculty.

The 13 respondents were then asked to indicate, on a list of 15 possible described methods, the types of collection analysis techniques utilized at their institutions. In a number of cases, individuals selected more than one answer; these responses are presented in rank order in Table 3.

The most frequently cited technique was the impressionistic method, chosen by 10 respondents (76.9 percent). Seven individuals (53.9 percent) selected the checklist approach and another 7 respondents (53.9 percent) utilized the shelflist analysis. Statistics on collection size were chosen by 6 people (46.2 percent), whereas in-house use, circulation records, and citation analysis were each chosen by 5 participants (38.5 percent). Four people (30.1 percent) utilized use studies; three people each (23.1 percent) selected analysis of interlibrary loan records, use studies, and comparisons with other library holdings. Two respondents (15.4 percent) indicated that standards established by accrediting bodies were used. The formula method and the document delivery test were each mentioned once (7.7 percent); no person mentioned the shelf availability test.

All respondents were then asked to indicate if any library functions were automated. Twenty-eight (60.9 percent) replied "Yes" and 17 (37.0 percent) an-

Table 3.   Rank Order of Responses: Indicating the Types of
Collection Analysis Methods Utilized

Method	#	%
Impressionistic	10	76.9
Checklist	7	53.9
Shelflist analysis	7	53.9
Statistics on the collection size	6	46.2
In-house use	5	38.5
Circulation records	5	38.5
Citation analysis	5	38.5
User studies	4	30.1
ILL records	3	23.1
Comparisons with other holdings	3	23.1
Use studies	3	23.1
Comparisons with standards established by other accrediting bodies	2	15.4
Formula	1	7.7
Document delivery test	1	7.7
Shelf availability tests	0	0.0

Table 4. Rank Responses Identifying
Automated Library Functions

Activity		%
Cataloging	17	60.7
Circulation	12	42.9
Acquisitions	8	28.6
Serials	6	21.4
On-line data bases	4	14.3
Interlibrary loan	2	7.1
Reserve holdings microcomputer	1	3.8
Implementation of an ILS	1	3.8

swered "No"; one individual (2.1 percent) did not respond. Of those who replied positively, 5 represented institutions whose LIS collections were not isolated but combined with larger campus-wide holdings.

In an open item that followed, those individuals indicating that their library used automated functions were asked to identify these operations. Respondents were free to report any number of activities. The rank order of these answers is provided in Table 4.

The activities most mentioned were cataloging functions (60.7 percent), and these were linked with such utilities as OCLC and UTLAS. Circulation (42.9 percent) was the second-most-recorded operation. Followed by acquisitions (28.6 percent) with 8 individuals reporting. Six respondents (21.4 percent) indicated that serial operations were automated and 4 (14.3 percent) listed on-line retrieval systems. The least-mentioned activities included interlibrary loan, utilization of the microcomputer for listing reserve materials, and the implementation of an Integrated Library System (ILS).

The 13 respondents who had conducted an analysis of their collections were then asked if the evaluation was assisted through mechanized methods. Ten (76.9 percent) responded negatively and 3 (23.1 percent) provided no answers. The data seem to indicate that managers have not yet utilized automated resources in the evaluation of library holdings.

DATA INTERPRETATION AND CONCLUSIONS

As depicted in Table 5, some calculated medians were compared to examine a number of related variables for the purpose of observing patterns in the data. The median values seem to indicate that few variations exist between the number of faculty members on staff and the number of students enrolled at those institutions where collections were not evaluated and those entities where an analysis did occur. In observing the medians for all reporting cases, there seem to be few differences as well.

Examining the medians for the number of monograph volumes and the number of serial titles held by these institutions, the data again demonstrate similarities

Table 5. Medians of Selected Data Responses

Category	Subcategory	Medians		
		All responses	Evaluators	Non-evaluators
Faculty	Full-time	9	9	9
	Part-time	4	5	3
Students	Master's, Full-time	47	42	52
	Master's, Part-time	58	45	59.5
	Master's, total	132	128	132
	Doctoral	15	0	0
Monographs (Vols.)	Master's Programs	29,000	29,000	23,000
	Master's/Ph.D programs	49,000	42,000	52,000
Serials (Titles)	Master's Programs	345	380	315
	Master's/Ph.D programs	367	400	340

among the responses for all reported cases—those indicating that their holdings had been evaluated and the nonevaluators. The most significant differences in these medians seem to exist in the monograph holdings held in institutions offering doctoral degrees and monographic collections that support only master's programs. By contrast, the number of serial titles does not seem to vary greatly between these two types of educational facilities.

Data on the various collection analysis methods utilized by the 13 evaluators was reorganized and depicted in Table 6. The purpose of this step in the analysis was to determine if any configuration could be observed from these reported responses.

With only 13 respondents (28.3 percent) indicating they had evaluated their holdings, these findings seem to confirm the initial assumptions of the researchers. Collection analysis is not an integral activity associated with the management of LIS libraries. Some of the reasons linked with the lack of evaluation activity involved shortages in staff, time, and money.

Examining the replies of the evaluators, the data indicate that personnel utilize multifaceted approaches in analyzing their holdings. These data further indicate a sophistication and curiosity by responsible librarians in striving to comprehend the nature of their collections.

There seem to be no obvious patterns in the choice of evaluation methods. The selection of techniques may be influenced by the same factors that influenced the nonevaluators (i.e., lack of funds, staff, and time). In addition, the selection of a technique may be related to the bias of the librarian in charge, which may in turn be associated with such variables as personal familiarity with a particular approach or an inclination toward an anticipated outcome. However, these com-

Table 6. Methods of Analysis Used by Evaluators

RESPONDENT	Impressionistic	In-House use	Size of collection	Interlibrary loan	Circulation records	Checklist	Compare library holdings	Standards	Formula	Citation analysis	Document delivery	Use studies	User studies	Shelf availability	Shelflist analysis	Number of Methods Utilized by Each Respondent
A	X	X	X	X		X	X			X		X	X			9
B	X		X			X		X	X	X			X		X	8
C	X	X	X	X	X		X			X	X					8
D	X	X	X		X	X						X			X	7
E	X		X	X	X	X									X	6
F	X		X			X		X					X		X	6
G	X				X	X				X					X	5
H						X				X		X			X	4
I		X			X		X									3
J	X												X			2
K	X	X														2
L															X	1
M	X															1
Total Number per Type of Evaluation	10	5	6	3	5	7	3	2	1	5	1	3	4	0	7	

Type of Method

Total Number per Type of Evaluation

ments are only possible explanations, which may be addressed in future research projects.

The authors suggest that accreditation standards should be restated in a fashion to reinforce the importance of the LIS collections. Furthermore, *adequacy* needs to be defined more explicity than do the general terms currently employed. Under the leadership and stimulus of the American Library Association, a list of core materials could also be prepared to identify essential titles that are critical in enhancing library education on the master's level. Such a list would not only be helpful in evaluation but also in the selection and weeding processes. In conclusion, the researchers support the opinion that collection evaluation increasingly should play a more important role in the management of LIS collections, to insure the excellence of learning resources in the training of future professionals.

NOTES

1. David Kaser, "Library School Libraries," *Journal for Education for Librarianship* 5 (Summer 1964); 17.

2. Jean Kindlin and June Engle, "Library School Libraries," in Allen Kent, Harold Lancour, and Jay E. Daily, eds., *Encyclopedia of Library and Information Science*, Volume 16 (New York: Marcel Dekker, 1975), 4–5.

3. Rudolf Jacob Penner, "Measuring a Library's Capability," *Journal of Education for Librarianship* 13 (Summer 1972): 29.

4. Eva L. Kiewitt, "Reference Collections of Accredited Library School Programs," *Journal of Education for Librarianship* 19 (Summer 1978): 55.

5. Ibid., 59.

6. Paul H. Mosher, "Collection Evaluation or Analysis: Matching Library Acquisitions to Library Needs," in Robert D. Stueart and George B. Miller, eds., *Collection Development in Libraries* (Greenwich, CT: JAI Press, 1980), 531.

7. Ibid., 530.

8. American Library Association, *Guidelines for Collection Development* (Chicago: American Library Association, 1979), 9.

9. Guy R. Lyle, *The Administration of the College Library*, 4th ed. (New York: Wilson, 1974), 293.

10. Ibid., 294.

11. Edward G. Evans, *Developing Library Collections*, (Littleton, CO: Libraries Unlimited, 1979), 234.

12. Lyle, *The Administration of the College Library*, 300.

13. Ibid., 238.

14. Priscilla Rose, "Innovations and Evaluation of Libraries and Library Service," *Drexel Library Quarterly* 7 (January 1971): 32.

15. Catherine Yancheff, *Criteria for Collection Analysis in the Academic Library* (Arlington, VA: Educational Resources Information Center, 1978), 17.

16. Robert N. Broadus, "Evaluation of Academic Library Collections: A Survey of Recent Literature," *Library Acquisitions: Practice and Theory* (1977): 153.

17. Ibid., 154.

18. Mosher, "Collection Evaluation or Analysis," 528.

19. Ibid., 529.

20. Mae L. Holt, "Collection Evaluation: A Managerial Tool," *Collection Management* 3 (Winter 1979): 279.

21. Evans, *Developing Library Collections,* 238–239.

22. F. W. Lancaster, *The Measurement and Evaluation of Library Service* (Washington, DC: Information Resources Press, 1977), 174.

23. George S. Bonn, "Evaluation of the Collection," *Library Trends* 22 (January 1974): 283.

24. Mosher, "Collection Evaluation or Analysis," 533–534.

25. American Library Association, *Guidelines for Collection Development,* 14.

26. F. W. Lancaster, "Evaluating Collections by Their Use," *Collection Management* 4 (Spring/Summer 1982): 24–27.

27. C. Harris, "A Comparison of Issues and In-Library Use of Books," *ASLIB Proceedings* 27 (March 1977): 125–126.

28. William E. McGrath, "Correlating the Subjects of Books Taken Out and Books Used Within an Open-Stack Library," *College and Research Libraries* 32 (July 1971): 280, 284.

‾29. Dorothy E. Christiansen, C. Roger Davis, and Jutta Reed-Scott, "Guide to Collection Evaluation through Use and User Studies," *Library Resources and Technical Services* 27 (October/December 1983): 437.

30. Ibid., 438.

31. Bonn, "Evaluation of the Collection," 267.

32. American Library Association, *Guidelines for Collection Development,* 15.

33. Bonn, "Evaluation of the Collection," 268.

34. Lancaster, *The Measurement and Evaluation of Library Services,* 165, 168.

35. Barbra Golden, "A Method for Quantitatively Evaluating a University Library Collection," *Library Resources and Technical Services* 18 (Summer 1974): 269–270.

36. Stella Bentley, "Academic Library Statistics: A Search for a Meaningful Evaluation Tool," *Library Research* 1 (Summer 1979): 144–151.

37. Bonn, "Evaluation of the Collection," 270–271.

38. Doris E. New and Retha Zane Ott, "Interlibrary Loan Analysis as a Collection Development Tool," *Library Resources and Technical Services* 18 (Summer 1974): 277, 280, 282–283.

39. Bonn, "Evaluation of the Collection," 273.

40. Lancaster, *Measurement and Evaluation,* 185.

41. Lancaster, "Evaluating Collections by their Use," 16–23.

42. Richard W. Trueswell, "Determining the Optimal Number of Volumes for a Library's Core Collection," *Libri* 16 (March 1966): 59.

43. Christiansen, Davis, and Reed-Scott, "Guide to Collection Evaluation," 435.

44. Mosher, "Collection Evaluation or Analysis," 537.

45. Cynthia Comer, "List-Checking as a Method for Evaluating Library Collections," *Collection Building* 3 (1981): 27–32.

46. Herbert Goldhor, "Analysis of an Inductive Method of Evaluating the Book Collection of a Public Library," *Libri* 23 (March 1973): 6, 13.

47. Bonn, "Evaluation of the Collections," 274–275.

48. John Whaley, "An Approach to Collection Analysis," *Library Resources and Technical Services* 25 (July/September 1981): 332.

49. Evans, *Developing Library Collections,* 240–241.

50. American Library Association, *Guidelines for Collection Development,* 12.

51. Evans, *Developing Library Collections,* 242–243.

52. Mosher, "Collection Evaluation or Analysis," 539.

53. John J. Knightly, "Overcoming the Criterion Problem in the Evaluation of Library Performance," *Special Libraries* 70 (April 1979): 176.

54. American Library Association, *Guidelines for Collection Development,* 18.

55. Knightly, "Overcoming the Criterion Problem," 176.

134   RENEE TJOUMAS and ESTHER E. HORNE

56.   Bonn, "Evaluation of the Collection," 284, 290.
57.   Charles M. Allen, "Trends in the Accreditation of Higher Institutions," in Herbert Goldhor, ed., *Research Methods in Librarianship: Measurement and Evaluation,* (Champaign, IL: University of Illinois Graduate School of Library Science, 1968), 48.
58.   Helen M. Brown, "College Library Standards," *Library Trends* 21 (Summer 1972): 212–213, 216.
59.   American Library Association, *Guidelines for Collection Development,* 15.
60.   Verner W. Clapp and Robert T. Jordan, "Quantitative Criteria for Adequacy of Academic Library Collections," *College and Research Libraries* 26 (September 1965): 371, 373, 380.
61.   Lancaster, *The Measurement and Evaluation of Library Services,* 169–172.
62.   R. Marvin McInnis, "The Formula Approach to Library Size: An Empirical Study of Its Efficacy in Evaluating Research Libraries," *College and Research Libraries* 33 (May 1972): 191, 193.
63.   Bonn, "Evaluation of the Collection," 268–269.
64.   Evans, *Developing Library Collections,* 244.
65.   Ibid., 244–245.
66.   Ibid., 244–245.
67.   Ibid., 244–246.
68.   Robert L. Burr, "Evaluating Library Collections: A Case Study," *The Journal of Academic Librarianship* 5 (November 1979): 257.
69.   "An Evaluative Checklist for Reviewing a College Library Program," *College and Research Library News* 40 (November 1979): 315.
70.   American Library Association, *Guidelines for Collection Development,* 15.
71.   Bonn, "Evaluation of the Collection," 269.
72.   American Library Association, *Guidelines for Collection Development,* 15.
73.   Travis G. White, "Quantitative Measures of Library Effectiveness," *The Journal of Academic Librarianship* 3 (July 1977): 132–133.
74.   American Library Association, *Guidelines for Collection Development,* 17.
75.   Christiansen, Davis, and Reed-Scott, "Guide to Collection Evaluation," 438.
76.   Shirley A. Fitzgibbons, "Citation Analysis in the Social Sciences," in Robert D. Stueart and George B. Miller, eds., *Collection Development in Libraries,* 321.
77.   Christiansen, Davis, and Reed-Scott, "Guide to Collection Evaluation," 437.
78.   F. W. Lancaster, "Evaluating Collections by their Use," 28–31.
79.   American Library Association, *Guidelines for Collection Development,* 18–19.
80.   Penner, "Measuring a Library's Capability," 8, 19.
81.   Richard Orr et al., "Development of Methodologic Tools for Planning and Managing Library Services: II. Measuring a Library's Capability for Providing Documents," *Bulletin of the Medical Library Association* 56 (July 1968): 242–258, 266.
82.   Yancheff, *Criteria for Collection Analysis in the Academic Library,* 8.
83.   Mosher, "Collection Evaluation or Analysis," 539–540.
84.   Jasper G. Schad et al., "The University of Pittsburgh Studies of Collection Usage: A Symposium," *Journal of Academic Librarianship* 5 (May 1979): 60–61.
85.   Ibid., 70.
86.   Ibid., 67.
87.   American Library Association, *Guidelines for Collection Development,* 17.
88.   Bonn, "Evaluation of the Collection," 279–283.
89.   Knightly "Overcoming the Criterion Problem," 176.
90.   Whaley, "An Approach to Collection Analysis," 333.
91.   George S. Bonn, "Library Self-Surveys," *Library and Information Sciences,* no. 9 (1971): 118–119.
92.   Charles M. Armstrong, "Measurement and Evaluation in the Public Library," in Herbert Goldhor, ed., *Research Methods in Librarianship, Measurement and Evaluation* (Champaign, IL: University of Illinois Graduate School of Library Science, 1968), 17.

93. Mosher, "Collection Evaluation or Analysis," 534.

94. Christiansen, Davis, and Reed-Scott, "Guide to Collection Evaluation," 433.

95. Lancaster, "Evaluating Collections by their Use," 35.

96. Robert Goehlert, "Book Availability and Delivery Service," *Journal of Academic Librarianship* 4 (November 1978): 368.

97. Paul B. Kantor, "Availability Analysis," *Journal of the American Society for Information Science* 27 (September 1976): 318.

98. John A. Urquhart and J. L. Schofield, "Measuring Readers' Failure at the Shelf in Three University Libraries," *Journal of Documentation* 28 (September 1972): 233.

99. Christiansen, Davis and Reed-Scott, "Guide to Collection Evaluation," 437.

100. Mosher, "Collection Evaluation or Analysis," 535–536.

101. Whaley, "An Approach to Collection Analysis," 337.

102. Robert L. Burr, "Evaluating Library Collections: A Case Study," *The Journal of Academic Librarianship* 5 (November 1979): 258.

103. Yancheff, *Criteria for Collection Analysis in the Academic Library*, 15.

104. C. J. Power and G. H. Bell, "Automated Circulation, Patron Satisfaction and Collection Evaluation in Academic Libraries—A Circulation Analysis Formula," *Journal of Library Automation* 11 (December 1978): 366.

105. Peter Simmons, "Improving Collections through Computer Analysis of Circulation Records in a University Library," *Proceedings of the American Society of Information Science* 7 (1970): 62.

106. Lancaster, "Evaluating Collections by their Use," 41.

**In the questionnaire, LIS collection was identified as either a separate library or a collection where materials were held together on the topic of library and information science.*

REFERENCES

Allen, Charles M. "Trends in the Accreditation of Higher Institutions." In Herbert Goldhor, ed., *Research Methods in Librarianship: Measurement and Evaluation*, pp. 40–50. Champaign, IL: University of Illinois Graduate School of Library Science, 1968.

Altman, E. O. "Collection Evaluation—What it Means; How It's Done." *The U*N*A*B*A*S*H*E*D Librarian*, no. 35 (1980): 13–14.

American Library Association. *Guidelines for Collection Development*. Chicago: American Library Association, 1979.

American Library Association. *Standards for Accreditation*. Chicago: American Library Association, 1972.

Armstrong, Charles M. "Measurement and Evaluation in the Public Library." In Herbert Goldhor, ed., *Research Methods in Librarianship: Measurement and Evaluation*, 15–24. Champaign, IL: University of Illinois Graduate School of Library Science, 1968.

Association for Library and Information Science Education. *Library and Information Science Education Statistical Report*. State College, PA: ALISE, 1984.

Association of American Law Schools. *Association Information*. N. p., Association of American Law Schools, 1983.

Association of Research Libraries. Office of Management Studies. *Annual Report 1982*. Washington, DC: OMS, 1982.

Beasley, Kenneth E. "A Theoretical Framework for Public Library Measurement." In Herbert Goldhor, ed., *Research Methods in Librarianship: Measurement and Evaluation*, 2–14. Champaign, IL: University of Illinois Graduate School of Library Science, 1968.

Bentley, Stella. "Academic Library Statistics: A Search for a Meaningful Evaluation Tool." *Library Research* 1 (Summer 1979): 143–152.

Bonn, George S. "Evaluation of the Collection." *Library Trends* 22 (January 1924): 265–304.
Bonn, George S. "Library Self-Surveys." *Library and Information Science,* no. 9 (1971): 115–21.
Broadus, Robert N. "Evaluation of Academic Library Collections: a Survey of Recent Literature."
    Library Acquisitions: Practice and Theory 1 (1977): 149–155.
Brown, Helen M. "College Library Standards." *Library Trends* 21 (October 1972): 204–218.
Burr, Robert L. "Evaluating Library Collections: A Case Study." *The Journal of Academic Librari-
    anship* 5 (November 1979): 256–260.
Cassata, Mary B., and Dewey, Gene L. "The Evaluation of a University Library Collection: Some
    Guidelines." *Library Resources and Technical Services* 13 (Fall 969): 450–457.
Christiansen, Dorothy E.; Davis, C. Roger; and Reed-Scott, Jutta. "Guide to Collection Evaluation
    through Use and User Studies," *Library Resources and Technical Services* 27 (October/
    December 1983): 432–440.
Clapp, Verner W., and Jordan, Robert T. "Quantitative Criteria for Adequacy of Academic Library
    Collections." *College and Research Libraries* 26 (September 1965): 371–380.
Cline, Gloria S. "Application of Bradford's Law to Citation Data." *College and Research Libraries*
    42 (January 1981): 53–61.
Comer, Cynthia. "List-Checking as a Method for Evaluating Library Collections." *Collection Build-
    ing* 3 (1981): 26–34.
"An Evaluative Checklist for Reviewing a College Library Program." *College and Research Library
    News* 40 (November 1979): 305–316.
Evans, Edward G. *Developing Library Collections.* Littleton, CO: Libraries Unlimited, 1979.
Fitzgibbons, Shirley A. "Citation Analysis in the Social Sciences." In Robert D. Stueart and George
    B. Miller, eds., *Collection Development in Libraries,* 291–344. Greenwich, CT: JAI Press,
    1980.
Gardner, Richard K. *Library Collections: Their Origin, Selection and Development.* New York:
    McGraw-Hill, 1981.
Goehlert, Robert. "Books Availability and Delivery Service." *Journal of Academic Librarianship* 4
    (November 1978): 368–371.
Golden, Barbra. "A Method for quantitatively Evaluating a University Library Collection." *Library
    Resources and Technical Services* 18 (Summer 1974): 268–174.
Goldhor, Herbert. "Analysis of an Inductive Method of Evaluating the Book Collection of a Public
    Library." *Libri* 23 (March 1973): 6–17.
Goldhor, Herbert, ed. *Research Methods in Librarianship: Measurement and Evaluation.* Cham-
    paign, IL: University of Illinois Graduate School of Library Science, 1968.
Harris, C. "A Comparison of Issues and In-Library Use of Books." *ASLIB Proceedings* 27 (March
    1977): 118–126.
Holt, Mae L. "Collection Evaluation: A Managerial Tool." *Collection Management* 3 (Winter
    1979): 279.
Kantor, Paul B. "Availability Analysis." *Journal of the American Society for Information Science*
    27 (September 1976): 311–319.
Kaser, David. "Library School Libraries." *Journal of Education for Librarianship* 5 (Summer
    1964): 17–19.
Kent, Allen et al. *Use of Library Materials: The University of Pittsburgh Study.* New York: Marcel
    Dekker, Inc., 1979.
Kiewitt, Eva L. "Reference Collections of Accredited Library School Programs." *Journal of Educa-
    tion for Librarianship* 19 (Summer 1978): 55–59.
Kindlin, Jean, and Engle, June. "Library School Libraries." In Allen Kent, Harold Lancour, and Jay
    E. Daily, eds., *Encyclopedia of Library and Information Science,* vol. 16, pp. 1–22. New York:
    Marcel Dekker, 1975.
Knightly, John J. "Overcoming the Criterion Problem in the Evaluation of Library Performance."
    Special Libraries 70 (April 1979): 173–178.

Lancaster, F. W. "Evaluating Collections by Their Use." *Collection Management* 4 (Spring/Summer 1982): 15–43.

Lancaster, F. W. "Measurement and Evaluation." *ALA Yearbook 1982*. Chicago: American Library Association, 1981.

Lancaster, F. W. *The Measurement and Evaluation of Library Services*. Washington, DC: Information Resources Press, 1977.

Levine, Marilyn M. "The Circulation/Acquisition Ratio: An Input–Output Measure for Libraries." *Information Processing and Management* 16 (1980): 313–315.

Liaison Committee on Medical Education. *Accreditation of Medical Colleges*. N.p., 1979.

Liaison Committee on Medical Education. *Accreditation of Schools of medicine: Policy Documents and Guidelines*. N.p., n.d.

Lopez, Manuel D. "A Guide for Beginning Bibliographers." *Library Resources and Technical Services* 13 (Fall 1969: 462–470.

Lyle, Guy R. *The Administration of the College Library*, 4th ed. New York: Wilson, 1974.

McGrath, William E. "Correlating the Subjects of Books Taken Out and Books Used Within an Open-Stack Library." *College and Research Libraries* 32 (July 1971): 280–285.

McInnis, R. Marvin. "The Formula Approach to Library Size: An Empirical Study of Its Efficacy in Evaluating Research Libraries." *College and Research Libraries* 33 (May 1972): 190–198.

Mosher, Paul H. "Collection Evaluation in Research Libraries: The Search for Quality, Consistency, and System in Collection Development." *Library Resources and Technical Services* 23 (Winter 1979): 16–32.

Mosher, Paul H. "Collection Evaluation or Analysis: Matching Library Acquisitions to Library Needs." in Robert D. Stueart and George B. Miller, eds., *Collection Development in Libraries*, pp. 527–545. Greenwich, CT: JAI Press, 1980.

National Architectural Accrediting Board. *1976/1977 Annual Report*. New York: National Architectural Accrediting Board, n.d.

National Association of Schools of Music. *A Basic Music Library for Schools Offering Undergraduate Degrees in Music*. Reston, VA: National Association of Schools of Music, 1970.

National Association of Schools of Music. *Handbook 1981*. Reston, VA: National Association of Schools of Music, 1981.

National Council for Accreditation of Teacher Education. *Standards for the Accreditation of Teacher Education*. Washington, D.C.: National Council for Accreditation of Teacher Education, 1982.

National League for Nursing. *Criteria for the Appraisal of Baccalaureate and Higher Degree Programs in Nursing*, 4th ed. New York: National League for Nursing, 1977.

New, Doris E., and Ott, Retha Zane. "Interlibrary Loan Analysis as a Collection Development Tool." *Library Resources and Technical Services* 18 (Summer 1974): 275–283.

Nisonger, Thomas E. "An Annotated Bibliography of Items Relating to Collection Evaluation in Academic Libraries, 1969–1981." *College and Research Libraries* 43 (July 1982): 300–311.

Nisonger, Thomas E. "An In-Depth Collection Evaluation at the University of Manitoba Library: A Test of the Lopez Method." *Library Resources and Technical Services* 24 (Fall 1980): 329–338.

Orr, Richard H. et al., "Development of Methodologic Tools for Planning and Managing Library Services: II. Measuring a Library's Capability for Providing Documents." *Bulletin of the Medical Library Association* 56 (July 1968): 241–267.

Orr, Richard H., and Schless, Arthur P. "Document Delivery Capabilities of Major Biomedical Libraries in 1968: Results of a National Survey Employing Standardized Tests." *Bulletin of the Medical Library Association* 60 (July 1972): 382–422.

Ottersen, Signe. "A Bibliography on Standards for Evaluating Libraries." *Colleges and Research Libraries* 32 (March 1971): 127–144.

Penner, Rudolf Jacob. "Measuring a Library's Capability." *Journal of Education for Librarianship* 13 (Summer 1972): 17–30.

Power, C. J., and Bell, G. H. "Automated Circulation, Patron Satisfaction and Collection Evaluation in Academic Libraries—A Circulation Analysis Formula," *Journal of Library Automation* 11 (December 1978): 366–399.

Rose, Priscilla. "Innovation and Evaluation of Libraries and Library Services." *Drexel Library Quarterly* 7 (January 1971): 28–41.

Schad, Jasper G. et al. *Journal of Academic Librarianship* 5 (May 1979): 60–70.

Simmons, Peter. "Improving Collections through Computer Analysis of Circulation Records in a University Library." *Proceedings of the American Society of Information Science* 7 (1970): 59–63.

Stankus, Tony, and Rice, Barbra. "Handle with Care: Use and Citation Data for Science Journal Management." *Collection Management* 4 (Spring/Summer 1982): 95–110.

Subramanyam, Kris. "Citation Studies in Science and Technology." In Robert D. Stueart and George B. Miller, eds., *Collection Development in Libraries*, pp. 345–372. Greenwich, CT: JAI Press, 1980.

Trueswell, Richard W. "Determining the Optimal Number of Volumes for a Library's Core Collection." *Libri* 16 (March 1966): 49–60.

Urquhart, John A., and Schofield, J. L. "Measuring Readers' Failure at the Shelf in Three University Libraries." *Journal of Documentation* 28 (September 1972): 233–241.

Whaley, John H. "An Approach to Collection Analysis." *Library Resources and Technical Services* 25 (July/September 1981): 339–338.

White, G. Travis. "Quantitative Measures of Library Effectiveness." *The Journal of Academic Librarianship* 3 (July 1977): 128–136.

Yancheff, Catherine. *Criteria for Collection Analysis in the Academic Library.* Arlington, VA: Educational Resources Information Center, 1978.

INTEGRATED LIBRARY SYSTEM AND PUBLIC SERVICES

Marcia L. Sprules

INTRODUCTION

Automation of library processes has been a great concern to the profession for a long time. Typewriters and photocopy machines, for example, changed technical services profoundly by eliminating the hand-written catalog card. Quick duplication of cards made it possible to have multiple copies of the unit-card at appropriate entry points in the catalog, rather than only one "main entry." Possible applications of computer technologies have been of considerable interest to at least one generation of librarians. As technological improvements have made computing power more affordable, interest is spreading from the largest research libraries to the smallest libraries. As computing power increases, our ambitions and expectations rise as well, until we ask for an integrated library system that will do everything.

Advances in Library Administration and Organization
Volume 5, pages 139–154
Copyright © 1986 by JAI Press Inc.
All rights of reproduction in any form reserved.
ISBN: 0-89232-674-3

As an operating definition of an *integrated library system* we may use "an automated system that performs multiple library functions from a shared, common database." Such systems frequently include both technical services functions (such as acquisitions, cataloging, or serials check-in) and public service functions (circulation and an on-line catalog). Other services frequently included are film bookings or room scheduling. The breadth of the system is limited only by the imagination of the library staff, not by technical requirements of the computer hardware.

It is important to state at the outset that the true integrated system does not yet exist. Advertisements from vendors use the phrase very glibly to describe all sorts of products, but all have more limitations than the ideal. Numerous systems are available that perform several functions from one database, but the user will always want more. OCLC is a familiar example of a system that began by automating one function (cataloging) and has subsequently added others (acquisitions, interlibrary loan), but it, too, does not (yet) do everything.

The development of these systems is going to bring profound changes in the way the library performs its role in society. During this transition period it is important that we reconsider what we do, how we do it, and why we do it that way. At the end of this transition period, librarians would certainly hope to provide better service to our users than we have in the past. This paper focuses on changes that are likely to occur in public services, but those changes are going to be dependent on actions and changes that take place in technical services. Thus, continued dialog between the two is going to be necessary, and will probably need to occur with greater frequency and greater depth. Although parts of this paper are rather speculative and conceptual, it is hoped that some of the questions raised will spark this needed reassessment.

THE DATABASE

Because all of the functions in the system are going to share a database, they will all stand or fall on the quality of the database created. Essentially the library already has a database describing its holdings: the card catalog. Both the strengths and the weaknesses of the traditional card catalog are well known and do not need to be repeated here. However, it would not be either wise or good library service exactly to replicate the card catalog in an automated form. Its features need to be reconsidered.

The early automated catalog systems did essentially replicate the card catalog and have only the same approaches already familiar in card files. In effect, they do the same thing, only they do it faster. Given hardware constraints that existed previously and the high cost of memory capacity, such limitations were undoubtedly necessary. Furthermore, such systems continue to provide acceptable catalogs where they are installed. Also due to the high cost of memory, some of the early catalogs have abbreviated records, perhaps as sparse as author, title, date, and call number. Such records serve their systems well, but cannot be upgraded to allow searching by subject.

Hardware costs have been reduced dramatically in recent years. It is now feasible and affordable to store the full MARC record, which averages about 750 characters, in a reasonably sized computer. There is no longer any question but that the full record should be stored. At the initial design stage, not every library will necessarily have an immediate use for each and every field, but after several years the system may expand in directions not originally imagined, and in directions that require additional elements of the MARC record. In such a case, the programming and implementation of the expanded features will be greatly simplified if the data are already there. Rekeying the record to augment sparse data is prohibitively expensive, not to mention foolhardy.

CONTENT OF DATABASE

There are currently eight MARC formats supported by the Library of Congress: monographs, serials, maps, audiovisuals, manuscripts, machine-readable data files, scores, and sound recordings. There is no technical reason why library materials in any of these formats should be excluded from the integrated system.

Most libraries have at least a few "special collections" that are not listed in the main card catalog. As an extreme example, when they started to create an on-line catalog, California State University at Chico discovered that they had 57 separate and unique collections, not listed in the main catalog.[1] A smaller library would probably have fewer, but no one has none. Librarians are so used to this fact of life that we do not often question the wisdom of the separate collection, but the users probably do. I doubt whether many of them have the patience and perseverance to look in 57 separate places for the information or material they need.

Some of these special collections, such as the pamphlet file, are separate because the materials are not substantial enough to justify full cataloging. It is not necessary to perform full cataloging to add materials to the integrated database. For vertical file materials, a single entry which says

245– Wounded Knee Massacre

710– Wounded Knee Massacre

590– For additional material on this topic, see the pamphlet file

would probably suffice. All that is needed is enough information to alert the user to the fact that the library has materials of interest that are not necessarily in book

form. Very simple author-and-title cataloging should be sufficient for many of
these collections:

110 Minnesota Mining and Manufacturing Co.

240 Annual Report

590 Latest three years kept behind Reference Desk

Addition of such special materials to the database is necessary if the new system is to deserve the title "integrated." What is even more basic to librarianship,
addition of such records to the catalog will do a lot to foster the goals espoused
by the Paris Principles and other fundamental documents of cataloging practice.
At present, the card catalog does not truly bring together and list all of the materials the library has. Reference librarians often observe that users leave the library after looking only in the card catalog, thinking the library does not have
what they wanted, when in fact the material was in an uncataloged location.

Such discouragement among users does not enhance the library's standing in
the community. To the average user, libraries must look rather chaotic. Apparently, it is not possible to go in and look in one place to find out what the library
has. Some users must wonder how the staff knows what they have. Low social
esteem and unfavorable stereotypes follow naturally from such unpleasant experiences and from apparent chaos. Likewise, the popular opinion that anyone can
run a library follows logically from the fact that we seem to do it so poorly.

An integrated library system, then, should serve a dual purpose: to improve
the quality of library service we offer to users, and their ease in obtaining service, and to enhance our professionalism.

AUTHORITY CONTROL

In order to reflect accurately the collection of a library, the card catalog must
provide authority control records for both main entries and subject headings.
Cross-references on cards are confusing to some users, and they may overlook
some potentially useful material. A good automated catalog should display results from a valid heading even though the user enters the invalid form. Either
"Twain, Mark" or "Clemens, Samuel Langhorne" should produce the same list
of materials owned. Whenever there is a simple one-to-one cross-reference, this
should occur.

However, in the case of a *see also* record, the choices of headings should be
displayed so the user can choose the most appropriate. This should be true of
alternate subject headings, as well as for multiple pseudonyms of some prolific
authors and name changes of corporate bodies.

ACCESS POINTS

Once the record is in the database, methods of access need to be considered. Traditionally, the card catalog offers three: named person or corporate body, titles by which the work is known (including alternate titles, earlier titles, and series title), and subject headings. However, additional access points become possible with the automated system. Title access is currently possible by the first word only; the record will be lost if that critical first word is lost. Subtitles often are more memorable than their main title, for example. It might be beneficial to make subtitles, as well as main titles, searchable.

Some interesting research has been done on what exactly users know about a book when they come to the library and what they remember about a book they have previously used. William S. Cooper[2] did quite an exhaustive study of memorability by having a group of volunteers look over a collection of books, then sometime later try to pick out the ones they had previously seen. In essence, he found that nonstandard characteristics, such as color, can partially aid such retrieval, but they work best in combination. Depending on the number of factors remembered, the number of cards to be scanned could be reduced by as much as a 500-to-1 ratio.

Clearly, as Don R. Swanson has pointed out, "future catalogs should incorporate principles of redundancy and multiple access routes to a much greater extent than they do presently."[3] This research project on design of future catalogs also considered user perseverance and search length as factors contributing to eventual success. In only 26 percent of experimental catalog searches was the item found in a search of less than 10 cards. When a subject search was performed, the average search length was 156 cards.

Some of this nonstandard information is already on the catalog card (therefore in the MARC record); examples are the presence of an index, bibliography, or illustrations, number of pages, height, or whether or not the work is a translation. We hope that the users of the card catalog will scan the cards and use such clues to help them decide which books to look at on the shelves. During the late 1960s, Ben-Ami Lipetz and others did a great deal of work on the best method of incorporating such clues into an automated catalog. Although many of their works and their speculations were constrained by then-existing hardware and attendant costs, some of the ideas are probably applicable to today's systems. In essence, they visualized a system in which the user would specify the author's name or the subject desired, and the computer would create a temporary set of records fulfilling that request. Against this subject of the larger database, the desired limitations could be checked. Current systems can do this sort of checking much more effectively and faster than can older ones. The major database search vendors offer this limit capability in their systems, and it does indeed aid in pinpointing retrieval.

USER APPROACHES TO THE CATALOG

There is an appalling dearth of research on how library users translate a perceived information need into a query at the reference desk or a first entry into the card catalog. The literature deals with how the reference librarian can translate the questions as stated back to the underlying need. The studies of card catalog users that do exist begin after the decision has been made to approach the catalog by author, title, or subject; they do not deal with how that decision was made. Many of them are poorly done and their findings cannot be accepted without question.[4]

Certainly the most comprehensive study of the card catalog was carried out at Yale University from November 1967 to January 1969.[5] It attempted to study both the user's approach to the catalog (author, title, or subject) and his or her underlying information need. Their results support the conclusion that the user's first approach to the card catalog does not necessarily reflect the true information need. At the first attempt to find something, 73 percent of users are attempting a document search (author or title), while 16 percent are attempting a subject search. Given the well-known fact that the card catalog is better at known-item retrieval than at subject retrieval, such behavior is eminently reasonable. But, underlying this behavior, the research staff discovered that only 56 percent of the searches are really for a document as an end in itself; the remaining 17 percent are using a known item as a starting point for a subject search. Thus, the number of subject searches is not 16 percent, but 31 percent.

One possible explanation was recently suggested by Stephen F. Stoan: The primary literature in any subject field indexes itself.[6] To scholars this use of the catalog appears eminently reasonable.

This report also contains some final speculations on the possible use of computerized catalogs to enhance search capabilities. However, human adaptability in changing search approaches cannot so easily be mechanized. Human users both accept and reject catalog cards on the basis of clues contained therein. Both capabilities must be incorporated into a computerized system, or an unacceptable number of false drops will be retrieved.

One final conclusion of this paper bears out the overall need for an integrated library system. The study found that 10 percent of the attempted document searches fail because the item is really not listed in the catalog. However, within one year, one-fifth of those items had been added to the catalog. Most probably, at the time of the initial search the item was "on order" or "in process." Although such items may not always be available to the user when needed, at least it is good public relations for the library if the system will show to the user the on-order and in-process records. It says, "We anticipated your need and are trying to fill it."

This research is independently confirmed by a study at the University of Michigan by Tagliacozzo and Kochen at approximately the same time.[7] They found that in the University's General Library (which would be comparable to Yale), 71.7 percent of the searches were for a known item and 22.2 percent were subject searches. In the undergraduate and medical libraries, there was a slight reduction in known-item searches (to 68.0 percent and 65.5 percent respectively) and a slight increase in subject searches (to 26.4 percent and 32.4 percent respectively). In the Ann Arbor Public Library, however, the ratio was much more nearly even (49.5 percent known-item searches to 41.6 percent subject searches). Of course, it is not a startling discovery that public library users are different from academic library users. However, this does point out that in a multitype library consortium, catalog records must be designed to accommodate several types of users.

This study further confirms that some known-item catalog searches may be subject searches. A follow-up questionnaire given to users of the medical library and the undergraduate library revealed that 80.8 percent and 76.5 percent (respectively) of searchers had browsed additional titles on the shelf they had not found in the card catalog. Of these browsers, 39.5 percent and 27.4 percent (respectively) had actually checked out at least one book located by browsing and not through the card catalog at all. Although the authors of the article do not so state, it is possible that some of these users came to the library with a subject search disguised as a known-item search, intending to use a document they already knew as an entré to the subject.

There are many other studies of card catalog users that I will not discuss here. However, none of them are as well done or as reliable as the two cited in this paper. Apparently, no studies at all have tackled how users formulate a strategy for locating information. Empirical observation would suggest that information-seeking behavior is ad hoc and relatively unplanned. Tagliacozzo and Kochen, too, were forced to comment on the naive users they encountered. They feel that the user's attitude has at least as much to do with searching success as does previous experience or skill.

The Council on Library Resources recently funded an exhaustive and detailed study of the existing on-line catalogs.[8] The data they gathered were largely demographic and attitudinal. The report tells us who is likely to prefer the on-line catalog and how users and nonusers feel about the catalog, but it does not tell us how these same users approach the catalog or what their habits are when they are seeking information.

CHOICE OF ACCESS POINT

The preceding research implies that at least some users try to do subject searches through a known document. Some naive library users try to look under subject for a work whose author and/or title they know from a course reading list or other printed bibliography. Both of these anomalous behavior patterns underscore the need for continuing user training. User behavior is unlikely to change when the catalog is automated, but it can be anticipated to some extent.

Some of the newer systems available already allow searching on individual words in authors, titles, and subject headings. Such an enhancement to the traditional catalog allows for minor lapses of memory on the part of the user. Is the correct title of that book *Handbook of Physics and Chemistry* or *Handbook of Chemistry and Physics?* Now the physicist can have his or her subject mentioned first, and the chemist can simultaneously have his or hers mentioned first.

Keyword searching would also be a great help in cases when subtitles are especially memorable. Because the search words can occur in any order, the difference between title proper and subtitle is blurred, for both user and system.

Keyword searching of the author field will enhance retrieval under two frequent and frustrating conditions: works with multiple authors when only the surnames are known, and corporate authors with extensive hierarchy. Everyone refers to a famous college chemistry textbook as "Sienko and Plane." The computer can match the lists of the two authors's books much faster than anyone can scan cards to look at added entries on the bottom. United States government agencies can be very difficult to locate because of the multiple layers of bureaucracy included in the main entry. If a user wants a congressional committee dealing with aging, it could be located with "Congress" and "Aging" rather than with the more formidable "U.S. Congress. House. Select Committee on Aging." In both of these cases, the likelihood of the user finding the material desired is enhanced by the speed of the computer when it matches two lists.

Subject retrieval in the card catalog would not be possible without some list of authorized headings to ensure that materials on any given topic will be listed together in one place. Some of the headings lists used employ terminology no longer in common use. As with titles, if the first word of the established heading is not known, nothing can be retrieved in our current card files. If subject headings are searchable by individual words, the user needing material on how television affects children can ask for the combination of "Television" with "Children" and never know that the actual heading used is "Television and Children."

In order for the search just described to work, the system will need the capability to perform Boolean operations on lists of entries. So many libraries now offer remote database searching through one of several vendors that many reference librarians take for granted the added retrieval capabilities of Boolean logic. An automated card catalog without an equal retrieval capability will seem primitive to the staff by comparison. However, the programs that allow Boolean searching to occur are long and complex; in addition, they require a much greater temporary memory space to process the request before forming the final set of answers. When computer storage and memory capacity were the limiting factors on the cost of a system, Boolean searching was too expensive for all but the largest systems. For this reason, the early automated catalogs did not offer it. But the state-of-the-art system we now want needs it.

At the very least, it should be possible to perform keyword searches on subject headings. A user should not be required to remember the precise heading "Indians of North America" but should be able to retrieve material by entering "Indians and America" or some other variation. Indeed, in a library such as the University of South Dakota, which extensively collects materials on Native Americans, we probably need to use more specific headings, such as the tribal name "Sioux Indians," or even the subtribe (at least for Sioux).

Such a finer division would make it possible for the library user to pinpoint the materials of greatest interest, without wading through the thousands of subject cards in two-and-one-half drawers. Consider the following cards:

INDIANS OF NORTH AMERICA.

E   Cattermole, E   G
85   Famous frontiersmen, pioneers and scouts;
C3.6   the vanguards of American civilization . . .
1884   including Boone, Crawford, Girty, Molly
             Finney, the McCulloughs . . . Captain Jack,
             Buffalo Bill, General Custer with his last
             campaign against Sitting Bull, and General
             Crook with his recent campaign against the
             Apaches. By E. G. Cattermole . . . Chicago, The
             Coburn & Newman publishing company, 1884
                xvi, [17]-540 p. front., illus. (incl.
             ports) 20 cm.

INDIANS OF NORTH AMERICA—BASKET MAKING.

         Morris, Earl Halstead, 1889-
98   Anasazi basketry, Basket maker II through
B3   Pueblo III, a study based on specimens from the
M7   San Juan river country [by] Earl H. Morris [and]
         Robert F. Burgh . . . Washington, D. C. [Carnegie
         institution of Washington] 1941.
            viii, 66 p. front., 43 pl. (incl. fold. map,
         tables) on 27 ⟨. 29 × 23 cm. (Carnegie insti-
         tution of Washington. Publications 533)
            Part of the plates accompanied by leaf with
         descriptive letterpress, not included in the
         paging.
            "References": p. 65-66.
            1. Indians of   North America—Basket
         making. I. Bur   gh, Robert Frederic,
         1907-   II.   Title.

In the first case, there should be a subject heading for each of the individuals named in that long subtitle. Otherwise, the catalog does not really bring together all of the books the library owns on Sitting Bull. In the second case, a heading for the Anasazi (an extinct people) would distinguish this book from others on contemporary basket making.

SEARCHABLE PARAGRAPHS

In the traditional card catalog, users expect to be able to look for a book in any one of three ways. When establishing a new system, it will be necessary to choose which fields of the MARC record are to be searched for the desired records and which should be displayed in the result but not searched. In order to equal the manual card catalogs, all author, title, subject, and added entry fields need to be searched (MARC tags 1—, 2—, 6—, 7—, 8—, 9—). In addition, there is much valuable information in series titles (which are often neglected in card catalogs) and in notes, such as earlier titles, original titles, contents of a collection, and others. Although usually there has not been room for the additional cards in the wood cabinets, or staff time available to file them, valuable information supplied by the catalogers has been lost. It would be well to consider adding those fields to the searchable part of the database.

It is true that more access points will require a larger computer memory to run the system and that the cost of the hardware is still a consideration in picking a system. At some point it becomes necessary to balance cost against desired services, but such balancing should be done with a critical eye on the status quo and should not assume that past practices are necessarily best.

UPDATING THE DATABASE

Technical services staff are going to be using this integrated system, as well as the public. Therefore, it will be possible to add new records to the public catalog the same day they are cataloged. Meeting user demand for popular new titles has always been a race against the wind. Daily updating of the database would help.

The acquisition staff will be adding records as well. These may be incomplete, as full cataloging data is not always available if a book is ordered at or before the time of publication. Such records, partial though they be, should be added to the public database. It is good public relations for the library if the user wanting a new bestseller finds a record in the library's catalog saying, "We anticipated your request and are trying to meet it." Paper files of on-order requests have usually been inaccessible to the public, back in the technical services area.

Pennsylvania State University's LIAS allows these partial acquisitions records to be upgraded by properly authorized staff to full cataloging.[9] Although this process is occurring behind the scenes, the material is available to circulate if anyone wants it. Careful analysis of work flow and procedures has considerably streamlined operations.

Frequency of updating the database is also an important question. If the library does its cataloging through a utility, the records must be transferred from the utility computer to the local computer. Technologically, this is relatively easy to do; politically, it is very difficult. Extra contractual arrangements are necessary to obtain authorization to reuse data from the utility. Archival tapes are often available, containing the input of one's own institution. But often these tapes are sent at irregular intervals or at long intervals (monthly, for example).

An automated catalog that is updated only monthly is not an improvement over the manual system. The new books (the very ones users will ask for) won't be included. Pennsylvania State University's library does a great deal of input themselves, despite using the utilities to locate copy. This local inputting is necessary in order to perform frequent updating (daily would be ideal).

OTHER NECESSARY FEATURES

Most of the features discussed so far are primarily for the use of the public catalog facet of the system. However, other departments such as circulation will be keeping their records on the same system. Therefore, the database must include additional fields of information not normally found in the card catalog, but necessary in order to circulate the item. These include, for example, an identifying number for each copy of a work (if multiple copies are owned), or for each volume of a multivolume set, or for each bound volume of a journal, or for each circulating piece of media.

Such numbers do not need to display to anyone except the circulation department staff at the time of charging or discharging the item. However, the on-line catalog should inform the user if an item is checked out. How frustrating it is to find what one wants in the catalog only to find it is out, after the user has walked all the way to the stacks! If the library has multiple branches throughout the city or around the campus, the circulation records for all branches should be accessible in all other locations so that copies can be made available if they are needed elsewhere.

INTERLIBRARY LOAN

Interlibrary loan librarians have been using systems like OCLC to ascertain locations of books for a decade or more. In a multilibrary system, such as the Minnesota State University System, it is most beneficial if the interlibrary loan staff can ascertain not only who owns the title, but whether it is available. A request to borrow sent to a library other than the closest may produce the material more expeditiously than a request to the nearby library whose copy is out. It may not be necessary for the general public to use this information all the time, but only authorized staff. Anything that can be done to speed delivery of the document to the user's hands can only help our library service.

TRAINING OF USERS

Because teaching users to use the traditional card catalog and other library tools usually has fallen to the public services staff, they can expect to bear the brunt of training users with the new automated catalog as well. One hears and reads a lot of speculation about how best to train users to use "the terminal." This question has been stated in the wrong terms; many of our users are already familiar with terminals. Children use microcomputers in school, adults have terminals of many kinds at their workplace, many families have a personal computer at home. Some colleges even require that all students purchase a personal computer for their course work. The mechanics of using the terminal should come easily to such persons.

The problem is the same one we have always faced: how best to teach people the intellectual process of locating something in the catalog. An automated system will not change this task. The scope of the undertaking is truly Herculean: to train all those users how to ask a question. Because no research has been done on how users formulate their questions, there is little foundation available on which to build. The research on user questions posed at the reference desk deals with how the reference librarian can best approach the questions as posed, and how to ascertain the true information need disguised as a question. The studies of card catalog users, as discussed earlier, deal with requirements to locate a known item either from a printed bibliographic reference or from previous exposure. But it will be necessary to extend this work one additional step backward to the user's first perception of needing some material, if we are to know how the questions originate.

Automated catalogs can be much less forgiving of minor errors than the card catalog is. Spelling errors are an obvious example. The computer will not "know what you mean" if there is an error in the question, in the way that another person will. In many cases, seeing the word spelled properly on a card will jog the memory of the user to the correct spelling, and he or she can alter the search strategy immediately. No rekeying is necessary to alter the approach with cards.

Some of the on-line catalogs available on the market today require the user to specify whether the search term is the author's name, the title, or the subject. The user who does not enter the field specification at all will get no results; the user who specifies the wrong one will get an erroneous negative answer. In the dictionary card catalog, the user will find the entry if he or she gets to the right part of the alphabet. The kinds of distinctions catalogers have always made among types of entries will become more important with the advent of the on-line catalog.

Mankato State University (Minnesota) reports very great success with peer instructors—students employed by the library and trained to assist other students using the on-line catalog. Because students (all library users) will ask questions everywhere except at the reference desk, this method of user assistance is a natural. Informally, it occurs anyway. Many libraries report that users help each other liberally with catalog terminals. Such peer assistance should be encouraged. If students already employed in the library are given additional training in using the on-line catalog, they can assist their peers and relieve some of the pressure on the reference librarian.

An ongoing and intensive user-awareness campaign should begin well before the system is installed. Users should be encouraged to submit comments and suggestions to the library staff. The University of California, Berkeley, had a particularly effective campaign called "Ask Cat-Fiche." Cat-Fiche was the mascot for their system, a wise-looking feline; he appeared on all promotional and instructional aids prepared for the system. Disguised as Cat-Fiche, librarians would respond to user inquiries concerning real difficulties actually experienced in using the system. Questions of general interest were answered in more general announcements. In this way the user community was kept informed of system progress.

One thing is certain, however: it is necessary to start now. Before the terminals are installed and while the system is still in the design phase, the staff member in charge of user education should be at work developing new instructional materials and developing a methodology to deliver instruction to as many people as possible.

Before the system is installed, there will be some anxieties to allay, particularly among users who are attached to the traditional ways of doing things. Those who have computer anxiety in other aspects of life (such as banking) will exhibit anxiety about the library's computer also. In such cases, it may help to point out that the new system will continue to do all the things that the old card catalog did but will add to those additional features not previously possible. If the staff have a positive and enthusiastic attitude, users will probably be positive and enthusiastic as well.

To keep staff attitudes positive and enthusiastic, it is necessary to keep *all* staff informed of the development of the system. If some staff feel left out or threatened by the computer, they will communicate their fears to the public. Another facet of Berkeley's Cat-Fiche campaign was an attempt to help staff members answer user questions accurately. Anticipated and actual questions were included in the staff newsletter, with suggested answers. These answers were designed to be not only accurate and informative but also were given in a positive, upbeat manner in order to convey enthusiasm on the part of the staff. Nothing will undermine the public relations campaign as quickly as an unenthusiastic staff member.

Among reference librarians who offer on-line database searching, there is some debate over the wisdom of teaching end users to perform their own searches. With an on-line catalog, the issue does not arise; end users must do their own searches, just as they do in the current card catalogs. For this reason the "dialog" between the user and the computer is very important. Charles Hildreth of OCLC has written a very fine summary and critique of the existing systems, their capabilities, and their dialog modes.[10] To an astounding degree, the dialogs currently available are replete with "biblish," terms and jargon of librarianship that are jibberish to the users.

An on-line help function is essential in a public use system. Well-written help messages will take some of the burden off the reference staff by enabling the user to solve his or her problem independently. Poorly written help messages will add to the burden of the reference staff, as they will be asked to interpret the help screen as well as to solve the user's initial problem. It is surprisingly difficult and time-consuming to write help screens that are both jargon-free ("user friendly"), accurate, and helpful to the user.

Turnkey systems should, of course, include a "Help" function before a purchase. Authorization to change the messages, should an improvement suggest itself, will keep the system current to changing needs. Some of the current systems require the purchasing library to write all the screens from nothing. This is not an ideal arrangement, as most librarians will not be expert at the semantic and syntactical subtleties necessary to create effective help screens. Some guide or starting point is extremely helpful when trying to create tailored screens.

It is surprising how many different screens are necessary if the help offered is to be situation specific. The user will encounter different problems with subject searches than with author searches, and the help screens should be appropriately different in those two situations. Northwestern University's NOTIS catalog includes 27 different help screens in its system in order to be as situation specific as they wish to be. The more functions are included in the total system, the more screens will be necessary. As "on-order" and "in-process" records are added to the database, additional explanatory material must be added to the help screens, or additional screens must be created.

A tutorial program to guide novice users through a sample search should be another part of the system. Such a tutorial allows people to learn at their own pace and at a convenient time. As with any other computer-assisted-instruction (CAI) module, a point can be repeated until it is mastered, with only occasional help from a staff member.

After the initial learning process, users are quick to assist each other in further learning. The library staff should probably encourage it. Often several people can figure out a problem collectively better than a solitary individual can. If the staff are available as resource persons to solve some of the difficult problems or to explain some of the quirks of the system, they can be of great help to the users. At the same time, they will not get bogged down in the routine matters of doing simple look-ups for everyone.

CONCLUSION

Many fine systems are available on the market for the library wishing to automate. Some of these now provide multiple functions from a single, shared database (such as circulation and an on-line public-access catalog). But the true integrated system, one that will do everything from a single terminal, does not yet exist. Like the sun rising on a cloudy morning, it looms beyond the horizon, illuminating our efforts but not yet directly visible.

Large research libraries have been using and seriously researching automation for approximately 15 years. Advances in hardware technology have simultaneously increased the power and reduced the costs of computers large enough to process the textual records a library requires. As a result, automation is now being seen in medium-sized and even in small libraries. There is a danger that the profession may use the new automation to do the same things faster, but in the same traditional way as before. As long as routines are changing anyway, to incorporate the new equipment, it is a good time to ask "why," as well as "how," things are done. We have been offered the opportunity to improve the quality, as well as the speed, of our services to users. In order to take full advantage of the opportunity, however, we need to ask some fundamental questions of Why? and to question long-sacred precepts of the profession. It is never easy to ask those questions, let alone to answer them.

But once the new databases are created and the systems installed, it will again be prohibitively expensive to make very many substantial, after-the-fact changes. The opportunity will not last forever, and is too good to lose.

NOTES AND REFERENCES

1. William E. Post, and Peter G. Watson, eds., *Online Catalog: the Inside Story, A Planning and Implementation Guide*. Chicago: (Ryan Research, 1983).

2. William S. Cooper, "The Potential Usefulness of Catalog Access Points Other than Author, Title, and Subject." *Journal of the American Society for Information Science* 21 (March-April 1970): 117–127.

3. Don R. Swanson, "Requirements Study for Future Catalogs." *Library Quarterly* 42(3) (July 1972): 302–315.

4. For a representative list and critical discussion of such studies, see ibid.

5. Ben-Ami Lipetz, *User Requirements in Identifying Desired Works in a Large Library* (New Haven: Yale University, 1970).

6. Stephen F. Stoan, "Research and Library Skills: An Analysis and Interpretation." *College and Research Libraries* 45(2) (March 1984): 99–109.

7. R. Tagliacozzo, and M. Kochen, "Information-Seeking Behavior of Catalog Users." *Information Storage and Retrieval* 6 (1970): 363–381.

8.   Joseph R. Matthews; Gary S. Lawrence; and Douglas K. Ferguson, eds., *Using Online Catalogs A Nationwide Survey* (New York: Neal-Schuman, 1983).

9.   David C. Genaway, ed., *Conference on Integrated Online Library Systems Proceedings* (Canfield, Ohio: Genaway & Associates, 1983).

10.   Charles R. Hildreth, *Online Catalogs: The User Interface* (Columbus, Ohio: OCLC, Inc., 1983).

BIBLIOGRAPHIC INSTRUCTION (BI):
EXAMINATION OF CHANGING EMPHASIS

Fred Batt

INITIAL CONSIDERATIONS: THE BI LITERATURE

Why another instruction paper? Noting the inherent controversy, Watson wrote, "The reference librarian who ventures to address the subject of library use instruction does so at the considerable risk of alienating at least half of his or her readers."[1] If that's not discouraging enough, Coleman's words add some guilt. "Reference departments . . . would do well to stop feuding about library instruction and start reaping its benefits."[2] Should I persist?

What else can be written about BI? How can the praises be sung one more time? How many "how we did it good" articles can be published? An examination of 934-item selective bibliography on library instruction published in 1979 displays how round and round we were going up to a half dozen years ago. Even the editor, Deborah Lockwood, points out the redundancy of much of the materials, a lack of conceptual framework, and an abundance of "how-to" articles.[3]

Advances in Library Administration and Organization
Volume 5, pages 155–178
Copyright © 1986 by JAI Press Inc.
All rights of reproduction in any form reserved.
ISBN: 0-89232-674-3

Sometimes I believe that the BI literature is barking up the wrong tree. Rather than "how-to," I'd like to read more of "how not to." Rather than "how we did it good," I'd like to read "how we failed." I've dreamed of a library science text or series titled something like "Great Plans, High Expectations: How We Goofed," perhaps a *Journal of Negative Results* approach. For BI, it might be instructive to learn by negative example. I recently heard a library administrator mention at a workshop that her best training was from observing what was ludicrous in the administrative approaches of her previous directors. (Everyone scampered to her biography.) Roberts wrote that her book was "the result of a thoughtful analysis of what, over the years, has been tried and has worked."[4] Perhaps a careful analysis of what hasn't worked might also yield constructive information. Bodi recently reinforced my feelings in the conclusion of her "Research Note." Rationalizing why she was writing about a BI program that has yet to be proven successful, she noted, "If it's a flop, I certainly won't write about it."[5]

I often feel frustrated with both the BI literature and BI itself. First I'll deal with the literature. I suppose librarians write about BI and reinvent the wheel so frequently because it is so obvious. Anyone who has spent time at a college or university reference desk, particular a busy one, is quickly hit over the head with the need for some type of mass education. Even my use of the term BI could create disagreement among some groups of library instruction connoisseurs. In the process of going around in circles, agreement on even basic nomenclature is difficult. I recently listened to an individual interviewing for a position who received her MLS in the late 1960s and an Advanced Study Degree in 1984. She mentioned her recent discovery and surprise that "they were talking about BI in the 1970s." I wanted to interrupt and tell her about the century plus of academic library-user-education analysis offered by Tucker,[6] or W. F. Poole's words in 1893 about the relations of the university library to university education,[7] or Peyton Hurt's 1934 article treating the need for library-use instruction,[8] or Hopkin's analysis of a century of bibliographic instruction,[9] and many other references reaching back to the nineteenth century.

Yet, her unawareness of the past brought back memories of my own naiveté a dozen years ago when I thought I had discovered BI. I wrote a short article in late 1972, submitted it to a journal in 1974, and finally discovered it published in the journal three years later. Like most people who wrote about instruction, I did make some sense. I couldn't understand how an integral part of education could "not include the location of past, present, and future information." I believed that

the library should be a more integral part of the teaching program" and proposed "one interrelated information system coordinating teaching faculty, research faculty and information specialists . . . For any given course a student would have to interact with each of these three sources of information . . . The end result would hopefully be a student who has a knowledge of the subject matter as well as a feel for the most efficient methods of locating information.[10]

Pie in the sky? Ironically, I've noticed similar articles before and after my contribution in the same journal.

The BI literature can literally drive you mad. Initially my strategy for this paper was to completely analyze the literature, and then step back from it to analyze the concepts that really need to be conveyed to different levels of academic library users and how this might best be accomplished. This approach presents two problems: (1) My space would have been filled up by just a bibliography. Anyhow, readers of this publication should already be familiar with the literature, and (2) My submission, as I retired from the library field in a strait jacket, would have probably been sent from the State Hospital. In the span of a few months of the literature, I found articles vehemently noting how BI should be administered completely outside the confines of reference services but other articles reasoning how closely interrelated BI and reference service were. I read a series of articles pushing for a theoretical understanding of library research by students instead of an emphasis on specific research tools (i.e., teaching how to use specific indices has been criticized). Then I read an article stating that "stimulating intellectual interest in scholarly communication and bibliographic structure is an exciting and worthwhile goal, but its value is diminished if the learner acquires only a theoretical understanding without practical skills" and that "the acquisition of basic library skills should serve as the cornerstone of bibliographic instruction."[11] Contradictions abound. Repetition abounds.

I would love to have a dollar for every time someone wrote or said that instruction is meaningless unless it is "course-related." It reminds me of a psychological word-association game. A bunch of librarians who do book reviews upon hearing the words *collection of papers,* would immediately respond *uneven.* In the same manner, the letters *BI* would elicit the response *course-related* from the majority of BI librarians.

Admittedly, things have improved somewhat since Lockwood's desire for BI conceptual frameworks. Although we are still barraged by BI literature, it is beginning to change. A recent book edited by Oberman and Strauch provides a number of theoretical frameworks by a variety of contributors.[12] Parson desires to make critical thinking a top BI priority and offers a "new paradigm . . . to move libraries from their passive stance to proactive orientation."[13] Roberts offers a "holistic approach in which users take the responsibility for meeting their own information needs, and in which librarians are the educators, teachers, and facilitators."[14] Tuckett and Stoffle treats the self-reliant library user by incorporating a cognitive learning theory model into BI methodology.[15] Many others could be cited. This new wave of BI literature includes some eloquent writing and good logic that holds some promise for the future, but is often hard to apply for the librarian in a large university trying to offer some kind of systematic instructional program with limited time and shrinking resources. Some individuals also believe that these new conceptual frameworks don't really change our instruction behavior. We keep on doing basically the same things, perhaps with a bit more confidence.

I've decided not to spend much space examining thousands of pages of testimonies and conceptual pieces in a wide array of library and related journals (including *Research Strategies* devoted completely to BI and journal issues devoted specifically to BI, for instance, *Library Trends, The Reference Librarian, Catholic Library World*); numerous newsletters; proceedings of 14 Library Instruction Conferences at Eastern Michigan University, The Southern Conference on Approaches to Bibliographic Instruction, many regional and state conferences with BI themes; publications, policy statements, model statements of objectives, etc. of ALA, ACRL, and other organizational round tables, sections, and task forces; numerous ERIC documents; edited books of readings; monographs (hundreds of clusters in the book file of RLIN); foreign publications; collections at LOEX as well as other depositories and clearing houses. All of this information about the powers of BI for self-reliance, life-long learning, truth, justice, and the American way becomes wearisome. It doesn't need a bibliography, but a concordance. My apologies to those whom I don't cite in my selective appraisal of the literature throughout this paper.

It might be useful here to describe my BI background. I've done well over a thousand BI sessions, reaching tens of thousands of students in a wide variety of subject areas (primarily social and behavioral sciences), using virtually every BI approach, at five academic institutions. My BI techniques have been highly evaluated at each institution and I've received dozens of unsolicited letters from faculty praising my efforts and letting me know how much information they picked up. I've had the luxury of experience at a smaller institution with a large enough staff so that I was able to reach most of the students in my assigned areas up to three times (general instruction, specialized instruction in major areas, and a few prior to graduate school). I've been at a large university with a small staff where formally reaching every student was nearly impossible and systematic levels of instruction were only a dream. My three other situations fell somewhere in between. When I think of myself in relation to BI, I think of success. Yet, through all of this, I've always had the continuous feeling that something is not quite right. There must be a better way. Many other librarians whom I hold in esteem have expressed similar feelings.

The remainder of this paper will (1) provide a short summary of what I philosophically think BI should offer in the ideal environment, (2) come back to realism by treating a series of concerns, frustrations, and even feelings of helplessness endemic in much BI, (3) examine some model BI programs, (4) present a conceptual approach to BI (i.e., what really needs to be communicated), and (5) finally present a proposal for a changing BI emphasis when the environment doesn't lend itself to the model situation.

BI IN MY IDEAL ENVIRONMENT

In my ideal environment, students want to learn, teachers want students to know, and librarians all know how to effectively teach research techniques. BI in my ideal environment should be mandatory and not dependent on the whims and bi-ases of the teaching and research faculty or even the soliciting and P.R. abilities of librarians. BI in my ideal environment should prepare the individual to effec-tively pursue research requirements during college as well as after formal educa-tion. BI should be built into the curriculum or course of study, a requirement to be met in various stages. BI in my ideal environment should also take the burden of repetition of basic techniques away from the reference desk and allow refer-ence personnel more time to pursue more complicated questions and happily to flourish in important and self-fulfilling projects. BI in my ideal environment should drastically add to the knowledge and capabilities of the librarians. Note: The best exercises I've ever had (including library school) have been what I have learned in preparation for advanced BI. You realize what you know and what you need to learn when you attempt to teach it to others. I've been thankful ever since.

BI PROBLEMS, CONCERNS, FRUSTRATIONS

My ideal environment is essentially visionary. We all work in situations that are far from perfect. Below I will treat problems, constraints and concerns that sepa-rate most situations from the ideal.

Administrative Concerns and Opinions:

Most administrators, I pray, recognize the need for some type of BI. Actually, I'm kidding myself because I know this is not always true. As financial con-straints increase, some library directors might love to have back some of the money that has been invested in elaborate BI programs. They are not certain that the return has been worth the cost in staff, time, and equipment, yet most are hesitant to write or speak negatively about something as popular as BI. Some are too isolated from day-to-day operations and too overwhelmed with other prob-lems and responsibilities to pay much heed to BI details. Others actually put in some time at the front (e.g., reference desk), but come away with an opinion somewhat differing from what BI librarians would desire. I have heard adminis-trators say that BI is "not all it is cracked up to be." Deep down I agree. At times it isn't. I've heard administrators note that "some students don't really need to be reached." I agree again, albeit a minority. There are times when I know that I'm wasting my efforts with some students. These individuals often tell us (both verbally and nonverbally) that they have no need for what we are offering. I read statements of college presidents concerned that librarians "have exaggerated the difficulty and importance of bibliographic instruction."[16] There are days when I feel there is an element of truth here too. Sometimes the propo-nents of BI carry things too far and espouse its merits out of proportion. It is important that library and university administrators realize that BI has enough value to pursue and that in some cases it can make a major difference (see section on student retention later in this paper). But we should avoid counterproductive overkill.

Administrators who realize the values of BI range from individuals who do everything in their power to develop a successful program, for example, Farber,[17] to others who support such a program with as little as a nod of the head and the words "Do it." They should be interested that the communications and P.R. accompanying initial contacts, discussions, and planning are being conducted effectively by the right people. They should be concerned that specific needs of the university community are determined and met with the teaching of specific skills and tools using effective and logical means. They should realize and plan for the effects that BI will have on staffing patterns, even perceived unevenness of position responsibilities. They should be aware of the potential effects of BI on reference desk demands, ILL, computer searching, time spent by reference staff on other projects, faculty opinions, future P.R., equipment needs, university community awareness of collection assets and deficiencies, signage, needs for instruction space, and a variety of other library functions. A BI program requires careful analysis, planning, and implementation. It has a ballooning effect that should not catch the library administration and staff by surprise.

Financial Constraints

BI coordinators and participants feel particularly helpless when they can't fulfill program expectations because of limited staffs (often preoccupied with many other responsibilities) paired with crippling financial constraints. As Dougherty notes, "There has been neither a shortage of opportunities nor a lack of enthusiasm among reference librarians to undertake new initiatives. What impedes our progress is a lack of venture capital."[18] I feel most helpless when I realize that a multilevel and cohesive program that gives every student what he or she needs could never happen in a specific situation. Miller hits the nail on the head. "Librarians must always have known subconsciously that if such large-scale instructional programs never [sic] took root, chaos would result. Now it has."[19] There must be a better way!

BI Artificiality

I wonder if part of our constant uphill battle has something to do with our attempts at overkill as well as our defensive postures, that is, always trying to defend the need for BI and our right as librarians to provide it. Do other disciplines do as much justification? Might this appear artificial to others? I also hear concerns about building BI into an already overflowing library school curriculum. It is as if library school faculty don't really believe in BI or mention it in class. Do other disciplines besides education offer specific courses on teaching techniques in their advanced degree programs? Although we've all had our share of college professors who were not adept at teaching, I would think that the basic skills for BI could be handled within the existing curriculum. In my opinion, a separate course is overkill.

There is even a flavor of artificiality in the BI newsletters, journals, etc., which are literally pleading and groping for new initiatives, new ideas, and reasons for existing. It appears to me that they are pushing too hard, perhaps trying to convince themselves that the BI movement, if a movement, is still expanding. Although new considerations such as end-user searching should be explored, if there is nothing new under the sun, don't fill space.

BI Variability—Keeping in Control and Related Factors

Control of a program where responsibilities are divided among many librarians leads to a variety of problems. Individual differences in teaching style and effectiveness come into play. If you strive for excellence, some individuals should just not be put in front of a class (just as some individuals are not capable of performing excellent on-line searches). Mandating a specific style can also lead to less effective rather than improved instruction. If the content varies, then we are not doing justice to the students. If we can agree on content for specific groups or levels, then my experience tells me that allowing for variations in the actual teaching approach is rational. Professors in other disciplines approach the same materials in different manners.

''Teaching'' at the reference desk is also difficult to control. Any given reference staff may include librarians with experience ranging from less than a year to tens of years. Styles develop and change over time. Some librarians are natural teachers with a knack for knowing precisely when to just provide information, when to add a degree of instruction to the process, and when to instruct the patron how to pursue the question independently. Some librarians tend to point too much, others tend to overinstruct—for example, they waste instruction at the desk on certain patrons who want (and perhaps deserve) information, not pedagogy. Some are excellent jugglers under pressure, others fall apart. Some have built up a storehouse of knowledge and trivia concerning the location of all types of information, others specialize in some areas but tremble in fear if a question in others comes their way. Some know precisely when to refer a question to another individual, others feel that sending a question to another librarian is a sign of weakness (to the detriment of library patrons). Some are extremely effective in a one-to-one situation but fall apart in front of a class, others love being on stage but have little patience for leading an individual through the research maze. It is up to reference administrators to help librarians develop a good feel for optimum responses, that is, a philosophy of reference service, and to work with individuals staffing the desk to modify their approaches so that patrons can anticipate even and accurate reference instruction and service. This is a task that never goes away. It is a daily battle to offer cohesive reference service as well as cohesive BI.

Other variability factors can provide frustration for BI programs. Both external and internal influences can play havoc with programs, such as changes in library administration, staff changes, losses of staff not replaced due to financial difficulties, changes within cooperating academic departments, and so forth. Students vary dramatically with regard to levels of library skills and previous BI experiences. It's difficult to teach when you are repetitive to some and have already lost others. Many classes have only a percentage of students showing up, often the wrong ones.

Another instance of variability is simply making sense of the total BI picture. There is such variation from school to school in administrative commitment, faculty approaches, BI history, predispositions, collections, funding, staffing, institution size, and other factors. The best approach for one school may be totally irrational for another. A school of 1,000 and a school of 25,000 are two different BI worlds, not even considering the varying academic levels of the institutions. What you can do along the lines of BI in an institution that accepts anyone who breathes as opposed to an institution filled with National Merit Scholars and the top 2 percent of high school classes is like the difference between night and day. However, either situation can provide a librarian with much satisfaction and a sense of accomplishment. Some teachers are best suited for work with the intellectually gifted, others can work wonders for students who are struggling or deficient. It is difficult to speak in generalities. The many step-by-step, "how-to" guides for BI program development (e.g., Beaubien, Hogan, and George),[20] and the various guidelines for academic library BI programs (i.e., ACRL)[21] are useful for providing procedures, administrative guidelines, concepts, techniques, and so forth, and can liberally be applied in certain situations but can be frustrating for an institution without adequate administrative, financial, or staff support. For some it is close to reality, for others wishful thinking.

Library Assignments

The closer librarians work with faculty in constructing assignments to accompany BI programs, the more effective students will apply the information. (This assumes that librarians know effective assignments when they see them.) The results of decent instruction can be dampened if the assignment is to "write a three-page paper using two references from *Reader's Guide.*" An improvement, although far from perfection, would be a slightly longer paper using sources from a general index, a specialized index, perhaps an abstract, a newspaper index, a specialized encyclopedia, a source from a bibliography, and so on, particularly if there is a logical strategy conveyed for attacking this variety of sources. Even so, this type of assignment is artificial.

Another type of library assignment that is artificial and counterproductive is one that is meant to prove the student's research competency but is really a test of the frazzled librarian—the library treasure hunt. Fleury says it well: "Faculty are often inclined to make their sole library assignment into a sort of benighted treasure hunt, in which students hop from one unrelated source to the next in their search for trivial and unconnected bits of information."[22]

I've heard and read many times how important it is to attach an assignment to your BI. I've observed many students completing their assignments (by hook or by crook). In more cases than not, the goal has been just to get it completed—to fulfill the requirement—and to get rid of it. It is an artificial, busy-work endeavor. My best BI experiences were with groups who were motivated by intellectual interest (pursuing papers in an advanced research class), or motivated by the future (a group of second semester seniors all going on to graduate school), or motivated by a severe need (a group of foreign students just trying to survive). We should apply the reasons for these successes into our BI programs, in other words, isolate when BI really works and pursue these situations (as I will attempt to do in my conclusion).

Premature Competence

This goes hand-in-hand with artificial or ineffective library assignments. At many institutions students are lucky if they experience one orientation session (perhaps to learn locations of the card catalog, reference books, reserve materials, areas to smoke, areas to eat, areas to hide, as well as to make a mental note about the best places to pick up or get picked up by members of the opposite sex) and one BI session. After completing whatever assignment is connected with this session, students may be led to believe that they now have library competence. Unless they are fortunate later to have a research methods class in their major area that examines library research techniques and sources, or if they ask the right questions of the right librarian, their library education may be essentially over. The end result is that they believe they are expert library users but in actuality do poor research. It's a case of a little learning being a dangerous thing.

Faculty Use and Abuse—Faculty Perceptions and Motivations

This is an extremely complex issue. There are many interrelated reasons for faculty reactions to BI programs proposals, some having virtually nothing to do with the content of the BI. Some of my perceptions are simply that—raw perceptions. There have been times when I would love to probe the mind of a faculty member who is behaving irrationally with respect to a librarian or a library-related proposal. Perhaps he or she is thinking along the lines reflected by the words of Davinson: "Much of the vast empire which is Library User Education has grown for no other reason than that such programmes are an entry point to a form of respectability of status for inferiority-complex-ridden librarians."[23] What follows may sound extremely negative, but I have perceived these faculty behaviors at least once at the five institutions where I've worked: (1) resistance based on negative opinions of faculty status for librarians, (2) resistance based on negative perceptions of a service group formally teaching information to classes, (3) resistance based on fear that BI may ultimately result in required BI for credit, thus perhaps creating competition for credits or less credits offered by their own departments, (4) resistance based on perceptions that library use is easy and doesn't require any kind of formal education, (5) resistance based on confusions between librarians and library science faculty, (6) resistance based on selfishness, arrogance, vanity, jealousy, need for power where each discipline is convinced that they alone are important, deserve support, and resent anyone else pushing for support, (7) resistance based on the thought that a librarian might be better able to teach skills than they (I've seen letters in the *Chronicle of Higher Education* relating these egotistical fears of appearing weak), (8) resistance based on protection of turf, (9) resistance based on the fact the faculty member got through without BI—so can their students, (10) resistance based on nonavailability of course time, and (11) resistance based on aroused "suspicion as to just what librarians are doing if they need to go around like traveling sales-man trying to drum up business."[24]

Now I will relate two thoughts that I've rarely verbalized, let alone written. First, I've perceived quite a bit of the reverse behavior, that is, librarians behaving irrationally toward faculty and displaying preconceived notions and re-sistance that are not well founded. It is a two-way street. Second, some of the faculty whom I've seen fighting against a library course or other BI proposals were some of the brightest, most well-respected members of the academic com-munity as well as effective library users. Some of the faculty who rallied behind librarians, flattered me with letters extolling my wonderful instruction, and were excessively impressed by everything that librarians did or said, were not among the best thinkers or most respected individuals on campus, in fact, they often displayed ineffective library research skills or were not really library users at all. Realize that this is *some,* far from *all,* but still it leaves me bewildered. Also realize that far more faculty react positively than negatively to library efforts. Many are sincerely interested in their students' acquisition of research skills.

One situation to avoid within the context of BI is falling into the helpless trap of having a class dumped on you while the instructor is "out of town." It is not fun to face a group of 15 students (out of 30—15 didn't show up when the word *library* was mentioned despite the threat of an attendance sheet) without an as-signment or reason for being in the library, or as Peele describes, "25 bodies in a lecture hall, only 5 of whom are interested in what we are saying."[25] Generally, I refuse to do a class without the instructor present. Student interest correlates highly with a visible instructor holding them in some way responsible for the information.

Pre-College Preparation

This is an often-voiced concern that can make a major difference. Fortunately, I perceive a trend toward an increased conveyance of library skills not only in some secondary schools but even in elementary schools. If BI could systematically become part of school curriculum and if students could acquire basic library skills prior to attending college, this would be a tremendous asset for those who don't attend college as well as for academic librarians, who can concentrate more on research strategies and the conveyance of bibliographic concepts rather than having to start from the "beginning." I have run into high school students using academic libraries who display much better skills than typical college students and ask far more probing questions at the reference desk. A number of pre-college BI programs are described in the literature, such as one for acquainting high school seniors with resources available in university libraries.[26]

Evaluation of Instruction

Studies of varying quality have demonstrated that programs of library instruction improve library skills of undergraduate students both within one institution (students with and without the BI experience) and across institutions (students experiencing a BI program at one institution versus students not having BI at another). The biggest difficulty I've had with some of this research is of the "so-what" variety. I expect students provided with instruction to do significantly better than those who didn't receive any instruction (on any measurement device reflecting what the students were taught). One can say the same thing about the posttest–pretest paradigms.

Considering the money, staff, and time involved, many librarians believe that evaluation is a necessary evil. You need to prove that your efforts have produced something of value. (I've had a few colleagues and administrators mention that they would rather put BI's "lifelong learning" to the test, i.e., test library competency years later.) Many articles and books deal with reasons, procedures, and proposed models for BI evaluation, usually built into the program (not an afterthought) and based on a series of goals and objectives. Yet, "evaluation in library instruction is not highly developed, and there is no model for evaluative techniques."[27] Referring to Library User Education, Davinson notes: "There is a large measure of self-delusory belief that it is a good thing for library users but proof of the assertion, where attempted, usually amounts to self-fulfilling prophecy if analyzed." He adds that "there has been little serious effort to evaluate User Education in terms of either cost to benefit for student or cost to loss of other opportunities to Libraries themselves."[28] I love Mimi Dudley's words:

> When I read the articles on evaluating library instruction programs . . . I long to remind the
> writers that they don't need to justify what they are doing . . . . We are librarians, we believe
> in libraries, we know to the very core of our beings that it is a good thing to be able to make
> use of our library resources. We also know that it is not a measurable, a quantifiable good.[29]

I couldn't agree with her more, but perhaps, unfortunately, we do have to try to
justify the good to our teaching and research faculty, university administrators,
and, yes, even library administrators!

Impact and Use of Computer Technology

Computers have both long-term and immediate implications for BI. We have
to consider two different elements of computer use: (1) as a mode of obtaining
information either via an intermediary (the librarian) or as an end user, and (2) as
a mode of providing instruction.

A large percentage of the information published during the last 10 years is
accessible on-line in hundreds of databases offered by a number of vendors. In
addition, an individual entering a typical university library is barraged by computers, for example, on-line catalogs, on-line circulation systems, interactive
database searching mentioned previously, microcomputers available for a variety
of reasons, terminals hooked up to the university mainframe computers, national
databases such as OCLC and RLIN, and so forth. If this is all intimidating for
cyberphobic (fearing computers) librarians, imagine what it does to library
patrons. Various modes of BI must effectively explain the use of these systems:
what they do, what they don't do, when to use them, how to use them.

As a vehicle for providing BI, computer-assisted instruction (CAI) has played
a role at many institutions. Computers are also used to generate BI exercises and
to do data analysis for BI evaluation. I anticipate the microcomputer to have major future input on BI.

I want to emphasize one major point in anticipation of the future. On-line access will continue to increase as an integral part of reference services. Unlike the
many librarians who feel that computers have been thrust upon them, the next
generation eats, sleeps, lives, and dreams computers. It is already second nature
to many elementary school children. On-line access will be no big deal. In addition, many previous patrons of library on-line search services as well as individuals in all fields of endeavors who haven't previously experienced on-line access
are beginning to use their own microcomputers with modems and printers to do
their own searching and, in some cases, to order their own articles, thereby
bypassing the library completely. Software is rapidly becoming available that allows the searcher to formulate the strategy off-line, go on-line and search, store
the retrieved references on a disk, and edit and print the information after discon-
necting.[30] Other computer systems lead the searcher through the whole search
process.[31] One vendor offers a microsoftware package that provides multiple sys-

tem access (to four major vendors) plus the ability to maximize the features unique to each system.[32] This is only the beginning.

BI programs must take this new technology into account. Librarians must acknowledge that people will do their own searching. On-line access is no longer just in the librarian's domain. Our roles will change. I envision that reference librarians will still provide on-line access to some individuals but will also spend time facilitating the on-line searching by end users. We will still be teaching others the skills to do research, but in a different manner. Hunter writes that end users "should be able to recognize when they need help and know that they can get it from their library. The library's job is to ensure that end user searchers need not wind up with poor results, for whatever reason."[33] BI must take heed.

Student Retention

The potential importance of BI for the individual student should be stressed. Many students arrive on campus without the skills necessary to complete their required assignments effectively. The academic careers of some students can be in jeopardy because of frustrations inherent in undertaking these assignments without the needed research competencies. Some of the best, most meaningful teaching for the individual student can go on outside of the classroom. Librarians are in a position to recognize students who are floundering, help them out, point them in the right direction, and make a real difference in a specific outcome of their academic career. They are "at the front" and can be trained to recognize apparent difficulties and to act constructively.

I believe that the library should be an important cog in the wheel of college-wide responsibilities for student retention. Professors can be useful during their office hours. Career services, commuter organizations, tutoring centers, self-help groups, academic advising, study-skills opportunities, and the like are all helpful if the student avails himself or herself of these types of services. But the librarian is in a different situation. The librarian sees the student trying to cope with assignments, research papers, and so forth. The librarian can be in a position to sense when an assignment is ineffective and tactfully try to work with the instructor to modify it. The librarian can see a student who is on the verge of giving up. The librarian at a reference desk can become a counselor, a provider of good advice to students in distress.

BI programs also can play an important role in the retention of students. Traditional library programs offer a student a recourse to learn how to find information. Given that frustrating library experiences could be a strong contributing factor to a student's decision to give up, librarians can attempt to isolate specific groups of students (e.g., foreign, specific academic areas, specific academic levels, specific handicaps, etc.) and offer services (e.g., term paper clinics, special programs, special availability of an individual librarian, on-line demonstrations, etc.) that are geared toward decreasing the level of risk in high-risk students. Group and individual library programs can make a strong contribution to the overall success of a student and ultimately affect dropout rate.

BI Modes

Many excellent articles and books offer detailed descriptions of advantages and disadvantages of the many approaches for providing BI, for example, Roberts' text.[34] It will serve no function to repeat details here. Instead I will provide terse perceptions of selected modes based primarily on my experience.

Slide-Tape Presentation

Effective for mass education but with inherent difficulties. Time consuming to prepare. Professional help useful. Since libraries change constantly, slide-tapes are quickly out of date. I've been involved with two fairly well done slide-tape presentations, yet in each case the librarians became so tired of hearing the vocal accompaniment that they eventually showed the slides at their own pace and talked instead! I like Davinson's words, "The idea that an itty-bitty tape-slide sequence shown to a class of freshers is an adequate surrogate for careful, sympathetic individual user assistance with a real problem in literature use is absurd."[35] I do find slide-tapes useful if accompanied by a "live librarian" for out-of-library orientation (not instruction), P.R. presentations, and detailed analysis (usually commercial) of the use of specific sources.

Term Paper Clinics

Nice to offer to those who missed other instruction or need additional help. If timed well, provides an opportunity to catch students when they really need help. Advertising, timing, and enough participating librarians are crucial.

Library Guides

Essential no matter what your BI program involves. Can be used in conjunction with other BI modes. Minimally should include a general guide introducing the complete library service, a guide on finding books, a guide on using indexes and locating journals, a guide on on-line access, a guide on microforms, a guide for major special collections (e.g., government documents), and guides for branch libraries.

Tours

Fine for orientation, getting one's bearings, and P.R. Not for instruction unless tour follows a presentation, reinforces information previously provided, or demonstrates tools within their library context. Many varieties such as round robin library tours (groups cycled around stations), general tours at fixed times, football morning tours, and the like.

Computer-Assisted Instruction and Other Self-Paced Instructional Packages

Some students take well to these approaches, for others progress may be impeded. Useful as an option but not as a complete program. CAI does have the advantage of offering an interactive learning situation.

Signs and Point-of-Use Instruction

Effective sign systems can relieve much patron frustration. Many patrons also appreciate information about the use of specific tools kept with the sources, whether published guides or handmade. Patrons should also be made aware of user guides published within many sources.

Faculty Instruction

I've found faculty fairly receptive to group instruction, particularly when it deals with a specialized system (e.g., on-line access demonstrations) or specific new tools in their subject areas. Faculty may also be instructed to provide BI to their students.

Programmed Texts

I've seen but not experienced programmed texts in BI. Kenney and MacArthur believe that this is a more effective teaching tool for lower-level cognitive skills and is preferred by students as compared with lectures. It "can teach basic skills more effectively and less tediously than a librarian with a truckful of books"[36]

Self-Guided Tours

I've been involved with two of these. Both required much preparation, were appreciated by some students, but were not heavily used.

Self-Paced Workbooks

Most of these efforts, such as Penn State's implementation, are adopted from Miriam Dudley's efforts.[37] Self-paced workbooks provide a feasible way to reach a large number of students in an active learning situation with minimal staff and time. The real challenges are effective implementation and control. Also crucial is the cooperative designing of a vehicle by teacher and librarian that accomplishes its goals. There are a variety of approaches for use of a workbook; for example, students at Slippery Rock University receive a one-credit library research course designed around a workbook/exercise module and bibliography assignment. Faculty believe that the students learn essential library skills as well as gain an improved attitude toward the library.[38] Arizona State University takes self-paced workbooks one step further. Their Comprehensive Self-Instruction compliments rather than competes with the college curriculum. For further analysis, consult Richardson.[39]

Reference Desk Instruction

In theory, reference desk instruction is most effective for the individual student. It is where I believe I make the best impact when the desk is not busy and I can lead a patron through an array of manual and on-line tools. In practice, instruction at a reference desk staffed by librarians, classified staff, graduate assistants, and even administrators is at best uneven.

Group Discussions and Seminars

These provide a flexible approach with active participation. Workable in small groups. Students, librarian, and teacher discuss research methods and materials. Morton believes that this approach results in "students who are more excited about digging for information, and who are better able to assimilate and interpret that information in their papers."[40] I would love for my instruction attempts to be in a group-discussion format. Unfortunately, Morton's Carleton College with under 2,000 students is a different world from a large university.

Required Courses and Optional Courses

Optional courses are generally attended by too few students to be considered anything more that just part of the overall BI program, that is, one of many alternatives. A required course has been considered the best of all worlds, resolving a multitude of problems. However, if it doesn't touch all of the right bases or is too removed in time from a student's real research needs, the course may not be totally effective. Even the required course has to be considered part of the overall BI program reinforced by later subject- and research-related efforts.

Course-Related and Course-Integrated Instruction

Course-Related instruction typically provides students with procedures for locating information and strategies for research to meet the requirements of a course, usually via the lecture-tour-exercise and/or paper route. This is the system I've most frequently experienced. On a couple of occasions I've been able to go one step further, work closely with the instructor, and offer course-integrated instruction—that is, when the library instruction is a necessary part of the course. Although time consuming, this experience provided the most satisfaction I've ever had with BI. The students demonstrated the most effective use of the library, compared with similar classes in previous years that received a one-hour course-related experience. There are many approaches to integrated instruction ranging from my isolated experience with one professor, to Mellon's integration of the levels of library abilities with parallel stages of the writing process,[41] to Farber's total integration at Earlham.[42] Carlson and Miller note that the integrated model does involve high costs in time and personnel, as well as extensive coordination, scheduling, and materials development. It is also critically dependent on teaching faculty, involves inconsistent programs of instruction, and a problem of transference of library knowledge from one course to another.[43]

It appears that no one BI system provides all of the answers. Some barely scratch the surface and can confuse more than help (e.g., the rapid-fire show-and-tell), others perhaps carry it too far (e.g., a required first-year library course for credit). It seems obvious that a combination is needed. As for the preferred mode, I don't really believe there is yet a substitute for a librarian in front of a group, interacting with them, providing a human contact, and gearing the information to their specific needs. Casbon says it well. Her two major BI goals "are to communicate enthusiasm for the potential assistance the library and its resources can offer and to let the students know of the existence of the Reference Department and the librarians' willingness to help." She finds the "lecture method of teaching, given the right personality and style of the lecturer, a successful method of communicating these ideas."[44] This "affective" aspect not available in the mechanical modes of BI can make a difference.

BI Librarian Burnout

The burnout literature across every discipline parallels the BI literature in sheer volume, in fact, I'm burned out about reading about burnout. I do believe that burnout is a real BI phenomenon and is a function of one or more of the following: repetition, pressure, perceived extra workload, attempting to do well in the face of many obstacles, staffing constraints, lack of librarian cooperation, financial constraints, faculty status pressures (e.g., trying to publish, build a BI program, and fulfill your responsibilities in the library and on campus), etc. I will leave the library literature to offer solutions.

MODEL BI PROGRAMS

It is a useful exercise to examine the model BI programs for elements that can be applied to one's own situation. Unfortunately, BI programs similar to those at Earlham, Swarthmore, Sangamon, and others are just a pleasant dream for many academic institutions. Major differences include a special administration, size of the institution, and nature of the university community. A colleague asked a librarian in a private school in my state that suddenly developed an array of BI programs (obviously involving a large financial investment) how it happened. The answer was, "We had a mandate from the Provost." This can be hard to take when your own state institution is biting the bullet for the third straight year and the only mandate passed down is to "freeze." To make possible the implementation of a model program, it helps to have a special situation such as an administrative mandate and the support that goes with it. When you get a competent and innovative individual directing a library who envisions a specific pioneering direction for his or her library and hires staff specifically for this purpose, the potential for extreme success dramatically increases. Some libraries emphasize specific collections, some emphasize on-line access, some pioneer with computer systems, some put their efforts into fund raising, some do everything above average, and some unfortunately lag behind on all fronts. Earlham College was blessed with the perfect academic environment and with Evan Farber, whom most consider the foremost BI pioneer. His success has been a boon for all of us because he travels widely discussing BI as well as offers frequent BI workshops at Earlham emphasizing faculty involvement (and, more recently, additional components such as on-line searching and end-user instruction).

This brings us to the other major difference besides an innovative director such as Farber—institutional size and the nature of the university community. There are not-so-subtle differences between what can be accomplished at larger universities versus smaller college environments, between, 1,000 academically minded students in the total institution versus thousands of incoming freshman, half harboring major goals involving parties and football. This is a fact of life. The sheer numbers of students do not mean correspondingly higher numbers of librarians. Emphasizing BI would mean totally ignoring other important services. There is also a difference in the teachers you cooperatively work with to implement BI. At a small school, the professor often teaches the course, has a vested interest in the institution, instructs smaller classes, and fosters a closer relation with a smaller and more manageable library. In a large university setting, transient graduate students often teach the courses that should involve BI, are themselves intimidated by the multimillion-volume library, have less of a vested interest in the program or the future success of the students, often have bigger egos than some of the professors, and even occasionally perceive the librarians as intruders. For them, BI may be mandated down the rigid chain of command. I believe that graduate teaching assistants provide less stability with regard to liaisons with the library and, subsequently, less success for BI. Farber admits that Earlham provides a "closely knit sense of community and very informal relationships among students, faculty, administration and staff," a favorable situation for fostering an effective BI program.[45] Despite these major differences, there is much to be learned from these model programs.

A CONCEPTUAL APPROACH TO BI

If you boil down all the information needed for basic BI into a list of raw concepts—what a student minimally should know to acquire enough of a foundation on which to build more complex library skills—the minimal content to be reckoned with is not overwhelming. There should be ways to convey this information without impinging on anyone else's turf, or depending on a number of individuals (where a weak-link effect can damage the process), or intimidating students, faculty, or administration. The previously mentioned college president who thought that librarians have exaggerated the difficulty and importance of BI may have been partially referring to a syndrome of overdoing both the content and the means to the end in attempt to reach our goals.

What concepts are available?

1. There are books. Books are checked out _____. Access to these books is via a card and/or on-line catalog organized by author, title, or subjects. The list of subject headings is _____. The information on the card and/or screen is _____. The idiosyncrasies of this catalog are _____. The catalog reflects the following branches, collections _____ located _____ . We use the _____ classification system(s) arranged in this library as follows _____. Consult this library guide.

2. There are periodical, journals, magazines _____. Some have general, research, theoretical articles _____. In this library they are arranged _____ . Our circulation policy is _____. To determine where to find specific titles, consult _____. Access is via indexes and abstracts. Indexes such as *Readers' Guide* work like _____. Abstracts work like _____ . Indexes and abstracts are arranged _____. Specific indexes and abstracts of note are _____. Consult this library guide.

3. There are newspapers. They are kept _____ and arranged _____. We own the following indexes to newspapers _____. This one works like _____, etc. Consult this library guide.

4. There are reference books that don't circulate, such as encyclopedias, dictionaries, reference microfiche sets, _____, in which to look up information such as _____. There is a catalog for reference books by author, title, and subject.

5. We offer on-line access to _____ by subscribing to the following vendors _____. Our policy about computer searching is _____ explained in this library guide. We also have access to the following on-line national databases _____. Patrons can search by themselves in _____ using the following guide(s). These systems do _____. These systems do not do _____. Consult this library guide.

6. We offer interlibrary loan. The procedure is _____. Costs are _____ .

7. This is our reference and/or information desk(s). Ask here for _____. The desk is staffed by friendly and helpful _____ during _____. Other services are _____.

8. Please consider the following strategies for researching _____. One approach might be to _____, another might be to _____.

I realize that this is grossly simplified. However, this body of information can be systematically covered in under an hour, reinforced with library guides and a subsequent 20-minute tour. This might sound ludicrous, but it is done every day at hundred of institutions. Some students come away bewildered, albeit with a sense of what is available as well as who and where to ask to try to figure it out. Reinforcing the information with the use of library guides (which should be readable and designed to lead the students through your own particular library maze) and with other available modes of BI help the overall process. Although the content of this body of information requires more time to really do it justice, it doesn't really compare to the body of knowledge in introductory courses throughout the curriculum. BI is a necessary skill that cuts across disciplines but doesn't approach the scope of a course on American History or Introduction to Physics or Elements of Conducting or even Government Documents. Remember, we are just attempting to convey the basics, to provide something that is more than orientation but not the content of a library-school course. (Even a library-school course cannot delve into the tricks, strategies, and complexities that are learned only by experience.) Although the basics do not justify a required credit course, it would make a marvelous optional course, valid for students who desire to delve deeper into research techniques and tools. However, most students really want and need just the basics to get them through, not a course. As Rettig notes, "Most people function quite well in their everyday business and personal lives without knowing beans about library research methods."[46]

BI—A CHANGING EMPHASIS

"Tell me, I'll forget. Show me, I may remember. But involve me and I'll understand." This Chinese proverb is the key to what I perceive as a necessary emphasis change for BI at many institutions. Perhaps students should be *involved* in the decisions about how they obtain basic library skills. Also, students who are *involved* with research and motivated by intellectual interest should be provided with additional instruction, instead of forcing additional BI on students who don't need the skills, or providing the advanced skills with artificial assignments. Rettig states, "BI can be justified, but only when directed at groups with both an immediate and a long-range need for such knowledge."[47]

We have an obligation and a need to provide all students with the means and opportunities to acquire basic library skills. We have at least an equal obligation to provide more-specialized and higher-level BI to those groups of students with immediate research needs. I believe many academic libraries, particularly those at the larger institutions, have been putting too much emphasis on the first category and not doing justice to the second. If I ask myself who really needs BI the most, the answer seems obvious: (1) individuals working on theses or dissertations, (2) new graduate students, (3) undergraduates who are going on to graduate school, have made a research commitment to a profession, and will soon be involved in research at an extensive library, and (4) faculty needing information for their research and teaching. These four groups really need to know about citation indices, sources for proceedings, specialized bibliographies, important modes of on-line access, the wealth of information and data in government documents, approaches for gaining access to the obscure, and so forth. These are the individuals who can't afford to work in isolation and should depend on the skills of reference librarians efficiently and effectively to pursue their research.

I believe we have to redirect our energies and provide instruction to these groups (as well as to other groups of students with specific library research needs) via seminars, sessions in research/methods classes, demonstrations, and whatever other BI modes fit the challenge.

But what about the naive freshman who has no feel for the flow and organization of information in libraries. How can we divert our efforts to the people who most need our expertise, without making short shrift of our undergraduates? If the library is fortunate enough to have more than adequate staff to cover both ends of the spectrum with "live" approaches, it is worth the effort to use librarians for beginning instruction. Otherwise, we can work toward restructuring our efforts to give them more or less. With an initial heavy work load followed by occasional routine maintenance, librarians can offer new students an array of possibilities to gain competency.

Let me first backtrack. With many lecture-related systems, even though I consider lectures the most efffective BI mode, many students are not really reached. Absenteeism is generally high. Students not paying total attention to the lecture and/or tour is a common occurrence. Even the student who is nodding at the librarian with a reinforcing gesture may be really lost in totally unrelated thought or fighting sleep. Also, cheating and cooperating on related library assignments is notoriously common, often at the expense of really learning. Assignments are treated as (and often are) busy work. To say that we really effectively reach 50 percent of the students might be an overestimation. (Of course, this percentage depends on the style of the librarian, the attitude of the professor, the particular pressure placed on the class to acquire library skills, the self-motivation of the students, and other factors.) Then there is the luck of the draw. Depending on their courses and instructors, some students may never set foot inside the library except to get reserve (which the professor calls reference) materials. Other students find themselves in more than one class that comes to the library for essentially the same information. Some students appreciate the repetition, others react with "Oh no, not the library again!"

There are ways around these problems of effectively reaching too few students and missing others, while duplicating services to still others. One common approach is to latch on to a course all students are required to take and to offer all basic instruction only in that course. Among the pitfalls are departmental cooperation, taking someone else's course time, and essentially not reaching students who don't make it to the session or don't pay attention. What might work is a university commitment to basic library competency, perhaps even stated in the college catalog. It doesn't have to be a noxious or threatening situation. It doesn't have to take hours away from anyone else's classes. It doesn't even require credit. All that is needed is a simple statement that all students will understand, noting that the acquisition of basic or core library skills is *required* by a specific point in the student's academic career, and that the library offers the following BI modes to prove such competency—for example, testing out, self-study with library guides leading to testing out, completing a self-paced workbook, completing a CAI module, passing an optional course, attending one of the sessions offered by librarians throughout the year (advanced sign up) that include an exercise or competency test, and so forth. Because no one BI method seems to meet the needs of every student in every situation, learning theorists would probably agree that giving a student a choice makes sense. Also, student feelings toward the library may be enhanced if they are able to pick their own mode of learning. If they don't prove competency by the given date, then they must participate in an instruction session/exercise offered near the end of the allotted time period.

I believe that librarians would be willing to help devise the necessary workbooks, texts, exercises and share the instruction load as well as find feasible approaches for dealing with the bookkeeping and other mechanics. Although more students would ultimately be reached, librarians would not have to deliver the same lecture hundreds of times and instead would be able to offer more interesting and advanced BI (as well as important on-line access) to the individual really in need. If a university commitment is not feasible, it could be a library policy—less clout but still effective. Basic skills acquired during the first year via a variety of modes would be followed later on by formal personal contact between the student and the research specialist at a time of greater need, thus providing a progressive approach. This fits well with studies that demonstrate how workbooks and other nonlecture approaches are more effective for basic information, and with studies documenting how lecture students perform better than workbook participants at higher competency-level skills.

Although I don't find this solution better than fully integrated BI systems, I believe that it might be a more effective and better use of manpower for the many institutions where the fully integrated system is not feasible.

Still another option might be to encourage the instructors assigning papers in basic courses to convey these skills themselves. Offer your handouts, self-paced workbooks, slides, etc. Beware, however, that bad instruction is worse than no instruction. Instructors have difficulty reinforcing and instilling skills that they don't have themselves. Recent investigations have demonstrated that instructors welcome assistance from librarians.[48] Detailed BI for the instructors to enable them to provide BI to their students might be an approach. Another option might be to hire graduate students (library school, if available) whom you can train to take some of the load of basic instruction off of the librarians' backs.

In the larger college or university situations, where freshman instruction is systematically emphasized and the needs of advanced students are handled more randomly, any approach that can redirect librarian BI efforts toward individuals involved in library research without ignoring the needs of the new college students is worth pursuing.

NOTES AND REFERENCES

1.   Melissa R. Watson, "No Royal Road," *The Reference Librarian*, no. 10 (Spring/Summer 1984): 227–232.

2.   Kathleen Coleman, "Library Instruction and the Advancement of Reference Service," *The Reference Librarian*, no. 10 (Spring/Summer 1984): 241–252.

3.   Deborah L. Lockwood, *Library Instruction: A Bibliography* (Westport, Conn.: Greenwood Press, 1979).

4.   Anne F. Roberts, *Library Instruction for Librarians* (Littleton, Colo.: Libraries Unlimited, 1982).

5.   Soni Bodi, "Relevance in Library Instruction: The Pursuit," *College and Research Libraries* 45 (January 1984): 59–65.

6.   John Mark Tucker, "User Education in Academic LIbraries: A Century in Retrospect," *Library Trends* 29: (Summer 1980) 9–27.

7.   W. F. Poole, "The University Library and the University Curriculum," *Library Journal* 18 (November 1893): 470–471.

8.   Peyton Hurt, "The Need of College and University Instruction in Use of the Library," *Library Quarterly* 4 (July 1934): 436–448.

9.   Frances L. Hopkins, "A Century of Bibliographic Instruction: The Historical Claims to Professional and Academic Legitimacy," *College and Research Libraries* 43 (May 1982): 192–198.

10.   Fred Batt, "Education is Illogical," *Improving College and University Teaching* 25 (Summer 1977): 188.

11.   Larry L. Richardson, "Teaching Basic Library Skills: Past Tense, Future Perfect," *Reference Services Review* 12 (Spring 1984): 67–76.

12.   Cerise Oberman and Katina Strauch, eds., *Theories of Bibliographic Education: Designs for Teaching* (New York: Bowker, 1982).

13.   Willie L. Parson, "User Perspective on a New Paradigm for Librarianship," *College & Research Libraries* 45 (September 1984): 370–373.

14.   Roberts, *Library Instruction for Librarians*.

15.   Harold W. Tuckett and Carla J. Stoffle, "Learning Theory and the Self-Reliant Library User," *RQ* 24 (Fall 1984): 58–66.

16.   Susan Brandehoff, "Academic Libraries: Sifting Fact from Fiction,"*American Libraries* 15 (May 1984): 334–335.

17.   Evan Farber, Director of Earlham College, Richmond, Indiana.

18.   Richard M. Dougherty, "Reallocating Resources and Reordering Priorities at the Reference Desk," (Editorial) *Journal of Academic Librarianship* 10 (November 1984): 255.

19.   William Miller, "What's Wrong with Reference: Coping with Success and Failure at the Reference Desk," *American Libraries* 15 (May 1984): 303–322.

20.   Anne K. Beaubien, Sharon A. Hogan, and Mary W. George, *Learning the Library: Concepts and Methods for Effective Bibliographic Instruction* (New York: Bowker, 1982).

21.   ACRL's Bibliographic Instruction Task Force developed *Guidelines for Bibliographic Instruction in Academic Libraries* in 1977. These are currently being updated (as of late 1984) by the ACRL Bibliographic Instruction Section.

22.   Bruce E. Fleury, "Lectures, Textbooks, and the College Librarian," *Improving College and University Teaching* 32 (Spring 1984): 103–106.

23.   Donald Davinson, "Never Mind the Quality, Feel the Width," *The Reference Librarian*, no. 10 (Spring/Summer 1984): 29–37.

24.   Joseph Rosenblum, "Reference Service in Academia—Quo Vadis?" *Journal of Academic Librarianship* 6 (July 1980): 151–153.

25.   David Peele, "Librarians as Teachers: Some Reality, Mostly Myth," *Journal of Academic Librarianship* 10 (November 1984): 267–271.

26.   Juanita W. Buddy, "Orientation to the University Library—The Missing Link," *NASSP Bulletin* 66 (December 1982): 99–101.

27.   Roberts, *Library Instruction for Librarians*, 85.

28.   Davinson, "Never Mind the Quality," 29–30.

29.   Mimi Dudley, "A Philosophy of Library Instruction," *Research Strategies 1 (Spring 1983): 58–63*.

30.   For example, Pro-Search offered by Menlo Corporation.

31.   For example, EASYNET offered by Telebase Systems, Inc.

32.   SDC's ORBIT Searchmaster.

33.   J.A. Hunter, "When Your Patrons Want to Search—The Library as Advisor to Endusers . . . A Compendium of Advice and Tips," *Online* 8 (May 1984): 36–41.

34.   Roberts, *Library Instruction for Librarians*, 40–45, 61–66.

35.   Davinson, "Never Mind the Quality," 33–34.

36.   Patricia Ann Kenney and Judith N. McArthur, "Designing and Evaluating a Programmed Library Instruction Text," *College and Research Libraries* 45 (January 1984): 33–42.

37.   Miriam Dudley, *Workbook in Library Skills* (Los Angeles: University of California University Library, 1974).

38.   Richard J. Wood, "The Impact of a Library Research Course on Students at Slippery Rock University," *The Journal of Academic Librarianship* 10 (November 1984): 278–284.

39.   Richardson, "Teaching Basic Library Skills," 71–76.

40.   Bruce Morton, "Beyond Orientation: The Library as Place of Education and the Librarian as Educator," *Improving College and University Teaching* 27 (1979): 161–163.

41.   Constance A. Mellon, "Process not Product in Course-Integrated Library Instruction: A Generic Model of Library Research," *College and Research Libraries* 45 (November 1984): 471–478.

42.   Evan Farber, "Library Instruction Throughout the Curriculum: Earlham College Program," in John Lubans (ed.), *Educating the Library User* (New York: Bowker, 1974), 145–162.

43.   David Carlson and Ruth H. Miller, "Librarians and Teaching Faculty: Partners in Bibliographic Instruction," *College and University Libraries* 45 (November 1982): 483–491.

44.   Susan Casbon, "The Efficiency of the Library Lecture . . . and a Few Other Statements," *Research Strategies* 1 (Spring 1983): 86–87.

45.   Evan Farber, "Library Instruction Throughout the Curriculum."

46.   James Rettig, "The Crisis in Academic Reference Work," *Reference Services Review* 12 (Fall 1984): 13–14.

47.   Ibid.

48.   Eugene A. Engeldinger and Barbara R. Stevens, "Library Instruction Within the Curriculum," *College and Research Libraries News* 45 (December 1984): 593–598.

THE UNIVERSITY LIBRARY DIRECTOR IN BUDGETARY DECISION MAKING

Susan E. McCargar

The effectiveness of the library director in budgetary decision making and in obtaining adequate financial resources for the library has become increasingly more important during the 1980s. During the fifties and sixties, academic institutions experienced a period of growth and expansion. During the 1970s, colleges and universities faced the problem of declining enrollments and a decrease in federal and state funding. As part of the new depression in higher education, academic libraries were confronted with the rising costs of library materials, an "information explosion" in the publishing industry, the necessity of competing with other academic units for diminishing financial resources, and the demand for justification of budgetary allocations.[1] Academic libraries will continue to experience problems of inflation, budgetary reductions, and declining enrollments through the 1980s. These factors are contributing to a climate of uncertainty and accountability.[2]

Advances in Library Administration and Organization
Volume 5, pages 179–205
Copyright © 1986 by JAI Press Inc.
All rights of reproduction in any form reserved.
ISBN: 0-89232-674-3

Earlier studies have indicated that the effectiveness of the library director in influencing budgetary decision making within the governing process is of great concern to the library profession. During the 1960s, McAnally and Downs reported that library directors whose institutions possessed membership in the Association of Research Libraries experienced a loss of power due to the shifting management patterns in higher education as well as the inability to achieve an effective national system for resource sharing.[3] With the increasing demand for accountability and access to information, the effective allocation of resources becomes increasingly more important. According to Axford, improved effectiveness can be reached through reestablishing the credibility of library directors within academic governance and working toward more sympathetic budget hearings both in and outside the university environment.[4] Bolton perceived new roles for the library director—planner, fund raiser, and innovator.[5] In the face of financial distress and relatively inadequate budgeting, the library director must be responsive to the need for new skills and techniques.

The Association of Research Libraries-sponsored study, *Problems in University Library Management,* recommends that library managers make the most effective justification, allocation, and use of limited resources in relation to the needs and objectives of the university.[6] According to Lynch, the match between the library's goals and objectives and the goals and objectives of the university will enhance the library's overall effectiveness.[7]

Webster points out that a major issue in the 1980s is maintaining quality in academic libraries while dealing with financial problems. He reiterates the need for libraries to provide access to information—solving their financial difficulties with new strategies of financial management and organizational development. Additionally, libraries need to pursue a more influential role in institutional decision making.[8]

Recent investigative studies have shown that the role of the academic library director is changing. In his study, Whitbeck found that college librarians occupied a peripheral status in the academic community in relation to specific areas of decision making: budgeting, development of the curriculum, and making key appointments.[9] Respondents in his study included administrators, faculty, fiscal officers, deans, library directors, and other academic librarians. In questioning respondents concerning their role in budgetary decision making, Whitbeck found that a strong correlation existed between the hierarchical level of respondent and the degree of influence in decision making. Respondents with administrative responsibilities (vice presidents, fiscal officers, deans, library directors) possessed greater influence. Concerning budgetary decision making within a department, it was found that the teaching faculty possessed greater involvement in their own departments than did librarians within the library.[10]

Lee addressed the issue of the function of library administrators in her study concerning conflict and ambiguity in the role of the library director. She interviewed 20 directors in Northeastern colleges and universities to find out how they define their roles. The respondents reported conflicting roles as internal library manager and as "ambassador for the library."[11] They also indicated that success or failure in their responsibilities depended heavily on their relationships with external constituents. Most of the directors interviewed felt that the person to whom they are immediately responsible was very important in determining the budgetary allocation to the library.[12]

Metz has recently conducted a study using empirical evidence from a large sample of library directors to determine the role of the library director, both within the library and his or her various activities with resources and constituents outside the academic institution.[13] Metz's data reveals that internal library affairs constitute the major portion of a director's time. Data further indicated little priority was given to relationships with constituents outside the academic institution.[14] Metz hypothesized that organizational size would be a significant factor in determining the library director's role. Analysis of the data revealed that the library directors more likely to represent the library in external affairs are found at larger, more complex institutions.[15]

The study of the academic library director within the framework of political analysis is suggested by Runyon. He feels that the library will occupy an increasingly more powerful role in the future, due to the nature of an information-rich society.[16] Runyon also recommends that librarians create new forms of library power by expanding the roles of the librarian. Due to greater involvement in more intensive conflict possibilities, the library director needs new skills in negotiation and political action in order to deal with these conflicts.[17]

The purpose of this study was to examine the effectiveness in budgetary decision making within the context of academic governance of library directors whose institutions are members of the Association of Research Libraries. Power was also a major component of the study. The investigation explored the relationship of the type of power and the amount of influence exerted by library directors to the governance model operating within the institutions. The degree of political activity within academic institutions was also analyzed.

The objectives of the study were as follows:

1. Identify the perceptions of power and the amount of influence exerted by the library director in budgetary decision making as perceived by five distinct groups: chief administrative officers, chief academic officers, chief financial officers, library directors, and associate library directors.
2. Identify the type of governance model operating at each institution based on the perceptions of the five selected groups of individuals.
3. Determine the amount of political activity operating in each governance model.
4. Identify the relationships between the personal characteristics of the library director and the library budget.[18]

Perceived power is a factor in French and Raven's definition of *power* as "potential influence."[19] Perception is also evident in Lewin's field theory definition of power, which includes the potentiality of one individual to influence another individual.[20] The study of perceived power in relation to academic governance has not been widely investigated; however, a number of researchers have examined power or the use of influence within academic institutions.

In an assessment of university goals, Gross and Grambsch attempted to determine a generalized distribution of power across the total university organization. To gather evidence about perceived power, respondents in their study were asked to rate the amount of influence exerted by certain groups, persons, or agencies on major decisions within the university. Results showed that the president was perceived as the most influential, followed by the regents, vice presidents, deans, faculty, and so on down the hierarchy.[21]

Hill and French designed a study to measure the perceived power of department chairpersons by faculty members and to determine whether variations in power were associated with variations in the satisfaction and productivity of the departmental faculty. Their results showed that the greater the power of the chairperson, the greater the faculty level of satisfaction and productivity.[22]

In their study of American faculty, Parsons and Platt found evidence to suggest that the distribution of influence might be affected by institutional status. They found that faculty at more prestigious institutions were more influential than faculty at less prestigious institutions.[23]

Baldridge and associates investigated patterns of influence within the university, based on the responses of administrators and faculty. Their survey indicated that administrators have a great deal of influence over a number of issues. Deans were also found to possess a great deal of power.[24]

Although many researchers have defined power, such as Tannenbaum, and Katz and Kahn,[25] the theoretical definitions of power set forth by French and Raven have provided the basic typology for further studies of the basis of power. French and Raven defined power in terms of influence. *Influence* was defined as change in a person's psychological field—including behavior, opinions, attitudes, goals, needs, and values.[26] The bases of power developed by French and Raven provide the following theoretical definitions of major types of power that a person might have as a basis of influence:

1. *Legitimate power*. O, a social agent, by virtue of role or position, has the right to prescribe power over P, another person.
2. *Referent power*. P identifies with O.
3. *Reward power*. O has the ability to mediate rewards for P.
4. *Coercive power*. P perceives that O has the power to mediate punishment for P.
5. *Expert power*. P attributes superior knowledge or ability to O.[27]
6. *Information power*. Information power is based on the content of O's communication of knowledge.[28]

Researchers in higher education who have used French and Raven's power typology for study have employed the power bases as descriptive tools rather than as a theoretical concept to be tested.[29]

In her study of the student personnel administrator in the budgetary process, Moxley tested French and Raven's theoretical definitions of power. Moxley hypothesized that the effectiveness of the types of power used by the student personnel administrator in attempts to gain funds is related to the governance model that prevails at the institution. Using a selection of influence activities, Moxley tested these six types of power utilizing factor and cluster analysis to determine whether French and Raven's six power bases represented a reality-based structure. A new power structure, derived from the factor and cluster analysis, was considered by Moxley to be a more comprehensive structure.[30] The new power structure is defined by six types of power:

1. *Person power.* Derived from an influencing agent's characteristics and ability to respond to the needs and traits of others (e.g., the library director demonstrates oral and/or written communication skills).

2. *Sanction power.* The agent has the ability to mediate awards or punishments (e.g., the library director threatens cutback of library services if budget requests are not granted).

3. *Task power.* Expertise of the agent is related to the domain of influence (e.g., the library director demonstrates expertise in budget development skills).

4. *Functional role power.* Derived from those resources available, or perceived to be available, to an influencing agent due to his or her organizational functions (e.g., the library director demonstrates skills and knowledge of the library profession).

5. *Associational role power.* Derived from contacts or associations an influencing agent establishes (e.g., the library director gains the support of influential people outside the library—trustees, governing board, state legislature).

6. *Reposeful power.* Derived from the influencing agent's inactivity in using power resources (e.g., the library director gives the appearance of nonaction, does not "rock the boat" or raise any conflict-producing issues.[31]

The bureaucratic and the collegial models were chosen to represent the models of governance examined in the study. The bureaucratic model, based on Weber's treatise on bureaucracies, has greatly influenced the study of colleges and universities. The university, viewed as a bureaucratic structure, is hierarchical, linked together by formal chains of command and systems of communication. Stroup identifies several characteristics of colleges and universities possessing the nature of the bureaucracy: rank is recognized and respected; salaries are fixed and paid directly by the institution; officials are appointed, not elected; and competence is used as a criterion for appointment.[32]

Although bureaucratic elements are found in colleges and universities, and the bureaucratic model provides an excellent framework for the study of authority (defined by Baldridge as legitimate, formalized power[33]), Baldridge maintains that the bureaucratic model does not assist in a study of nonformal forms of power and influence. The bureaucratic model describes structure, but very little about processes, such as decision making; it also does not deal with policy formulation, or with political issues, such as the struggles of groups within the institution who want to force policy decisions toward their own special interests.[34]

The collegium or community-of-scholars model is extensively discussed by Millett, a major proponent of this model. The collegium model assumes an equality of interest among administrators, faculty, and students. A participatory process of decision making, involving the governing board, administrators, faculty, and students, replaces the bureaucratic model where authority rests with the bureaucratic officials.[35] Baldridge suggests that collegial discussion through a round-table type of decision making is not an accurate description of the college and university, but rather a goal yet to be attained.[36] Millett emphasizes the "dynamics of consensus" as a method of decision making,[37] but, according to Baldridge, fails to take into account that consensus usually follows a prolonged battle. Consequently, the collegium model neglects to deal adequately with the problem of conflict.[38]

The political model—a third, and more recent, model used to study colleges and universities—is advanced by Baldridge. This model has as its basis conflict and theories concerning power.[39] Baldridge conducted a single case-study investigation and formulated a political model from his observations having five points of analysis:

1. *Social structure*. Various interest groups with divergent goals and values; the difference between these groups often leads to conflict.
2. *Interest articulation*. Groups with conflicting goals must translate them into effective influence in order to obtain favorable action by legislative bodies. Interest groups must be identified as well as the methods used to exert pressure.
3. *Legislative stage*. Three basic questions are raised: Who makes the decisions? What are the areas of influence? How are decisions made? Answers to these questions clarify the process by which various pressures are translated into formal policy.
4. *Formulation of policy*. Articulated interests have gone through conflict and compromise; legislative action is taken.
5. *Execution of policy*. Inevitably results in a feedback cycle generating new interests and a new cycle of conflict.[40]

Recent studies by Childers and by Moxley utilized these three models of governance—the bureaucratic, collegial, and political—in relation to decision making in colleges and universities.[41] Childer's study indicated that the bureaucratic and collegial models comprised one structural construct while the political model was identified as a process. The political process seemed to be independent but related to the bureaucratic–collegial construct. Childers suggests that more precise conceptualizations are needed and raises the question, "What is political about bureaucratic/collegial decision-making?"[42]

When Moxley examined power in relation to the three models of governance, she found that the collegial and the bureaucratic models did indeed exist in higher education, separately, as well as merged with each other. The political model, alone, however, was rarely found within the institutions Moxley surveyed. Her research disproved Baldridge's theory that the political model was the principal approach to a study of academic governance. Moxley recommends that a more precise definition of the term *political* be pursued.[43]

Certain elements that can be characterized as political exist in higher education: special interest groups, which work toward forcing policy decisions in their favor;[44] and conflict, especially where competition for resources exists.[45]

This study examined the relationship between a political process, or activity, and the two models of governance—collegial and bureaucratic—with regard to budgetary decision making in those institutions belonging to the Association of Research Libraries. The power typology developed by Moxley was also studied in relation to the two models of governance.

Based on the premise that budgetary decision making, with regard to the university library director, can occur within these governance models, two research hypotheses were formulated:

1. The type of power and amount of influence exerted by the library director in attempts to gain budgetary resources is related to the governance model operating at the institution.
2. The degree of political activity will be greater in a bureaucratic model of governance in academic institutions than in a collegial model of governance.

To facilitate an understanding of various terms used in this study, definitions are provided in Appendix A. The population of this study consisted of the 89 universities in the United States having membership in the Association of Research Libraries as of May 1981. The respondents for this investigation consisted of 89 chief administrative officers, 89 chief academic officers, 89 chief financial officers, 89 library directors, and 89 associate library directors (or equivalent).

Due to the total number of individuals, a questionnaire was considered the most appropriate and feasible method of data collection. Two questionnaires were developed. One was for distribution to library directors; it included a Status of Library Budget sheet and a Personal Information Sheet. The second questionnaire was for distribution to the other four groups of participants. Both questionnaires are shown in Appendix B. The questionnaires were developed from (1) a review of the literature and research concerning the use of power by academic administrators and governance in academic institutions;[46] (2) criticism from individuals consulted; and (3) the results of a pretesting of the questionnaires.

The purpose of the questionnaires was to compare the perceptions of the five groups of respondents regarding the type of power and the amount of influence exerted by the library director in attempts to gain budgetary resources, and the degree of political activity at each institution.

The questionnaire was mailed during May 1982 to each individual. A second mailing, sent in June 1982 as a follow-up to those individuals who did not previously respond, included 225 questionnaires. Table 1 shows a breakdown of the responses. Of the questionnaires mailed, 239 were received and considered usable, a total of 53.7 percent. Library directors provided the highest rate of return with 77.5 percent; the lowest percentage of returns came from chief administrative officers—28.1 percent.

Initially, the academic institutions were categorized according to the prevailing governance model—bureaucratic or collegial—by analyzing the collective responses to two questions pertaining to policy and decision making from all individuals at each institution. The one-way analysis of variance was used for testing the data. The significance level for all statistical data was set at .05.

The two models of governance were operationally defined by the respondents' answers to Questions 1 and 2 in Section A of the questionnaire. Those institutions whose respondents perceived the president and/or a president's council being primarily responsible for budget decision-making policies and budget-allocation decisions were categorized as bureaucratic. Those institutions whose respondents perceived a budget committee and/or a governing body (i.e., faculty senate) being primarily responsible for budget decision-making policies and budget-allocation decisions were categorized as collegial.

Based on the perceptions of the respondents, 66 institutions were categorized as bureaucratic. Of these, there was disagreement at only one institution about who primarily determines budget decision-making policies and budget-allocation decisions. Ten institutions were categorized as collegial; of these, there was disagreement among the respondents at two institutions. Where disagreement occurred, the governance model was categorized according to how the majority of respondents at an institution answered the questions.

The six types of power chosen for the study were analyzed. Respondents were given a list of 17 influence activities, to rate the effectiveness of each activity when used by the library director in attempts to gain budgetary resources for the library (Hypothesis One). This set of influence activities represented the six types of power being studied: person power, functional role power, task power, associational role power, sanction power, and reposeful power. The influence activity statements are listed in Appendix A. The response categories given for each statement were: ''don't know,'' ''not used at all,'' ''negative effect,'' ''no effect,'' ''effective,'' and ''very effective.''

Table 1. Analysis of Returns Received by Mailings
(Total Sent = 445)

Respondents	1st Mailing				2nd Mailing				Total			
	Number received	%	Number usable	%	Number received	%	Number usable	%	Number received	%	Number usable	%
Administrative officer	40	44.9	20	22.5	9	10.1	5	5.6	49	55.1	25	28.1
Academic officer	44	49.4	36	40.4	11	12.4	7	7.9	55	61.8	43	48.3
Financial officer	49	55.1	39	43.8	14	15.7	8	8.9	63	70.8	47	52.8
Library director	73	82.0	67	75.3	2	2.2	2	2.2	75	84.3	69	77.5
Associate library director	54	60.7	46	51.7	13	14.6	9	10.1	67	75.3	55	61.8
Totals	260	58.4	208	46.7	49	11.0	31	6.9	309	69.4	239	53.7

Total number unidentifiable = 5.

The numbers in Table 2 represent the total number of responses to the questions representing each type of power by each group of respondents. All standard deviations are the standard deviation of the sample.

Table 2 shows the results of the one-way analysis of variance when the collective responses for all groups of respondents were analyzed between the two types of governance. The mean scores indicated that three types of power—functional role power, person power, and task power—are effective in both the bureaucratic and collegial models of governance. Reposeful power and associational role power were perceived to have no effect in either model of governance. Sanction power, while perceived as having no effect in a bureaucratic model, was perceived to have a negative effect in a collegial model of governance.

For sanction power, the analysis of variance revealed a significant difference in the perceptions of all groups between the bureaucratic and collegial models of governance. No statistically significant differences were found for the other five types of power between the two governance models. The six types of power were then tested with the one-way analysis of variance for four groups of respondents—chief academic officers, chief financial officers, library directors, and associate library directors (or equivalent)—between the two governance models. (When the institutions were categorized according to the prevailing governance model, no responses from chief administrative officers for collegial institutions were found.)

Statistically, there was little difference between the two governance models. When looking at the perceptions of the respondent groups of the type of power and degree of influence exerted by the library director in attempts to gain budgetary resources, even where there was a statistically significant difference, the actual means were similar. Table 3 presents a summary of these mean scores.

No statistically significant differences were found between the two governance models for any of the six types of power as perceived by the chief academic officers. Person power, functional role power, and task power were perceived to be effective in both bureaucratic and collegial institutions. Associational role power and reposeful power were perceived to have no effect when used by the library director in attempts to gain budgetary resources in both types of governance models. Sanction power was perceived to have no effect in bureaucratic institutions, but a negative effect in collegial institutions.

Chief financial officers also perceived functional role power, person power, and task power to be effective in both models of governance. Associational role power was perceived to have no effect when used by the library director. Although reposeful power and sanction power were perceived to have no effect in bureaucratic institutions, both types of power were perceived to have a negative effect in collegial institutions. No statistically significant differences between governance models were found for any of the six types of power.

There were no statistically significant differences between the two models of governance for any of the six types of power when perceived by the library di-

Table 2. Collective Responses for the Two Types of Governance

Types of Power	Bureaucratic			Collegial			
	Mean*	Number	Standard Deviation	Mean[a]	Number	Standard Deviation	F-ratio
Functional role	4.25	573	.58	4.14	84	.60	2.57
Person	3.95	555	.69	3.95	75	.68	0.00
Task	3.93	523	.69	3.96	72	.68	.06
Associational role	3.48	420	.75	3.44	55	.83	.19
Reposeful	2.82	210	.64	2.74	23	.75	.35
Sanction	2.65	333	.85	2.31	35	.58	5.13[b]

$F_{.05} = 3.84$.

[a] The mean scores are based on the effectiveness ratings: 2 = negative effect, 3 = no effect, 4 = effective, and 5 = very effective. "Don't know" and "not used at all" responses were not included in the calculations.

[b] $p < .05$.

189

Table 3. Mean Scores of the Four Groups Between Governance Models

Types of Power	Chief academic officer		Chief financial officer		Library director		Associate library director		Collective responses	
	$Mean_B$	$Mean_C^a$	$Mean_B$	$Mean_C$	$Mean_B$	$Mean_C$	$Mean_B$	$Mean_C$	$Mean_B$	$Mean_C$
Functional role	4.38	4.17	4.30	4.17	4.18	4.21	4.18	4.00	4.25	4.14
Person	3.84	3.85	3.81	3.73	4.15	4.00	3.98	4.20	3.95	3.95
Task	4.01	4.00	3.89	3.91	3.99	4.00	3.86	3.87	3.93	3.96
Associational role	3.47	3.36	3.41	3.13	3.43	3.69	3.63	3.44	3.48	3.44
Reposeful	2.57	2.80	2.77	2.25	2.85	2.80	3.02	3.00	2.82	2.74
Sanction	2.53	2.32	2.51	2.13	2.64	2.20	2.87	3.00	2.65	2.31

^{a}B = Bureaucratic; C = Collegial.

The mean scores are based upon the effectiveness ratings: 2 = negative effect; 3 = no effect; 4 = effective; and 5 = very effective. "Don't know" and "not used at all" responses were not included in the calculations.

rectors themselves. Task power, functional role power, and person power were perceived to be effective in both bureaucratic and collegial institutions. Associational role power, perceived to have no effect in bureaucratic institutions, was perceived by library directors to be effective in collegial institutions. Reposeful power was perceived to have no effect in either governance model. Sanction power was perceived to have no effect in a bureaucratic model of governance, but a negative effect in a collegial model.

Associate library directors perceived functional role power, person power, and task power to be effective in both types of governance. Associational role power was also perceived to be effective in bureaucratic institutions, but to have no effect in collegial institutions. Reposeful power and sanction power were both perceived to have no effect when used by the library director in both bureaucratic and collegial institutions in attempts to gain budgetary resources for the library. There were no statistically significant differences between governance models for any of the six types of power.

Prior to the investigation, it was expected that the type of power and the amount of influence exerted by the library director in attempts to gain budgetary resources for the library would be related to the governance model—bureaucratic or collegial—that was operating at the institution. As Figure 1 indicates, three types of power—functional role power, task power, and person power—were perceived to be effective in both bureaucratic and collegial institutions. Associational role power and reposeful power were perceived by the library director to have no effect in both types of governance in attempts to gain budgetary resources. Sanction power was perceived to have no effect in bureaucratic institutions but a negative effect in collegial institutions. Although a statistically significant difference was found between the two governance models for sanction power when perceived by all respondents collectively, the results of this investigation did not support the initial premise concerning power and its relationship to governance.

The one-way analysis of variance was also used to test the second research hypothesis: The degree of political activity will be greater in a bureaucratic model of governance in academic institutions than in a collegial model of governance. Respondents were given a list of 10 constituents and asked how influential they perceived each constituent to be in determining budgetary allocations to the library. These constituents were president, vice president for academic affairs, chief budget officer, budget committee, library director, heads of academic departments, library committee, internal special interest groups, state legislature, collective bargainers, and an "other" category. The response categories were as follows: 0 = "not applicable," 1 = "no influence," 2 = "minor influence," 3 = "moderate influence," 4 = "considerable influence," and 5 = "maximum influence."

Prior to an analysis of the data, the amount of agreement or disagreement among the respondents concerning the presence of political activity within insti-

Figure 1.   The Effectiveness of Power Between Governance Models

Bureaucratic Institutions (N = 66)			
Very effective	Effective	No effect	Negative effect
	Functional´role power		
	Person´power		
	Taskpower		
	Associatîonal		
		Role power	
		Repôseful power	
		Sanctiôn power	

Collegial Institutions (N = 10)			
Very effective	Effective	No effect	Negative effect
	Functional role power		
	Persoñ power		
Task pôwer			
	Associatîonal		
	role power		
		Reposeful power	
		Sanctioñ power	

Note: "ˆ" represents the actual mean of each type of power.

tutions was observed. Of the 66 institutions categorized as bureaucratic, the respondents at 41 of these institutions disagreed about the presence of political activity occurring within their institutions. The respondents at two of the collegial institutions disagreed about the presence of political activity at their institutions. The responses of all participants were weighted for the analysis of political activity. The range of responses was from "no influence" to "moderate influence."

The analysis of variance test revealed no significant differences in the degree of political activity between the two models of governance. Table 4 displays the findings of the testing. The mean scores of the two governance models also indicates that political activity has minor influence in the determination of budgetary allocations to the library.

A number of researchers have written about studying colleges and universities in a political context.[47] Baldridge advocates that a political analysis should be a primary approach to a study of governance in colleges and universities.[48] The findings of this investigation, along with Moxley's, however, indicate that political activity is not as prevalent as the literature might suggest.

This investigation was undertaken on the belief that Association of Research Library directors need to develop more effective techniques in attempts to gain

Table 4. Political Activity Between Governance Models

Governance model	Number	Total[a]	Mean[b]	Standard deviation
Bureaucratic	229	403	1.76	.827
Collegial	31	53	1.71	.824
Total	260	456		

F = .102 $F_{.05} = 3.84$

[a]The total score is the sum of the ratings of the two statements used to define political activity (Section A: question 3 of the questionnaire).
[b]The mean scores are based upon the influence ratings: 1 = no influence; 2 = minor influence; 3 = moderate influence; 4 = considerable influence; and 5 = maximum influence. "Not applicable" responses were not included in the calculations.

resource allocations for the library. It was felt that the type of power and the amount of influence of the library director was related to the governance model predominant within the institution. It was also expected that the amount of political activity related to the determination of budgetary allocations to the library would be greater in a bureaucratic model of governance in academic institutions than in a collegial model of governance.

The groups of respondents for this study were chosen with the expectation that they would be in a position to observe the use of power exerted by the library director in attempts to gain budgetary resources for the library. This investigation revealed that, statistically, there was only one significant difference in the perceptions of the respondents—when the collective responses were analyzed.

Based on the results of this investigation, three types of power were found to be effective when used by library directors in those libraries with membership in the Association of Research Libraries:

1. *Functional role power.* The professional expertise and the resources of the library director as a result of his or her role constitute functional role power. Functional role power ranked first as the most effective power base in both bureaucratic and collegial institutions. This ranking was supported by comments provided by some of the respondents. One administrator stated, "The importance of the Library Director maintaining a high positive profile with the campus top administrators is crucial." Another academic officer commented: "Our University Librarian is effective in keeping the needs of the library before the University Administration and the Deans."

2. *Person power.* Person power is based on the library director's personal characteristics and his or her ability to respond to the needs and traits of others. The mean scores of person power showed that person power was ranked second in effectiveness as perceived by the collective responses of all groups and the library directors and associate library directors. Person power was ranked third in effectiveness by chief financial officers and chief academic officers. One academic officer commented on the person power utilized by the library director:

"He strives to obtain [a] fair share for Libraries but at the same time does not make unreasonable demands and does not encourage pressure groups to intervene for the libraries."

3. *Task power.* Task power is related to the library director's domain of influence within the context of budgetary decision making in colleges and universities. Task power pertains to the skills of financial management and budget development, and the ability of the library director to obtain external funding for the library. Task power was ranked second in effectiveness, after functional role power and person power, by the chief academic officers and chief financial officers. The mean scores showed that task power ranked third in effectiveness as perceived by library directors and associate library directors. The importance of the use of task power when utilized by the library director was illustrated by these statements from some of the respondents: "Third-party funding grants is critical"; "We could not function with a Library Director . . . who did not possess adequate budgetary skills."

4. *Associational role power.* Associational role power of the library director is derived from contacts or associations established by the library director. Overall, associational role power, when used by the library director, was perceived as having no effect in attempts to gain budgetary resources. No supporting statements were provided by respondents to indicate that this type of power had any effect on the decision-making process. Metz's study of 215 academic institutions revealed that library directors spend a greater portion of their time on internal library matters than in dealing with other individuals outside the library and the institution. Respondents in his study, library directors, indicated that only 11 percent of their time was spent with external constituents—foundations, donors, other librarians, and other people.[49]

5. *Reposeful power.* Reposeful power is derived from the library director's inactivity in any form of power. Reposeful power was perceived to have no effect when used by the library director in either governance model. One respondent commented about the use of resposeful power: "Director definitely operates on a 'don't rock the boat' principle." This comment by an administrative officer makes it understandable why a library director might act in a passive manner: "The largest share of the budget is formula driven and depends on the health of the state's revenues. The Library Director has almost no control over either of these and therefore is a passive actor in allocations." A number of other respondents also indicated that the allocation of resources rests with the legislature.

6. *Sanction power.* When utilized by the library director, sanction power involves the use of coercion in an effort to gain budgetary resources. Sanction power was perceived primarily to have a negative effect when used by the library director in seeking budgetary resources.

An investigation of political activity in relation to the allocation of resources to the library revealed that this variable holds minor influence in those libraries holding membership in the Association of Research Libraries, whether a bureaucratic or collegial model of governance is operating at an institution.

Political activity was defined as influence exerted by two sets of constituents in determining budgetary allocations to the library. Respondents were asked to rate these two sets of constituents in relation to several others (president, vice president for academic affairs, heads of academic departments, library committee, etc.) in order to determine the degree of political activity.

The findings of the study did not support the second research hypothesis that the degree of political activity would be greater in a bureaucratic model of governance than in a collegial model. The mean scores, representing the perceptions of the respondents, were 1.76 for bureaucratic institutions and 1.71 for collegial institutions—indicating minor influence for political activity in the determination of budgetary resources for the library.

This investigation was limited to examining the effectiveness of library directors in the budgetary decision-making process at those academic institutions having membership in the Association of Research Libraries. It is hoped that this study will encourage similar investigations across and within other types of institutions in higher education (e.g., liberal arts colleges, community colleges) in order to determine if the effectiveness of the library director in budgetary decision making is contingent upon institutional mission and control as well as the decision-making structure. It is also hoped that this study will provide a foundation for further studies concerning the role of the library director within governance.

APPENDIX A

Definition of Terms

1. *ARL Libraries.* Educational institutions, excluding Canadian institutions and research and public libraries, having membership in the Association of Research Libraries as of May 1981.
2. *Library director.* The individual having administrative responsibilities for the overall direction of the library.
3. *Associate library director.* The individual whose title is most closely related to internal library technical operations/budgeting, where there exists more than one associate library director, or to that single individual who possesses the title of associate or assistant library director.
4. *Chief administrative officer.* The individual having administrative responsibility for the overall direction of the institution.
5. *Chief academic officer.* The individual having responsibility for the academic and/or educational programs of the institution.
6. *Chief financial officer.* The individual who has the responsibility for institutional budgeting.

7. *Bureaucratic models.* Institutions whose budget decision-making policies and budget-allocation decisions are primarily determined by the chief administrative officer and/or a council composed of top level administrators.

8. *Collegial models.* Institutions whose budget decision-making policies and budget-allocation decisions are primarily determined by a budget committee and/or a governing body, such as a faculty senate.

9. *Political activity.* Refers to the influence of internal special groups and collective bargainers in determining budget decision-making policies and budget-allocation decisions within the institution.

10. *Power structure.* Seventeen influence activities have been developed to describe the six types of power utilized by the library director in budgetary decision making.

Person power

a. The library director demonstrates oral and/or written communication skills.

b. The library director displays a broad awareness of institutional activities.

c. The library director displays interpersonal-relation skills (tact, understanding, tolerance, etc.).

Task power

a. The library director demonstrates an ability to obtain outside funds (e.g., grants, endowments).

b. The library director demonstrates expertise in financial management.

c. The library director demonstrates expertise in budget development skills.

Functional role power

a. The library director demonstrates skills and knowledge of the library profession.

b. The library director supplies the administration with information concerning expanding library services, etc.

c. The library director relates the goals and objectives of the library to those of the institution.

Associational role power

a. The library director involves the library staff in the development of the library budget and in establishing funding priorities.

b. The library director gains the support of influential people outside the library (e.g., trustees, governing board, state legislature).

Reposeful power

a. The library director gives the appearance of nonaction, does not "rock the boat" or raise any conflict-producing issues.

b. The library director encourages the library staff to teach on a voluntary basis, with the expectation that budgetary funds would be supplied to the library in exchange.

Sanction power
a. The library director overspends appropriated library funds in order to gain a larger budget for the next year.
b. The library director brings external pressure to bear on an issue (e.g., possible unionization).
c. The library director threatens cutback of library services if budget requests are not granted.

APPENDIX B

Section A: Budgetary Decision Making Models of Governance

Please indicate your *perceptions* of how budgetary decision making operates at your institution by circling the appropriate responses.

1. Budget decision making *policies* within the institution are primarily determined by: (Circle the one that best characterizes your situation)
The president. 1
A president's council (e.g., composed of top level administrations). . . . 2
A budget committee 3
A governing body (i.e., faculty senate) 4
Special interest groups or individuals who exert pressure informally
"behind the scenes". 5
Collective bargainers 6
2. Budget allocation *decisions* within the institution are primarily determined by: (Circle the one that best characterizes your situation)
The president. 1
A president's council (e.g., composed of top level administrators). 2
A budget committee 3
A governing body (i.e., faculty senate) 4
Special interest groups or individuals who exert pressure informally
"behind the scenes". 5
Collective bargainers 6
3. How influential do you *perceive* the following constituents to be in determining budgetary allocations to the library? (Circle "0" = Not Applicable if the constituent is not represented at your institution)
Maximum influence _____
Considerable influence _____
Moderate influence _____
Minor influence _____
No influence _____
Not applicable _____

 1. President 0   1   2   3   4   5
 2. Vice President for Academic Affairs 0   1   2   3   4   5
 3. Chief budget officer 0   1   2   3   4   5
 4. Budget committee 0   1   2   3   4   5
 5. Library director 0   1   2   3   4   5
 6. Heads of academic departments 0   1   2   3   4   5
 7. Library committee 0   1   2   3   4   5
 8. Internal special interest groups 0   1   2   3   4   5
 9. State legislature 0   1   2   3   4   5
10. Collective bargainers 0   1   2   3   4   5
11. Others, please specify:

_____ 0   1   2   3   4   5

_____ 0   1   2   3   4   5

Section B: Influence in Budgetary Decision Making

(Form for Non-Library Director)

How effective is each of the following when used by the library director when attempting to gain budgetary allocations for the library? Circle the number that most closely represents your situation. (Please respond in terms of how effective the activity *actually is*, not how effective it should be).

Very effective _____

Effective _____

No effect _____

Negative effect _____

Not used at all _____

Don't know _____

 1. Demonstrates expertise in financial management .. 0   1   2   3   4   5
 2. Demonstrates an ability to obtain outside funds   0   1   2   3   4   5
    (e.g., grants, endowments) ....
 3. Gives the appearance of non-action; does not   0   1   2   3   4   5
    "rock the boat" nor raise any conflict-producing
    issues ....
 4. Demonstrates skills and knowledge of the library 0   1   2   3   4   5
    profession ....
 5. Overspends appropriated library funds in order to 0   1   2   3   4   5
    gain a larger budget for the next year ....
 6. Demonstrates expertise in budget development   0   1   2   3   4   5
    skills ....

7. Brings external pressure to bear on an issue (e.g.,   0   1   2   3   4   5
possible unionization)......................

8. Demonstrates oral and/or written communication   0   1   2   3   4   5
skills ....

9. Supplies the administration with information con-   0   1   2   3   4   5
cerning expanding library services, etc..........

10. Involves the library staff in the development of the   0   1   2   3   4   5
library budget and establishing funding priorities .

11. Displays interpersonal relation skills (tact, under-   0   1   2   3   4   5
standing, tolerance, etc.) ....

12. Gains the support of influential people outside the   0   1   2   3   4   5
library (e.g., trustees, governing board, state
legislature ....

13. Displays a broad awareness of institutional   0   1   2   3   4   5
activities ....

14. Encourages library staff to teach on a voluntary ba-   0   1   2   3   4   5
sis, with the expectation that budgetary funds
would be supplied to the library in exchange .....

15. Threatens cutback of library services if budget re-   0   1   2   3   4   5
quests are not granted ....

16. Strives for membership of self and library staff on   0   1   2   3   4   5
strategic committees ....

17. Relates the goals and objectives of the library to   0   1   2   3   4   5
those of the institution......................

Comments

The space below is provided for you to write any comments you have regarding this investigation and questionnaire.

Section B: Influence in Budgetary Decision Making

(Form for the Library Director)

How effective is each of the following when you use it in your attempt to gain
budgetary allocations for the library? Circle the number that most closely represents your situation. (Please respond in terms of how effective the activity *actually is*, not how effective it should be).

Very effective _____

Effective _____

No effect _____

Negative effect _____

Not used at all _____

1. Demonstrate expertise in financial management .. 1   2   3   4   5
2. Demonstrate an ability to obtain funds (e.g., 1   2   3   4   5
    grants, endowments)........................
3. Give the appearance of non-action; does not "rock 1   2   3   4   5
    the boat" nor raise any conflict-producing issues. .
4. Demonstrate skills and knowledge of the library 1   2   3   4   5
    profession ....
5. Overspend appropriated library funds in order to 1   2   3   4   5
    gain a larger budget for the next year ....
6. Demonstrate expertise in budget development 1   2   3   4   5
    skills ....
7. Bring external pressure to bear on an issue (e.g., 1   2   3   4   5
    possible unionization).....................
8. Demonstrate oral and/or written communication 1   2   3   4   5
    skills ....
9. Supplie the administration with information con- 1   2   3   4   5
    cerning expanding library services, etc..........
10. Involve the library staff in the development of the 1   2   3   4   5
    library budget and establishing funding priorities .
11. Display interpersonal relation skills (tact, under- 1   2   3   4   5
    standing, tolerance, etc.) ....
12. Gain the support of influential people outside the 1   2   3   4   5
    library (e.g., trustees, governing board, state
    legislature)...............................
13. Display a broad awareness of institutional 1   2   3   4   5
    activities ....
14. Encourage library staff to teach on a voluntary ba- 1   2   3   4   5
    sis, with the expectation that budgetary funds
    would be supplied to the library in exchange .....
15. Threaten cutback of library services if budget re- 1   2   3   4   5
    quests are not granted ....
16. Strive for membership of self and library staff on 1   2   3   4   5
    strategic committees ....
17. Relate the goals and objectives of the library to 1   2   3   4   5
    those of the institution.....................

Section C: Status of the Library Budget

1. What percentage of the total institutional budget was allocated to the library? (Please write in)

   1979-80   _____%

   1980-81   _____%

   1981-82   _____%

2. Who is responsible for the internal allocation of the library's budget? (Circle the most representative answer)

   The library director   1

   The library director, with consultation with other library members   2

   The library director, library staff and with faculty input   3

   The library director, with input from the academic deans   4

   Other, please specify: _____

   _____ 5

Section D: Personal Information Sheet

(Library Director)

Instructions:

Perceptions and behaviors about decision making are often shaped and affected by earlier experiences and current status. This section collects this kind of information concerning you. Please circle the proper numbers and fill in the appropriate spaces.

1. What title does your present position carry?

   Director of Library   1   Vice President   4

   Dean of Libraries   2   Other _____

   Librarian   3   _____ 5

2. How many years have you had your present position?

   0 - 5 years 1

   6 - 10 years 2

   11 - 15 years 3

   16 - 20 years 4

   Over 20 years 5

3. How many years of service have you as a library director in a college or university?

   0 - 5 years 1

   6 - 10 years 2

   11 - 15 years 3

   16 - 20 years 4

   Over 20 years 5

4. To whom do you report most directly within the administration?

    President   1 Assistant Provost   4
    Vice President for   Other _____
       Academic Affairs   2 _____ 5
    Provost   3

5. How many of your professional writings have been published or accepted
    for publication (including joint authorship) in the last five years?

    b. Books _____

    a. Articles _____

	a	b
1 - 3	1	1
4 - 6	2	2
7 - 10	3	3
11 +	4	4
None	5	5

6. What is your present rank?
    Faculty rank and title (Professor, etc.)   1
    Equivalent rank (Librarian, etc.)   2
    Assimilated rank (Librarian with rank of Professor)   3
    Other (please supply) _____   4

7. What is your age?
    Under 31 1
    31 - 40 2
    41 - 50 3
    51 - 60 4
    Over 60 5

8. Your sex: Female 1   Male 2

9. List the academic degrees (beginning with the most recent) which you have
    been awarded and the year each was obtained.

Degree	University	Year

10. On what campus-wide committees do you serve?

        Appointed/Elected   *Voluntary*

    _____   _____

    _____   _____

    _____   _____

    _____   _____

11. To what professional associations do you belong?

    _____   _____

    _____   _____

    _____   _____

Comments

Please feel free to attach a sheet with comments you have regarding this investigation and questionnaire.

If you would like to receive an abstract of this study upon completion, please indicate: Yes _____ No _____

NOTES AND REFERENCES

1. Richard De Gennaro, "Austerity, Technology and Resource Sharing," *Library Journal* 100 (May 15, 1975): 919.

2. Miriam A. Drake, "Management Control in Academic Libraries," in Robert D. Stueart and Richard D. Johnson, eds., *New Horizons for Academic Libraries* (New York: K.G. Saur, 1979), 91–95; Robert H. Simmons and William O. Van Arsdale III, "Academic Libraries Fall on Hard Times," *Southeastern Librarian* 31 (Fall 1981): 103–104.

3. Arthur M. McAnally and Robert B. Downs, "The Changing Role of Directors of University Libraries," *College and Research Libraries* 34 (March 1973): 105.

4. H. William Axford. "The Interrelations of Structure, Governance, and Effective Resource Utilization in Academic Libraries," *Library Trends* 23 (April 1975): 560.

5. Earl C. Bolton, "Response of University Library Management to Changing Modes of University Governance and Control," *College & Research Libraries* 33 (July 1972): 309–310.

6. Booz, Allen & Hamilton, Inc., *Problems in University Library Management* (Washington, DC: Association of Research Libraries, 1970), 5.

7. Beverly P. Lynch, "Options for the 80s: Directions in Academic and Research Libraries," *College & Research Libraries* 43 (March 1982): 129.

8. Duane E. Webster. "Issues in the Financial Management of Research Libraries," *Journal of Library Administration* 3 (Fall/Winter 1982): 13.

9. George W. Whitbeck. *The Influence of Libraries in Liberal Arts Colleges in Selected Decision Making Areas,* (Metuchen, N.J.: The Scarecrow Press, 1972), 120–121.

10. Ibid., 121.

11. Susan A. Lee, "Conflict and Ambiguity in the Role of the Academic Library Director," *College and Research Libraries* 38 (September 1977): 396–403.

12. Ibid., 399.

13. Paul Metz, "The Role of the Academic Library Director," *The Journal of Academic Librarianship* 5 (July 1979): 148.

14. Ibid., 149.

15. Ibid., 150.

16. Robert S. Runyon, "Power and Conflict in Academic Libraries," *The Journal of Academic Librarianship* 3 (September 1977): 200.

17. Ibid., 201.

18. For a discussion of the findings concerning the relationship between the personal characteristics of the library director and the library budget, see Susan Elaine McCargar. "The University Library Director in Budgetary Decision Making: A Study of Power, Influence, and Governance" (Ph.D. diss. The University of Michigan, 1984), chap. IV.

19. B. Raven, "Social Influence and Power," in I. D. Steiner and M. Fishbein, eds., *Current Studies in Social Psychology* (New York: Holt, Rinehart and Winston, 1965), 371.

20. Kurt Lewin, *Field Theory and Social Science* (New York: Harper and Bros., 1951).

21. Edward Gross and Paul V. Grambsch, *University Goals and Academic Power* (Washington, D.C.: American Council on Education, 1966).

22. Winston W. Hill and Wendell L. French, "Perceptions of the Power of Department Chairmen by Professors," *Administrative Science Quarterly* 11 (March 1967): 548–574.

23. Talcott Parsons and Gerald Platt, *The American Academic Profession* (Washington, D.C.: National Science Foundation, 1968).

24. J. Victor Baldridge et al., *Policy Making and Effective Leadership* (San Francisco: Jossey-Bass, 1978), 73.

25. A. S. Tannenbaum, *Control in Organizations* (New York: McGraw-Hill, 1968), 33; Daniel Katz and Robert L. Kahn, *The Social Psychology of Organizations* (New York: Wiley, 1966), 218–220.

26. J. R. P. French, Jr. and B. Raven. "The Bases of Social Power," in Dorwin Cartwright, ed., *Studies in Social Power* (Ann Arbor: Research Center for Group Dynamics, Institute for Social Research, The University of Michigan, 1959), 150–151.

27. Ibid., 151–164.

28. Informational power was described as informational influence by French and Raven, "Bases of Social Power," 163–164 and Raven, "Social Influence and Power," 372–373.

29. Parsons and Platt *American Academic Profession;* Gerald Platt and Talcott Parsons, "Decision-making in the Academic System: Influence and Power Exchange," in C. E. Kruytbosch and S. L. Messinger, eds., *The State of the University: Authority and Change* (Beverly Hills: Sage, 1968); R. G. Cope, "Bases of Power, Administrative Preferences, and Job Satisfaction: A Situational Approach," *Journal of Vocational Behavior* 2 (April 1972): 457–465.

30. Linda Sue Moxley, "The Student Personnel Administrator in the Budgetary Process: Decision Structures, Power, and Purse Strings" (Ph.D. diss. The University of Michigan 1980), 21, 259–260.

31. Ibid., 265.

32. Herbert H. Stroup, *Bureaucracy in Higher Education* (New York: The Free Press, 1966), 42–44.

33. J. Victor Baldridge, *Power and Conflict in the University: Research in the Sociology of Complex Organizations* (New York: Wiley, 1971), 11.

34. Ibid.

35. John D. Millett, *The Academic Community: An Essay on Organization* (New York: McGraw-Hill, 1962), 234–235.

36. Baldridge, *Power and Conflict,* 14.

37. Millett, *The Academic Community,* 234.

38. Baldridge, *Power and Conflict,* 14.

39. Ibid., 19–20.

40. Ibid., 21–25, 192.

41. Marie E. Childers, "What is Political about Bureaucratic-Collegial Decision-Making?" *The Review of Higher Education* 5 (Fall 1981): 25–45; Moxley, "The Student Personnel Adminstrator," 31–46.

42. Childers, "What is Political," 41–43.

43. Moxley, "The Student Personnel Administrator," 71, 369.

44. Baldridge, *Power and Conflict,* 23; Childers, "What is Political," 25–45.

45. Richard C. Richardson. "Governance Theory: A Comparison of Approaches." *Journal of Higher Education* 45 (May 1974): 344–354.

46. Portions of Moxley's instrument were modified for the purposes of this study—fewer questions were used to identify the governance models; the influence activities of the library director were adapted from those developed by Moxley for the student personnel administrator—fewer influence activities were used in the questionnaire.

47. Baldridge, *Power and Conflict,* 20; Baldridge et al., *Policy Making and Effective Leadership.*

48. Baldridge, *Power and Conflict,* 15.

49. Metz, "The Role of the Academic Library Director," 149.

GETTING FROM HERE TO THERE:
KEEPING AN ACADEMIC LIBRARY IN OPERATION DURING CONSTRUCTION/ RENOVATION

T. John Metz

INTRODUCTION

The literature provides excellent material on almost all of the stages of library planning, from assessing the need for expansion to planning the dedication ceremony. The product is, after all, the thing, and most writers wish to document the physical achievement and the conceptual, organizational, and architectural planning that went into it. However, the librarian who has expended the tremendous effort involved in selling the idea of a new building, planning it, getting it funded, and has reached a point where a contractor is engaged and work is ready to begin, will find little in the literature to help in working out arrangements for

Advances in Library Administration and Organization
Volume 5, pages 207–219
Copyright © 1986 by JAI Press Inc.
All rights of reproduction in any form reserved.
ISBN: 0-89232-674-3

maintaining services for a year or more in a building that is being renovated and/or having an addition added. This can be a difficult period, and one that tends to be forgotten in the excitement and activity of occupying and adapting to new quarters. However, if the library is as necessary to the functioning of an academic institution as we would all like to think it is, it becomes rather important that materials continue to be acquired and made available and that library services be provided throughout the construction process. It is the purpose of this article to describe the stages of planning required, the options that may be available, and some of the problems that need to be resolved in order to keep a library operating during a period of construction.

ALTERNATIVES

We will assume that the alternative of a totally new building has been rejected. The remaining alternatives include moving the library into temporary quarters outside the building, moving some library functions or materials to temporary quarters outside the building, eliminating or reducing some library functions during construction, compacting and/or storing some materials within the building, reconfiguring the library to fit into available space, and phasing the moves of functions and materials within the building with the construction and demolition schedules so that services continue to function and access to materials is retained throughout the process. Moving into temporary quarters may be an attractive alternative for smaller libraries. For a sizable library, however, moving materials and dismantling and erecting shelving twice can be a very lengthy and costly process that could more than double the time and labor requirements of the move. Moreover, most campuses do not have suitable vacant space sufficient to accommodate a large library in a location easily accessible to users. In most situations, we are faced with a combination of the remaining alternatives. Before a decision can be made as to which alternatives can be used and to what extent each should be used, the librarian needs to gather a substantial amount of information about the library, explore some concerns with the contractor, and have at least the preliminary construction schedule in hand.

PRELIMINARY STEPS

In preparation for construction planning, the librarian should gather the following information, which will be needed to plan moves and to schedule the work to be done:

1. Review every library space and function and determine the minimum amount of space that each requires—often, this will be the amount of space it now occupies. For each function, also note the requirements for

power, telephone, cable, and other utilities, and critical relationships to other areas and functions.

2. Identify and prioritize those spaces and functions that could be eliminated or moved out during construction—public and staff lounge areas, language lab, AV center, reserve book room, browsing, archives, rare books, mending and binding, etc. On-line access to holdings could increase the mobility of some functions.

3. Know *exactly* the number of yards of shelving every division of the classification and every collection of materials would occupy if it were to be compacted as tightly as possible. This information should be gathered by someone experienced in laying out stacks and estimating linear space occupied by books—not arbitrarily assigned to whatever students happen to be available.

4. Know the annual rate, in yards, at which materials are being added to each collection and each division of the classification. If you are reclassifying, know the number of linear yards of reclassified books that will go in each division of the classification.

5. Find out how long it takes to move a given quantity of books in the library, both on the same floor and between floors.

6. From the foregoing information, determine the very least amount of space in square footage that is needed to keep the library operational and the least quantity of shelving that can hold library collections. Minimum square footages for stacks, for user space, and for functions and services should be precisely determined.

Besides gathering information for the move, the following work should be completed before the busy period of planning, moving, and construction arrives:

1. Dispose of or locate a temporary home for everything in library storage that will not be needed during the construction period. If the library has been storing materials or objects belonging to others, return them. If anyone not essential to the library operation is occupying office or other space in the library, move them out.

2. Remove to outside storage everything occupying active library space that is not essential to library operations—art work, display cases, plants, benches, large lounge furniture, AV equipment, and so forth.

3. Order or borrow a sufficient quantity of sturdy, high-capacity booktrucks. Do not skimp here. These trucks will see several lifetimes of normal use during the move, and it is essential that they not break down. Higher capacity means fewer trips. Workers should spend their efforts moving materials, not wending their way through the clutter of a construction site and waiting for elevators.

ESTABLISHING BASIC RELATIONSHIPS

In order for construction to proceed efficiently and for the library to remain functional during construction, it is critical that the librarian establish very close working relationships based on mutual respect and trust with three key people: the person responsible for coordinating the project for the institution, the architect, and the construction supervisor. If the librarian cannot do this, someone who can establish these relationships should be found to manage the project for the library. The earlier in the planning process these four key people can begin working together, the better. All members of this team need to be tolerant, flexible, and imaginative in accommodating both library and construction needs. All must be sensitive to the need to work through channels, to keep all parties informed, and to not upset complex relationships between institution, library, library staff, users, architect, contractor, subcontractor, and suppliers. In order to know what is being planned that will affect the operation of the library and to keep others aware of library needs, the librarian must insist on being an active participant in any regular meetings held between contractor, subcontractors, engineers, institutional representatives, and the architect. In effect, administration of the building is shared between the librarian and the construction supervisor, and they both need all the information they can get about each other's plans and activities. It is the responsibility of the librarian to learn the relationships between all concerned interests and to know the circumstances under which problems can be discussed directly with a workman or subcontractor, and those that require going to the construction supervisor, institutional representative, or architect. Always err on the side of caution. The librarian can make an invaluable contribution, but final responsibility for the project rests with the institution's project coordinator, the contractor, and the architect. Don't try to assume any of their prerogatives.

BASIC CONCERNS

Some essential matters need to be resolved or reviewed before either the contractor or the library can develop a plan:

1. *How will public access and library exit control be maintained throughout the construction period?* It may take a degree of imagination to resolve this problem. In a recent project, where all regular and emergency exits to the existing building were blocked and the contractor needed to move equipment and materials around the remaining perimeter, an entrance was broken into a stack floor at the third level and a bridge was built across to the parking lot of an adjoining building, leaving space for construction equipment to move beneath it. Some stack ranges were removed to make room for circulation and exit control at the new entrance, and the bridge served as access to the main entrance for over a year.

2. *How will code requirements regarding emergency exits and stairways be met during construction?* Complying with safety codes could require maintaining pathways to emergency exits through library work and/or construction areas, constructing temporary stairways, building some elements of new construction before their logical sequence, and the like.

3. *How will the library maintain continuing access to electrical control panels, alarms, signals, etc.? Also, how will umbilical cords to services such as OCLC be kept intact?* Solutions to these problems may include temporary wiring, temporary walls and offices, leaving lights on continuously in some areas for certain periods, or temporary switching.

4. *How will heat, ventilation, power, access to restrooms, and so forth, be maintained?* These are needs the contractor must keep in mind as construction planning proceeds, but for which detailed plans may not be made in advance.

5. *How can vehicular access to the building be maintained to allow for regular deliveries, trash pickup, etc.?*

6. *How will elevator access be arranged?* The library needs almost continual elevator access to move materials, and the contractor will need at least periodic access. A possible solution is to schedule library moves after construction hours, assuming only one shift is being used.

OTHER CONCERNS

Other points that need to be discussed include the following:

1. The contractor needs to be made aware of, and to make the workers aware of, the continuing need for a level, unobstructed path for booktrucks for their entire route. Even a large electrical cord can effectively block the passage of booktrucks.

2. Security for library materials and contractor's equipment needs to be arranged.

3. Provisions for protecting library materials and equipment from dust and other damage need to be considered.

4. The need to protect library personnel from dust, fumes, noise, etc. should be discussed. Protective devices such as dust masks, hearing protectors, and hard hats should be made available to staff who may need them to pass through certain areas or to work near a demolition site.

5. Constraints on construction workers who may not be accustomed to working in or near occupied library space should be pointed out. The contractor should establish rules on smoking, radios, leaving doors and windows open, and so forth, before the work begins.

6. Access to the construction site by library personnel and to the library space by construction personnel during various phases of construction

should be reviewed. There will be times, particularly during renovation, when it will be almost impossible to completely separate library from construction space.

7. Constraints on library personnel who are moving materials should be resolved. Are they restricted to moving materials, or can they also remove shelving from and install shelving on uprights and perform tasks such as removing empty boxes and other construction trash that may be in the way? Can they move through construction areas to reach the elevator? Answers to these questions will determine to what degree and in what ways library workers can be utilized, may effect the sequence in which spaces are exchanged between contractor and library, and could alter the scheduling of demolition or installation of elevators.

LIBRARY REQUIREMENTS

In addition to the basic concerns, the librarian must also help the contractor to understand the following library requirements:

1. When library use is critical and when it is not—not just vacation and exam periods, but days of the week, times of the day, etc. This will help the construction supervisor to identify both large and small blocks of time when demolition and other work that might be very disruptive to the library might be scheduled.

2. Library operational requirements, preferences, and options and their relative importance. These include the minimum square footage needed to maintain library operations in terms of stack space, user space, and space for functions and services; areas the library prefers to keep in place and areas that are relatively easy to move; critical relationships between different parts of the library; the sequence of moves and relinquishment and occupation of spaces that would be least disruptive to the library.

3. The library's need to move in an orderly sequential fashion. Contractors sometimes do not understand that when library materials are being moved in sequence it is often not possible to speed up the process by assigning more people to the task, and that it is very difficult to make up time lost through interruptions. Contractors are not accustomed to working at a regular pace. Their normal operating procedure is to add workers as needed to maintain schedules and to work everywhere at once, doing all the wiring, then all the plastering, then all the painting, etc. It is inefficient to bring in workmen to do only a small amount of work in one area, even though the library will prefer to have spaces completed in sequence, one at a time. It is helpful to identify and attempt to resolve these differences early on. The contractor will organize the construction work around library requirements to the degree possible, but staff and users

must recognize that construction must proceed efficiently, that it is very costly to do otherwise, and that unforeseen problems will arise. It is highly unlikely that a major addition and renovation will move at the even pace and in the orderly sequence to which most library personnel are accustomed, and many surprises, changes, and disruptions of plans should be expected. Both the construction and the library plans need to have as much flexibility and as many options and plans for contingencies as possible.

THE LIBRARY PLAN

When the preliminary construction schedule is completed, it should be reviewed with the construction supervisor to identify "tight spots" where certain work has to be accomplished in order to proceed, leaving few or no alternatives. The library plan should be kept as flexible as possible at these points, and as the library plan evolves the contractor should be made aware of junctures in the library plan that are relatively inflexible. The next step is to identify the periods in which the least amount of space will be available for stacks, users, and operations. If these spaces are below the minimum space requirements established earlier, some negotiation between the librarian and the construction supervisor is in order. These periods of maximum restriction of library operations may indicate times when fewer options are open for library moves. If at all possible, such periods should be scheduled when library usage is low.

Having compiled data on all library functions and space needs, resolved and/or reviewed basic concerns, and reviewed the preliminary construction schedule to identify what spaces the library can use during the course of construction, it can now be determined which library functions can be retained in the building, which functions need to be moved out or discontinued, what materials need to be compacted or stored within the building, and how moves of library materials and functions might be planned and arranged in sequences that mesh with the construction schedule.

Adhering to the following principles can facilitate the process of moving and temporary space utilization:

1. The fewer moves the better. Work toward the final configuration and try to move most things only once—nothing more than twice.
2. People, offices, and furniture are much easier to move than library materials.
3. Moving staff functions is less disruptive and confusing than moving user-oriented functions. Keep the perspective of the user in mind when planning moves.
4. Stack space, if near capacity, is probably already being utilized at close to maximum efficiency and should be left alone as much as possible.

5. It is usually more difficult to move materials out of and back into a building than within a building, unless there is a level path between the buildings and the elevators involved.
6. No materials should be moved between floors more than once.
7. Shelved materials should be kept in sequence on shelving and moved with booktrucks. Avoid packing and unpacking containers whenever possible.
8. Avoid erecting and dismantling temporary shelving if at all possible.

In addition to the final plan for occupying the finished building, several other plans may be needed to move a library through a construction/renovation project. If the construction plan indicates one or more phases where library functions and materials remain in place for a substantial period of time while construction activities occur in space separate from the library, the problem is to evolve an interim configuration that will allow the library to carry on its normal activities and provide user access to materials. The library arrangement for these static phases is worked out through normal library-space-planning techniques, keeping in mind the principles suggested for planning moves and temporary utilization of space, the configuration for the next static phase of construction, and the final library plan.

It is probable that the space available to the library during construction will be more limited than existing space, at least during the earlier of the static phases. The most essential library materials and functions need to be organized within the available space, and the remainder relocated or eliminated. It is important that temporary configurations that will be in place for some time work well, especially if they occur during periods of normal library use. Available space should be viewed as open space, and planning should not be constrained by the presence or absence of doors, walls, ventilation, power, etc. If a workable plan cannot be developed without requiring temporary construction, wiring, ventilation, or some demolition, so be it. There is, of course, more constraint on the modifications that can be made in newly constructed space than in space slated for later renovation or demolition, but often, more total space is available for library purposes by the time new construction is being occupied by the library.

Example 1 is a plan for temporary occupation of space that may help to illustrate the process. This plan allowed most stacks and most public functions to remain in place. It included only those areas that actually needed to be moved or to be changed.

The plan outlined in Example 1 allowed all essential functions to retain approximately the amount of space they formerly occupied. Most of the 300 square feet lost in the temporary plan was through the elimination of consultation tables and traffic circulation space in the card catalog area. Card cabinet tops then served as a surface for consulting card trays.

A different kind of planning is required for phases of construction during which the library is evacuating old spaces and moving into new spaces at the

Example 1. Plan for Temporary Library Space

Function	Space in Old Quarters	Space in Temporary Quarters	Location of Temporary Quarters/ Modifications Needed
Cataloging	1005 SF	1012 SF	Present enclosed card catalog area. Move card catalog out, install door.
Acquisitions	1258 SF	1100 SF	Present circulation area and half of Main Lobby. Build wall to allow traffic to pass through area from main stair to reference room.
OCLC terminals	included above	200 SF	Elevator lobby between cataloging and acquisitions, 4th level.
Interlibrary Services	364 SF	288 SF	Staff Lounge and elevator lobby on 3rd level.
Administration	154 SF	144 SF	Present small study in 3rd level stacks
Document Preparation	252 SF	264 SF	Move microfilm materials and equipment closer together on 2nd level. Construct room in space gained.
Rare Books	154 SF	192 SF	Compact oversized books on 3rd level. Remove 12 d.f. stack sections and 3 study carrels. Construct room.
Browsing	484 SF	576 SF	Move shelves and books into study area on first level.
Student Lounge	484 SF	—	Eliminate.
Main Lobby	680 SF	—	Eliminate the half not used for Acquisitions.
Staff Lounge	200 SF	—	Eliminate.
Circulation	650 SF	657 SF	3rd level stacks. Remove 39 d.f. stack sections and 3 carrels at east end. Compact 3rd level books to clear needed stack sections. Open exterior door in east wall and construct bridge to parking lot.
Card Catalog	1012 SF	630 SF	Center aisle of reference room in one row, back to back. Remove consultation tables to make space.
Reference Office	99 SF	150 SF	Construct office at north end of reference room center aisle.
	6896 SF		
	—	—	
	less 1374 eliminated		
	—		
	5532 SF	5231 SF	

same time that the contractor is preparing other new spaces for library occupancy. This kind of active situation requires a plan for what is, essentially, a prolonged move from an existing library arrangement to either an interim or final library configuration. The object is to plan the most efficient sequence of steps to get from here to there, while allowing the maximum number of options and alternatives to cope with the unexpected. It requires a much closer relationship with the contractor, and probably, a merged plan for construction and library activities. This is a disruptive phase during which most arrangements are quite temporary, and it is probably more important to get through it as quickly as possible than to try to maintain an ideal functional configuration. If possible, active phases should be scheduled during periods of low library use. In any case, staff and users should be made aware that they can expect temporary inconveniences during active phases.

A typical active sequence involves renovation of stack areas—library removes books; contractor dismantles shelving; electricians remove old fixtures; floor covering comes off; plaster repairs are made; painters paint walls and ceilings; electricians install new fixtures; shelving is installed; library moves in books. Hopefully, this already-complex sequence is not further complicated by specifying that stacks rest on carpet or tile, in which case the entire operation becomes dependent on delivery and installation of floor covering.

Example 2 shows a portion of a schedule for an active phase of construction to illustrate the kind of planning required:

Some general principles for planning moves previously have been stated. Some specific procedures have also been proven useful. For example, it is helpful to divide the space to be evacuated and the space to be occupied into a grid—if you have a modular building, a bay is a good size to work with and can be precisely identified as to location. For each bay to be evacuated, list every-

Example 2. Portion of a Schedule for an Active Phase of Construction

Permanent	Spring	1.	Relocate ARCHIVES and RARE BOOKS to First Floor.
			A. Requires early finish in West end new construction including carpet.
			B. Requires early delivery and installation of NEW BOOKSTACKS.
Permanent	Spring	2.	Relocate GOV DOCUMENTS to Third Floor West End—3 people 38 hours = 5 days.
			A. Requires early finish in West end new construction. Defer CARPET installation.
			B. Requires early delivery and installation of NEW BOOK-STACKS (including end panels and lighting/switching installation).
			C. Move from First Floor allows early First Floor renovation (with 3 below).
Temporary	Spring	3.	Relocate (compactly) BOUND PERIODICALS at East end of First Floor—2 people 61 hours = 8 days.
			A. Locate in existing stacks (existing locations) in NEW STORAGE 152.
			B. Move from First Floor location.
			C. Allows early First Floor renovation at stacks 150.
			D. Allows availability of existing stacks from First Floor to be relocated to Level 2, West end.

Note: Numbers indicate library moves. Letters indicate notes to library moves and other work that must be completed.

Example 3. Steps for Preparing a Bay for Temporary Use

4th Level, Second Bay from South
Move public copying machine to 3rd floor circulation area.
Move office copying machine and photocopiers to 3rd level elevator lobby.
Move all lobby display equipment, furniture, and art objects to outside storage.
Install phone connections for OCLC terminals and cable connections for local VAX terminals in 4th level elevator lobby.
Construct a temporary acoustic and dust barrier across the three bays open to the south bay.
Enclose the main stairwell to permit air conditioning of the space.
Install artificial lighting to permit office work in the area.
Install electrical connections for the several work stations.

thing that has to be moved and indicate the bay or other location it is to be moved to. For bays to be occupied, list all wiring, plumbing, cabling, lighting, etc., that will be needed, along with all objects to be moved into the bay. From the lists for each bay, one can then separate out the various kinds of work that need to be done and develop schedules for temporary construction, mechanical work, and for the actual moves. Sequences to accomplish the work and the moves need to be worked out by the construction supervisor and the librarian together. Example 3 is a list of steps to be completed to prepare a bay for temporary occupancy.

In planning the moving of books and other library materials, divide the materials to be moved into small segments, arrange the segments into the most efficient sequence from the standpoint of the library, and then develop alternative sequences to meet contingencies. There should always be several alternative locations in which moving crews can be working, and they should easily be able to shift their activities to another location for an hour, a day, or whatever period construction activities dictate.

IMPLEMENTING THE PLAN

The contractor will view the general plan of construction as a guide, the details of which will change whenever circumstances provide an opportunity to save time and/or reduce costs. The plan will also change due to unforeseen problems in modifying the existing structure, delays in deliveries of materials, shortages of personnel, work that is finished ahead of or behind schedule, and last but by no means least, the weather. Barring a disaster such as a strike, or a supplier of some vital material going out of business, the general construction plan will probably be followed in broad outline, but details will vary enormously, and many of the details will affect library plans. The librarian should be prepared to be on the site early in the morning daily to meet with the construction supervisor and review plans for the day for both construction and library activities. Modifications will occur almost daily, and the librarian will need to learn to adapt to the mode of operation of the contractor, continually modifying plans as ways are found to reduce labor, increase options, and save time.

Usually, new construction is more susceptible to planning and less disruptive than demolition and renovation. The most disruptive work often involves vertical elements that penetrate all floors—stairways, air ducts, and the like—in existing construction. The construction superintendent will be aware of library needs and constraints and will do what can be done to communicate them to subcontractor and workmen, but the librarian should observe what is happening and what preparations are being made in areas near library operations. If a workman is preparing to drill into a stone wall next to an open window adjacent to books, contact the supervisor—fast. The contractor should make the workers aware that advance notice to library staff and some flexibility in scheduling of jackhammering or turning off a utility can minimize the disruptive effect. Staff and patrons usually can work around a problem they are warned about, but people do not like their work abruptly interrupted. Notices on the entrance door, though generally frowned on in normal circumstances, are a good way to communicate information about utility shut-offs, and the like, on short notice. Some disruptive work may need to be scheduled very early in the morning, and the library may wish to consider reducing hours of opening during construction hours and increasing evening and weekend hours if this does not create major problems for the staff.

As plans for moving books change and stack space becomes limited, make sure stacks are being fully utilized in areas where books are compacted. Although books should be kept in order on shelves, the order of the classification does not necessarily need to be maintained for temporary compaction. If the space can be better utilized or a move between floors avoided by putting BX temporarily between QR and LB, do so. One can also compact a portion of the classification across the bottom or top shelves of a section of materials that have been expanded and placed in permanent locations. Get materials as early as possible onto the floors they will occupy permanently, to avoid delays that can be created by obstructions caused by construction activity and heavy elevator traffic. When quantities of materials are being moved, it may save time to designate one person as elevator operator, responsible for loading, operating, and unloading the elevator. This can save enormous amounts of time that would be wasted if each worker had to wait their turn to use the elevator and spend time riding up and down it. This does, of course, assume a well-thought-out system of marking book trucks and their destinations.

Finally, there is no substitute for the librarian or other person responsible for the library plan being constantly available to coordinate, modify, and oversee library activities during construction. His or her position is, on the library side, comparable to that of the construction superintendent. There must be continuous review, checking, rechecking, analysis, observation, and consultation. The site should be thoroughly inspected when construction activities cease each day, and it should be toured several times in the course of the day. By doing this, many potential problems can be identified and resolved before they interfere with the work, and opportunities for reducing work and/or improving efficiency will be discovered. This role must be assumed by one person who sees the whole picture; it cannot be easily shared or delegated.

CONCLUSION

In a renovation/addition to a library that must remain in operation, both contractor and library are forced into a relationship that is difficult at best. The climate created by the mix of physical constraints, institutional policies and operating procedures, local construction codes, union regulations, background and experience of the principals involved, and so forth, produces problems that are unique to each project. No individual can possibly have experienced all of the situations that can arise. This essay is an attempt to identify, from very specific experiences on specific projects, the general procedures that have worked and some guidelines that might be helpful to those faced with maintaining library operations through the construction period. Hopefully, it may serve to motivate others who may have faced totally different problems in similar situations to make further contributions to the literature on this important but neglected topic.

THREE STUDIES OF THE ECONOMICS OF ACADEMIC LIBRARIES

Paul B. Kantor

INTRODUCTION

The economic problems of academic libraries always merit attention. This is particularly true in times of transition. Computer technology and telecommunications have transformed technical processing. They are transforming the catalog, and they are expected to change many aspects of publishing itself.

Although the library's goals remain unchanged in the deepest sense, its scope expands and the details of its policies and procedures drastically change. To assure adequate support during these transitions, the library must have a concrete and objective understanding of its economic needs, and of the relation between those needs and the services the library renders. Economic information and in-

Advances in Library Administration and Organization
Volume 5, pages 221–286
Copyright © 1986 by JAI Press Inc.
All rights of reproduction in any form reserved.
ISBN: 0-89232-674-3

sights are essential to protect the interests of libraries, their institutions, and their readers.

Library economics may be studied in at least three ways. The broadest view is given by econometric studies[1,5,6,7,8] which compare cost and service statistics for many libraries. The best possible product of an econometric study is an average expenditure formula, relating the budgetary needs to the recognized activities of the library. Any such formula is surrounded by statistical caveats regarding its precision and the variability of individual library expenditures in relation to the predicted average.

A sharper view of economics is given by a functional cost analysis, or unit cost analysis.[7,11,13,18,21] Cost analysis may be done at a single library. It may also be done, using consistent procedures and principles, at several libraries jointly. In either case, the result is a rational determination of the cost of providing a single unit of each service. The results may be thought of as "fair costs" for the services. If a library were to sell its services, charging fees equal to the unit costs, it would exactly cover its expenses. When several libraries use the same methods, it makes sense to compare the unit costs and to find representative values such as the mean or median for particular services.

A third, microscopically precise, view of library economics is given by detailed study of specific processes[12,14]. The specificity must be so great that inputs of labor, equipment, and other resources are uniquely defined. The outputs must also be defined very precisely. The result of such a study is detailed understanding of where costs originate. This understanding is the foundation for reviewing and improving the organization and management of specific processes. The value of detailed cost analysis is enormously enhanced when several libraries adopt the same analytic techniques. The results become truly comparable, permitting the determination of representative value and ranges of variation.

Between 1981 and 1984, over 100 academic libraries have participated in one or more of these kinds of studies. The studies, taken together, reveal some surprising and significant features of the economics of academic libraries and show that it is very hard to budget for the future. The average costs of services or processes do not describe all libraries with sufficient precision. Costs for specific processes at one particular library may be twice (or half) as great as the median or average cost for that process. This variability applies to the finest details, such as the cost of placing a single order; it applies to the cost of visible services, such as circulation or reference; it applies to total library budgets.

Possible explanations of this enormous variability, and its significance for planning and budgeting, are discussed at the conclusion of this paper.

Historical Note and Acknowledgments

As often occurs in research, the facts summarized in this paper were discovered in the most perplexing order. The econometric study was done first, during the academic years 1981–1982 and 1982–1983. It was supported by the National Science Foundation Division of Information Science and Technology, and the project team included Dr. Judith Wood, Dr. Prəsert Shusang, Mr. J. J. Lee, and Ms. Marla Bush. The unit cost study became possible while the econometric study was under way, and was suggested by Professor Jacob Cohen of the University of Pittsburgh. It involved 32 libraries, and took place during the academic year 1982–1983. The detailed study of costs for technical processing was done under contract to the Council on Library Resources during the summer and fall of 1984.

Each study was externally funded, but the libraries involved contributed substantial effort in gathering new primary data on costs, efforts, and outputs. The names of the libraries and key personnel are listed in Appendix 3. Without their efforts these projects would not have been possible. Particular thanks are also due to Ms. Helene Ebenfield and Dr. Charles Brownstein of the National Science Foundation, and to Mr. Warren J. Haas, Ms. Deanna Marcum, and Dr. Martin Cummings at the Council on Library Resources. The special analysis of ARL libraries was supported in part by the Association of Research Libraries, through its Statistics Committee, chaired by Mr. Herbert Johnson. The accretion of economic data is a colorless task whose product is more often questions than answers. Both vision and persistence are required to support such research.

UNIT COSTS OF SOME TECHNICAL PROCESSES

This study is a detailed look at the costs (other than purchase price) of choosing a book, ordering it, and providing catalog access to it[12]. The data represent eight libraries and are focussed on a very specific part of the collection: books in English and Western European languages.

Studying a small part of one aspect (technical services) of library operations is analogous to a medical tissue biopsy. It may indicate highly localized disease or health. It may also indicate the general health of the entire organization.

The Generalized Acquisition Cycle

Because the situation is enormously complex, we concentrate in this study on hard order (also called single order, or unitary order, or unit order) monographic acquisitions. We exclude those materials that arrive as part of a regular series, or on a blanket order, standing order, or approval plan. Because of this, our study may exclude a majority of the monographic materials at your library. However, this restriction provides us with a basis for making sensible comparisons of one library to another. If we did not focus on a specific type of order, then the difference in mix of materials at different libraries would almost surely invalidate our conclusions.

Our analysis is based on the "universal simplified flow" chart for the acquisitions process. I call it "universal" because, although it is wrong in any particular case, it does capture the key features of monographic acquisition at any large library. The cycle is shown in Figure 1 and is built up as follows.

The beginning steps of the cycle (Step A) have to do with book selection. This may involve action by the faculty with review by the staff of the library requests also may originate with the staff of the library, or they may review approvals or make other book-in-hand decisions.

Step B is the pre-order search to determine that the material, if it is indeed suitable for acquisition, has not already been acquired. Of course a certain number of items are found to be already in the collection.

Step C is the placing of an order. This involves designating fund codes and vendors, as well as preparation of the physical order.

The next step (Step D) is the responsibility of the vendors who, in their own good time, send at least some of the ordered books to the library.

Step E represents the physical receiving operation, the mail room or unpacking area. From there, of course, the picture is a little complicated. Approvals, which are now book-in-hand, go to the selectors, while the hard order monographs of interest in this project go to some operation that I generally will call accounting.

Accounting (Step F) involves checking to see that the materials are indeed what was ordered, matching them with invoices, and authorizing payment. The materials themselves then go into a rather complicated family of operations represented here by Steps G, H, and I.

Step G is the activity called copy cataloging, or on-line cataloging, or something of the sort. It involves a search for materials in whatever utilities or databases are used. If the materials are found, they are promptly cataloged and the books themselves go on to Step J, marking or labeling, while the cards go to Step L, which is their final placement in the catalog.

However, if material is not found in the on-line system, it then is either passed on for original cataloging, (Step I), or put into some kind of a holding area.

Almost every library has a substantial "dungeon" filled with books in process. According to a variety of strategies (Step H), materials are withdrawn from holding either to be checked again in copy cataloging or to be handled by original catalogers.

In any case, eventually books are cataloged and wind up at Step J to be labeled. Having been labeled they are finally delivered to the shelves and the cycle is completed. In fact, associated with labeling is a small additional cycle for bindery preparation and binding, which is shown here as a little add-on in Figure 1.

We believe that the universal simplified flow chart represents the key features of hard order monograph acquisition and, with some adaptation, it describes these features at each of the eight libraries in the study.

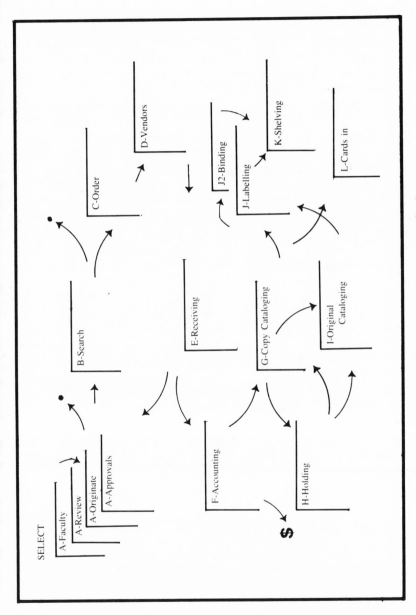

Figure 1. The Generalized Acquisition Cycle

225

Data Collection

The libraries gathered data on both the individual effort and the supporting costs for computers, purchased services, and overhead costs. Data were gathered at every "station" defined in the generalized cycle. If the task was divided into several parallel (or serial) parts, data from those parts were aggregated to represent the task in standard form. For a series, overall efforts and delays are a simple sum. For parallel operations, the overall efforts and delays are weighted averages.

All of these data were integrated into spreadsheets (see Exhibit 1) for each library. The final line in each spreadsheet is the delay data, by task. Effort, in hours per 100 items, was calculated separately for professional, technical, and student personnel. Data were collected every day, on general-purpose data forms, customized to each subtask at each library. Most commonly used descriptions have different meanings at individual libraries. In some cases, the local acronym has been used for so long that many workers do not know its meaning. Therefore "customization" was essential to ensure that the data are truly comparable. Delays were calculated using techniques described in the ARL manual *Objective Performance Measures for Academic and Research Libraries*.[22]

Data-collection periods ranged from a high of 10 weeks at several libraries to a low of 2 weeks at one of the libraries. Data collection was done during the summer of 1984. It was essential to record daily to capture variations in work flow and effort. Special statistical techniques were used to estimate the underlying variation in the effort required to perform single tasks. It was found that the underlying effort is highly variable. Thus the effort data reported in the spreadsheet are averages, but they are not true of every single item processed.

Selected lines from these spreadsheets were assembled and processed together. This permits comparison of the actual hours of labor, for particular tasks, and of the salary and wage scales. Other tables permit the comparison of other cost components, such as overhead, space, computers and so on. These tables appear in Appendix 1.

The Effect of Wage Scales

The most general conclusions are drawn by comparing the costs with each other, task by task. To make these comparisons, we must remove the effect of significant variation in the wage scales. For professional staff, the range of salary plus fringe is $11.07 to $15.87 per hour. (These data were provided by the financial officer at each library. We interpret these as annual salary divided by a nominal 2,000-hour work year. The number of so-called productive hours varies with library practices governing leave, professional development, and even coffee breaks. The wage per productive hour generally will be somewhat higher than the wage per nominal hour.) For technical staff, the range is $9.71 to $13.91; for students it is $1.84 (presumably subsidized) to $4.68 per hour. These figures include the effect of fringe rates, which vary from 10.85 percent to 24 percent.

For comparative analysis, the effects of varying wage scales are removed by using an average wage for each class of staff (professional = $13.80/hr.; technical = $7.50/hr.; student = $3.70/hr.). These salaries also carry an overhead burden ranging from 36.30 percent to 57.63 percent (library L8 did not report the university share of the overhead). Combining the labor costs, calculated at these standard rates, with overhead calculated at the actual rate for each library, and all other costs as reported, gives the comparable costs shown in Exhibit 2. They form the basis for our most important conclusions.

Because libraries have been assured of total confidentiality, we cannot list the characteristics of each library in single table. That is, knowing which library is in OCLC but not in Solinet, or which is a member of RLG but does not use computerized order processing, would compromise confidentiality. With a few libraries unveiled, all would soon be unveiled. We will refer frequently to some library characteristics, which we call "profile variables." These are:

Form of support: P = public I = independent
Acquisition system: M = manual B = batch C = on-line R = RLIN
Copy cataloging system: C = independent S = Solinet O = OCLC R = RLIN

For example, we will report

	Low	High
	PPII	IIII

to indicate that of the four low-cost libraries, two are publicly supported, and two are independent, etc.

Comparative Cost Data

Task A: Book Selection

Seven libraries reported on the selection task. The highest reported level of effort is 15.94 technical hours per 100 items considered, or 5.87 professional hours per 100 items considered (not at the same library). The number of items considered, if not separately tallied, was assumed to be twice the number of items ordered. This ratio is based on data from those libraries that did tally both items considered and items ordered. The highest labor cost was $2.65 per item. The highest nonlabor cost was $0.36 per item, and the representative figure is

The combined cost and effort data for CLR project

Example
L0
24-Jan 03:45 PM Labor Data in Hours Per Hundred Items

For library Prepared by: Hrs/100	Wage	Fringe	:A:Select	B:Search	C:Order	E:PhysRec	F:AccRcv	G:CopyCat	H:Holding	I:Orignl	J:Mrkng	L:CardsIn
Prof:	$11.50	16:	4.37		0.81	1		0		63.13	0	0
Tech:	$6.23	16:		0.84	5.41		3.17	26.18		34.18	1.86	0.903
Stdt:	$3.50	4:		0.43	2.65	0.4	2.57	0		0	1.86	0
					Cost of Direct Labor Per Single Item							
$/Item Prof:			$0.58	$0.00	$0.11	$0.00	$0.00	$0.00	$0.00	$8.42	$0.00	$0.00
Tech:			$0.00	$0.06	$0.39	$0.07	$0.23	$1.89	$0.00	$2.47	$0.13	$0.07
Stdt:			$0.00	$0.02	$0.10	$0.01	$0.09	$0.00	$0.00	$0.00	$0.07	$0.00
Direct:			$0.58	$0.08	$0.60	$0.09	$0.32	$1.89	$0.00	$10.89	$0.20	$0.07
					Overhead on Labor in Dollars Per Item							
Overheads Univ:	8.40		$0.05	$0.01	$0.05	$0.01	$0.03	$0.16	$0.00	$0.91	$0.02	$0.01
Libry:	15.10		$0.09	$0.01	$0.09	$0.01	$0.05	$0.29	$0.00	$1.64	$0.03	$0.01
Divsn:	5.60		$0.03	$.00	$0.03	$.00	$0.02	$0.11	$0.00	$0.61	$0.01	$.00
Dept:	14.05		$0.08	$0.01	$0.08	$0.01	$0.05	$0.27	$0.00	$1.53	$0.03	$0.01
Total:	43.15		$0.25	$0.03	$0.26	$0.04	$0.14	$0.82	$0.00	$4.70	$0.09	$0.03
					Combined Cost of Labor/Fringe and Overhead							
Sal + Fring + Ovhd:			$0.83	$0.11	$0.85	$0.12	$0.46	$2.71	$0.00	$15.59	$0.29	$0.09
					Calculation of Non-Labor Costs							
Annual Output Stat:			95,000	95,000	46,319	103,140	90,000	15,761	1	882	35,343	271,500

		A:Select	B:Search	C:Order	E:PhysRec	F:AccRcv	G:CopyCat	H:Holding	I:Orignl	J:Mrkng	L:Cards-
Cost Data: (Annual)	Computers:		10,734	2,000	6,000	2,000	0	0	0	4,262	4,262
	Supp SVC:								4,262	0	0
	Space CST:	72,198	72,198	39,969	39,969	12,349		21,235			
	Oth Dirct:						61,797		6,257		
	Non-Assignable:										
					**** Non-Labor Costs in Dollars Per Item ****						
Per Item:	Computers:	$0.00	$0.11	$0.04	$0.06	$0.02	$0.00	$0.00	$0.00	$0.00	$0.00
	Supp SVC:	$0.00	$0.00	$0.00	$0.00	$0.00	$0.27	$0.00	$4.83	$0.12	$0.02
	Space CST:	$0.76	$0.76	$0.86	$0.39	$0.14	$0.00	*****	$0.00	$0.00	$0.00
	Oth Dirct:	$0.00	$0.00	$0.00	$0.00	$0.00	$3.92	$0.00	$7.09	$0.00	$0.00
	Non-Assignable:	$0.00	$0.00	$0.00	$0.00	$0.00	$0.00	$0.00	$0.00	$0.00	$0.00
Nonlabor	Total Per Item:	$0.76	$0.87	$0.91	$0.45	$0.16	$4.19	*****	$11.93	$0.12	$0.02
Labor	Total Per Item:	$0.83	$0.11	$0.85	$0.12	$0.46	$2.71	$0.00	$15.59	$0.29	$0.09
Combined	Total Per Item:	$1.59	$0.98	$1.76	$0.57	$0.62	$6.90	*****	$27.52	$0.41	$0.11
In		A:Select	B:Search	C:Order	E:PhysRec	F:AccRcv	G:CopyCat	H:Holding	I:Orignl	J:Mrkng	L:Cards-
	Delay (days)	0	0.3	1	0	0.5	22.81	490	46.3	1.2	36.9
	Output*Labor	$55,381	$7,254	$27,582	$8,955	$29,037	$29,819	$0	$9,606	$7,144	$17,718
	Output*Ovrhd	$23,897	$3,130	$11,902	$3,864	$12,530	$12,867	$0	$4,145	3,082	$7,645
	Rate:	0.432	0.431	0.431	0.432	0.432	0.432	ERR	0.431	0.432	0.432

Exhibit 1. The spreadsheet for reporting unit costs, cost components, and delays for the tasks in the acquisition cycle.

229

		Select	Search	Order	Physi-cal	Account-ing	Copy-cat	Hold-ing	Orig-inal	Mark-ing	Cards in	Sum cost
L1 Total Cost/Item	13	$0.96	$3.21	$7.99	$0.27	$0.81	$6.43	$0.00	$22.25	$0.68	$1.58	$44.18
L2 Total Cost/Item	13	$2.03	$0.00	$2.58	$0.00	$1.82	$4.50	$0.60	$22.99	$0.55	$0.26	$34.73
L3 Total Cost/Item	13	$2.09	$2.87	$1.42	$0.07	$2.33	$6.64	$0.00	$22.51	$0.95	$0.13	$39.02
L4 Total Cost/Item	13	$0.86	$0.22	$0.96	$0.19	$0.49	$7.79	$0.00	$14.84	$0.18	$0.00	$25.52
L5 Total Cost/Item	13	$4.00	$1.08	$1.34	$0.41	$2.68	$8.58	$0.92	$46.91	$1.21	$0.21	$66.42
L6 Total Cost/Item	13	$1.37	$3.59	$1.20	$0.40	$2.08	$8.55	$0.00	$29.62	$0.42	$0.11	$47.35
L7 Total Cost/Item	13	$1.33	$0.30	$3.44	$0.12	$0.49	$6.89	$0.00	$13.17	$0.11	$0.91	$26.76
L8 Total Cost/Item	13	$0.00	$2.81	$1.46	$0.00	$4.51	$3.94	$0.11	$22.07	$0.84	$0.00	$35.62
Mean		$1.58	$1.76	$2.55	$0.18	$1.90	$6.66	$0.20	$24.30	$0.62	$0.40	$39.95
Std ERR		$1.11	$1.41	$2.20	$0.15	$1.26	$1.61	$0.33	$9.79	$0.36	$0.52	

12/08/84 11:44:00

	Select	Search	Order	Physi-cal	Account-ing	Copy-cat	Hold-ing	Orig-inal	Mark-ing	Cards in
Unit costs in Size place:	$0.00	$0.00	$0.96	$0.00	$0.49	$3.94	$0.00	$13.17	$0.11	$0.00
	$0.86	$0.22	$1.20	$0.00	$0.49	$4.50	$0.00	$14.84	$0.18	$0.00
	$0.96	$0.30	$1.34	$0.07	$0.81	$6.43	$0.00	$22.07	$0.42	$0.11
	$1.33	$1.08	$1.42	$0.12	$1.82	$6.64	$0.00	$22.25	$0.55	$0.13
	$1.37	$2.81	$1.46	$0.19	$2.08	$6.89	$0.11	$22.51	$0.68	$0.21
	$2.03	$2.87	$2.58	$0.27	$2.33	$7.79	$0.11	$22.99	$0.84	$0.26
	$2.09	$3.21	$3.44	$0.40	$2.68	$8.55	$0.60	$29.62	$0.95	$0.91
	$4.00	$3.59	$7.99	$0.41	$4.51	$8.58	$0.92	$46.91	$1.21	$1.58
Mean of mid 4	$1.43	$1.77	$1.70	$0.16	$1.76	$6.94	$0.03	$22.46	$0.62	$0.18
Range of mid 4	$1.07	$2.57	$1.24	$0.20	$1.53	$1.36	$0.11	$0.93	$0.42	$0.15

Using New Wages
Prof $13.80
Tech 7.50
Student $3.70

Exhibit 2. Summary of unit costs by station and library. In the upper table the unit costs are shown by library and station. The mean and standard error for each column are shown beneath the table.

In the lower table the unit costs for each station are arranged in order of increasing cost. To provide a more stable estimate of the mean, we have calculated the average of the middle four entries in each column. The degree of variation is shown by the range of those four entries. For example, for accounting, the mean of .81, 1.82, 2.08 and 2.33 is 1.76 and the range (2.33–.81) is 1.53. (There are small rounding effects in the numbers reported here.)

$1.43 (the average of the four central values.) The low-cost and high-cost profiles are:

Selection cost: $1.43

	Low	High
Support	PII	PIII
Copy catalog	OSR	SSRR
Acquisition	CBR	MCCR

No clear differences in profiles appear here.

Task B: Searching

This task includes searching done prior to the decision to recommend purchase and that done prior to placing the order. Many of the libraries have at least two searches. When a utility is searched, the selector may learn that the item under consideration is already held at another institution. In no case was "resource sharing" interpreted through rules of the form "do not buy because another library already holds the item."

The highest effort levels reported were 27.46 technical hours per 100 items, and 16.70 student hours per 100 items (not at the same library). The highest labor cost was $2.14 per item; the highest value for other costs is $0.85. The representative figure is $1.77 per item. The profile of other properties is:

Search cost: $1.77

	Low	High
Support	PPII	IIII
Copy catalog	OSRR	CRSS
Acquisition	CCRR	CCMB

The fact that both publicly supported libraries are in the low batch is not statistically important. The RLIN acquisition system appears in the low-cost group, while the manual and batch systems appear in the high-cost group.

Task C: Ordering

Ordering includes fund assignment, if not done by selectors, and vendor assignment. The highest effort levels reported were 51 technical hours per 100 items; 4.4 student hours per 100 items, and 7.11 professional hours per 100 items (not at the same library). The highest labor cost was $4.01 per item; the highest figure for other costs was $3.07 per item. (This number is an extreme outlier. The next highest is $0.58 per item.) The representative value for the order cost is $1.70 per item. The profile of other properties is:

Ordering: $1.70

	Low	High
Support	PIII	PIII
Copy catalog	OSRR	SSRC
Acquisition	CCMR	BCCR

As with book selection, there is no clear pattern in the profile variables.

Tasks D; E; H: Receiving; Accounting, and Holding

The meaning of these tasks depends on details of the local procedures.

Although the mail room and neighboring spaces are sometimes used to store exotica, at the libraries studied they were not used systematically to hold the monographs under consideration here. The effort levels do not vary greatly. The representative cost is $.16 per item.

Holding areas may be more or less remote. In many cases, the effort associated with retrieval is divided among many people, or otherwise inextricable from other tasks. For these reasons our effort to obtain consistent data on the availability of these materials, and the access effort associated with retrieval, was not successsful.

Accounting interfaces with the university accounts payable office, and the amount of work required from the library, varies from institution to institution. The representative cost figure is $1.76 per item.

All of the cost and delay figures for these tasks appear in Exhibit 2, and we will not analyze them further here.

Task G: Copy Cataloging

Copy cataloging is the preparation of catalog records for materials already cataloged in the machine-readable database used. Labor costs include professional supervision and editing of records. Nonlabor costs include system charges which are, at present, based on the agreement that a system renders a library service when the library first accesses a record, adopts it, and reports to the system that it now holds the item.

The highest efforts reported for copy cataloging are 10.67 hours of professional time per 100 items and 40.89 hours of technical time per 100 items (not at the same library). The highest labor cost is $3.36 per item, and the highest nonlabor cost is $4.19 per item. The representative value is $6.94 per item. The profile of other variables is:

Copy Cataloging: $6.94

	Low	High
Support	PIII	PIII
Copy catalog	CSSS	ORRR
Acquisition	CCCB	CRRM

The concentration of RLIN libraries in the higher cost range may reflect higher charges or the fact that users of the RLIN utility are faced with more options among which to choose. The latter explanation is not borne out by detailed analysis of the labor charges. It is also paradoxical that the SOLINET system, which adds charges, consistently falls in the lower-cost group. We therefore conclude that the profile variables and particularly the utility used is NOT a determining factor in the variation of cost for copy or derived cataloging. At one of the SOLINET libraries, data were kept separately on the use of Library of Congress records and records contributed by other libraries. There was no significant difference in the effort or cost levels.

Task I: Original Cataloging

Original cataloging is the construction of new catalog entries when there are no existing records, and includes supervisory, editorial, and data-entry work as needed. The highest reported effort levels are 157.18 professional hours per 100 items and 92.46 technical hours per 100 items (not at the same library). The latter represents an unusual situation because there were no professional staff available during the study period; the work during the study period did not include creation of totally new records. Only items for which some copy exists in printed form were processed. The next highest technical effort level was 34.18 hours per 100 items. The highest reported labor cost was $23.54 per item.

This is lower than the figure that would be obtained by dividing labor cost of the original cataloging department by the number of items cataloged. There are several reasons for this. First, our study excludes area studies, exotic languages, and materials obtained under PL 480, which often present extreme cataloging problems. Second, we have isolated certain work that is done by professional catalogers, but which contributes to the accessibility of all materials (for example, authority control).

The highest figure for nonlabor costs (which includes that portion of authority control prorated to the items requiring original cataloging) is $12.50. The representative cost figure is $22.46 per item. The profile of other variables is:

Original Cataloging: $22.46

	Low	High
Support	PIII	PIII
Copy catalog	CORS	SSRR
Acquisition	BCOR	CCMR

and does not show any significant pattern.

Task J: Marking

Marking includes the marking of fore-edge, insertion of labels and tattle-tapes, and call number. The details are generally comparable, except for one library that performs part of these tasks together with Task F (accounting). The highest efforts reported are 12.75 student hours per 100 items and 7.42 technical hours per 100 items (not at the same library). The highest labor cost reported is $0.56 per item, and the highest nonlabor costs are $0.46 per item.

The representative value is $0.62 per item, and the profile of other variables is unimportant here.

Task L: Cards In

This task includes receipt of cards from the utility sorting, filing and revising (checking), and ends when the cards are dropped. It does not apply to libraries where the card catalog has been closed. It is not possible to attach this particular cost directly to a single book because the number of cards per item cataloged will vary. The high labor cost is $0.66 per card. The high value for other costs is $.03 per card. The representative value is $0.18 per card dropped. The profile of other variables is unimportant in this task.

Combined Data on Costs

There is no simple way to combine all of these data into a single measure of performance, even for the highly specialized task of "buying hard order monographs." One approach is to sum all of the individual task costs. This ignores the fact that no book receives both copy cataloging and original cataloging, and the fact that books require several cards. The result, without the cost of "holding" (whose meaning remains obscure) is shown as "sum cost" in the last column of Exhibit 2.

When dealing with widely varying data, a semiquantitative analysis is possible, using ranks. Using ranks suppresses the actual magnitude of the cost figures, and deals only with their rank among the libraries studies. Each entry in Exhibit 2 is replaced by its rank in the column to which it belongs. The result (Exhibit 3) represents each library by its rank with regard to every one of the tasks (1 = lowest cost; 8 = highest cost). This is similar to the format used in presenting the ARL statistics.

We go one step further and calculate the average rank for each of the eight libraries. This is shown in the second column of Exhibit 3. It is clear from a study of Exhibit 3 that no library is most (or least) costly in every category. The average rank does, however, show a significant range, from a low of 2.6 to a high of 6.6. Although no library has found the least costly way to do every task, some of them have found many low-cost strategies.

Using this "average rank" concept, we see a gap between the four low-rank libraries (averages 2.6, 3.7, 3.7 and 4.0) and the four high-rank libraries (average ranks 5.1, 5.2, 5.2 and 6.6). The preceding task-by-task review shows that the profile variables do not provide an overall explanation of the cost variations.

	Avg	Std err	Select	Search	Order	Physical	Accounting	Copycat	Holding	Original	Marking	Cards in
L1	5.2	2.0	3	7	8	6	3	3	1	4	5	8
L2	4.0	2.1	6	1	6	1	4	2	7	6	4	6
L3	5.1	1.4	7	6	4	3	6	4	2	5	7	4
L4	2.6	1.6	2	2	1	5	2	6	3	2	2	1
L5	6.6	1.9	8	4	3	8	7	8	8	8	8	5
L6	5.2	2.0	5	8	2	7	5	7	4	7	3	3
L7	3.7	2.3	4	3	7	4	1	5	5	1	1	7
L8	3.7	2.3	1	5	5	2	8	1	6	3	6	2

Exhibit 3. Library rank with regard to unit cost, for 10 stations. Each library's rank (1-lowest) is shown for each station, and the average rank, and its standard deviation are shown for each library. For example, L2 ranks 4 in accounting costs (dollar value $1.82/item). L2 has an average rank of 4.0, with a standard deviation of 2.1.

Relation of Average Cost Rank to Volumes Added

Using the ARL statistics for 1982–1983, we have divided the libraries into two groups according to the number of volumes added per year (gross). The correlation is significant: the four libraries with low average rank for cost are precisely the four libraries which add the most volumes (gross) per year. The four libraries with the highest average rank for cost are the ones adding the fewest volumes per year.

The likelihood that this correlation occurs purely by chance is only 1 in 70. That is, we are 98.6 percent confident in rejecting the notion that volume of activity has nothing to do with the average cost rank. Our data do not permit a more detailed model of the relation between costs and volumes added. The result is nonetheless significant both statistically and managerially. This pattern would be expected in a production industry, where automation and division of labor lead to economies of scale.

Delays Associated With Tasks

Our information on processing delays is summarized in Table 1.7 (Exhibit 4). The variation is enormous, and its interpretation is clouded by variations in bibliographic accessibility. With an integrated system, such as NOTIS at Northwestern, the record corresponding to a book is available, in some form, as soon as the book is ordered. With a dedicated computer, as at Georgia or Illinois, the information is available at least to the library staff. Short records may be used to alert patrons to the availability of materials in the holding area, and so on.

Bearing all of this in mind, we review the representative delay figures. (As for costs, we drop the two highest and two lowest, and average the remaining delays.) For selection, delay only refers to those items proposed to the selector at some definite time. The representative figure is 5.3 days, with a high of 45. For searching the representative delay is 3.7 days, and for ordering, 1.5 days. Thus, in a hypothetical "representative library" approximately 12 working days elapse from the time a book is suggested until the order goes out.

The vendors' response time is presumed not to vary among the libraries. Data from several libraries indicate that six months is a representative figure.

Physical receipt introduces essentially no delay; accounting causes a delay of 8.5 days. The representative time for copy cataloging is 17.8 working days. The representative time for original cataloging is 64.7 days. The true impact of resource sharing is the reduction of three-fourths in the delay time, as well as the lowering of costs.

The impact of holding is difficult to assess. The obvious performance measure is the average holding time, 205 working days, or more than one academic year. However, this must be interpreted in the light of the degree of patron access to items in holding, and the number of items that are consigned to holding each working day. Further work would be needed to assess completely the impact of present holding practices on patron access to new materials.

Conclusions

Large variations occur in the costs of specific tasks and in the combined costs of all tasks. There are significant differences in the averaged performance (averaged rank) of libraries. These differences are strongly correlated with the number of items processed. Computer-supported (derived) cataloging is much less expensive than original cataloging. The impact of resource sharing appears to be a savings of $15.52 per item cataloged, and a decrease of 47 working days (more than two months) in processing delays.

This comparison overstates the cost impact of sharing because, in the past, derived cataloging was done using printed aids such as the *National Union Catalog*. A more accurate picture includes both delays and costs.

Discussion

An inverse relation between unit costs and volume processed is found in many production industries. This may be due to the greater flexibility of organization and management possible with a large work flow. It suggests that the large variability in individual processing times does not reflect an essential variability in the nature of the work. Perhaps the observed variability of individual processing time is due to the random occurrence of unrecorded interruptions unrelated to the task at hand (such as conversations or coffee).

This study of technical libraries reflects a classical view of the library—the library acquires and stores books. We have studied how efficiently the library acquires books, without regard to the purchase price of the books or to the quality of either the books or the cataloging record. To get clear results we have had to apply a "microscope." It would be impossible, and of doubtful value, to extend such studies to cover every aspect of library operation.

When this study was begun, it was hoped that microscopically detailed examination would remove the disturbing variability reported in existing cost studies. These studies (nearly all unpublished) show variations of as much as a factor of six in the cost of putting a book on the shelf. Using the "sum" as an indicator, one could say that we have reduced that range to something like a factor of about two and two-thirds, from $25.00 to $66.00. However, for the detailed tasks themselves we find much larger variations.

As a general rule, variations of this type are most likely to originate with management, organization, and quality of personnel. It is less likely that they are due to differences in the quality with which, for example, books are matched against invoices and orders.

Raw Data:

Library	Select	Search	Order	Physical	Accounting	Copycat	Holding	Original	Marking	Cardsin
L1	11.00	33.10	3.80	0.00	13.80	50.30	0.00	102.50	8.90	31.60
L2	3.3	33.9	20.8	1.5	30.1	10	415.2	152.5	1.8	17.9
L3	39.3	0.3	0.2	0	5.4	2.6	X	11.9	0	18
L4	0		1		0.5	3.2		2.8	1.2	0
L5	45.8	10.2	3.2	0	10.9	10.5	278.1	18.3	0	
L6	6.975	0.4	0		0.5	22.81	490	46.3	1.2	36.9
L7	0	0.5	0.1	0.3	4	60.9	128.9	141	1	
L8		3.6	1.5		19.9	27.82	1021.3	91.76	3.7	36.4

Rank for Costs	Library	Avg. Delays Rk	Rank for Delay	Select	Search	Order	Physical	Accounting	Copycat	Holding	Original	Marking	Cardsin
6.5	L1	6.2	8	6	7	7	6	6	7	3	6	8	6
4	L2	5.0	7	4	1	8	2	8	3	6	8	6	4
5	L3	4.1	2	7	8	3	8	4	1	2	2	1	5
1	L4	2.3	1	2	2	4	5	1	2	1	1	4	1
8	L5	4.6	4	8	6	6	4	5	4	5	3	2	3
6.5	L6	4.3	3	5	3	1	3	2	5	7	4	5	8
2.5	L7	4.8	6	3	4	2	7	3	8	4	7	3	7
2.5	L8	4.7	5	1	5	5	1	7	6	8	5	7	2

Delays (in days) arranged in order of increasing size.								
0.0	0.3	0.0	0.0	0.5	2.6	X	2.8	0.0
0.0	0.4	0.1	0.0	0.5	3.2	0.0	11.9	0.0
3.3	0.5	0.2	0.3	4.0	10.0	128.9	18.3	1.0
7.0	3.6	1.0	1.5	5.4	10.5	278.1	46.3	1.2
11.0	10.2	1.5		10.9	22.8	415.2	91.8	1.2
39.3	33.1	3.2		13.8	27.8	490.0	102.5	1.8
45.8	33.9	3.8		19.9	50.3	1,021.3	141.0	3.7
		20.8		30.1	60.9		152.5	8.9
Mean of mid 4								
5.3	3.7	1.5	0.0	8.5	17.8	205.6	64.7	1.3
Half of range of mid								
5.5	4.9	1.5	0.0	4.9	8.9	207.6	42.1	0.4

Exhibit 4. Delays and rankings. Available data on delay at various stations are reported in the lower portion of the table. The ranks are shown in the upper portion, together with the average rank for each library.

The impact of networks is clearest in the cataloging process, with substantial savings in cost and delay. The shared order-production facility does no better or worse than stand alone computer systems, and the function is, by nature, local. If it were regarded as a shared function, a substantial impact on materials budgets could result. Specifically, with searches on either RLIN or OCLC one could find that items are held at designated "partner" institutions, and forego purchase. This strategy would increase the scope of the joint holdings, with some corresponding increase in the original cataloging load. Because it would not provide local ownership of the desired materials, it diverges widely from the classical view of the library.

The customizing of the data-collection instruments involved the pleasant experience of visiting the technical services divisions of eight major research libraries. Some impressions were formed, above and beyond those supported by hard numerical data. The most important of these is that facilities, and to a lesser extent, personnel and organization, are not ideally matched to the power that computation and telecommunication offer.

For example, the order and order-checking process involves keying in the order number and other identifiers several times. Bar code systems could be developed to eliminate all of this and reduce the incidence of error. Vendors could surely be encouraged to attach peel-off labels to their invoices, if assured that this facilitates prompt payment. The technology of the public library and of the supermarket could reduce the operating costs of the academic library as well.

Most often, the terminal for an order system is found in the place deemed ideal when orders were processed by hand. Terminals are often clustered in an out-of-the-way space, with difficult access. The most skilled and highly trained personnel are usually not in closest contact with the resource sharing systems. It is clear that these systems have produced cost savings, by permitting less-expensive personnel to assume some tasks. There is great potential for further improvement by linking the best-trained personnel with the power of these systems.

One such possibility is searching by selectors authorized to accept the fact that another library holds material, as a satisfactory alternative to purchase. Another possibility is a form of teleconferencing among original catalogers, permitting each person to tackle the materials he or she can best handle. These seem highly speculative today (January 1985), but the experience in both science and industry is that the computer serves most capably when it is in the most capable hands. Whatever specific procedures are developed, a further integration of the computer and resource-sharing systems into library operations can only result in improved scope of resources and improved access for readers.

STUDY OF THE UNIT COST OF SERVICES

The most important tool for obtaining a rational understanding of the relations between costs and services is the determination of unit costs.[9,11,18] Unit costs are

derived from specific data on levels of service and on the allocation of staff effort. They are fair to the library, which means that if they were charged as fees
they would completely support the library. As an intermediate step in the determination of unit costs we also determine the share of the total budget that supports each of the primary services delivered to readers.

There has been no prior study of unit costs at several libraries simultaneously.
Some prior studies have costed a particular technical service[14] or have allocated
all costs to circulation[13]

The Libraries Studied

The study sample was drawn from the 119 libraries participating in the
econometric study described in the next section, "An Average Budget Formula
for Academic Library Units." Only the 60 that were able to report full fringe,
space, and overhead costs were invited. Of these, 32 prepared the unit costs analysis form (Exhibit 5). The data recorded there, together with data on services
rendered, permit calculation of unit costs.

The libraries involved here are fairly large, with an average total budget of 1.6
million dollars. They include 6 private and 26 publicly supported libraries. Private colleges and universities are underrepresented compared to the econometric
study (39 private; 96 public), but not significantly so. (The probability of this
large a difference in proportions is at least 10 percent.) Geographically, they
come from 21 states: 6 from the Pacific Coast; 8 from central states, 8 from the
Midwest, 7 from the Northeast, and 3 from the South.

The Method of Determining Unit Costs

Techniques have been developed permitting uniform unit cost analysis for varying libraries[21]. These techniques take into account the fact that nearly all of the
direct budget contributes to more than one service (book stock and technical services are a kind of overhead), and that details of cost allocation depend on the
actual levels of service rendered. The latter dependence is expressed by a book
use equivalency (BUE) factor.

The BUE factor represents the number of distinct books that are used in providing a unit of output. The BUE is 1 for circulation. Based upon interviews with
reference librarians (primarily anecdotal evidence), we have taken the average
number of items per reference query to be 2. Based on somewhat more systematic, but limited, studies of the relationship between reshelving counts and hours
of in-house use, we have taken 3 books per hour as the BUE for in-house use.
Due to the specific mathematics of the unit cost calculation, the final results are
fairly robust against small variations in the BUE.

Note that we invoke the "use until satisfaction" principle in allocating equal

Library Name: _____

Unit Cost: Time and Space   Contact Person: _____   Phone: (_____) _____

Name	Salary	Fringe	ILL	Circ	Ref	TechSvs	GenAdm
		0|					
		0|					
		0|					
		0|					
		0|					
		0|					
		0|					

Sums:

Fringe: $\|$ = _____ % of Salary

Sum of: $\|$ = _____ + _____ + _____ = _____
                  ILL   Circ   Ref   Reading

Space Use

Catalog $\|$ _____
Abst/Ind $\|$ _____
TechSvcs $\|$ _____
Materls $\|$ _____
= _____
  GenAdm

Exhibit 5. Extracted from the Unit Costs Manual

weight to a 20 minute in-house use of a book and the borrowing of a book for weeks or months.

The outline of the unit cost calculation is as follows:

1. All administrative costs are allocated to nonadministrative salaries.
2. Technical services salaries and space (processing, stacks) are added to the direct cost of materials.
3. The resulting sum is allocated to the principal services using the BUE factors.
4. Public service salaries and space costs are added to this allocation.
5. All other direct costs are allocated to these sums.
6. Institutional overhead is allocated to salaries or total costs as appropriate.
7. The total cost of each service is divided by the volume of service delivered.

We have applied this procedure to 30 participating libraries that were willing to collect the required data. The type of report sent to each library is illustrated by EXHIBIT 6, which is a report for a branch with only three staff members.

The specific unit costs have been reported to the libraries participating in the study. Without violating the confidentiality of which they were assured, we can report the statistical distributions of those unit costs. These provide the first uniformly defined view of both the magnitude and the variability of unit costs of public services at academic libraries, and the beginnings of a baseline that other libraries may use for evaluation and planning.

Principal Results

Total Cost of Services

The allocation of costs to the principal services is calculated as a weighted average of data from the 32 libraries. Thus it is not necessarily typical of any individual library.

The most interesting result is that in-house use represents a very substantial fraction of the allocated costs. This is due to the high level of reading that occurs in academic and research libraries. (This is so despite the fact that use of the

Table 1. Allocation of Costs to Services

In-house use	50%
Circulation	27%
Reference	20%
Interlibrary Loan	3%

Cost Analysis for Libraries #999 Example Library
Fiscal year Begin: 7/81   End: 6/82
Analysis of Salaries:

		Personnel		Public Services				Technical Services		ILL	Others	
	Name	Salary	Fringe	AVCirc	OthrCirc	On-Line	OthrRef	Catlgng	Acqstn	ILL	GenAdm	Excluded
a.	Librn	$25,764	$6,518			4	2		20	3	34	
b.	Librn	$21,304	$5,390			4	3	10			2	
c.	Lib Asst	$15,672	$3,965		2		1					
d.	I TC	$1,268	$321		3		0.5			0.5		
e.	Clerk	$21,064	$5,329		5		1					
f.		$0	$0									
g.		$0	$0									
	Sums:	$85,072	$21,523									

Fringe: 0   or   25.3% prcnt
Total:

Materials Budget:
Total =   Monograph + Periodcl + OthrSerl + AudioVsl + OthrMatl
104600   24600   70000   0   10000   WO AV
                                                                  104600

All other direct expenses:
Total =   On-Line +   ILL +   AVCirc   + The Rest
10804   4000   0   6804

Cost of Space: $ 38 /sqft/yr   OR $ 1   Total, per year
Maintenance of space, if not given above: $ 0   Total/yr

ASSIGNMENT OF SPACE

SPACE		Total Assignable:				Cost:		
			2100 sq. ft.					$79,800
Materials	68	% OR	??	sq. ft.	Catalog	0.05	sq. ft. $	% OR ??
Abstr&Ind	5	% OR	??	sq. ft.	TechSvcs	6.48	sq. ft. $	% OR ?? 28552.29
Total of these 4:	78	% OR						
	Audio Vis						sq. ft. $	28552.29 28552.29
	Reference						sq. ft. $	0 0
	Circulatn						sq. ft. $	0 0
	Adminstrm	140					sq. ft. $	51247.70 51247.70
	Reading						sq. ft. $	0 0
	Excluded						sq. ft. $	0 0
	Miscellan	218					sq. ft. $	0 Adjusted
	Total:	2100					sq. ft. $	79800 79800

244

Rate is: % of the salaries
Rate is: % of the salaries wo fringe
Rate is: 28.87483   % of the total direct cost
Total overhead is   1.288748
                        0.288748
Library cost is: $301,799

BOOK USE

EQUIVALENCY:			LEVELS OF ACTIVITY:			
Circultn:	1	vol/chkt	10204	Circs	1560 ILL:	1560 ILL: Borrowed / Lent
In-house:	5	vol/hour	6970	Hours	812	On-line Searches
Refernce:	2.5	vol/qury	1870	Queries		

Aud-Vis — Impacts 1 / 1

DISTRIBUTION OF SALARIES

AVCirc	OthrCirc	On-Line	OthRef	Catlgng	Acqstn	ILL (On-line)	GenAdm	Excluded
0		3228.229	1614.114			9818.508	27439.94	0
0		2737.837	2053.377			198.6005	1368.918	0
0	6545.672		3272.836	6844.592	13689.18			0
0	1191.603		198.6005					0
0	21994.32		4398.865					0
0								0
0								0
Sums: 0	29731.60	5966.066	11537.79	6844.592	13689.18	10017.10	28808.86	0
Sums: 0	60330.93	12106.25	23412.32	13888.94	27777.89	20326.57	AdmSpc: 51247.70	Distrbted 0

Adm Space

Allocation of Costs to Services

New heads	AVC	OthrCirc	On-line	OthRef	Matrls	In-house	ILL	Excluded
Sal:	0	60,331	20,757	23,412	41,667	None	20,327	0
Space:	0	0	None	0	28,552	0	None	0
Matls:	0	35,872	None	16,435	Dist	122,513	None	None
OthDir:	0	1,396	4,000	640		4,768	0	0
Sums:	0	97,599	16,106	40,487		127,281	20,327	0

New heads	AVC	OthrCirc	On-line	OthRef	Matrls	In-house	ILL	Excluded
Total Cst	$0	$125,780	$20,757	$52,177		$164,033	$26,196	$0
Impact:	1	10,204	812	1,870		6,970	3,120	1
Unit cost	$0.00	$12.33	$25.56	$27.90		$23.53	$8.40	$0.00
Per	Impact	Circ	Search	Query		Hour	Item	Service

Line Budget

Salary	85,072
Ovhd	0
Fringe	21,523
Ovhd	0
Matrls	104,600
Space	79,800
OthDir	10,804
Ovhd	87,144
Totals	388,943
Balance:	100
Space:	100

: Ovhd 388,943

Exhibit 6.

library materials, considered here, typically represents only 30 percent of the
reading in such a library. The rest is "study hall" use of the library.)

To see how the impact becomes so great, suppose that an average of 200 students are in the library (recall that the average library in this study is rather large)
over a span of 8 hours. Together they use

$$30\% \times 200 \times 8 \times 3 \ (\text{books/hour}) = 1440$$

items. Over a year of 200 days this represents 290,000 items used. It is the
materials-intensive quality of in-house use that brings it to the head of the list.

Circulation is next, slightly ahead of the more labor-intensive reference service. This is because there are many more circulations than reference transactions at the libraries studied. Interlibrary loan, which attracts much attention because of its potential for resource sharing, and its high direct costs, accounts for
only 3 percent of the total at this time.

The Units Costs of Services

The actual unit costs are shown in stem-and-leaf diagrams in Exhibit 7. These
diagrams are discussed in an Association of Research Libraries Publication,[22] and
may be read either as histograms (by turning them sideways) or as an ordered list
of the actual cost results.

Summary of the Data

The unit costs for circulation are fairly well grouped. Those for in-house use
are more varied, and the unit costs for reference and inter-library loan vary
widely. This is probably due to the responsive nature of these services, and the

0.	63
1.	27 48*
2.	07 15 27 28 38 59 65 66 74 88 97
3.	08 17 27/43 55 93 95
4.	12 39 78
5.	36 96
6.	22 53*68
6.	00
8.	
9.	25
10.	91
11.	

The "/" represents the median. The "*" represents the upper and lower 1/6th points.

Exhibit 7: Figure 2a.   Circulation costs

1.	66
2.	43 82*
3.	36 70
4.	34 66 92 98
5.	18 24 28 79
6.	38 71 73
7.	56/
8.	36 60 81 89
9.	37 75 93
10.	
11.	
12.	91
13.	59
14.	72
15.	
16.	03
17.	
18.	64
19.	*
20.	76
21.	
22.	93
23.	
24.	26
25.	

Exhibit 7: Figure 2b.   In-house costs per hour of reading

fluctuating load. A library may have to maintain a high capacity to provide reference service, even in times when demand is slight. If the variation in demand could be predicted, and if personnel could move freely from technical to public services, this problem would not be so great.

The data shown in the stem-and-leaf diagrams may be summarized by a table of statistics (Table 2).

The fact that the balance point K is larger than the median M shows that all of these distributions have "long tails." We have not tried to calculate an average

Table 2.   Statistics of the Distributions of Unit Costs

		Service			
		Circulation	*Reference*	*In-house*	*ILL*
Average A		$3.72	11.93	7.70	NA
Median M		3.35	14.00	8.00	13.00
Upper 1/6th	U	6.60	23.00	20.00	23.00
Lower 1/6th	L	1.50	6.00	3.00	4.20
(U + L)/2	K	4.05	14.50	11.50	13.60

4.	93
5.	39 80*
6.	04 37
7.	04 68
8.	32 55 59 79 92
9.	01
10.	12
11.	
12.	78
13.	06 07/
14.	84 86
15.	
16.	01
17.	07
18.	32
19.	
20.	04 63 77
21.	53
22.	26
23.	03*
24.	
25.	03
26.	
27.	51
28.	77
29.	

Above range: 38,256.

Exhibit 7: Figure 2c. Unit costs of reference, per query

for interlibrary loan because of the large number of unbelievable results. It is presumed that they trace to severe underreporting of the service statistics.

Explanatory Variables

The analysis of many variables that might influence the unit costs reveals only one with substantial explanatory power. This is the "public" versus "independent" distinction. We find that libraries at private college and university libraries tend to lie above the median:

Table 3. Distribution of Unit Costs at Private Institutions

Service	Number above median	Number below median
Circulation	4	2
Reference	5	1
In-house	4	2
Interlibrary loan	4	2

Below Range: 0.80 1.87
4.	13*25 54
5	
6.	73 93 96
7.	56
8.	00 12
9.	52 56
10.	74 87
11.	14 22
12.	21 52/
13.	
14.	27
15.	19 75 96
16.	26 32
17.	
18.	
19.	
20.	29
21.	
22.	04 53*
23.	

Above range: 28.45 36.09 54.41 243.11

Note: For interlibrary loan, only those items lent out are included in the calculation. When one library borrows from another the costs to the borrowing library are much lower because it is not making use of its own materials.

Exhibit 7: Figure 2d. Unit costs of interlibrary lending, per volume

With such a small number of private libraries, none of these results is statistically significant. Taken together, however, they suggest that private institutions have higher costs for the delivery of services to readers. This notion is also supported by the econometric results discussed in a later section of this paper.

Unit Costs at ARL Libraries

ARL units represent 16 of the 32 units for which this data was collected. Compared to the median, the ARL libraries have lower unit costs:

	Less Expensive	More Expensive	Significance
Service:			
In-house	12	4	95%
Circulation	12	4	95%
ILL	12	4	95%
Reference	10	6	40%

Notes: All the results taken together have a very high significance. Although there are 12 libraries below the median for the first three services listed, they are not the same 12 libraries. In other words, a library may be above the median cost for one service, and below the median for others.

Conclusions

Unit costs can be studied uniformly at academic libraries. The results show that reference and interlibrary loan are quite costly, with median costs of \$14.00 per query and \$13.00 per interlibrary loan. In-house use is next, at \$8.00 per hour of reading. Circulation is lowest, at \$3.35 per item borrowed. The hour of in-house reading is selected as a unit because it is very easily measured.[8] If a more cumbersome reshelving count is used, the unit of measure becomes the item used in-house. The corresponding unit cost will be \$2.33.

Discussion

There is very significant variation in the unit costs, even when they are determined by completely uniform procedures. Although some part of that variation might be attributable to variations in service quality, a more likely cause is variations in the management of academic libraries. Other libraries, undertaking such studies, should regard unit costs above these medians as a flag indicating the possibility of improvements in staffing patterns and other library procedures.

Unit costs studies drive home the point that library services are not a "free good." They represent a mechanism by which a college or university buys services that contribute to its overall missions. The costs are calculable, and significant. They are large compared to the financial resources of many students. A student who reads the library's books for 2 hours per day, for 40 weeks, receives a support service worth:

2 hrs. $\times$ 5 days $\times$ 40 weeks $\times$ \$8.00 = \$3,200

Within limits, increasing the use of the library will drive costs down, because the library budget is fixed in advance. Publicizing the great value available, in crude dollar terms, may provide the stimulus to bring readers into the library.

From the management point of view, an increase in use may create a decrease in the quality of the service process. This can be appraised using the techniques given in the ARL manual.[22] In planning and budget justification, a careful manager will want to determine the unit costs at her or his own library or branch rather than using the medians, or other representative values from the widely varying distributions reported here.

We firmly recommend that future studies of the economics of academic libraries build on the uniform analysis of unit costs. Detailed comparison of the factors contributing to unit costs, within and between institutions, will provide a rational basis for modification of service level, budgets, or both. Detailed analysis of unit cost is needed to extract the management information that relates costs of operation to the services rendered.

AN AVERAGE BUDGET FORMULA FOR ACADEMIC LIBRARY UNITS

We have seen wide variation in the unit costs of technical and "delivered" or public services. We may ask what happens if the representative values for the cost of public services are used to build a model of services and budgets for a larger group of libraries. The third study reported here answers that question. In brief, the results are statistically very satisfactory, and they enhance and emphasize the conclusions of the two studies already reviewed.

The Concept of a "Cost Function"

The Cost Function for Academic Libraries (CFAL) study is an opening wedge in the very difficult problem of the measurement and interpretation of library outputs. Although the term *outputs* has been applied (in the public library field) to describe certain measures of service quality,[23] its most appropriate application is to the measurement of service quantity, as well as quality. The CFAL study has helped us to refine efficient techniques for the measurement of quantity, and tools for its interpretation.

The interpretation of output data is subtle because it must involve a model for the relationship between outputs and other key variables (such as resource inputs, potential demand, levels of quality, etc.). If the model is explicit, the interpretation will be rather mathematical and forbidding. If the model is implicit (supplied, for example, by the regression routine of a computer package), the model may be inappropriate and the conclusions misleading.

Economic theory defines the *cost function* of a mixture of goods and services as the minimum price at which that mixture can be produced. If many competitors offer the same goods and services, those with inefficient methods will either improve or drop out of the market. Thus, in a mature market, the observed relation between costs and product will reveal the nature of the cost function.[17]

The CFAL project applied this concept to the mixture of services provided by academic libraries, in the hope that the cost of operating the library would reveal the minimum cost for provision of three principal services.

Libraries in the Sample

With the support of the National Science Foundation, we studied a random sample of 119 academic library units. Several library directors asked that other branches be included in the study and, whenever possible, this was done. (Some of these nonrandom libraries are among the 32 for which unit costs were determined.) An average formula was derived from the 119 random libraries, but our charts and tables include the units that were not selected at random. The names of the libraries appear in Appendix 3. The unit of observation in this study, as in the unit cost study, is the individual branch or department. The libraries range in size from budgets of less than $50,000 to over $2,000,000.[18] (See Table 3 of Appendix II).

Libraries belonging to the Association of Research Libraries are quite heavily represented in the sample, which permits us to draw a number of subsidiary conclusions. The study used a stratified sampling in which the chance that a library would be chosen is proportional to the library budget. Of the 119 libraries that were drawn from a frame of 1,800, 43 belong to the ARL libraries. In fact, even within the ARL there is a skewed distribution. As indicated by the ARL index (of 35 libraries consenting to release their names), 15 fall in the top third, 11 in the middle third, and 9 in the lower third.

The Mathematical Model

The overall mathematical form is a slight extension of a model used with statistical success in the description of costs and outputs of scientific and technical libraries.[8] It builds on the presumed relation between costs and services, starting from the expression:

$7.70 * RDGHRS + $3.72 * CIRC + $11.93 * REF

RDGHRS	=	thousands of hours of in-house use (*S*-variable)
CIRC	=	thousands of circulations (*C*-variable)
REF	=	thousands of informational queries (*R*-variable)

This expression is the cost expected if libraries provide only these three services, at the average costs determined in the unit cost study, and there are no economies of scale or scope. (An economy of scope is a savings in the delivery of one service due to the fact that another is also provided.)[2] Following statistical practice we add an unknown constant, to allow for start-up costs and services not included. The expression is then:

7.70 * RDGHRS + 3.72 * CIRC + 11.93* REF + X

Logarithmic Variables

It is well known that library statistics do not show a normal distribution unless a logarithmic transformation is used,[2,3,4] so we have required that the formula predict the logarithm of the direct budget. Finally, we introduce two more unknowns: Y, representing the effect of economies of scale, and Z, which corrects the precise dollar amounts for those effects, if they are present. The final formula looks like this:

log (direct budget) =

$Y * \{Z + \log (7.70 * \text{RDGHRS} + \$3.72 * \text{CIRC} + \$11.93 * \text{REF} + X\}$

(We would have preferred to use the sum of all costs, including space, fringe, and overhead, but half of the libraries were unable to report these important data.)

The unknowns themselves are determined by a nonlinear regression analysis. The effect is to find that average budget formula that is both consistent with the unit cost study and closest, across all libraries, to the actual budgets.

It can be shown that, in this model, the unit costs of services increase or decrease together, so that their ratio is always in proportion to their average values. If Y is greater than 1, the unit costs increase with library size. If it is less than 1, they decrease. If it is equal to 1, the model reduces to a linear model, and unit costs are independent of size.

Specification of the Best Fit Model

The model is "specified" by adjusting the unknowns—X, Y, and Z—until the formula is in the best possible agreement with the reported data. The result is: $X = 52,000$; $Y = 1.06$; $Z = -0.832$.

The contribution of X is unimportant for all but the smallest library units in the study. The value of Y, being slightly greater than 1, indicates that the cost per unit of service rises gradually as the library size increases. The coefficient Z permits the marginal unit costs to vary while their ratio remains fixed. It is adjusted to give the best possible fit over the full range of library budgets.

The formula can be simplified by combining Z into the coefficients, using logarithms. The resulting formula for the total direct budget in 1982 dollars is:

BDIR (in $1,000) =
    [3.35 * S (in 1,000 hours of reading) +
    + 1.61 * C (in 1,000 circ/year) +
    + 5.16 * R (in 1,000 queries/year) +
    + 22.63]$^{1.06}$

Application of the Formula

For example, if a library provides 10,000 hours of reading, 7,000 circulations, and answers 5,000 queries, the predicted budget is:

BDIR (in $1,000) =
    ($3.35 * 10 + 1.61 * 7 + 5.16 * 5 + 22.63)$^{1.06}$
    = $(93.2)^{1.06}$
    = 122.34 or:
BDIR = $122,340/year.

Evaluation of the Model

The model can be evaluated on three criteria: goodness of fit, specificity of the unknowns, and variation of the residuals.

Goodness of fit. This is a statistical notion regarding the fraction of the observed variation in the (logarithm of) the direct budget that is explained by the formula. That fraction is called the R-squared value. The formula explains the data with an R-squared value of 81.9 percent, which is quite satisfactory from a statistical point of view. In fact, if the numbers that are fixed here (7.70, 3.72, and 11.93) are allowed to change, the best possible fit has an R-squared value of 82 percent. In other words, the fit that is based on unit costs is essentially just as good as the best possible fit for a model of this general form. This is the best fit that has yet been obtained in any effort to relate library costs to library outputs.[5,6,7,8,9]

Specificity of the unknowns. This refers to how definitely X, Y, and Z have been determined. In particular, if other values of these unknowns give just as good a fit, then the specificity of the model is low. We find that very substantial changes may occur, while still meeting criterion (1). From the technical point of view, this ambiguity originates in the fact that the mix of services (the ratio of S to C to R) does not vary greatly from one library to another.

Distribution of the residuals. When a best fit, or average expense formula, is found, roughly half the libraries will have higher costs and roughly half will have lower costs. The discrepancy is called the residual cost, or budget variation. From the statistical point of view, the residuals in this situation are quite satisfactory (that is, they are distributed according to the normal law of probability.) However, from the points of view of library management, they are not satisfactory.

Specifically, one-third of the libraries in the study deviate from the average formula by more than 60 percent. Translated into managerial terms, the results so far enable a director to say: "Based on our levels of service, our operating budget for next year will have to be $122,000." But, when pressed, he or she would have to admit: "Well, I'm 66 ⅔ percent confident that it should be somewhere between $195,000 and $76,000." The university will quickly opt for the lower price.

This leads us to a more careful study of the residual variation. Before proceeding, we outline the happier path "that might have been."

Management Value of a Sharply Defined Formula

If the residuals were sharply distributed according to the normal law of probability and the unknowns were sharply determined, then every library could use the cost formula for planning and review. For example, if two-thirds of the residuals were less than plus or minus 10 percent, then (with 95 percent confidence) any library that is 20 percent off the average formula merits special attention to determine why. In other words, only 1 in 20 would be that far off for random reasons. With this precision, a cost formula may be used for planning, review, and incentive.

This was the underlying motivation behind the CFAL study. As it turns out, the study has not determined the cost function but, rather, has determined that the cost function is not yet determinable. Of course, if the whole problem had been a cut-and-dried one, there would be no reason for the National Science Foundation to have regarded it as "research." It would simply have been a routine economic analysis of a typical "industry."

Reserve Capacity and Overload: The Residual Variation

To study the residual variation, we define a hypothetical capacity for each library (in terms of the budget) by the rule:

The CAPACITY is any mix of services (*S, C,* and *R*) that, under the average formula given above, exactly matches the library's direct budget.

Mathematically, this definition does not specify the amount of *S, C,* and *R*. They could change to *S'* (the prime ['] denotes a hypothetical alternative), *C'* and *R'*, so long as the particular combination:

CAPACITY = \$3.35 * *S'* + \$1.61 * *C'* + \$5.16 * *R'*

remains compatible with the actual budget. That is, so long as:

BDIR = (CAPACITY + 22.63)$^{1.06}$

In fact, the library delivers actual services, in amounts denoted by *S, C,* and *R*. From these values we can calculate the combined service load:

LOAD = 3.35 * *S* + 1.61 * *C* + 5.16 * *R*.

In the example discussed earlier the load was 93.2.

The library will be exactly average if and only if:

LOAD = CAPACITY

Specifically, if it is overloaded, we measure the amount of overload by:

OVERLOAD = (LOAD − CAPACITY)/CAPACITY.

If it is underutilized (or overbudgeted) we measure the amount of reserve capacity by:

RESERVE = (CAPACITY − LOAD)/CAPACITY.

The Distribution of Reserve Capacity and Overload

The complete distribution of these results for 132 libraries is shown in Exhibit 7. As would be expected, half the libraries lie above the average budget formula and half lie below, We also see that 22 have a reserve capacity of 40 percent or more, and 22 have overloads of 78 percent or more. This illustrates the lack of precision we noted in both of the other studies. Because of it, the average budget formula is not yet a satisfactory management tool.

Possible Causes of Residual Variability

Several possible explanations of the large variation have been considered. The most important are:

1. Perhaps libraries with reserve capacity are delivering services at higher quality levels, which accounts for their higher cost per unit volume.
2. Perhaps the variation is due to bad data, bad models, or problems in the econometric analysis.
3. Perhaps the variation is due to other characteristics of the libraries, or of the universities that they serve.
4. Perhaps budgets simply do not have a sharp and consistent relation to services rendered.

Possibility 1 seems ruled out by the specific position of the 62 ARL libraries in study (there are 62 library units at the 43 institutions). They are substantially (in the ratio 2:1) below average in cost and above average in load. We do not believe that they are giving poorer quality of service than the 70 non-ARL libraries.

With regard to the possibility of bad data, it is possible (in fact, almost a cer-

Overload (in %)
420   WING
328 302
288 270 242 222 204
186 161 150 146 113 101

89 84 83 83
79 79 78 78 73 63
59 58 55 53 47 46 45 41
39 37 36 34 33 30 28 25 23 23 21 21 21 20
19 18 17 15 15 13 13 12 11 11 8 7 6 5 5 5 4 4 4 2
ZERO ---
 2 4 5 5 6 6 7 9 10 11 13 13 14 14 16 16 16 16 19 19
20 23 24 24 25 26 28 28 29 29 30 32 33 33 33 34 34 35 36 36 37 37 38 39
40 40 41 43 45 47 48 49 50 50 51 52 55 56 57 59 59
64 66 74 76 78

Reserve Capacity (in %)

Exhibit 7.

tainty) that some of the data are inaccurate. We asked each library to doublecheck the data we reported back to them, particularly in the case of low scaling factors (a measure of how busy the sample week was) and/or extreme deviation from the average formula. We received very little response. Unfortunately, this may only mean that the libraries are not sure how to check the data or are fearful of releasing the data for internal scrutiny.

At any rate, on the information available as of January 15, 1984, the residual variations are not due to "bad data."

As for the quality of the model, it has a logical simplicity and is of an econometric form called "constant elasticity of substitutions" models. The parameter determination was done using several different optimization packages and the results are consistent.

We are fairly sure that budget deviation is not determined by properties of the library or institution as a whole (such as are reported in the ARL statistics). We examined 15 library units at one ARL institution, and found that they are split 9 to 6 between overload and reserve. This is essentially the same as the 40 to 22 split for ALL of the ARL libraries. Clearly, the differences among these 15 libraries cannnot be explained by university statistics, because they all share the same statistics.

(The fact that the ARL library units are more likely to show an overload than a reserve capacity is statistically significant. The chance of the observed 40 to 22 split, if ARL libraries obey the same formula as all libraries, is 1.5 percent. We conclude that the ARL library units are significantly more cost effective than academic libraries in general; however, they also exhibit some high cost behavior. In fact, some have a reserve capacity of over 50 percent.)

Variables Affecting Deviation From the Average Formula

The original study design anticipated the possibility that other variables might control variation from the average formula. For this reason, libraries were asked to supply a good deal of additional information on interlibrary loan, computerization, and the composition of the collection. Of all those variables,[20] only computerization of the acquisitions process was significant (at 98.7 percent confidence.) The difference between public institutions and private was also significant at the 99 percent level. The results can be summarized in terms of the average overload or reserve:

Type	Average deviation from formula*	
Public	− 13%	(Overload)
Private	+ 22%	(Reserve)
Computerized ACQ	− 22%	(Overload)
Non-Comp ACQ	+ 7%	(Reserve)

Note: The deviation is measured by the logarithm of CAPACITY/ LOAD. This differs only slightly from the reserve capacity or overload.

These differences are small compared to the plus-or-minus 60 percent spread that characterizes all of the libraries. Thus, although they are statistically significant, they are not a full explanation. We turn then to the fourth possibility.

Nonexistence of the Cost Function

The remaining possibility is that present library budgets are not in accord with an accurate cost function and, therefore, the study of these budgets will not reveal the cost function. We believe that this is the correct, and most important, conclusion of the project. We can identify (a posteriori) three reasons why this situation exists.

Reasons for the Absence of a Cost Function

1. The procedure for setting budgets does not take into account levels of service rendered. In fact, a budget is often set on the basis of history, at some fixed fraction of the university budget or the library budget.[20]
2. In the absence of a marketplace, library directors have no way of knowing whether their procedures are efficient. Hence the basic condition under which expenditures would reveal the "cost function" is not met.
3. The library maintains a capacity to serve (through its purchases of labor and materials), but the levels of use depend on the demand expressed by the students and faculty of the university. Therefore it may not be possible for a library to adjust its service load to match the capacity it has established.

An Alternative Model of Library Budgets

We have found[10] that collection size is a better explanatory variable for library budgets than is service delivered. (It explains 89 percent of the [logarithmic] variation in library budgets.) This reflects a historic view of the library as a collection of books. Libraries funded on this historical assumption will find it hard to maintain their budget levels as the nature of services changes. In fact, many small libraries may become access points to large files located elsewhere, and maintain only a small "ready reference" collection.

Possible Changes in Library Management Procedures

Changes in the Budget-Setting Process

In principle, the budget process could be changed, so that it would reflect levels of service. This is particularly important in view of the long-range transformation in modes of information storage and retrieval.

If the budget process is linked to current (or recent) levels of service delivered, the situation becomes an economic game, in which branches or libraries compete for funds under a known formula. This provides a clear service incentive that is lacking in the present funding structure. It also creates the possibility that a poorly designed budget formula will encourage an undesirable mix of services. This problem is almost certain to become important in 7 to 10 years. An analogous approach to the distribution of state or county funds to public library systems is now under investigation.[16]

Information Sharing to Improve Service

The absence of information can be remedied by the systematic collection and exchange of output information among academic libraries of similar type and/or purpose. When interpreted with correct models (such as by unit cost analysis), this data will enable libraries to identify various norms and to share techniques that promote greater effectiveness.

We strongly urge that such data collection and exchange be initiated. It is a delicate procedure because, at any time, half of the libraries will be below the average, and that fact can be used against them by critics who lack the patience needed for evolution of better procedures.

From a purely statistical point of view, it may well be that the average expense formula that we have found is close to the true cost formula and, as libraries share management information and procedures, the variation of budgets will become smaller, around the same central formula. However, from a managerial point of view, we expect that the sharing of procedures will result in a drift toward higher effectiveness and a better (lower) cost formula. Because the cost formula represents the price that universities pay for the library services they receive, this drift will represent an improvement in the library's contribution to the university mission.

Modification of Demand

Even without information sharing, any library can improve its performance by increasing the demand for its services. The situation depends on the particular library and its context. For example, no university maintains a special collection in the expectation that students and faculty will pack the reading room soaking up arcana. On the other hand, almost all "college reading collections" are maintained in the expectation that they will be heavily used. There are four possibilities, depending on the flexibility of the demand, and the university expectation of the library.

The four possibilities can be formed into a table:

	University Expectation	
	High usage	*Other reasons*
Library can:		
Control demand	OK	OK
Not control demand	Bad	OK

We see that only one of four situations is troublesome when budgets are linked to current or recent service levels. If the university expects to see high usage, and the library has no control over that usage, then branches or libraries with significant reserve capacity may expect to see their budgets cut. Although this situation is unpleasant for managers and staff of such branches it is, arguably, beneficial to the library as a whole, and to the university that supports it.

SUGGESTIONS FOR FUTURE DEVELOPMENT

The three studies presented here have established that unit cost studies can be done uniformly, even at very large libraries. They can be done for both technical and public services. They can provide a statistically adequate formula for the description of budgets. However, a statistically adequate formula (one with a high R-squared value) is not always managerially adequate. The most important contribution to library management is that studies of this kind provide new information about library operations and services. The information helps managers to monitor the services they provide to the college or university. It provides concrete support in the quest for the funds needed to manage the library in transition.

Information Sharing

We strongly recommend that libraries work toward gathering and sharing this information. The resulting data can not be openly published, as are the ARL statistics, because they refer to branches and units, rather than to the library as a whole. More important, they are extremely sensitive, because many critics do not really understand that half of the units must be below the median, and they will attack. However, the benefits in improved management and in budget justification may outweigh the risks.

In a related spirit, the ARL could report aggregate service (of all ARL university libraries) without placing any of them at risk. This would move colleges and universities toward thinking of libraries in terms of service, rather than as collections of books.

Research Opportunities

There are also a number of research studies that could contribute to the improvement of library statistics as a tool for management and budgeting. Theoretical studies may be done, on the impact of the game-theoretic situation that formula budgeting could create. Additional data could be gathered to examine a variety of question suggested by the large variability of library costs, at every level.

For example: Is there any link between subjective estimates of quality and budget variation? Is there any relation between budget variation and the size of the potential user population for a given library unit? Is there a correlation between the deviation from the budget formula and the director's professional evaluation of whether a unit is underworked or overworked? If there is, the formula provides a valuable back-up in presenting such information to a skeptical administration, and in justifying transfers of personnel to the staff itself. Is there a relation between the budget variation and the university expectation for the particular library unit?

Conclusions

These three studies have established the potential of certain techniques for output measurement and analysis. They have also revealed that the "library industry" is not yet in the economic state that permits determination of fundamental costs from a statistical analysis of overall operating budgets.

Our present discussion takes place in a climate of immediate change and at the leading edge of a long-range transformation in library operations. In the short range, techniques of office automation, applied to library operations, may produce substantial savings in time and effort, improvements in control, and reallocations of personnel and funds. They affect, primarily, the intermediate outputs (technical and management services) of a library. The effect on services delivered to the user (public services) is likely to lie in improved quality, rather than in changes in cost or quantity.

In the longer range, electronic storage and retrieval of information will change the (public) services that are delivered. That is, while a reader will still gain access to the information that he or she seeks, the access may be through on-line use of an optical disk, rather than through borrowing or browsing in a book. These changes will make many of our customary indicators of library activity obsolete, while producing costs savings in lines (such as space) that frequently are not even posted in the library budget. To successfully weather this revolution, libraries need a clear picture of what they provide to the university, how much it really costs, and why.

The three studies described here have sought to refine some tools and to define some models for the understanding of services and costs. The nature of the difficulties and the steps to be taken next seem clear. In a nutshell, there is enormous variation in the price that universities pay for the services their libraries provide. Better collection and sharing of management and cost information will enable libraries to reduce this variation and arrive at precise and accurate models for the relation of costs to services.

Every university should be prepared to add a modest sum to its library budgets, to permit the library to manage more scientifically during the current changes in technical services and the coming transformation in information storage and retrieval. The added expenditure on library management will be quickly recovered through savings in the cost of library services rendered to the readers.

ACKNOWLEDGMENTS

This work is supported in part by the National Science Foundation, the Council on Library Resources, and the Association of Research Libraries. Any views or opinions expressed are those of the author, and do not necessarily reflect the opinions of the supporting organizations.

NOTES AND REFERENCES

1. W. J. Baumol, and M. Marcus *Economics of Academic Libraries* (Washington, D.C.: American Council on Education, 1973).

2. The notion of economy of scope was used by Baumol and Braunstein, *"Scale Economies, Production Complementarity and Information Distribution by Scientific Journals,"* (New York: New York University, Center for Applied Economics, 1976).

3. We worked directly from the tapes. The suurvey has been published in summary form: Richard M. Beazley, *Library of Statistics of Colleges and Universities, 1979: Institutional Data.* (Washington, D.C.: National Center for Educational Statistics, 1979). Available as NTIS publication number PB82-169087.

4. C. West. Churchman, *The Systems Approach* (New York: Dell, 1972).

5. M. Cooper, "The Economics of Library Size: A Preliminary Inquiry," *Library Trends* 28 (1979).

6. M. D. Cooper, "Economies of Scale in Large Academic Libraries," *Library and Information Science Research* (1984): 321–333. Cooper reports even higher levels of r-squared than are found in the present study. The reader must note that Cooper's sample is restricted to libraries in a narrow size range, so that it is not directly comparable with the CFAL project. It is also noteworthy that Cooper's formulas indicate that total library budgets are reduced when the library is open longer. This point, which is misinterpreted in Cooper's paper, defies rational interpretation. It may arise from the colinearity of the independent variables, which makes all of the coefficients only poorly defined.

7. R. Hayes, "The Management of Library Resources: The Balance Between Capital and Staff in Providing Service," *Library Research* 1 (1979): 119–142, and personal communications.

8. The report of the study of Scientific and Technical libraries appears in Paul B. Kantor, "Levels of Output Related to Costs of Operation of Scientific and Technical Libraries, Parts I and II," *Library Research* 3(1), (1981): and 3(2) (1981): 141–145.

9. Paul B. Kantor, with Judith B. Wood, Marla Bush, Prasert Shusang, and Linda Karaffa, *Analytical Study of the Users and Use of Health Sciences Libraries in the United States in 1982* (Cleveland, OH: Tantalus Inc., 1982). Copies of this report may be ordered from Tantalus Inc., Suite 218, 2140 Lee Road, Cleveland, OH 44118.

10. Paul B. Kantor, with Judith Wood, Marla Bush, Prasert Shusang and Jung Jin Lee, *An Average Expense Formula for Academic Libraries: The Final Report of the CFAL Project* (Cleveland, OH: Tantalus Inc., 1984). The full report (TANTALUS/GT-84/1, 2, 3). may by purchased from Tantalus Inc.

11. A concurrent study of Health Sciences Libraries has produced comparable data for 95 health sciences libraries of which 15 are located at academic institutions. Details appear in Paul B. Kantor, "Cost and Usage of Medical Libraries I: Economic Aspects," *Bulletin of the Medical Library Association* 72(July 1984): 274–286.

12. Paul B. Kantor, *Relation between Consortia, On-Line Services, and the Cost of Processing Monographs at Eight University Libraries"* (Council on Library Resources, November 1984).

13. Allen Kent, *A Cost Benefit Model of Some Critical Library Operations in Terms of Use of Materials* (Pittsburgh, PA: University of Pittsburgh, 1978). Final Report for NSF Grant #SIS75-11840

14. Joel A. Nachlas, and Anton R. Pierce, "Determination of Unit Costs for Library Services," *College and Research Libraries* 40 (May 1979): 240–247.

15.   A. D. Pratt, "Library Statistics," Library Quarterly 45 (1975): 275–286.

16.   A. Robert Rogers, and Paul B. Kantor, *Implications of Formula Budgeting for the Growth of Library Services*. A project of Kent State University and Tantalus Inc., supported in part by the State Library of Ohio. Project Director: Prof. A. Robert Rogers, Dean of the School of Library Studies (Kent, Ohio: Kent State University, 1985).

17.   See any textbook on microeconomics. The classic reference for contemporary mathematical economics is Paul A. Samuelson, *Foundations of Economic Analysis* (Cambridge, MA: Harvard University Press, Enlarged ed., 1983).

18.   Ralph M. Shoffner, and Paul B. Kantor, *Non-Resident User Survey for the King County Public Library System and the Seattle Public Library* (Beaverton, OR: Ringgold Management Systems, 1979).

19.   R. A. Stayner, "The Use of Empirical Standards in Assessing Public Library Effectiveness, in N. K. Kaske and W. G. Jones (eds.), *Library Effectiveness* (Chicago: LAMA, 1980), 352–372.

20.   Richard Talbott, University of Massachusetts, Amherst, private communication. (Based on a review of ARL data. Mr. Talbot has arrived as chair of the ARL statistics committee and as ARL President.)

21.   "Unit Cost for Library Services." Package is available as a consulting service from Tantalus Inc. Spreadsheets working under Lotus Symphony are available from the same source (Tantalus Inc., Suite 218, 2140 Lee Rd. Cleveland Ohio 44118).

22.   Paul B. Kantor, *Objective Performance Measures for Academic and Research Libraries* (Washington D.C.: Association of Research Libraries, 1984).

23.   Douglas Zweizig, and Eleanor Jo Rodger, *Output Measures for Public Libraries: A Manual of Standardized Procedures* (Chicago: American Library Association, 1982).

24.   Malcolm Getz, and Doug Phelps, "Labor Costs in the Technical Operations of Three Research Libraries" (Nashville, TN: Vanderbilt University, 1983). This work has been published in the *Journal of Academic Librarianship* (1984): 209–219.

APPENDICES

1.   Supplementary Tables for the Cost of Monographic Acquisition. All of these tables are extracted, with permission, from Reference [12c].

2.   Supplementary Tables for the Study of an Average Expenditure Formula for Academic Libraries. All of these tables are extracted, with permission, from Reference [10:a].

3.   Acknowledgments. There are many individuals to acknowledge for their generous commitment of time and effort to the projects reported here. The extent of our gratitude cannot be adequately represented by the simple listing here. These libraries, and the individual participants, are helping to bring the full benefits of modern management to academic and research libraries.

Appendix I

Tantalus-CLR Study of Processing Costs

The attached tables summarize the comparative statistics by station and library. The comparison tables differ from the totals reported to individual libraries for two reasons. (1) To facilitate comparison, we have used the same wage scales at every library. (2) We found so much variation in the space costs that we have omitted them from the comparison. Some general and specific comments help to understand the table.

The wage scales are given as reported by the libraries. Robert Hayes has pointed out that a wage, given as (annual salary)/(52 weeks) is an underestimate of the true cost of labor. The correction needed may range from a factor of (52/50) = 104% for staff with two weeks leave to as much as (52/46) for professional staff, including vacation time and leave for meetings and other reasons. This correction has not been applied.

The data for library L7 are based on a very short time span, selected by that library, and occurring during the Fall. Thus the numbers presented here for cost and delay may reflect the kind of variation seen in fortnightly data from the other libraries. For library L7, space figures for selection were not available. In addition, computer-support services were determined at L7 by a non-standard method, used in an internal study, whose details are not yet known to us. Finally, station I (original cataloging) at L7 includes all derived cataloging except LC.

In the determination of selection costs, some libraries collected good data on the number of items "seriously considered." For the others, we have estimated this number to be twice the number of orders placed. In general, zeroes appearing in the cost table represent unreported data, except for station L. Libraries 4 and 8 have closed their card catalogs. For library L8, the selectors chose not to report cost in comparable form. For library L2, search costs are included in the reported selection costs. Several libraries did not report costs associated with physical receiving, or with holding, shown as 0.

In the DELAY data, we have not included the delays associated with bindery preparation or in-house binding activities. These are judged not to be comparable between institutions.

Table 1.1. Hours per hundred items processed, of professional, technical and student labor. The average wage rate, and fringe (in %) are shown in the second and third column. The code is 1 = Professional; 2 = Technical; 3 = Student.

Library	Wages	Fr Rate	Line Nmbr	Select	Search	Order	Physical	Accounting	Copycat	Holding	Original	Marking	Cards in	True Wage plus fringe
L1	$10.77	17.5	1	4.51		0.00		0.00	1.21		81.07	0.00	0.22	$12.65
L2	$10.85	10.85	1	5.03		7.11		0.00			28.07		0.36	$12.03
L3	$9.71	14	1	6.2							99.06			$11.07
L4	$13.01	13.259	1	4.37	0.39	0.81			10.67		70.62	0.01	0.00	$14.73
L5	$13.92	20	1	3.62		1.00		0.00	5.28	0.00	157.82	0.00	0	$16.70
L6	$11.84	22	1	5.78		0		0.64	0		63.13	0	0	$14.44
L7	$12.80	24	1	5.87		0.10	0	0	1.62	0.01	68.77	0	4.44	$15.87
L8	$11.74	18.5	1			0.03		0	0		115.23	0		$13.91
L1	$5.33	17.5	2	0.00	17.39	51.35	2.31	6.03	21.34		92.46	5.30	9.77	$6.26
L2	$4.89	28.5	2	5.43		6.20		11.32	13.64			1.64	1.65	$6.28
L3	$6.17	11	2	0.52	23.12	6.11		16.06	29.54	2.54		7.42	0.26	$6.85
L4	$5.81	13.259	2		0.84	5.41	1	3.17	22.65		9.52	0.65		$6.58
L5	$8.27	20	2	15.94	3.65	5.77		13.84	21.90	0.01	23.47	0.00	1.73	$9.92
L6	$5.91	22	2	0.52	27.46	7.4		11.98	26.18		34.18	1.86	0.903	$7.21
L7	$6.31	24	2	1.53	2.88	3.35	1.13	3.45	40.89	0.03	0	1.07	0.59	$7.82
L8	$7.08	18.5	2		20.52	1.50		40.4	29.67		0	6.73		$8.39
L1	$3.57	0	3	0.00	16.70	4.37		1.89	6.48	5.25	0.89	1.11	7.06	$3.57
L2	$3.35	0	3	0.61		0.23		2.24			27.30	3.07	1.24	$3.35
L3	$3.51	7	3	11.63		0.8		3.6			0		0.29	$3.76
L4	$3.35	4	3	25.87	0.43	2.65	0.4	2.57	5.15		0	2.05		$3.48
L5	$3.63	20	3	0.52	0.32	0.36		0.14	0.00	5.88	0	12.75	0.00	$4.36
L6	$1.84	0	3	0.92	2.25	0		4.99	0		0	1.86	0	$1.84
L7	$3.50	0	3			0	0	0.09	0	0.61	0	0	0	$3.50
L8	$4.68	18.5	3		2.25	1.81		1.34	0.16	2.54	0	4.24		$5.55

265

Table 1.2. Summary of direct cost data, per item, for all libraries and stations.

4. Actual reported overhead (station by station) and weighted average rate (in %). Note that library L8 did not report university overhead.
5. Local computer costs.
6. Cost of support services including external network and communications charges.
7. Reported space costs.
8. Other direct costs. This category was used to collect any costs not otherwise reported.

Library	Wages	Fr rate	Line Nmbr	Select	Search	Order	Physical	Accounting	Copycat	Holding	Original	Marking	Cards in
L1	54.69	Avg:Ovrhd:	4	$0.34	$1.00	$1.99	$0.06	$0.18	$0.63	$0.00	$10.06	$0.15	$0.42
L2	55.31	Avg:Ovrhd:	4	$0.53	$0.00	$0.69	$0.00	$0.43	$0.67	$0.19	$5.59	$0.11	$0.08
L3	57.63	Avg:Ovrhd:	4	$0.67	$0.91	$0.26	$0.00	$0.71	$1.17	$0.00	$6.32	$0.29	$0.04
L4	41.84	Avg:Ovrhd:	4	$0.27	$0.03	$0.24	$0.03	$0.12	$1.36	$0.00	$4.62	$0.05	$0.00
L5	36.30	Total:	4	$1.20	$0.16	$0.27	$0.00	$0.50	$1.11	$0.09	$10.41	$0.20	$0.06
L6	43.30	Avg:Ovrhd:	4	$0.38	$0.88	$0.23	$0.00	$0.45	$0.82	$0.00	$5.02	$0.07	$0.03
L7	38.80	Avg:Ovrhd:	4	$0.42	$0.09	$0.11	$0.03	$0.11	$1.34	$0.01	$4.24	$0.03	$0.29
L8	20.49	Avg:Ovrhd:	4	$0.00	$0.37	$0.04	$0.00	$0.71	$0.51	$0.02	$3.29	0.16	$0.00
L1		Computers	5	$0.00	$0.05	$0.17	$0.00	$0.00	$0.09	$0.00	$0.12	$0.00	$0.00
L2		Computers	5	$0.21	$0.00	$0.13	$0.00	$0.18	$0.00	$0.00	$3.44	$0.09	$0.00
L3		Computers	5	$0.00	$0.00	$0.24	$0.00	$0.12	$0.00	$0.00	$0.00	$0.00	$0.00
L4		Computers	5	$0.00	$0.11	$0.04	$0.06	$0.02	$0.00	$0.00	$0.00	$0.00	$0.00
L5		Computers	5	$0.27	$0.41	$0.42	$0.30	$0.69	$3.68	$0.00	$8.28	$0.00	$0.00
L6		Computers	5	$0.00	$0.00	$0.00	$0.00	$0.00	$0.00	$0.00	$0.00	$0.00	$0.00
L7		Computers	5	$0.00	$0.00	$0.00	$0.00	$0.00	$0.00	$0.00	$0.00	$0.00	$0.00
L8		Computers	5	$0.00	$0.06	$0.03	$0.00	$0.05	$0.09	$0.00	$0.46	$0.00	$0.00

Line	Category	Grp										
L1	Supp SVC	6	$0.00	$0.19	$1.18	$0.00	$0.00	$3.86	$0.00	$4.78	$0.00	$0.00
L2	Supp SVC	6	$0.08	$0.00	$0.14	$0.00	$0.19	$1.36	$0.00	$0.32	$0.09	$0.00
L3	Supp SVC	6	$0.00	$0.05	$0.00	$0.00	$0.00	$2.90	$0.00	$0.23	$0.00	$0.00
L4	Supp SVC	6	$0.00	$0.00	$0.00	$0.00	$0.00	$3.02	$0.12	$0.00	$0.00	$0.00
L5	Supp SVC	6	$0.02	$0.04	$0.04	$0.02	$0.11	$0.07	$0.00	$1.00	$0.11	$0.01
L6	Supp SVC	6	$0.15	$0.29	$0.34	$0.40	$0.40	$0.27	$0.00	$4.83	$0.12	$0.02
L7	Supp SVC	6	$0.00	$0.00	$2.94	$0.00	$0.00	$2.03	$0.00	$0.00	$0.00	$0.00
L8	Supp SVC	6	$0.00	$0.73	$1.06	$0.00	$0.65	$0.70	$0.00	$1.48	$0.00	$0.00
L1	Space CST	7	$0.07	$0.06	$0.14	$0.06	$0.14	$0.31	$0.00	$0.71	$0.05	$0.05
L2	Space CST	7	$0.01	$0.00	$0.01	$0.00	$0.01	$0.02	$0.00	$0.12	$0.01	$.00
L3	Space CST	7	$0.00	$0.02	$0.08	$0.03	$0.01	$0.03	$0.26	$0.27	$0.01	$.00
L4	Space CST	7	$0.76	$0.76	$0.86	$0.39	$0.14	$1.18	$0.42	$2.21	$0.46	$0.00
L5	Space CST	7	$0.12	$0.09	$0.09	$0.05	$0.24	$0.16	$0.26	$2.19	$0.24	$0.01
L6	Space CST	7	$0.12	$0.24	$0.28	$0.33	$0.33	$0.22	$0.00	$3.99	$0.10	$0.01
L7	Space CST	7	$0.00	$0.00	$0.17	$0.15	$0.16	$0.47	$0.30	$0.44	$0.00	$0.00
L8	Space CST	7	$0.00	$0.29	$0.07	$0.00	$0.23	$0.26	$0.17	$2.98	$0.06	$0.00
L1	Oth Direct	8	$0.00	$0.00	$0.00	$0.00	$0.00	$0.00	$0.00	$0.00	$0.00	$0.00
L2	Oth Direct	8	$0.00	$0.00	$0.00	$0.00	$0.00	$0.00	$0.00	$0.00	$0.00	$0.00
L3	Oth Direct	8	$0.00	$0.09	$0.37	$0.07	$0.11	$0.22	$0.00	$0.71	$0.07	$.00
L4	Oth Direct	8	$0.07	$0.00	$0.00	$0.00	$0.00	$0.00	$0.00	$0.00	$0.00	$0.00
L5	Oth Direct	8	$0.00	$0.13	$0.13	$0.07	$0.35	$0.23	$0.38	$3.21	$0.35	$0.02
L6	Oth Direct (rlin)	8	$0.00	$0.23	$0.00	$0.00	$0.00	$3.92	$0.00	$7.09	$0.00	$0.00
L7	Oth Direct (chrg)	8	$0.00	$0.00	$0.13	$0.00	$0.13	$0.30	NA	$0.00	$0.00	$0.00
L8	Oth Direct	8	$0.00	$0.06	$0.14	$0.00	$0.10	$0.29	$0.00	$0.78	$0.04	$0.00

Table 1.3. Cost data for libraries L1.L8 in four categories, for 10 principal stations. The cost categories are:

9. Non-assignable: work which does not pertain to the processing of a particular item, such as catalog maintenance.
10. Wages/fringe: uniform labor costs, including fringe, based upon wages plus fringe of ($13.80, 7.50, 3.70) for the effort levels reported in lines 1, 2 and 3 of Table 1.1.
11. Overhead: four layers of overhead: department, division, library and university. The weighted average overhead rate is applied to the uniform labor cost.
12. Comp + Svcs + Other direct: all costs of domestic and purchased computer systems, and related supplies. The sum of lines 5, 6 and 8 in Table 1.2.
Note: in some cases supplies were assigned to overhead. They still appear in the final sums.
Space costs are not included here because there is no consistency in the scope of available cost information.

Library	Fr rate	Line Nmbr	Select	Search	Order	Physical	Accounting	Copycat	Holding	Original	Marking	Cards in
L1	Non-Assignable	9	$0.00	$0.00	$0.00	$0.00	$0.00	$0.00	$0.00	$0.00	$0.00	$0.00
L2	Non-Assignable	9	$0.00	$0.00	$0.00	$0.00	$0.00	$0.92	$0.00	$0.88	$0.00	$0.00
L3	Non-Assignable	9	$0.00	$0.00	$0.00	$0.00	$0.00	$0.02	$0.00	$0.02	$0.00	$0.00
L4	Non-Assignable	9	$0.00	$0.00	$0.04	$0.00	$0.00	$0.00	$0.00	$0.00	$0.00	$0.00
L5	Non-Assignable	9	$0.02	$0.04	$0.00	$0.02	$0.11	$1.37	$0.12	$2.32	$0.11	$0.01
L6	Non-Assignable	9	$0.00	$0.00	$0.00	$0.00	$0.00	$1.54	$0.00	$1.54	$0.00	$0.00
L7	Non-Assignable	9	$0.00	$0.00	$0.00	$0.00	$0.00	$0.00	$0.00	$0.00	$0.00	$0.00
L8	Non-Assignable	9	$0.00	$0.00	$0.00	$0.00	$0.00	$0.18	$0.02	$0.19	$0.01	$0.00
	Average	9	$.00	$0.01	$0.01	$.00	$0.01	$0.50	$0.02	$0.62	$0.01	$.00
L1	All wages/fringe	10	$0.62	$1.92	$4.01	$0.17	$0.52	$1.60	$0.00	$11.22	$0.44	$1.02
L2	All wages/fringe	10	$1.12	$0.00	$1.45	$0.00	$0.93	$1.43	$0.38	$11.82	$0.24	$0.17
L3	All wages/fringe	10	$1.32	$1.73	$0.49	$0.00	$1.34	$2.22	$0.00	$13.67	$0.56	$0.08
L4	All wages/fringe	10	$0.60	$0.08	$0.62	$0.09	$0.33	$3.36	$0.00	$10.46	$0.13	$0.00

L5	All wages/fringe	10	$2.65	$0.34	$0.58	$0.00	$1.04	$2.37	$0.22	$23.54	$0.47	$0.13
L6	All wages/fringe	10	$0.86	$2.14	$0.56	$0.00	$1.17	$1.96	$0.00	$11.28	$0.21	$0.07
L7	All wages/fringe	10	$0.96	$0.22	$0.27	$0.08	$0.26	$3.29	$0.03	$9.49	$0.08	$0.66
L8	All wages/fringe	10	$0.00	$1.62	$0.18	$0.00	$3.08	$2.23	$0.09	$15.90	$0.66	$0.00
	Average	10	$1.02	$1.01	$1.02	$0.04	$1.09	$2.31	$0.09	$13.42	$0.35	$0.27
L1	Average overhead	11	$0.34	$1.05	$2.19	$0.09	$0.29	$0.88	$0.00	$6.14	$0.24	$0.56
L2	Average overhead	11	$0.62	$0.00	$0.80	$0.00	$0.52	$0.79	$0.21	$6.54	$0.13	$0.09
L3	Average overhead	11	$0.76	$1.00	$0.28	$0.00	$0.77	$1.28	$0.00	$7.88	$0.32	$0.05
L4	Average overhead	11	$0.25	$0.03	$0.26	$0.04	$0.14	$1.41	$0.00	$4.38	$0.05	$0.00
L5	Average overhead	11	$0.96	$0.12	$0.21	$0.00	$0.38	$0.86	$0.08	$8.54	$0.17	$0.05
L6	Average overhead	11	$0.37	$0.93	$0.24	$0.00	$0.51	$0.85	$0.00	$4.88	$0.09	$0.03
L7	Average overhead	11	$0.37	$0.08	$0.10	$0.03	$0.10	$1.28	$0.01	$3.68	$0.03	$0.25
L8	Average overhead	11	$0.00	$0.33	$0.04	$0.00	$0.63	$0.46	$0.02	$3.26	$0.14	$0.00
	Average	11	$0.46	$0.44	$0.52	$0.02	$0.42	$0.97	$0.04	$5.66	$0.15	$0.13
L1	Comp + Svcs + OthDir	12	$0.00	$0.24	$1.35	$0.00	$0.00	$3.95	$0.00	$4.89	$0.00	$0.00
L2	Comp + Svcs + OthDir	12	$0.29	$0.00	$0.27	$0.00	$0.37	$1.36	$0.00	$3.76	$0.10	$0.00
L3	Comp + Svcs + OthDir	12	$0.00	$0.14	$0.60	$0.07	$0.23	$3.12	$0.00	$0.94	$0.07	$.00
L4	Comp + Svcs + OthDir	12	$0.00	$0.11	$0.04	$0.06	$0.02	$3.02	$0.00	$0.00	$0.00	$0.00
L5	Comp + Svcs + OthDir	12	$0.36	$0.58	$0.58	$0.39	$1.15	$3.98	$0.50	$12.50	$0.46	$0.03
L6	Comp + Svcs + OthDir	12	$0.15	$0.52	$0.34	$0.40	$0.40	$4.19	$0.00	$11.93	$0.12	$0.02
L7	Comp + Svcs + OthDir	12	$0.00	$0.00	$3.07	$0.00	$0.13	$2.33	NA	$0.00	$0.00	$0.00
L8	Comp + Svcs + OthDir	12	$0.00	$0.85	$1.23	$0.00	$0.80	$1.07	$0.00	$2.72	$0.04	$0.00
	Average	12	$0.10	$0.30	$0.94	$0.12	$0.39	$2.88	NA	$4.59	$0.11	$0.01

APPENDIX II

Key to the Data Tables

Variables have been for the most part defined in the text, or by the data collection manuals. The meaning and units are summarized here.

Variable	Table	Meaning	Units of measure
BDIR	I	Direct budget	$/year (current)
INHOUSE USE	I	Reading matrls in lib	Hours rdng/year
CIRC	I	Circulations	Items/year
REF	I	Reference service	Info quer/yr
RES/OVD	I	Reserve cap or overld	%. Using Model I
RESIDUAL	I	Log (PRED BDIR/BDIR)	log units
LIBRARY NUMBER	I	number used to key other tables	
FISCAL YR	II	end of fiscal year	date
SALARY	II	total salary budget	$/yr
STAFF (FTE)	II	Staff (full time eq)	souls
SALARY/FTE	II	Crude mean salary	$/soul-year
SQUARE FEET	II	Area:assgnable space	sq ft
SQFT/FTE	II	Ratio of area to staff	sqft/soul
TOTALBUDGET	III	Direct budget again	$/yr
SALARY	III	as in Table II	
DIRECT-SALARY	III	non salary budget	$/yr
FRINGE	III	Fringe budget	$/yr
SP/MAINT	III	Cost of space	$/yr
OVERHEAD	III	Admin ovhd costs	$/yr

Table I.

Direct budget	Inhouse use	Circulation	Reference	+Res/-OVD	Residual	Library
17,398	10,909	3,582	5	−145.	1.46	1
29,565	2,541	6,116	514	6.	0.66	2
51,716	6,388	9,836	3,778	−204.	0.70	3
53,870	4,830	6,097	2,286	−83.	0.35	4
60,518	14,945	37,404	Unknown	−382.	1.18	5
64,607	2,830	1,705	218	57.	−0.41	6
71,587	13,902	25,492	4,459	−242.	0.95	7
78,008	1,254	2,026	135	78.	−0.72	8
88,561	6,276	25,116	2,358	−83.	0.47	9
102,200	9,672	8,409	2,225	2.	−0.02	10
102,692	1,921	12,072	1,672	28.	−0.24	11
108,660	38,403	38,137	26,466	−420.	1.49	12
110,847	7,814	20,292	741	−11.	0.09	13
111,596	6,530	11,972	2,394	11.	−0.09	14

Table I. (*continued*)

Direct budget	Inhouse use	Circulation	Reference	+Res/-OVD	Residual	Library
113,476	31,194	64,646	4,663	− 288.	1.21	15
115,420	7,120	11,526	277	30.	− 0.27	16
128,945	23,828	28,947	3,144	− 89.	0.55	17
132,037	12,189	19,414	2,893	− 15.	0.12	18
137,251	25,083	49,625	7,268	− 161.	0.87	19
141,260	26,107	32,439	1,839	− 78.	0.51	20
146,350	17,292	14,109	1,644	4.	− 0.03	21
146,445	13,299	3,410	1,342	45.	− 0.46	22
147,515	19,962	55,163	9,327	− 150.	0.84	23
167,510	8,671	16,980	Unknown	41.	− 0.44	24
172,806	22,749	25,616	9,842	− 55.	0.40	25
182,644	9,743	39,011	1,324	− 5.	0.05	26
196,355	18,053	26,833	13,461	− 41.	0.32	27
210,273	10,186	44,176	3,018	− 6.	0.05	28
216,830	43,185	28,252	1,379	− 33.	0.26	29
220,686	42,448	4,172	218	14.	− 0.14	30
221,669	32,478	174,833	8,707	− 270.	1.27	31
226,345	6,250	21,828	Unknown	55.	− 0.68	32
227,412	37,078	508	4,063	19.	− 0.19	33
233,857	26,354	39,538	5,802	− 25.	0.21	34
240,881	38,767	78,780	10,293	− 113.	0.73	35
253,820	26,586	25,782	2,597	14.	− 0.14	36
261,364	19,103	28,780	927	29.	− 0.32	37
261,796	19,505	24,929	10,717	5.	− 0.05	38
272,517	33,037	33,075	6,072	− 8.	0.07	39
272,549	15,742	24,784	1,659	40.	− 0.47	40
277,676	18,316	31,948	3,532	24.	− 0.25	41
281,280	21,518	46,473	6,019	− 5.	0.04	42
286,924	45,624	83,370	7,349	− 84.	0.59	43
304,172	72,717	62,156	5,053	− 79.	0.57	44
308,081	47,309	35,113	2,656	− 7.	0.07	45
321,072	81,237	39,695	1,145	− 46.	0.37	46
329,989	15,043	33,305	3,991	38.	− 0.44	47
352,160	64,473	6,458	435	20.	− 0.22	48
369,507	48,877	30,710	4,230	10.	− 0.11	49
375,613	39,400	Unknown	52,068	− 47.	0.38	50
382,668	31,159	31,310	29,315	− 18.	0.16	51
384,750	41,634	45,210	5,775	6.	− 0.06	52
397,161	63,282	71,643	17,559	− 58.	0.46	53
403,376	7,314	201,168	Unknown	− 78.	0.58	54
409,474	41,537	22,298	8,872	25.	− 0.28	55
412,226	30,206	40,897	119	37.	− 0.44	56
431,522	11,997	25,184	5,557	59.	− 0.85	57
436,828	34,551	77,675	7,646	− 5.	0.05	58
453,415	79,328	98,435	9,449	− 59.	0.46	59
470,000	132,832	72,370	9,685	− 79.	0.59	60
496,591	43,091	77,106	21,116	− 19.	0.18	61

Table I. (*continued*)

Direct budget	Inhouse use	Circulation	Reference	+ Res/-OVD	Residual	Library
507,262	50,474	28,766	10,536	26.	− 0.29	62
534,459	222,572	332,580	18,000	− 302.	1.43	63
556,199	39,934	32,635	8,626	40.	− 0.50	64
565,052	97,976	72,632	6,960	− 21.	0.19	65
588,442	82,626	95,038	13,683	− 28.	0.25	66
662,997	34,438	67,411	7,990	36.	− 0.44	67
703,299	19,285	31,964	7,476	66.	− 1.04	68
707,286	42,666	58,289	30,176	16.	− 0.17	69
717,955	104,341	160,340	Unknown	− 34.	0.29	70
719,804	39,563	42,828	8,065	50.	− 0.68	71
734,589	65,339	76,152	21,645	7.	− 0.08	72
780,767	25,798	60,788	13,644	47.	− 0.64	73
791,221	46,924	49,492	4,162	51.	− 0.72	74
1,018,004	58,941	101,750	11,561	34.	− 0.42	75
1,033,767	196,973	196,657	15,993	− 53.	0.44	76
1,098,325	65,400	98,614	56,355	6.	− 0.07	77
1,150,934	72,261	98,292	18,568	33.	− 0.41	78
1,200,964	194,111	156,400	18,193	− 21.	0.20	79
1,251,735	59,936	70,767	19,811	49.	− 0.69	80
1,261,022	168,954	167,024	121,075	− 73.	0.57	81
1,283,000	78,063	140,171	22,651	24.	− 0.29	82
1,468,934	129,346	144,562	14,190	23.	− 0.27	83
1,492,400	151,587	210,501	44,468	− 13.	0.12	84
1,546,624	104,346	190,345	34,734	13.	− 0.14	85
1,646,725	56,987	19,458	12,810	76.	− 1.44	86
1,673,939	119,450	159,265	1,796	37.	− 0.48	87
1,838,985	120,608	135,027	45,690	28.	− 0.35	88
1,858,950	108,420	221,184	37,870	19.	− 0.22	89
1,893,744	29,796	133,194	11,193	64.	− 1.06	90
2,016,454	159,605	152,391	32,346	29.	− 0.35	91
2,122,859	98,727	232,275	27,507	32.	− 0.41	92
2,212,204	66,852	486,725	77,331	− 17.	0.17	93
2,341,493	387,919	178,829	27,831	− 4.	0.04	94
2,570,201	239,047	470,000	25,684	− 11.	0.11	95
2,608,787	210,611	230,539	130,362	− 4.	0.04	96
2,663,028	375,526	334,673	93,927	− 30.	0.28	97
2,716,631	96,225	147,745	36,320	56.	− 0.84	98
2,838,338	99,905	322,810	41,638	33.	− 0.42	99
3,216,638	386,099	347,484	101,088	− 13.	0.13	100
3,358,521	232,577	428,173	124,174	− 4.	0.04	101
3,518,213	139,932	766,314	327	5.	− 0.05	102
3,711,192	311,853	327,055	113,051	9.	− 0.10	103
4,072,335	150,617	357,893	51,163	43.	− 0.58	104
4,107,432	532,473	471,050	126,042	− 21.	0.20	105
4,429,509	257,874	402,960	146,014	16.	− 0.18	106
4,436,400	342,747	437,149	86,116	16.	− 0.18	107
4,868,657	194,825	266,313	26,646	59.	− 0.92	108

Table II.

Library	Fiscal year	Salary	Staff (FTE)	Salary/FTE	Square feet	Sqft/FTE
1	6/30/82	11,673	1.6	7,296	5,200	3,250
2	6/81	13,565	2.0	6,783	1,000	500
3	6/82	36,246	3.3	11,153	3,550	1,092
4	6/30/82	22,870	2.3	10,164	2,571	1,143
5	6/82	44,932	3.0	14,977	5,538	1,846
6	6/82	31,993	2.8	11,634	2,454	892
7	6/82	37,434	4.0	9,359	4,261	1,065
8	6/30/82	25,518	3.7	6,841	5,907	1,584
9	6/81	57,500	4.8	12,105	3,922	826
10	6/82	33,000	3.0	11,000	1,200	400
11	6/82	34,492	3.0	11,497	5,960	1,987
12	6/81	84,785	9.0	9,421	16,000	1,778
13	6/81	42,634	2.8	15,503	4,400	1,600
14	6/82	59,226	3.0	19,742	25,000	8,333
15	6/82	88,048	10.0	8,805	6,210	621
16	6/82	51,920	4.8	10,931	11,592	2,440
17	6/82	24,635	4.3	5,729	5,800	1,349
18	6/30/82	81,984	7.0	11,712	7,500	1,071
19	6/82	68,367	8.0	8,546	5,845	731
20	6/81	99,368	7.4	13,356	7,500	1,008
21	6/82	37,861	5.0	7,572	6,980	1,396
22	6/82	54,487	4.5	12,108	2,359	524
23	6/82	89,715	7.5	11,962	10,664	1,422
24	6/82	55,050	4.5	12,233	2,800	622
25	1982	122,906	26.0	4,727	23,042	886
26	8/82	52,644	5.0	10,529	10,767	2,153
27	6/81	63,853	4.8	13,386	8,595	1,802
28	6/82	141,853	16.3	8,703	9,500	583
29	6/30/81	169,188	32.0	5,287	60,000	1,875
30	1982	97,391	5.0	19,478	8,096	1,619
31	6/82	100,982	9.5	10,630	11,159	1,175
32	6/82	157,000	12.0	13,083	1,800	150
33	8/81	120,546	8.0	15,068	Unknown	Unknown
34	1982	112,012	9.5	11,791	10,769	1,134
35	6/30/82	122,550	8.8	13,926	27,000	3,068
36	6/82	140,374	14.1	9,956	24,502	1,738
37	6/82	220,364	32.0	6,886	17,046	533
38	6/82	129,105	19.2	6,742	21,120	1,103
39	6/30/82	174,543	10.0	17,454	8,858	886
40	6/81	154,083	19.0	8,110	37,116	1,953
41	6/82	157,410	12.6	12,493	36,000	2,857
42	6/30/82	190,220	14.5	13,119	29,500	2,034
43	6/82	89,981	12.5	7,198	14,464	1,157
44	6/81	84,493	9.3	9,085	17,160	1,845
45	6/81	193,810	23.5	8,247	37,538	1,597
46	6/30/82	163,752	13.5	12,130	43,000	3,185
47	6/81	165,474	13.5	13,257	20,498	1,518

Table II. (continued)

Library	Fiscal year	Salary	Staff (FTE)	Salary/FTE	Square feet	Sqft/FTE
48	6/30/82	179,881	18.0	9,993	11,072	615
49	6/82	200,589	23.0	8,721	60,000	2,609
50	6/30/81	250,052	17.3	14,496	10,369	601
51	8/81	218,872	18.0	12,160	10,000	556
52	6/82	159,750	11.5	13,891	7,500	652
53	6/82	233,611	16.5	14,158	60,000	3,636
54	6/81	393,611	36.0	10,934	286,000	7,944
55	9/82	176,314	17.5	10,075	30,492	1,742
56	6/82	280,016	47.0	5,958	38,271	814
57	5/82	235,172	21.8	10,788	22,655	1,039
58	6/81	181,587	12.5	14,527	26,400	2,112
59	6/30/83	272,365	20.5	13,286	Unknown	Unknown
60	6/82	200,000	15.0	13,333	39,500	2,633
61	8/82	336,591	28.8	11,708	100,000	3,478
62	9/82	390,333	52.0	7,506	58,100	1,117
63	6/82	359,964	38.0	9,473	67,121	1,766
64	5/31/82	273,825	26.2	10,451	32,350	1,235
65	6/30/82	315,204	27.5	11,462	47,576	1,730
66	6/30/83	432,803	63.5	6,816	100,000	1,575
67	6/81	315,957	29.0	10,895	85,075	2,934
68	3/82	375,100	29.8	13,587	23,515	789
69	7/83	241,286	19.0	12,699	42,526	2,238
70	6/30/82	466,162	34.1	13,670	29,406	862
71	9/82	260,804	18.8	13,910	74,642	3,981
72	6/30/81	494,448	35.5	13,928	133,367	3,757
73	6/30/82	428,378	58.0	7,386	108,000	1,862
74	6/81	471,764	111.0	4,250	92,768	836
75	1981	579,555	40.2	14,417	120,000	2,985
76	6/81	560,939	45.0	12,465	108,000	2,400
77	6/81	785,712	68.9	11,399	64,092	930
78	6/82	355,416	28.0	12,693	75,780	2,706
79	6/82	597,519	39.1	15,270	120,678	3,084
80	6/82	538,751	37.5	14,367	71,648	1,911
81	6/30/81	708,524	62.8	11,291	125,161	1,995
82	6/82	596,000	51.0	11,686	127,280	2,496
83	1981	849,332	38.0	22,351	73,886	1,944
84	3/31/82	960,800	73.6	13,054	223,000	3,030
85	7/81	805,552	101.0	7,976	220,000	2,178
86	8/82	528,192	41.3	12,780	63,000	1,524
87	6/83	988,016	175.0	5,646	171,000	977
88	1982	1,086,210	130.0	8,355	56,000	431
89	6/81	874,263	68.0	12,857	89,539	1,317
90	6/30/82	1,008,430	84.3	11,962	115,777	2,373
91	6/81	726,040	40.5	17,927	106,777	2,636
92	6/81	1,185,727	112.0	10,587	80,050	715
93	6/81	1,196,542	101.9	11,739	177,131	1,738
94	6/82	1,547,945	124.5	12,433	231,348	1,858
95	6/82	1,565,648	16.0	13,497	165,000	1,422

Table II. (continued)

Library	Fiscal year	Salary	Staff (FTE)	Salary/FTE	Square feet	Sqft/FTE
96	8/82	1,465,943	134.0	10,940	272,000	2,030
97	6/30/81	1,215,313	149.0	8,156	213,707	1,434
98	8/31/82	1,346,634	116.0	11,609	239,000	2,060
99	6/30/82	1,713,918	96.8	17,706	128,600	1,329
100	6/81	1,904,544	181.0	10,522	123,000	680
101	6/81	1,762,629	137.8	12,791	185,868	1,349
102	6/30/81	2,266,615	156.5	14,483	177,256	1,133
103	6/82	2,360,179	130.1	18,141	184,340	1,417
104	6/81	2,228,050	173.0	12,879	87,009	503
105	6/81	1,874,478	221.5	8,463	294,939	1,332
106	9/81	2,737,780	249.0	10,995	252,600	1,014
107	6/82	2,490,419	208.0	11,973	266,000	1,279
108	6/30/82	2,399,457	171.0	14,032	152,958	894

Table III.

Library	Total budget	Salary	Direct-Salary	Fringe	Space Maintenance	Overhead
1	23,499	11,673	5,725	2,101	4,000	Unknown
2	37,871	13,565	16,000	2,889	1,891	3,526
3	66,320	36,246	15,470	3,964	6,240	4,400
4	55,974	22,870	31,000	Unknown	2,104	Unknown
5	99,173	44,932	15,586	5,427	33,228	Unknown
6	83,195	31,993	32,614	3,864	14,724	Unknown
7	101,675	37,434	34,153	4,522	25,566	Unknown
8	82,091	25,518	52,490	4,083	Unknown	Unknown
9	119,038	57,500	32,061	6,945	23,532	Unknown
10	117,040	33,000	69,200	11,000	3,840	Unknown
11	123,815	34,492	68,200	7,347	4,808	8,968
12	525,049	84,785	23,875	21,196	384,000	11,193
13	150,641	42,634	68,213	5,798	21,912	12,084
14	268,750	59,226	52,370	7,154	150,000	Unknown
15	238,493	88,048	25,428	24,865	15,525	84,627
16	171,177	51,920	63,500	5,126	Unknown	50,631
17	144,051	24,635	104,310	5,247	3,434	6,425
18	151,599	81,984	50,053	19,562	Unknown	Unknown
19	180,579	68,367	68,884	8,258	35,070	Unknown
20	198,548	99,368	41,892	10,328	35,838	11,122
21	169,536	37,861	108,489	8,064	5,278	9,844
22	167,180	54,487	91,958	6,581	14,154	Unknown
23	362,427	89,715	57,800	16,149	76,354	122,409
24	190,959	55,050	112,460	6,649	16,800	Unknown
25	264,283	122,906	49,900	13,309	Unknown	78,168
26	194,831	52,644	130,000	12,187	Unknown	Unknown

Table III. (*continued*)

Library	Total budget	Salary	Direct-Salary	Fringe	Space Main-tenance	Overhead
27	291,867	63,853	132,502	6,741	67,747	21,024
28	325,288	141,853	68,420	29,515	85,500	Unknown
29	327,782	169,188	47,642	Unknown	Unknown	110,952
30	382,606	97,391	123,295	Unknown	161,920	Unknown
31	300,821	100,982	120,687	12,198	66,954	Unknown
32	256,109	157,000	69,345	18,964	10,800	Unknown
33	247,458	120,546	106,866	20,046	Unknown	Unknown
34	280,364	112,012	121,845	20,554	25,953	Unknown
35	280,846	122,550	118,331	39,965	Unknown	Unknown
36	286,693	140,374	113,446	32,873	Unknown	Unknown
37	290,163	220,364	41,000	6,976	Unknown	21,823
38	409,823	129,105	132,691	22,108	76,437	49,482
39	926,063	174,543	97,974	46,254	558,054	49,238
40	415,149	154,083	118,466	18,100	124,500	Unknown
41	303,525	157,410	120,266	25,849	Unknown	Unknown
42	309,530	190,220	91,060	28,250	Unknown	Unknown
43	384,577	89,981	196,943	10,869	86,784	Unknown
44	327,926	84,493	219,679	23,754	Unknown	Unknown
45	350,422	193,810	114,271	42,341	Unknown	Unknown
46	377,997	163,752	157,320	22,925	34,000	Unknown
47	359,437	165,474	164,515	29,448	Unknown	Unknown
48	440,320	179,881	172,279	21,728	66,432	Unknown
49	401,776	200,589	168,918	32,269	Unknown	Unknown
50	454,303	250,052	125,561	30,204	48,486	Unknown
51	426,442	218,872	163,796	43,774	Unknown	Unknown
52	480,350	159,750	225,000	23,600	Unknown	72,000
53	661,700	233,611	163,550	38,832	43,500	182,207
54	2,166,920	393,611	9,765	47,544	1,716,000	Unknown
55	577,210	176,314	233,160	24,808	55,004	87,924
56	452,098	280,016	132,210	39,872	Unknown	Unknown
57	609,663	235,172	196,350	51,738	53,500	72,903
58	470,582	181,587	255,241	33,754	Unknown	Unknown
59	502,758	272,365	181,050	49,343	Unknown	Unknown
60	653,015	200,000	270,000	42,000	141,015	Unknown
61	579,544	336,591	160,000	33,322	49,631	Unknown
62	627,135	390,333	116,929	13,065	Unknown	107,808
63	980,665	359,964	174,495	43,480	402,726	Unknown
64	747,191	273,825	282,374	42,840	92,835	55,317
65	710,108	315,204	249,848	39,000	93,000	13,056
66	1,098,494	432,805	155,639	48,902	266,389	194,761
67	1,422,586	315,957	347,040	78,989	680,600	Unknown
68	933,405	375,100	328,199	106,116	84,654	39,336
69	1,065,900	241,286	466,000	38,415	10,000	310,199
70	883,027	466,162	251,793	78,924	86,148	Unknown
71	1,070,601	260,804	459,000	41,281	197,370	113,146
72	1,119,795	494,448	240,141	108,779	276,427	Unknown
73	1,893,705	428,378	352,389	85,674	290,182	737,082

Table III. (continued)

Library	Total budget	Salary	Direct-Salary	Fringe	Space Maintenance	Overhead
74	885,574	471,764	319,457	94,353	Unknown	Unknown
75	1,356,546	579,555	438,449	98,542	240,000	Unknown
76	1,657,828	560,939	472,828	98,257	169,560	356,244
77	3,139,099	785,712	312,613	263,263	1,153,656	623,855
78	1,458,035	355,416	795,518	81,509	216,892	8,700
79	1,582,186	597,519	603,445	111,978	269,244	Unknown
80	1,619,901	538,751	712,984	75,126	Unknown	293,040
81	1,891,803	708,524	552,498	99,987	Unknown	530,794
82	1,912,604	596,000	687,000	119,200	354,132	156,272
83	1,675,699	849,332	619,602	206,765	Unknown	Unknown
84	1,812,677	960,800	531,600	320,277	Unknown	Unknown
85	1,926,327	805,552	741,072	82,703	Unknown	297,000
86	1,866,425	528,192	1,118,533	84,200	Unknown	135,500
87	3,357,286	988,016	685,923	170,588	940,500	572,259
88	2,019,150	1,086,210	752,775	124,165	56,000	Unknown
89	2,530,277	874,263	984,687	114,850	407,637	148,840
90	2,043,534	1,008,430	885,314	149,790	Unknown	Unknown
91	2,706,030	726,040	1,290,414	102,750	58,420	528,406
92	2,361,212	1,185,727	937,132	238,353	Unknown	Unknown
93	2,744,151	1,196,542	1,015,662	205,134	326,823	Unknown
94	3,099,688	1,547,945	793,548	186,285	365,110	206,800
95	2,945,957	1,565,648	1,004,553	375,756	Unknown	Unknown
96	2,944,049	1,465,943	1,142,844	Unknown	335,262	Unknown
97	3,315,147	1,215,313	1,447,715	135,461	343,340	173,318
98	3,585,183	1,346,634	1,369,997	181,350	687,202	Unknown
99	4,343,968	1,713,918	1,124,420	411,832	665,477	428,321
100	4,448,287	1,904,544	1,312,094	259,018	612,435	360,196
101	4,592,163	1,762,629	1,595,892	530,493	703,149	Unknown
102	4,019,278	2,266,615	1,251,598	501,065	Unknown	Unknown
103	7,682,309	2,360,179	1,351,013	708,054	2,925,218	337,845
104	7,011,722	2,228,050	1,844,285	557,012	2,088,216	294,159
105	5,769,024	1,874,478	2,232,954	265,185	308,605	1,087,802
106	8,072,978	2,737,780	1,691,729	547,556	2,906,462	189,451
107	7,747,005	2,490,419	1,945,981	622,605	1,042,000	1,646,000
108	6,155,782	2,399,457	2,469,200	575,870	711,255	Unknown

ACKNOWLEDGMENTS

Appendix III

We wish to thank all the Directors: Mr. Hugh Atkinson, Director; University of Illinois Libraries; Mr. David Bishop, Director; University of Georgia Libraries; Dr. Malcolm Getz, Director; Vanderbilt University Libraries; Mr. Herbert F. Johnson, Director; Emory University Libraries; Mr. Louis E. Martin, Director; Cornell University Libraries; Ms.

Susan K. Martin, Director; Johns Hopkins University Libraries; Mr. John P. McGowan, Director; Northwestern University Libraries; Mr. Carlton C. Rochell, Dean of Libraries; New York University Libraries.

Thanks to the Project Managers: Mr. William Potter, Assistant University Librarian for Central Processing; University of Illinois Libraries; Mr. Barry Baker, Assistant Director of Technical Services; University of Georgia Libraries; Mr. Douglas Phelps, Director of General Technical Services; Vanderbilt University Libraries; Mr. Paul M. Cousins, Director of Fiscal and Administrative Services; Emory University Libraries; Mr. Ryburn M. Ross, Assistant University Librarian, Technical and On-Line Services; Cornell University Libraries; Ms. Johanna Hershey, Associate Director for Technical Services; Johns Hopkins University Libraries; Ms. Karen Horny, Assistant University Librarian for Technical Services; Northwestern University Libraries; Ms. Susan Kallenbach, Assistant University Librarian for Technical Services; New York University Libraries.

And a final word of thanks to: Mr. Richard McCoy and Mr. James Michalko at RLG, Mr. Frank Grisham and Mr. Furman Beckwith at SOLINET, Mr. Roland Brown, Ms. Mary Ellen Jacobs, Mr. Richard Green, Ms. Kate Nevins, Mr. Ron Gardner and Mr. Tom Sanville at OCLC.

Libraries	*Data Coordinators*
Ms. Rita Kane, Associate Director for Public Services Music Library University of California Berkeley, CA 94720	Michael A. Keller
Mr. Fred W. Ryan, Assistant Director Meriam Library California State University Chico, CA 95929	William Post
Ms. Ruth Hafter, Director Ruben Salzar Library Sonoma State University Rohnert Park, CA 94928	Ruth Haftner
Mr. Norman E. Tanis, Director Delmar T. Oviatt and South Libraries California State University Northridge, CA 91330	Clark Wong Jack Jaffe
Ms. Millicent D. Abell, Director Cluster Undergraduate Library Science and Engineering Library University of California - San Diego La Jolla, CA 92093	Mark Gittelsohn Beverly French
Dr. Calvin Boyer, Director University of California Library University of California Irving, CA 92713	Calvin Boyer

Ms. Betty J. Blackman, Director
Charles Von DerAhe Library   Betty J. Blackman
Loyola Marymount University
Los Angeles, CA 90045

Ms. Joanne R. Euster, Director
J. Paul Leonard Library   Fred E. Hearth
San Francisco State University
San Francisco, CA 94132

Mr. John Garralda, Director
Leslie J. Savage Library   John Garralda
Western State College of Colorado
Gunnison, CO 81230

Ms. Joan McConkey, Librarian
Engineering Library   Joan McConkey
Music Library   Joan McConkey
University of Colorado at Boulder
Boulder, CO 80309

Mr. Robert Massmann, Director
Elihu Burritt Library   Frank Gagliardi
Central Connecticut State College
New Britain, CT 06050

Mr. James A. Servies, Director
John C. Pace Library   William M. Lee
University of Western Florida
Pensacola, FL 32504

Mr. R. Max Willocks, Associate Director
Agriculture & Fine Arts Library   Anna L. Weaver
University of Florida
Gainesville, FL 32611

Mr. Herbert F. Johnson, Director
Robert W. Woodruff Library   Paul M. Cousins, Jr.
Emory University
Atlanta, GA 30322

Ms. Mildred Tietjen, Director
James Earl Carter Library   Mildred Tietjen
Georgia Southwestern College
Americus, GA 31709

Mr. David F. Bishop, Director
Science Library   Russell C. Pease
University of Georgia
Athens, GA 30602

Mr. Joel H. Holmes, Director
Simon Schwob Memorial Library   Joel H. Holmes
Columbus College
Columbus, GA 31993

Mr. Richard C. Pearson, Director
Joseph F. Smith Library   Richard C. Pearson
Brigham Young University
Laie, HI 96762

Ms. Marian E. Hubbard, Librarian
Chaminade University Library   Marian E. Hubbard
Chaminade University
Honolulu, HI 96816

Mr. Hugh Atkinson, Librarian
Circulation & Stacks   L. Probst
Reference Room & Documents   Sharon Van Der Laan
Applied Life Studies
Architecture & Art   Delores Wallace
Asian Library   Bill Wong
Biology   Elisabeth B. Davis
Classics   Barbara Nadler
Commerce
Education & Social Science   Barton M. Clark
English   Grete Krolihork
History & Philosophy   C. Bride
Library and Information Science   P. Stenstrom
Modern Languages   Pam Lindell
Rare Book Room   N. Frederick Nash
Undergraduate Library   David Kohl
University of Illinois
Urbana, IL 61802

Ms. Mary MacDonald, Acting Librarian
Norris L. Brookens Library   Florence Lewis
Sangamon State University
Springfield, IL 62708

Mr. Robert C. Miller, Director
Memorial Library   George E. Sereiko
Architecture Library   George E. Sereiko
University of Notre Dame
Notre Dame, IN 46556

Mr. B. Michael Wood, Director
Science Library   James F. Comes
Ball State University
Muncie, IN 47306

Dean Elaine F. Sloan, Director
Fine Arts Library

Geology Library

Indiana University
Bloomington, IN 47405

Stella Bentley
Lyn Korenic
Stella Bentley
Lois Heisen

Dean Jasper G. Schad, Director
Ablah Library
Wichita State University
Wichita, KS 67208

Jasper G. Schad

Ms. Antoinette Powell, Librarian
Agriculture Library
University of Kentucky
Lexington, KY 40546

Antoinette Powell

Dr. Earl Wassom, Director
Helm-Cravens Library
Western Kentucky University
Bowling Green, KY 42101

Chris Bixler

Dean Donald D. Hendricks, Director
Earl K. Long Library
University of New Orleans
New Orleans, LA 70122

Anthony Tassin

Mr. Willis Bridegam, Librarian
Robert Frost Library
Amherst College
Amherst, MA 01002

Willis Bridegam

Ms. Carol E. Fraser, Director
Cushing-Martin Library
Stonehill College
North Easton, MA 02356

Carol E. Fraser

Mr. Wolfgang M. Freitag, Librarian
Fine Arts Library
Harvard University
Cambridge, MA 02138

Wolfgang M. Freitag

Mr. Alan E. Erickson, Librarian
Cabot Science Library
Harvard University
Cambridge, MA 02138

Alan E. Erickson

Mr. Richard J. Talbot, Director
U. of Mass. at Amherst Library
University of Massachusetts
Amherst, MA 01002

Gordon Fretwell

Dean Roland H. Moody, Director
Northeastern University Libraries   Tom Cahalan
Northeastern University
Boston, MA 02115

Mr. Emerson Hilker, Director
Science Library   Emerson Hilker
Wayne State University
Detroit, MI 48202

Ms. Georgia Clark, Director
Arthur Neef Law Library   Georgia Clark
Wayne State University
Detroit, MI 48202

Mr. Thomas E. Albright, Assistant Director
Chemistry Library   Bernice Z. Wallace
Engineering Library   Jackson Yang
Geology Library   D. Baclawski
Mathematics Library   Berle G. Reiter
Michigan State University
East Lansing, MI 48824

Mr. Paul L. Anthony, Director
Cardinal Newman College Library   Paul L. Anthony
Cardinal Newman College
St. Louis, MO 63121

Mr. Robert D. Harvey, Director
Southwest Missouri State Library   Robert D. Harvey
Southwest Missouri State
Springfield, MO 65807

Mr. Elmer E. Rodgers, Director
George A. Spiva Library   Elmer E. Rodgers
Missouri Southern State College
Joplin, MO 64801

Mr. Dean Schmidt, Acting Director
Elmer Ellis Library   Mary Ryan
Engineering Library   Alfred H. Jones
University of Missouri
Columbia, MO 65201

Mr. Kilbourn L. Janecek, Director
Chemistry Library   Linda Schultz
North Dakota State University
Fargo, ND 58105

Mr. Edward S. Warner, Director
Geology Library   Mary Scott
University of Northern Dakota
Grand Forks, ND 58202

Ms. Barbara Lerch, Acting Librarian
Geisel Library   Barbara Lerch
Saint Anselm College
Manchester, NH 03102

Mr. Carlton C. Rochell, Dean of Libraries
Elmer Holmes Bobst Library   Nancy Kanich
Stephen Chen Library of Fine Arts   Evelyn Samuel
Grad School of Business Admin Library   Ron Dow
New York University
New York, NY 10012

Ms. Jane P. Franck, Director
Columbia University Library   Maureen Horgan
Teachers College
New York, NY 10027

Mr. Norman O. Jung, Director
College at Old Westbury Library   Norman Jung
State University of New York
Old Westbury, NY 11568

Ms. Ina C. Brownridge, Director
Main Library   Ina Brownridge
State University of New York - Binghamton
Binghamton, NY 13901

Mr. George C. Newman, Director
Edward H. Butler Library   Bruce L. Andrew
State University of New York   Mary C. Hall
    College at Buffalo
Buffalo, NY 14222

Mr. Allan Lentini, Director
    of Administrative Operations
Engineering Library   Susan Markowitz
Physical Sciences Library   Ellen Thomas
Cornell University
Ithaca, NY 14853

Rev. Lawrence A. Lonergan, Director
Loretto Memorial   Sister Marie Melton
Queens Library   Sister Marie Melton
Saint John's University
Jamaica, NY 11439

Mr. David C. Genaway, University Librarian
William F. Maag Library   Carol Wall
Youngstown State University
Youngstown, OH 44555

Mr. Dwight F. Burlingame, Dean
BGSU Library   Sharon Gilbert
Bowling Green State University
Bowling Green, OH 43403

Mr. Donald E. Oehlerts, Director
Science Library   Marian Winner
Miami University
Oxford, OH 45056

Dr. William W. Jernigan, Director
John D. Messick Learning Resources Ctr.   William W. Jernigan
Oral Roberts University
Tulsa, OK 74171

Dr. Roscoe Rouse, University Librarian
OSU Library   Norman L. Nelson
Oklahoma State University
Stillwater, OK 74078

Mr. George W. Shipman, Librarian
Architecture & Allied Arts Library   Reyburn R. McCready
University of Oregon
Eugene, OR 97403

Mr. Charles Weyant, Director
Williamette University Library   Charles Weyant
Williamette University
Salem, OR 97301

Mr. Leonoor Swets Ingraham, Director
Aubrey R. Watzek Library   Vicki Kreimeyer
Lewis & Clark College
Portland, OR 97219

Mr. Keith B. Cohick, Librarian
Johnstown Campus Library   Keith B. Cohick
University of Pittsburgh
Johnstown, PA 15904

Dr. Kenneth J. Oberembt, Librarian
Alumni Memorial Library   Kenneth J. Oberembt
University of Scranton
Scranton, PA 18510

Mr. Paul Pugliese, Director
Duquesne University Library   W. B. Spinelli
Duquesne University
Pittsburgh, PA 15219

Mr. Charles Myers, Director
School of Engineering &
  Applied Science Library
University of Pennsylvania
Philadelphia, PA 19104

Charles Myers

Mr. Joseph A. Boisse, Director
Ambler Campus Library
Temple University
Philadelphia, PA 19122

Esther Bloomsburgh
Sharon Hogan

Frankie H. Cubbedge, Director
Gregg-Graniteville Library
University of South Carolina
Aiken, SC 29801

Frankie H. Cubbedge
Susan I. Roberts
Jane H. Tuten

Ms. Ann T. Hare, Director
Larry A. Jackson Library
Lander College
Greenwood, SC 29646

Ann T. Hare

Mr. Donald R. Hunt, Director
James D. Hoskins Library
Agriculture & Veterinary Medicine Library
University of Tennessee
Knoxville, TN 37916

Marcia J. Myers
Marcia J. Myers

Ms. Exir B. Brennan, Director
Lamar Memorial Library
Maryville College
Maryville, TN 37801

Exir B. Brennan

Dr. W. Walter Wicker, Director
Clear Lake City Library
University of Houston
Houston, TX 77058

W. Walter Wicker

Mr. Robin Downes, Director
Anderson Memorial Library
University of Houston
Houston, TX 77004

Thomas Shaughnessy
J. L. Krevit

Ms. Linda Beaupre, Associate Director
Physics-Math-Astronomy Library
University of Texas
Austin, TX 78712

John Sandy

Mr. E. Dale Cluff, Director
Texas Tech University Library
Texas Tech University
Lubbock, TX 79409

Stewart Dyess
Donald Frank
Sibyl P. Morrison
Peggy Tooker

Mr. Craige S. Hall, Director
Stewart Library
Weber State College
Ogden, UT 84408

Sally Arway
Craige Hall
James R. Tolman

Mr. Roger K. Hanson, Director
Marriot Library
University of Utah
Salt Lake City, UT 84112

Bob Holley
John Meador

Mr. Joseph T. Popecki, Director
Saint Michael's College Library
Saint Michael's College
Colchester, VT 05404

Joseph T. Popecki

Mr. Steve Marquardt, Director
William D. McIntyre Library
University of Wisconsin
Eau Claire, WI 54701

Steve Marquardt

Mr. William M. Gardner, Director
Memorial Library

Science Library

Marquette University
Milwaukee, WI 53233

David Farley
Kathy Frymark
Kathy Frymark
Kevin Riggle

Dr. J. Daniel Vann III, Director
Forrest R. Polk Library
University of Wisconsin
Oshkosh, WI 54901

Joanne White

Ms. Sarah M. McGowan, Director
Ripon College Library
Ripon College
Ripon, WI 54971

Sarah M. McGowan

BIOGRAPHICAL SKETCH OF THE CONTRIBUTORS

Fred Batt, head of the Reference Department, University of Oklahoma Libraries, presented a paper at the Fifth International Conference on Contemporary Issues in Academic and Research Libraries in 1984 on faculty status for academic libraries. A frequent speaker at conferences, his talks center on online access to information.

Eleanore R. Ficke, formerly Executive Director of the Continuing Library Education Network and Exchange, Inc., is now self-employed. Active in the Library Administration and Management Association, her major fields of interest are public relations, library statistics and continuing education for librarians.

Esther E. Horne, Assistant Professor in the School of Library and Information Science of the Catholic University of America, teaches courses in Library Automation, Computer Technology and Special Libraries. She presented a paper "Core Curriculum and Innternational Aspects" at the American Society for In-

Advances in Library Administration and Organization
Volume 5, pages 287–289
Copyright © 1986 by JAI Press Inc.
All rights of reproduction in any form reserved.
ISBN: 0-89232-674-3

formation Science 46th Annual Meeting. Information Technology in Libraries and Information Centers is a strong professional interest.

Paul B. Kantor, President of Tantalus, Inc., has served as a Consultant to the Association of Research Libraries and the Council on Library Resources. Author of "Cost and Usage of Medical Libraries (M.L.A. Bulletin, July 1984) he takes the iconoclastic view that the most important principles of library management and economics apply with only very minor changes to all types of libraries.

Rashelle Schlessinger Karp, is an Assistant Professor in the College of Library Science at Clarion University of Pennsylvania. Active in the American Library Association, she serves on the Library and Information Technology Committee.

Joe W. Kraus, Director of Libraries Emeritus of Illinois State University, writes on the history of publishing. His *History of Way and Williams, Chicago, . . .* was published in 1983. In 1979 **Messrs. Copeland and Day, 69 Cornhill, Boston, 1893–1899** was issued. Recently he served as chairperson of the Editorial Board "ACRL Publications in Librarianship." Other interests include rare books and administration of university libraries.

Susan E. McCargar, librarian for the El Paso Herald Post, is a former head of the Acquisition Division, Albert R. Mann Library, Cornell University. Occasionally, she serves as a library consultant particularly for technical services operational analysis. She is also a member of the American Society of Information Science.

John A. McCrossan, chairperson and professor of the Department of Library, Media, and Information Studies at the University of South Florida, was recently President of the Florida Library Association. Formerly State Librarian of Vermont, he is active in the American Library Association. One of his recent publications was "Public Library Standards" in Encyclopedia of Library and Information Science, 1984 supplement.

T. John Metz, formerly Executive Director of the Midwest Regional Library Network, is College Librarian of Carleton College. He is a member of the Building and Equipment Section of the Library Administration and Management Association reflecting his interest in planning library facilities.

Ruth J. Person is Associate Dean of the School of Library and Information Science, of The Catholic University of America. In the Spring 1985 issue of *Library Trends,* her article "The Organization and Administration of Two-Year College Learning Resources" appeared. This is her second article for ALAO. She has taught courses in the management of information organizations, personnel management and community college learning resources. Other interests include management education, continuing education and long-range planning.

Joan M. Repp, Chair of Access Services, Jerome Library, Bowling Green State University, actively speaks and writes on topics related to cataloging, management and technology. In 1984, she prepared and presented the "Management in the Library Environment" workshop to the Dade County Library Association in Miami, Florida. She has prepared and participated in similar activities related to AACR2.

Marcia L. Sprules, author of "Online Bibliometrics in an Academic Library," *Online,* January 1983, is the Coordinator of the Computer-Assisted Bibliographic Service, in the I.D. Weeks Library of the University of South Dakota. A member of the American Library Association, she is active in the Reference and Adult Services Division.

Renee Tjoumas is an Assistant Professor in the Graduate School of Library and Information Studies of Queens College, The City University of New York. A member of the American Society for Information Science, she served as associate editor of *SIG: International Issues Newsletter*. She has had articles published in *Libri, an International Library Review*.

AUTHOR INDEX

Koenig, Michael, 45
Kostelanetz, Richard, 47
Kostiainen, Auvo, 47
Kraus, Joe W., 45
Krick, Robert, 45
Krikelas, James, 85
Kroeger, Karl, 46
Krohn, Ernst C., 46
Kruger, Linda Markson, 44
Krummel, D. W., 46
Kuehl, John, ed., 45
Kurian, George Thomas, 42

Lancaster, F. W., 81, 112, 115, 117,
    119, 121, 123
Larson, Judy L., 49
Lawrence, Gary S., 154
Lawry, Martha, 68, 72
Learmont, Carol L., 100, 101
Leclair-Marzolf, M., 23
Lee, Jung Jin, 223, 246
Lee, Marshall, 48
Lee, R. J., 15
Lee, Susan A., 181
Lemay, Harding, 45
Lenihan, G. O., 15
Levine, E., 17, 18
Lewin, Kurt, 182
Lindeman, E., 16
Lipitz, Ben-Ami, 75, 144
Lockwood, Deborah L., 155
Logan, G. K., 22
Lohe, Kenneth A., 43
Longeway, B., 19
Lorenz, Alfred Lawrence, 45
Lucas, I., 20, 26
Lucker, Jay K., 48
Lyle, Guy R., 111
Lyles, William H., 47
Lynch, Beverly P., 180

McAdams, Donald R., 47
McAnally, Arthur, 180

McArthur, Judith N., 169
McCargar, Susan Elaine, 181
McCullough, Ann Catherine, 45
McDonough, J. F., 1
McGrath, William E., 113
McInnis, R. Marvin, 117
Mckerrow, R. B., 34
McKittrick, David, ed., 49
McKinley, C., 23
McVey, Sheila, 48
Madison, Charles A., 43, 47
Magavero, Gerard, 42
Magnotti, Shirley, 39
Malinconico, S. Michael, 84
Mallinson, David Walker, 43
Markey, Karen, 85
Marshall, Joan K., 17
Martin, Henri-Jean, 34
Martin, Jean Krieg, 1
Martin, Murray S., 71
Massman, Virgil F., 120
Matthews, Joseph R., 78, 79, 145
Meckler, Alan Marshall, 48
Mellon, Constance A., 171
Metz, Paul, 181, 194
Meyer, Susan E., 49
Miller, Ruth H., 171
Miller, C. William, 45
Miller, William, 160
Millett, John D., 184
Mintzberg, Henry, 10
Molnar, John Edgar, 44
Monroe, Margaret E., 99
Moore, Carole Weiss, 83
Moore, John Hammond, 45
Moran, James, 49
Morse, John D., 50
Morton, Bruce, 170
Mosher, Paul H., 110, 111, 112,
    116, 120, 121, 122
Moss, Sidney P., 45
Moussa, L., 22
Moxley, Linda Sue, 183, 185

SUBJECT INDEX

FOUNDATIONS IN LIBRARY AND INFORMATION SCIENCE
A Series of Monographs, Texts and Treatises

Series Editors: **Evelyn Daniel,** Dean
School of Library and Information Science
Simmons College

Robert D. Stueart, Dean
Graduate School of Library and Information Science
University of North Carolina

Developing Collections of U.S. Government Publications
Peter Hernon and Gary R. Purcell

Library Management Without Bias
Ching-Chih Chen

Issues in Personnel Management in Academic Libraries
Murray S. Martin

Information Needs of the 80s: Library and Information Services' Role in "Bringing Information to People" Based on the Deliberations of the White House Conference on Library and Information Services
Edited by Robert D. Stueart

ALMS: A Budget Based Library Management System
Betty Jo Mitchell

Options for the 80s: Proceedings of the Second National Conference of The Association of College and Research Libraries (2 vols.)
Edited by Michael D. Kathman and Virgil F. Massman

The Library Services and Construction Act:
An Historical Overview from the Viewpoint of Major Participants
Edward G. Holley and Robert F. Schremser

Changing Technology and Education for Librarianship
and Information Science
Edited by Basil Stuart-Stubbs

Videotex and Teletext: New Online Resources for Libraries
Michael B. Binder

Research Libraries and Their Implementation of AACR2
Edited by Judith Hopkins and John A. Edens

Brochure Available Upon Request

JAI PRESS INC.
36 Sherwood Place, P.O. Box 1678
Greenwich, Connecticut 06836-1678

Editor
Peter Hernon
Graduate Library School
University of Arizona

Associate Editor
Charles R. McClure
School of Library and
Information Studies
University of Oklahoma

GOVERNMENT INFORMATION QUARTERLY

An International Journal of Resources, Services, Policies and Practices

Government Information Quarterly is an interdisciplinary journal that provides a forum for theoretical and philosophical analyses, the presentation of research findings and their practical applications, and a discussion of current policies and practices, as well as new developments at all levels of government.

Materials published in **GIQ** are of increasing importance to:
● **librarians** ● **researchers** ● **government administrators** ● **record managers** ● **students**

Articles from recent issues

Public Access to Congressional Records: Present Policy and Reform Consideration
Harold C. Relyea, *Library of Congress*

Increasing Reliance on the Decennial Census
John G. Keane, *Director, U.S. Bureau of the Census*

Federal Restrictions on the Free Flow of Academic Information and Ideas
John Shattuck, *Harvard University*

The Implications of Scientific and Technical Information on Congressional Policies and Actions
Jane Bortnick, *Library of Congress*

— —

Mail orders to JAI Press, Inc., Subscription Dept., 36 Sherwood Place, P.O. Box 1678, Greenwich, Connecticut 06836-1678 or call (203) 661-7602.

Published Quarterly. Subscriptions must be prepaid and are for the 1986 calendar year only. No institutional checks will be accepted for individual subscriptions.

☐ Institutions $65.   ☐ Individuals $35.   ☐ Members of GODORT, ALA $30.

Outside the U.S. add $5. for surface postage and handling; $10. for air mail delivery.

Name (please print) _____

Address _____

City _____ State/Country _____ Zip _____

☐ Enclosed is my check/money order for $_____

Please charge $_____ to my credit card account:

☐ American Express   ☐ MasterCard   ☐ VISA

Account Number_____ Expiration Date: _____

Authorizing signature_____

⅃ai JAI PRESS INC.
Greenwich, Connecticut   **London, England**